# TRUSTS 740-RISK MANAGEMENT APPLICATIONS

A comprehensive analysis of the risk management process and its impact on the individual, business, and the economy in the 21$^{st}$ century. Case studies on current trends in risk management will be presented in class

Nicholas Paleveda MBA J.D. LL.M, Adjunct Professor, Graduate Tax Program, Northeastern University, Boston, Adjunct Professor Campbell University North Carolina

## ABOUT THE AUTHOR

Nick Paleveda received his B.A. in 1977 and M.B.A. degree in 1979 from the University of South Florida. Mr. Paleveda received his J.D from the University of Miami in 1982. Next, Mr. Paleveda attended the University of Denver and received his Master of Laws in Taxation in 1984. During the summer, Mr. Paleveda attended programs in Oxford University for law in England and international business at Harvard University in the U.S. In 1984 he was admitted to practice law in the State of Florida, admitted before the U.S. Tax Court, and admitted before the 11th Circuit Court of Appeals. Mr. Paleveda founded the law firm Hampton, Paleveda, Murphy, Cody and Levy in 1984. Later, Mr. Paleveda was hired to work for Mutual Benefit Life. While at Mutual Benefit Life, Mr. Paleveda conducted over 1,000 Advanced Tax and Estate Planning Seminars throughout the U.S. in almost every major city. Mr. Pale Veda's client list included; the founder of Dunkin Donuts, the President of Phillip Morris, the President of Kimberly-Clarke, the founding family of Coca-Cola and others. In 1993 Mr. Paleveda returned to law practice at the firm of Paleveda and Rome in Atlanta. In 1997 Mr. Paleveda became a contributing author for "The Life Insurance Answer Book for Qualified Plans and Estate Planning" (1997) published by Panel Publishing now a division of ASPEN publishing. Mr. Paleveda was appointed the Adjunct Professor for Retirement Planning for the College for Financial Planning at Oglethorpe University in Atlanta. In 2001 Mr. Paleveda became a CEO for a pension administration firm in Seattle Washington. In 2006, Mr. Paleveda became CEO for an executive compensation consulting firm in Bellingham Washington and in 2010, the President of National Pension Partners. Mr. Paleveda is an avid chess and trivia player. Mr. Paleveda is a USCF chess master and the Florida State Chess Champion in 1977, 1978 and 1994. He was a top 10 player in Chess nationally in high school and placed 7th at the National Chess Competition in college after winning the Southern region. He currently plays for the State of Washington Chess Team in matches against British Columbia and Oregon. In Trivia, his Team won the Whatcom County Championship two years in a row. (One year with the help of Ken Jennings as his teammate). Mr. Paleveda is also a member of Infinity International Society a top 99.63% society. In 2009, Mr. Paleveda was admitted to practice before the 9th Circuit Court of Appeals and the Supreme Court of the United States. In 2011, Mr. Paleveda became an Adjunct Professor for the Masters in Taxation Program at Northeastern University, Boston. In 2011 Mr. Paleveda is scheduled to lecture for the University of Denver CPE CPA program, the Washington Society of CPAs, The Florida Institute of CPAs, and the New York Society of CPAs. He can be reached at Nick@nationalpensions.com

# Contents

**RMA/Wharton Advanced Risk Management Program** . Error! Bookmark not defined.
   Program Overview ............................................................. Error! Bookmark not defined.
   Impact & Experience ......................................................... Error! Bookmark not defined.
      The curriculum covers: ................................................. Error! Bookmark not defined.
   Who Attends This Program ............................................. Error! Bookmark not defined.
_____ ................ **Error! Bookmark not defined.**
   MIT-Advanced Risk Management Course ..................... Error! Bookmark not defined.
   Course Meeting Times ..................................................... Error! Bookmark not defined.
   Course Objective ............................................................. Error! Bookmark not defined.
   Prerequisites .................................................................... Error! Bookmark not defined.
   Course Format ................................................................. Error! Bookmark not defined.
   Grading ............................................................................ Error! Bookmark not defined.
   Additional References ..................................................... Error! Bookmark not defined.
   Topic Outline ................................................................... Error! Bookmark not defined.
      The Role of Risk Management ................................... Error! Bookmark not defined.
      The Tools of Risk Management .................................. Error! Bookmark not defined.
      The Business of Risk Management ............................ Error! Bookmark not defined.
      The Risk Management Function ................................. Error! Bookmark not defined.
   Calendar .......................................................................... Error! Bookmark not defined.
**Harvard** ............................................................................... Error! Bookmark not defined.
**Advanced Risk Management and Infrastructure Finance** ......... Error! Bookmark not defined.
   Schedule .......................................................................... Error! Bookmark not defined.
   Description ....................................................................... Error! Bookmark not defined.
   Stanford Advanced Risk Management ............................ Error! Bookmark not defined.
   Course Description .......................................................... Error! Bookmark not defined.
   Learn How To: ................................................................. Error! Bookmark not defined.
**Introduction** ....................................................................................................... 11
**1 Scope** ............................................................................................................ 13
**2 Terms and definitions** ................................................................................... 14
   Local Chapters ............................................................................................. 22
   Public Education ........................................................................................... 22
**SFSP** ................................................................................................................. 23
**About the Society of Financial Service Professionals** ................................... 23
   InsMark Product Line ................................................................................... 28

| | |
|---|---|
| Featured Products | 30 |
| Product Categories | **Error! Bookmark not defined.** |
| More Contact Options | **Error! Bookmark not defined.** |
| General Information | **Error! Bookmark not defined.** |
| What Types of Captives are available in Utah? | 34 |
| Pure Captives | 34 |
| Group Captives | 34 |
| Reinsurance Captives | 35 |
|     How Much Will It Cost to Create a Captive Insurer in Utah? | 35 |
| What are the capitalization requirements in Utah for a captive insurance company? | 36 |
| Are there any investment restrictions in Utah? | 37 |
| What fees are applicable for captives in Utah? | 38 |
| What taxes are applicable to captives in Utah? | 38 |
| Are Captives covered under Guaranty Funds? | 38 |
| What types of insurance can be written in a captive? | 38 |
| What must a Captive do to conduct business in Utah as a Utah domiciled Captive? | 38 |
|     Cutting off Liability using the Statute of Limitations | 94 |
| **UNITED STATES v. BESTFOODS** | 98 |
|     SOLE PROPRIETOR | 103 |
|     CORPORATION | 103 |
|     LIMITED PARTNERSHIP | 120 |
|     Hellman v. Anderson (1991) 233 Cal.App.3d 840,    284 Cal.Rptr. 830 | 127 |
|     LIMITED LIABILITY COMPANY (LLC) | 147 |
|         Classification | 151 |
|         Filing | 152 |
|     PERSONAL RISK MANAGEMENT-ASSET PROTECTION | 153 |
|     HOMESTEAD OR STATE LAW EXEMPTIONS | 153 |
|     Florida Constitution | 162 |
|     Florida Homestead Act | 167 |
|     Texas Homestead Act | 180 |
|     Other State Considerations | 188 |
|         Florida v. Texas: Which State Has Best Homestead Protection | 190 |
|     Fraud vs. Fraudulent Transfer | 192 |
|     Domestic Asset Protection Trusts | 193 |
|     Effective Trust Structures | 194 |
|     Trust Situs Considerations | 195 |

- ALASKA ..... 196
  - Alaska Statute: AS 34.40.110. Restricting Transfers of Trust Interests ..... 197
  - Delaware Statute ..... 203
  - Nevada ..... 216
  - DAPT Concerns ..... 226
  - Trustee Designation and Replacement ..... 228
    - In any event, the Federal Courts did not recognize the Alaska Statute when it came to Bankruptcy Proceeding before an Article I Judge ..... 232
    - UNITED STATES BANKRUPTCY COURT FOR THE DISTRICT OF ALASKA ..... 233
- MEMORANDUM DECISION ..... 233
  - DONALD MacDONALD IV ..... 241
  - United States Bankruptcy Judge ..... 241
    - U.S. Supreme Court ..... 245
  - Conclusion ..... 248
  - Offshore over DAPT ..... 248
  - "The"Anderson Case ..... 251
  - "The" Lawrence Case ..... 277
- **Fuel Hedging in the Airline Industry: The Case of Southwest Airlines** ..... 284
  - David Carter ..... 284
  - Daniel A. Rogers ..... 284
  - Betty J. Simkins ..... 284
- **Credit Risk Scoring Models** ..... 286
  - Gabriele Sabato ..... 286
- **Bear Stearns and the Seeds of its Demise** ..... 287
  - Susan Chaplinsky ..... 287
- **Modern Pension Fund Diversification** ..... 288
  - Marty Anderson-et. Al. ..... 288
- **Why Did U.S. Banks Invest in Highly-Rated Securitization Tranches?** ..... 289
  - Isil Erel ..... 289
  - Taylor Nadauld ..... 289
  - Rene M. Stulz ..... 289
- About the NAIC ..... **Error! Bookmark not defined.**
- Governance ..... **Error! Bookmark not defined.**
- The NAIC's History and Background  A Tradition of Consumer Protection ..... **Error! Bookmark not defined.**
- NAIC Office Locations ..... **Error! Bookmark not defined.**

The author wishes to thank Jay Adkisson for using the "matrix" provided in this Book. The author also thanks Professor Barry Nelson for his contribution to the "Homestead Act". These individuals are true 'mavens" in the Asset Protection Planning world.

# TRUST 740 Risk Management Applications

**Week 1 Introduction to Risk Management**

**Chapter 1 Problem of Risk**
**Chapter 2 Introduction to Risk Management**
**Chapter 3 Insurance Device**

> Risk and Insurance
> ISO 31000
> Enterprise Risk Management
> Solvency and Capital Reserves

**Dalton Q+A**

**Case Study #1** -Client owns a compound pharmacy company with $600,000 a month in profits. He is interested in the Captive Insurance company to lower this corporate tax and insure against risk. He plans on paying $70,000 to establish and $70,000 a year to maintain the captive.

What captive will you recommend?
What jurisdiction will it be located in?
What forms will you need to fill out?
Prepare for a presentation along with forms and a report to present to the board of directors..

---

**Week 2**

**Chapter 4 Risk Management Applications pp 61-71**
**Chapter 5 Private Insurance Industry**
**Chapter 9 Legal Framework**

Domestic Insurance Companies
Offshore Insurance Companies
Reinsurance companies and treaties
Life License-Annuity License-P+C Licenses
Balance Sheet

Income Statement
Subchapter L issues –DAC tax
Packaged Products
Broker Dealer Relationships
Capital-Surplus-Reserves
Income

**Dalton Q+A**

**Report on Case Study #1 Establishment of the Captive**

---

## Week 3

**Chapter 6 Regulation of the Insurance Industry**
**Chapter 7 Functions of Insurers pp 135-142 only**
**Chapter 8 Financial Aspect of Insurer Operations pp 146-150,161,162**

**Dalton Q+A**

**Case Study #2**
Major client gives your company a contract to work with their 1200 employees and 20,000 brokers across the USA. They would like to review your disaster recovery plan and cyber security plan.

What is your plan?
What software do you use?
How do you maintain privacy?
How do you comply with HIPPA?
Prepare report to present to the board of a $500 billion dollar company.

---

## Week 4

**Chapter 12 Life Insurance pp 231-235 &237-244**
**Chapter 18 Annuities pp 318-321 & 3223-328**

**Dalton Q+A**

Report on Case Study #2 Disaster Recovery plan and Cyber Risk Plan for the company

---

## Week 5

**Chapter 20 Disability Income insurance pp 360-367**
**Chapter 21 Health Insurance pp 378-384 & 389-394**

**Dalton Q+A**

**Case Study # 3**

Dr. and Mrs. Dunbar run a specialty Medical group out of Princeton NJ. Engages in Surgery and has about 1.9 million in K-1 and W-2 income. They owns real estate worth 2,000,000 a house worth $700,000 and other assets. They are interested in tax and asset protection planning to minimize risk

What plan do you recommend?
How do you use trusts to minimize risk?
How do you use corporations to minimize risk?
Prepare report to present to his CPA and attorney.
Improve on Asset Protection software

---

## Week 6

**Chapter 26 Other Property Insurance pp 483-492**
**Chapter 27 Negligence and Legal Liability pp 497-507**
**Chapter 28 General Liability Insurance pp 526-528**
**Homeowners and Surplus Lines**
**Chapter 33 Surety Bonds 633-638**

**Dalton Q+A**

**Report on Asset Protection Plan for Dr. Dunbar**

---

## Week 7

**Chapter 29 Automobile and its Legal Environment**

## Automobile Insurance

## Dalton Q+A

Case Study-Client age 65 has 3.0 million in an IRA from a pension rollover- you need to design a product portfolio and risk plan for assets in the portfolio. Needs income for life, but would also like to provide for spouse age 62 and children.

What investments will you use?
What is the overall risk of the portfolio?
What amount of income can be taken out safely?
Present plan to client

---

## Week 8

## Dalton Q+A

### Report on Portfolio Design with Risk assessment and Final exam

Required Reading-
Fundamentals of Risk and Insurance Vaughan 11$^{th}$ Edition
The Dalton Review Fundamentals and Insurance-Preparation for the CFP exam
Advanced Risk Management-Paleveda,
When Genius Fail- The Rise and fall of Long Term Capital Management.-Lowenstein

### Recommended reading-

**Dress for Success-Malloy**
**How to win Friends and Influence People-Dale Carnegie**
**Think and Grow Rich-Napoleon Hill**
**The Magic of Thinking Big**
**The Millionaire Next Door- Dr. Thomas Stanley**

# ISO 31000

ISO (the International Organization for Standardization) is a worldwide federation of national standards bodies (ISO member bodies). The work of preparing International Standards is normally carried out through ISO technical committees. Each member body interested in a subject for which a technical committee has been established has the right to be represented on that committee. International organizations, governmental and non-governmental, in liaison with ISO, also take part in the work. ISO collaborates closely with the International Electrotechnical Commission (IEC) on all matters of electrotechnical standardization.

International Standards are drafted in accordance with the rules given in the ISO/IEC Directives, Part 2.
The main task of technical committees is to prepare International Standards. Draft International Standards adopted by the technical committees are circulated to the member bodies for voting. Publication as an International Standard requires approval by at least 75 % of the member bodies casting a vote.
Attention is drawn to the possibility that some of the elements of this document may be the subject of patent rights. ISO shall not be held responsible for identifying any or all such patent rights.
ISO 31000 was prepared by the ISO Technical Management Board Working Group on risk management.

## Introduction

Organizations of all types and sizes face internal and external factors and influences that make it uncertain whether and when they will achieve their objectives. The effect this uncertainty has on an organization's objectives is "risk".
All activities of an organization involve risk. Organizations manage risk by identifying it, analysing it and then evaluating whether the risk should be modified by risk treatment in order to satisfy their risk criteria. Throughout this process, they communicate and consult with stakeholders and monitor and review the risk and the controls that are modifying the risk in order to ensure that no further risk treatment is required. This International Standard describes this systematic and logical process in detail.
While all organizations manage risk to some degree, this International Standard establishes a number of principles that need to be satisfied to make risk management effective. This International Standard recommends that organizations develop, implement and continuously improve a framework whose purpose is to integrate the process for managing risk into the organization's overall governance, strategy and planning, management, reporting processes, policies, values and culture.
Risk management can be applied to an entire organization, at its many areas and levels, at any time, as well as to specific functions, projects and activities.
Although the practice of risk management has been developed over time and within many sectors in order to meet diverse needs, the adoption of consistent processes

within a comprehensive framework can help to ensure that risk is managed effectively, efficiently and coherently across an organization. The generic approach described in this International Standard provides the principles and guidelines for managing any form of risk in a systematic, transparent and credible manner and within any scope and context. Each specific sector or application of risk management brings with it individual needs, audiences, perceptions and criteria. Therefore, a key feature of this International Standard is the inclusion of "establishing the context" as an activity at the start of this generic risk management process. Establishing the context will capture the objectives of the organization, the environment in which it pursues those objectives, its stakeholders and the diversity of risk criteria – all of which will help reveal and assess the nature and complexity of its risks.

The relationship between the principles for managing risk, the framework in which it occurs and the risk management process described in this International Standard are shown in Figure 1.
When implemented and maintained in accordance with this International Standard, the management of risk enables an organization to, for example:

- — increase the likelihood of achieving objectives;
- — encourage proactive management;
- — be aware of the need to identify and treat risk throughout the organization;
- — improve the identification of opportunities and threats;
- — comply with relevant legal and regulatory requirements and international norms;
- — improve mandatory and voluntary reporting;
- — improve governance;
- — improve stakeholder confidence and trust;
- — establish a reliable basis for decision making and planning;
- — improve controls;
- — effectively allocate and use resources for risk treatment;
- — improve operational effectiveness and efficiency;
- — enhance health and safety performance, as well as environmental protection;
- — improve loss prevention and incident management;
- — minimize losses;
- — improve organizational learning; and
- — improve organizational resilience.

This International Standard is intended to meet the needs of a wide range of stakeholders, including:

- a) those responsible for developing risk management policy within their organization;
- b) those accountable for ensuring that risk is effectively managed within the organization as a whole or within a specific area, project or activity;
- c) those who need to evaluate an organization's effectiveness in managing risk; and
- d) developers of standards, guides, procedures and codes of practice that, in whole or in part, set out how risk is to be managed within the specific context of these documents.

The current management practices and processes of many organizations include components of risk management, and many organizations have already adopted a formal risk management process for particular types of risk or circumstances. In such cases, an organization can decide to carry out a critical review of its existing practices and processes in the light of this International Standard.

In this International Standard, the expressions "risk management" and "managing risk" are both used. In general terms, "risk management" refers to the architecture (principles, framework and process) for managing risks effectively, while "managing risk" refers to applying that architecture to particular risks.

Figure 1 — Relationships between the risk management principles, framework and process

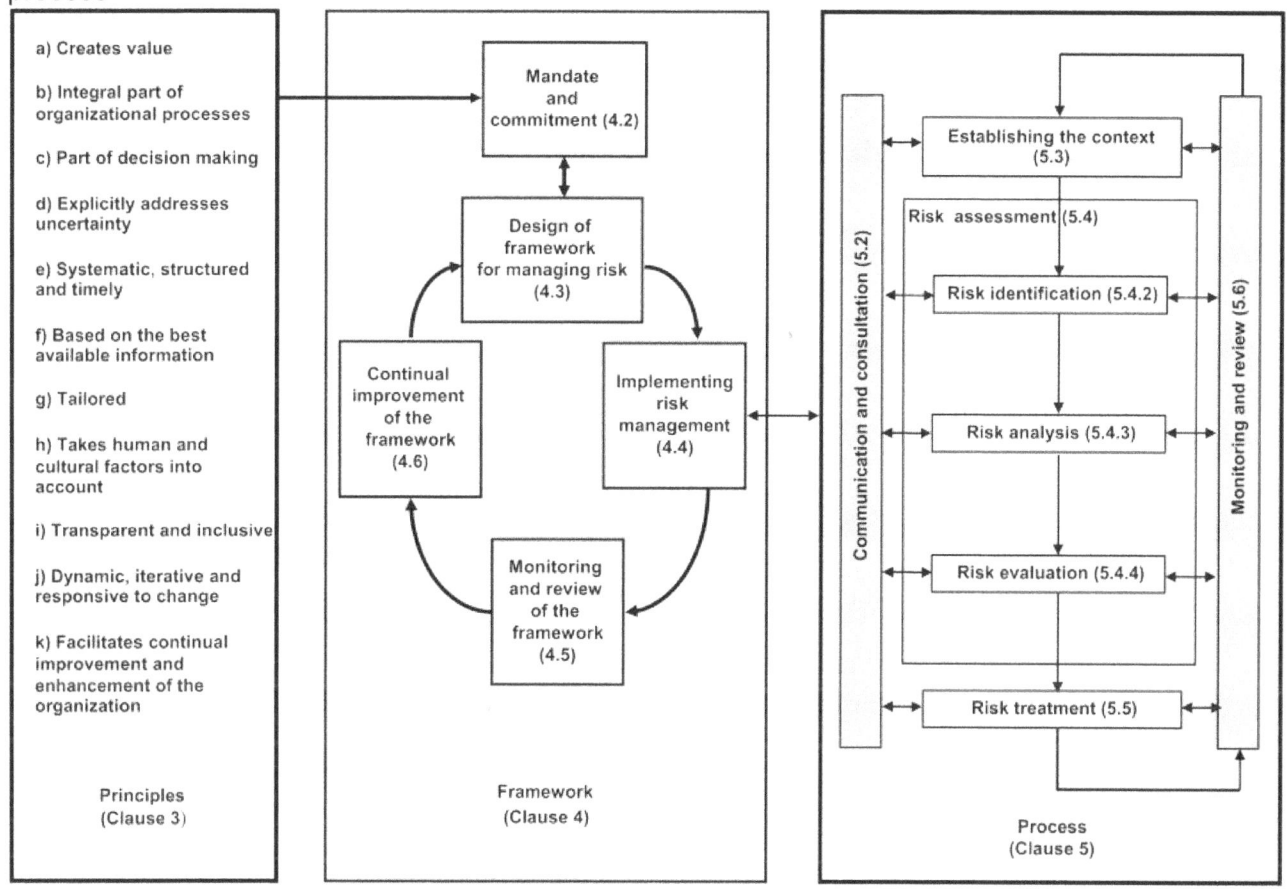

# 1 Scope

This International Standard provides principles and generic guidelines on risk management.

This International Standard can be used by any public, private or community enterprise, association, group or individual. Therefore, this International Standard is not specific to any industry or sector.

NOTE For convenience, all the different users of this International Standard are referred to by the general term "organization".

This International Standard can be applied throughout the life of an organization, and to a wide range of activities, including strategies and decisions, operations, processes, functions, projects, products, services and assets.

This International Standard can be applied to any type of risk, whatever its nature, whether having positive or negative consequences.

Although this International Standard provides generic guidelines, it is not intended to promote uniformity of risk management across organizations. The design and implementation of risk management plans and frameworks will need to take into account the varying needs of a specific organization, its particular objectives, context, structure, operations, processes, functions, projects, products, services, or assets and specific practices employed.

It is intended that this International Standard be utilized to harmonize risk management processes in existing and future standards. It provides a common approach in support of standards dealing with specific risks and/or sectors, and does not replace those standards.

This International Standard is not intended for the purpose of certification.

## 2  Terms and definitions

For the purposes of this document, the following terms and definitions apply.

2.1
risk
effect of uncertainty on objectives
Note 1 to entry: An effect is a deviation from the expected — positive and/or negative.
Note 2 to entry: Objectives can have different aspects (such as financial, health and safety, and environmental goals) and can apply at different levels (such as strategic, organization-wide, project, product and process).
Note 3 to entry: Risk is often characterized by reference to potential events (2.17) and consequences (2.18), or a combination of these.
Note 4 to entry: Risk is often expressed in terms of a combination of the consequences of an event (including changes in circumstances) and the associated likelihood (2.19) of occurrence.
Note 5 to entry: Uncertainty is the state, even partial, of deficiency of information related to, understanding or knowledge of an event, its consequence, or likelihood.
[SOURCE: ISO Guide 73:2009, definition 1.1]

2.2
risk management
coordinated activities to direct and control an organization with regard to risk (2.1)
[SOURCE: ISO Guide 73:2009, definition 2.1]

2.3
risk management framework
set of components that provide the foundations and organizational arrangements for designing, implementing, monitoring (2.28), reviewing and continually improving risk management (2.2) throughout the organization
Note 1 to entry: The foundations include the policy, objectives, mandate and commitment to manage risk (2.1).
Note 2 to entry: The organizational arrangements include plans, relationships, accountabilities, resources, processes and activities.
Note 3 to entry: The risk management framework is embedded within the organization's overall strategic and operational policies and practices.
[SOURCE: ISO Guide 73:2009, definition 2.1.1]

2.4

risk management policy statement of the overall intentions and direction of an organization related to risk management (2.2)
[SOURCE: ISO Guide 73:2009, definition 2.1.2]

**2.5**
**risk attitude**
organization's approach to assess and eventually pursue, retain, take or turn away from risk (2.1)
[SOURCE: ISO Guide 73:2009, definition 3.7.1.1]

**2.6**
**risk management plan**
scheme within the risk management framework (2.3) specifying the approach, the management components and resources to be applied to the management of risk (2.1)

Note 1 to entry: Management components typically include procedures, practices, assignment of responsibilities, sequence and timing of activities.

Note 2 to entry: The risk management plan can be applied to a particular product, process and project, and part or whole of the organization.
[SOURCE: ISO Guide 73:2009, definition 2.1.3]

**2.7**
**risk owner**
person or entity with the accountability and authority to manage a risk (2.1)
[SOURCE: ISO Guide 73:2009, definition 3.5.1.5]

**2.8**
**risk management process**
systematic application of management policies, procedures and practices to the activities of communicating, consulting, establishing the context, and identifying, analyzing, evaluating, treating, monitoring (2.28) and reviewing risk (2.1)
[SOURCE: ISO Guide 73:2009, definition 3.1]

**2.9**
**establishing the context**
defining the external and internal parameters to be taken into account when managing risk, and setting the scope and risk criteria (2.22) for the risk management policy (2.4)
[SOURCE: ISO Guide 73:2009, definition 3.3.1]

**2.10**
**external context**
external environment in which the organization seeks to achieve its objectives
Note 1 to entry: External context can include:

- — the cultural, social, political, legal, regulatory, financial, technological, economic, natural and competitive environment, whether international, national, regional or local;
- — key drivers and trends having impact on the objectives of the organization; and
- — relationships with, and perceptions and values of external stakeholders (2.13).

[SOURCE: ISO Guide 73:2009, definition 3.3.1.1]

**2.11**
**internal context**

internal environment in which the organization seeks to achieve its objectives
Note 1 to entry: Internal context can include:

- — governance, organizational structure, roles and accountabilities;
- — policies, objectives, and the strategies that are in place to achieve them;
- — the capabilities, understood in terms of resources and knowledge (e.g. capital, time, people, processes, systems and technologies);
- — information systems, information flows and decision-making processes (both formal and informal);
- — relationships with, and perceptions and values of, internal stakeholders;
- — the organization's culture;
- — standards, guidelines and models adopted by the organization; and
- — form and extent of contractual relationships.

[SOURCE: ISO Guide 73:2009, definition 3.3.1.2]

2.12
communication and consultation
continual and iterative processes that an organization conducts to provide, share or obtain information and to engage in dialogue with stakeholders (2.13) regarding the management of risk (2.1)
Note 1 to entry: The information can relate to the existence, nature, form, likelihood (2.19), significance, evaluation, acceptability and treatment of the management of risk.
Note 2 to entry: Consultation is a two-way process of informed communication between an organization and its stakeholders on an issue prior to making a decision or determining a direction on that issue. Consultation is:

- — a process which impacts on a decision through influence rather than power; and
- — an input to decision making, not joint decision making.

[SOURCE: ISO Guide 73:2009, definition 3.2.1]

2.13
stakeholder
person or organization that can affect, be affected by, or perceive themselves to be affected by a decision or activity
Note 1 to entry: A decision maker can be a stakeholder.
[SOURCE: ISO Guide 73:2009, definition 3.2.1.1]

2.14
risk assessment
overall process of risk identification (2.15), risk analysis (2.21) and risk evaluation (2.24)
[SOURCE: ISO Guide 73:2009, definition 3.4.1]

2.15
risk identification
process of finding, recognizing and describing risks (2.1)
Note 1 to entry: Risk identification involves the identification of risk sources (2.16), events (2.17), their causes and their potential consequences (2.18).
Note 2 to entry: Risk identification can involve historical data, theoretical analysis, informed and expert opinions, and stakeholder's (2.13) needs.
[SOURCE: ISO Guide 73:2009, definition 3.5.1]

2.16

risk source
element which alone or in combination has the intrinsic potential to give rise to risk (2.1)
Note 1 to entry: A risk source can be tangible or intangible.
[SOURCE: ISO Guide 73:2009, definition 3.5.1.2]

2.17
event
occurrence or change of a particular set of circumstances
Note 1 to entry: An event can be one or more occurrences, and can have several causes.
Note 2 to entry: An event can consist of something not happening.
Note 3 to entry: An event can sometimes be referred to as an "incident" or "accident".
Note 4 to entry: An event without consequences (2.18) can also be referred to as a "near miss", "incident", "near hit" or "close call".
[SOURCE: ISO Guide 73:2009, definition 3.5.1.3]

2.18
consequence
outcome of an event (2.17) affecting objectives
Note 1 to entry: An event can lead to a range of consequences.
Note 2 to entry: A consequence can be certain or uncertain and can have positive or negative effects on objectives.
Note 3 to entry: Consequences can be expressed qualitatively or quantitatively.
Note 4 to entry: Initial consequences can escalate through knock-on effects.
[SOURCE: ISO Guide 73:2009, definition 3.6.1.3]

2.19
likelihood
chance of something happening
Note 1 to entry: In risk management terminology, the word "likelihood" is used to refer to the chance of something happening, whether defined, measured or determined objectively or subjectively, qualitatively or quantitatively, and described using general terms or mathematically (such as a probability or a frequency over a given time period).
Note 2 to entry: The English term "likelihood" does not have a direct equivalent in some languages; instead, the equivalent of the term "probability" is often used. However, in English, "probability" is often narrowly interpreted as a mathematical term. Therefore, in risk management terminology, "likelihood" is used with the intent that it should have the same broad interpretation as the term "probability" has in many languages other than English.
[SOURCE: ISO Guide 73:2009, definition 3.6.1.1]

2.20
risk profile
description of any set of risks (2.1)
Note 1 to entry: The set of risks can contain those that relate to the whole organization, part of the organization, or as otherwise defined.
[SOURCE: ISO Guide 73:2009, definition 3.8.2.5]

2.21
risk analysis
process to comprehend the nature of risk (2.1) and to determine the level of risk (2.23)
Note 1 to entry: Risk analysis provides the basis for risk evaluation (2.24) and decisions about risk treatment (2.25).
Note 2 to entry: Risk analysis includes risk estimation.
[SOURCE: ISO Guide 73:2009, definition 3.6.1]

2.22

risk criteria
terms of reference against which the significance of a risk (2.1) is evaluated
Note 1 to entry: Risk criteria are based on organizational objectives, and external (2.10) and internal context (2.11).
Note 2 to entry: Risk criteria can be derived from standards, laws, policies and other requirements.
[SOURCE: ISO Guide 73:2009, definition 3.3.1.3]

2.23
level of risk
magnitude of a risk (2.1) or combination of risks, expressed in terms of the combination of consequences (2.18) and their likelihood (2.19)
[SOURCE: ISO Guide 73:2009, definition 3.6.1.8]

2.24
risk evaluation
process of comparing the results of risk analysis (2.21) with risk criteria (2.22) to determine whether the risk (2.1) and/or its magnitude is acceptable or tolerable
Note 1 to entry: Risk evaluation assists in the decision about risk treatment (2.25).
[SOURCE: ISO Guide 73:2009, definition 3.7.1]

2.25
risk treatment
process to modify risk (2.1)
Note 1 to entry: Risk treatment can involve:

- — avoiding the risk by deciding not to start or continue with the activity that gives rise to the risk;
- — taking or increasing risk in order to pursue an opportunity;
- — removing the risk source (2.16);
- — changing the likelihood (2.19);
- — changing the consequences (2.18);
- — sharing the risk with another party or parties (including contracts and risk financing); and
- — retaining the risk by informed decision.

Note 2 to entry: Risk treatments that deal with negative consequences are sometimes referred to as "risk mitigation", "risk elimination", "risk prevention" and "risk reduction".
Note 3 to entry: Risk treatment can create new risks or modify existing risks.
[SOURCE: ISO Guide 73:2009, definition 3.8.1]

2.26
control
measure that is modifying risk (2.1)
Note 1 to entry: Controls include any process, policy, device, practice, or other actions which modify risk.
Note 2 to entry: Controls may not always exert the intended or assumed modifying effect.
[SOURCE: ISO Guide 73:2009, definition 3.8.1.1]

2.27
residual risk
risk (2.1) remaining after risk treatment (2.25)
Note 1 to entry: Residual risk can contain unidentified risk.
Note 2 to entry: Residual risk can also be known as "retained risk".
[SOURCE: ISO Guide 73:2009, definition 3.8.1.6]

**2.28**
monitoring
continual checking, supervising, critically observing or determining the status in order to identify change from the performance level required or expected

Note 1 to entry: Monitoring can be applied to a risk management framework (2.3), risk management process (2.8), risk (2.1) or control (2.26).

[SOURCE: ISO Guide 73:2009, definition 3.8.2.1]

**2.29**
review
activity undertaken to determine the suitability, adequacy and effectiveness of the subject matter to achieve established objectives

Note 1 to entry: Review can be applied to a risk management framework (2.3), risk management process (2.8), risk (2.1) or control (2.26).

[SOURCE: ISO Guide 73:2009, definition 3.8.2.2]

# ADVANCED RISK MANAGEMENT-THE INSURANCE INDUSTRY

# Financial Service Industry Associations

# FPA

The Financial Planning Association® (FPA®) is the largest membership organization for CFP® professionals in the U.S. and also includes members who support the financial planning process. Working in alliance with academic leaders, legislative and regulatory bodies, financial services firms and consumer interest organizations, FPA helps connect all in our membership through a variety of unique and compelling ways. FPA members adhere to the highest standards of professional competence, ethical conduct and clear, complete disclosure to those they serve. FPA membership consists of CERTIFIED FINANCIAL PLANNERS™, educators, financial services professionals, students and more; FPA is compensation neutral and represents those from diverse backgrounds and business models. FPA's unique network of nationwide chapters encourage professional development and networking on a local level.

The Financial Planning Association is headquartered in Denver, Colo. and is governed by a volunteer Board of Directors who are charged with helping the organization reach its strategic goals. FPA's staff is dedicated to creating an unparalleled membership experience.

*Local Chapters*

A nationwide network of close to 100 chapters is the lifeblood of FPA. Each chapter promotes the advancement of knowledge in financial planning, supporting programs and projects that help the public learn the benefits of financial planning.

*Public Education*

FPA offers resources designed to help the public understand the importance of financial planning and the value of objective advice from a financial planner. Click here to search resources.

# SFSP

## About the Society of Financial Service Professionals

For more than 80 years, the Society of Financial Service Professionals has been helping individuals, families, and businesses achieve financial security.

With their strong commitment to delivering only those financial products and planning services that are in their clients' best interests, the Society's approximately 11,000 members nationwide are uniquely qualified to assist the public in reaching their future financial goals—today, tomorrow, and into the next millennium.

Society members can provide consumers expert assistance with: estate, retirement and financial planning; employee benefits; business and compensation planning; and life, health, disability, and long-term care insurance.

Society members have earned recognized professional credentials in the financial services industry, or are working towards attaining a professional credential.

If you are looking for a professional adviser who has experience, knowledge, and a strong commitment to ethical business practices, look for a member of the Society of Financial Service Professionals.

## NAIFA

One of the oldest and largest trade organizations in the insurance field, NAIFA was founded on June 18, 1890 in Boston as the National Association of Life Underwriters. NAIFA celebrated 100 years of industry leadership..

*Timeline*

- In 1928, NALU transferred its headquarters to New York City and eventually relocated to Washington, D.C., in 1956.
- In 1951, NALU created a conference, General Agents and Managers Association (GAMA), to enhance the quality and capability of the insurance industry's field management.
- In 1957, NALU formed the Association for Advanced Life Underwriting (AALU) to support advanced life insurance underwriters, agents engaged in complex areas of life insurance such as business continuation planning, estate planning, retirement planning, deferred compensation, and employee benefits planning.
- In 1990, a third conference of NALU, the Association of Health Insurance Agents (AHIA) was formed to sustain and enhance the business environment for health insurance agents and to improve the financing and delivery of health care in the United States.
- On September 29, 1999, the National Council delegates voted to change the association's name from the National Association of Life Underwriters to National Association of Insurance and Financial Advisors.
- NAIFA has been committed to improving the quality of life for Americans and addressing social problems since 1956 when the association first started developing community service programs. NAIFA local associations currently volunteer in social programs for health care, homelessness, youth education, AIDS awareness, drug/alcohol awareness, the family, senior citizens and U.S. crisis relief efforts. Between 1981 and 1989, NAIFA public service programs were honored six times by the Reagan and Bush Administrations' Private Initiatives Program.
- In May 2000, NAIFA moved into its new headquarters in Falls Church, Va., after 40 years at 1922 F Street, N.W., Washington, D.C.

# THE INSURANCE INDUSTRY

## NORTH CAROLINA DEPARTMENT OF INSURANCE-WEBSITE

- Consumer Services (Auto, Homeowners, Life and Other Insurance)
- Health Insurance Smart NC (Health Insurance)
- SHIIP (Medicare)
- Criminal Investigations (Insurance Fraud)

## EN ESPAÑOL

- We offer select information in the Spanish language (en Español). View available resources in the Spanish language.

## INSURANCE INDUSTRY

- Agent Services (Agents, Adjusters, Bail Bondsmen, Business Entities)
- Property and Casualty (Forms, Rates, Surplus Lines)
- Life and Health (Forms and Rates)
- Market Regulation
- Financial Evaluation
- Captive Insurance
- Alternative Markets (Captive Insurance, Medical Loss Ratio (MLR), Regulatory Actions, Unauthorized Plan Investigation)
- Actuarial Services
- Legislative Services (Bulletins)

# Product comparison

Male, Age 52, Std NT, Actual Prospect
**Comparison of Guaranteed Life Policy Illustration Values**
November 22, 2013

|  | **Liberty Select** | **FlexProtect II** | **National** |
|---|---|---|---|
| Annual Premium | $ 100,000.00 | $ 100,000.00 | $ 100,000.00 |
| *Premiums reduced* | | | |
| *13 th Yr Premium* | $ 77,052.00 | | |
| Guaranteed CSV @ Yr 13 | $ 1,303,307.00 | $ 850,698.00 | $ 1,025,238.00 |
| Non-Guaranteed CV @ Yr 13 | $ 1,359,847.00 | | |
| Net Insurance Yield | 3.31% | | |
| Net Annuity Yield | 3.00% | | |
| Guaranteed Death Benefit | $ 2,710,762.00 | $ 3,170,578.00 | $ 2,137,025.00 |
| **Comdex Rating** | 96 | 89 | 93 |
| **Guaranteed Paid Up Date** | 13 Yrs | Age 100 | Age 100 |

*All Illustrated with dividends to reduce premiums*

HomeStoreProductsCompanyEventsSupportContact Us

## Wealth In Motion

Wealth In Motion®
The Professional's Choice

Wealth In Motion® is the preeminent financial analysis tool in the industry today. Coupled with the proprietary training from LEAP SYSTEMS, Inc., you will have the benefit of over 30 years of financial industry experience in helping to enrich the lives of clients through a time-tested process. Capture a simultaneous view of a client's Protection, Savings, Growth, Debt, and Cash Flow components on one page to help clients to make the best financial decisions possible for them and their family.

**New License Only**
**$2,495**
Buy Now

| Overview | Features | Screenshot | Reports | Sys Reqs | FAQs |

## OVERVIEW

- Unique Personal Financial Simulation™ software
- PS&G Model® financial organizer helps to analyze and track on one page
- Proprietary, cutting edge technology differentiates your practice
- Supported with regional live training events and archived video tutorials
- Client presentation materials enhance the total experience*
- Integrated reports allow for long term retention of ideas and strategies
- Available WebCFQ™ provides a 24/7 access point for collecting and inputting financial data for clients and professionals/staff*

*May be available separately and for an additional fee

Advanced Risk Management

# InsMark Product Line

InsMark Illustration System

Licensing Fee: $899.00

Wealthy and Wise® System

Licensing Fee: $1,499.00

Loan-Based Split Dollar System

Licensing Fee: $1,299.00

-

    Leveraged Compensation System

    Licensing Fee: $1,299.00

-

    Premium Financing System

    Licensing Fee: $1,299.00

-

    Cloud-Based Documents On A Disk

    Licensing Fee: $399.00

-

    Life Plan System

    Licensing Fee: $149.00

-

Power Producer Platinum

Licensing Fee: $4,995.00

Power Producer Gold

Licensing Fee: $4,295.00

Power Producer Silver

Licensing Fee: $3,495.00

Power Producer Bronze

Licensing Fee: $2,995.00

*"The InsMark software is indispensable to my entire planning process because it enables me to show my clients that inaction has a price tag. I can't afford to go without it!"* David McKnight, Author of The Power of Zero, InsMark Gold Power Producer®, Grafton, WIFeatured Products

- InsMark Illustration System
- Wealthy and Wise® System
- Loan-Based Split Dollar System
- Leveraged Compensation System
- Premium Financing System
- Cloud-Based Documents On A Disk™
- Life Plan System
- Advanced Underwriting Registry

# ADVANCED RISK MANAGEMENT-CAPTIVE INSURANCE COMPANIES

Delaware Series LLC Micro-Captive Proforma

# CAPTIVE INSURANCE COMPANY PROPOSAL

**Introduction**

A Captive Insurance Company allows a corporation to **secure** insur**ance covering** risk **where insurance is** otherwise **is** unavailable or expensive to obtain by forming a company that is controlled by the parent company and **by then** purchasing risk **insurance** from the subsidiary company. Micro-captives that file an election under section 831(b) and follow the rules, as promulgated by the Internal Revenue Service and the U.S. Courts, are allowed to exclude from income up to $1.2 million in annual premium. This corporate tax incentive was placed into law in the Tax Reform Act of 1986. Rulings by the service to clarify the rules began in earnest in 2002. A Tax Court decision on January 14, 2014, in favor of the Captive helped clarify the rules. Today, according to Forbes, 90% of the Fortune 500 already ha**ve** established Captive Insurance Companies. Most captives today that are created are established in the USA and not offshore as states have modified their charters to accommodate the formation of captive insurance companies. The Tax Court will respect the separate taxable treatment of a captive unless there is a finding of sham or a lack of a business purpose. A captive must be created for significant and legitimate non-tax reasons. A captive should not have impermissible circular flow of funds. The captive must have adequate premium-to-surplus ratios. The captive must be a bona-fide insurance company.

In order for payments **to a Captive** to be a deductible expense **to the Parent**, the policies issued must involve insurance risk. This means there must be risk-shifting, the policies must distribute risk, and the arrangement must constitute insurance in the commonly accepted sense.

In Rent a Center v. Commissioner 142 T.C. 1 (Tax Court 2014), in a divided court, the Tax Court upheld a parent guarantee of the insurance subsidiary. In Rev. Rul. 2005-40 example 4, the Internal Revenue Service cites with approval the formation of a captive. In Rev. Rul. 2014-15 the IRS again cites with approval the unrelated party risk of a captive. However, captives that are abusive in nature, generally where disrespect for the entity takes place by borrowing funds out of the captive, may be designated a sham *see* Bancroft v. Scolari No. C11-507RBI (DC WA 2013), Salty Brine 1 v. U.S. (DC TX 2013).

# Captive Application Process

In order to obtain an application, interested parties must first complete some preliminary steps as follows:

1. Conduct a self- assessment to make a preliminary determination as to whether a captive insurance company is right for your business,
2. Obtain a qualified consultant to provide advice and conduct a feasibility study (see below for guidance),
3. Meet with the Department to obtain guidance and buy-in on the initial plan, and
4. Make an on-line request to the Department for an application.

It is imperative that these steps be completed before an application is filled out. Because these steps are so critical to the success of any captive, the Department limits access to the captive application forms until it is satisfied that this process has been completed. After we have met with the principals and the initial plans appear feasible, access to the application process will be provided by email.

### *What Types of Captives are available in Utah?*

Generally there are three types of captives in Utah:

- Pure Captives
- Group Captives
- Reinsurance Captives

### *Pure Captives*
**Single Parent (or Pure) Captive**
   A Pure Captive is owned and controlled by one company and insures that company and/or its affiliates.

**Branch Captives**
   A branch captive is an on-shore (US) arm of an off-shore captive. Branch captives are typically used to cover employee benefits under ERISA, which can only be offered by a US insurer and can only write the business that a pure captive may write.

**Special Purpose Captives**
   A special purpose captive is owned or controlled by a parent company and may only insure the risk of its parent.

### *Group Captives*

A Group Captive is a captive insurance company owned and controlled by two or more non-affiliated organizations insured by the captive.

There are several types of group captives available under Utah statutes. Each of these captives is briefly described below:

### Association Captives
An association captive is owned by members of a common industry or trade association. This type of captive is designed to insure the risks of that industry among its members. Participation is limited to members of the association.

### Sponsored Captives
Sponsored captives are a type of rent-a-captive and are also called Segregated Cell and Protected Cell Captives. These entities allow for assets and liabilities of one captive program to be legally segregated from the assets and liabilities of other captive programs. Sponsored Captives allow for entities to insure their own risks without establishing their own captive structure.

### Industrial Insured Captives
An Industrial Insured Captive is one formed to insure the risks produced by a group of industrial entities.

An Industrial Insured is an insured that procures the insurance of any risk or risks by use of the services of a full-time employee acting as an insurance manager or buyer and whose aggregate annual premiums for insurance on all risks is at least $25,000 and who has at least 25 full-time employees. Industrial entities may form a group and insure the risks produced by that group through an Industrial Insured Captive.

### Risk Retention Group (RRG)
A Risk Retention Group is one form or type of captive that is restricted to writing only liability coverage. An RRG may have either state or federal charters. A federal charter allows the RRG to write liability coverage directly in any state where it is registered without having to become a licensed carrier in each state or use a fronting company. This can significantly reduce the cost and effort of crossing state boundaries. However, they are restricted to writing liability coverage.

### *Reinsurance Captives*

The third type of Captive is a Captive Reinsurance Company. This Captive is a stock corporation formed to carry the risks of a qualifying reinsurance parent company. The captive must maintain at least $300,000,000 of capital or 10% of the reserves of the reinsurance parent company whichever is greater.

## How Much Will It Cost to Create a Captive Insurer in Utah?

An organization considering the captive alternative will need to incorporate the following initial setup costs and also the ongoing costs to manage a captive before making a final decision:

| Startup Activity: | Estimated Cost: |
|---|---|
| Prepare business plan and complete application. | Varies, but should not be |

|  |  |
|---|---|
|  | significant once feasibility study completed. |
| Filing of application | $200 per application |
| Review of application | $3,600 |
| Initial license fee | $5,000 **without proration** (as per rule R590-238-20 (2)), |
| Initial e-Commerce fee | $250 **without proration** |
| Incorporation | $52 w/ annual renewal of same. |
| Initial Capital: |  |
|    Pure Captive | $250,000 |
|    Association | $750,000 |
|    Industrial Insured | $500,000 |
|    Sponsored | $1,000,000 |
|    Any captive organized as Reciprocal | $1,000,000 |
| **Ongoing Maintenance:** | **Estimated Cost:** |
| Annual renewal fee | $5,000 **Due June 30th** |
| Annual e-Commerce fee | $250 **Due June 30th** |
| Taxes | None except property taxes |
| Independent Actuary - Reserve Opinion | $6,000 |
| Independent CPA - Annual Audit | $5,000 |
| Management Firm | Annual fee ($20,000+) |

In general it is estimated that initial startup costs for a captive would be $30,000 to $60,000 plus initial capital. Ongoing maintenance costs would be estimated at $60,000 to $70,000 annually. Of course these are just estimates and will vary depending on the size and complexity of each captive arrangement. Service provider costs will vary depending on the complexity and requirements of the engagement.

*What are the capitalization requirements in Utah for a captive insurance company?*

|  | Unimpaired Paid-in Capital | Free Surplus | Total Capital Requirement |
|---|---|---|---|
| Pure Captive (Stock) | 100,000 | 150,000 | 250,000 |
| Association Captive (Stock) | 400,000 | 350,000 | 750,000 |
| Association Captive (Mutual) |  | 750,000 | 750,000 |
| Association Captive (Reciprocal) |  | 1,000,000 | 1,000,000 |
| Industrial Insured Captive (Stock) | 200,000 | 300,000 | 500,000 |
| Industrial Insured Captive (Mutual) |  | 500,000 | 500,000 |
| Industrial Insured Captive (Reciprocal) |  | 1,000,000 | 1,000,000 |
| Sponsored Captive | 500,000 | 500,000 | 1,000,000 |

**Department Examination:**
Each Utah captive will be examined at least once every three years by the Utah Insurance Department. The cost of that examination will be born by the captive being examined.

**Annual Audit:**
All companies shall have an annual audit by an independent CPA authorized by the commissioner, and shall file the audited financial report with the commissioner on or before June 30 for the year ending December 31 immediately preceding. The annual audit shall be on the same basis as the annual report. The audit report should consist of:

1. Opinion of Independent Certified Public Accountant;
2. Audited Financial Statements (including balance sheet, statement of gain or loss from operations, statement of changes in financial position, statement of cash flows, and statement of changes in capital paid up, gross paid in and contributed surplus and unassigned funds (surplus), income statement, statement of stockholder's equity, cash flow statement, and notes to the financials);
3. Independent Auditor's Report On Internal Controls;
4. Accountant's Letter of Qualifications
5. Certification of Loss Reserves and Loss Expense Reserves (individual certifying must be approved by commissioner.

**Annual Report:**
Each Utah captive will be required to file a report of the financial condition of the captive insurance company (annual report) with the commissioner before March 1 of each year, verified under oath of two of the executive officers. The form of the report is as follows:

- A pure captive, sponsored captive, industrial insured captive, or producer reinsurance captive shall submit the annual report using the form prescribed by the commissioner as "Captive Annual Statement".
- An association captive or industrial insured captive shall annually submit to the commissioner a report using the applicable NAIC Annual Statement Blank.

## *Are there any investment restrictions in Utah?*

Association Captives, Sponsored Captives, and Industrial Insured Groups must comply with the same investment restrictions that a traditional insurance company must observe. Specific investment restrictions are contained in Utah Code Annotated (U.C.A.) Section 31A-18-105 and U.C.A. Section 31A-18-106.

A Pure Captive has no investment restrictions, except that the Department will not allow investments that threaten the solvency of the captive. Each captive insurer must file a description of their investment strategy as part of the initial application. The captive must notify the Department of any future changes to that investment strategy.

A Pure Captive is the only type of captive that may make loans to the parent company or an affiliate of the captive. However, such loans by a Pure Captive may not be made from the paid-in capital or the free surplus that is required by U.C.A. Section 31A-37-204(1) and U.C.A. Section 31A-37-205(1), respectively. While the Department may allow pure captives to make loans back to the parent, there could be significant tax implications. Therefore, a captive insurer should consult with appropriate tax advisors prior to making request of the Department to make loans back to the parent.

Advanced Risk Management

### What fees are applicable for captives in Utah?

Initial license application: $200
Initial license application - review: Actual costs incurred by outside reviewer
Initial license issuance: $5,000
Initial e-Commerce fee: $250
Annual renewal fee: $5,000
Annual e-Commerce fee $250

### What taxes are applicable to captives in Utah?

Except for personal and real property tax on property owned by the captive in Utah and an annual e-commerce fee, an annual assessment of $5,000 is the sole tax or fee assessed on a captive insurer in Utah.

### Are Captives covered under Guaranty Funds?

No, a captive insurance company is prohibited from contributing financially to a plan, pool, association, guaranty fund or insolvency fund not covered by the guaranty associations in Utah or elsewhere.

### What types of insurance can be written in a captive?

When permitted by its articles of incorporation or charter, a captive insurance company may apply to the commissioner for a certificate of authority to do ALL lines of insurance allowed by the insurance code, EXCEPT workers compensation insurance and personal motor vehicle or homeowners insurance, or any component of these coverage's. Reference Title See U.C.A Section 31A-37-202(1) (a) and (b) (iv).

A pure captive may only insure the risks of its parent, affiliates, or controlled unaffiliated business. Reference Title See U.C.A Section 31A-37-202(1) (b) (i)

An association captive may only insure the risks of association member organizations and affiliates of the association member organizations. Reference Title See U.C.A Section 31A-37-202(1) (b) (ii).

An industrial insured may only insure risks of the industrial insured's that comprise the industrial insured group and affiliates of the industrial insured's that comprise the industrial insured group. Reference Title See U.C.A Section 31A-37-202(1) (b) (iii)

### What must a Captive do to conduct business in Utah as a Utah domiciled Captive?

- Obtain from the commissioner a valid Certificate of Authority specifying the types of insurance authorized (i.e. go through the licensing process).
- Hold at least once each year in Utah a board of directors meeting, or in the case of a reciprocal insurer, a subscriber's advisory committee meeting.
- Maintain the principal place of business of the captive in Utah.
- Appoint a resident registered agent to accept service of process and act on behalf of the captive in Utah.
- Renew the Certificate of Authority annually by July 1 of each year.
- Comply with all other applicable statutes and rules.

## The Benefits of a Micro-Captive:

The Primary benefit of a captive is to purchase insurance at favorable costs or underwrite risks that generally cannot be underwritten. However, there are tax benefits as well.

Assumptions Written Premiums $1,200,000 Pool Participation 53% Pooling Fee & Atlas Reinsurance 2.488% Investment Return 4% Federal Income Tax Rate 43.4% (includes 2.9% Medicare tax plus 0.9% surcharge) State Income Tax Rate 5% Loss Ratio 10%

| | | | | |
|---|---|---|---|---|
| Income | $1,200,000 | | Income | $1,200,000 |
| Tax | 420,000 | | Claims | 120,000 |
| State | 60,000 | | Expenses | 75,000 |
| Net | $ 720,000 | | Net | $1,005,000 |

ILLUSTRATION

| Expense | | | | | |
|---|---|---|---|---|---|
| MGMT Fees | 39,500 | 39,500 | 39,500 | 39,500 | 39,500 |
| Pooling Fee | 29,856 | 29,856 | 29,856 | 29,856 | 29,856 |
| Actuary & Audit | - | - | - | - | - |
| Domicile Fee | 5,000 | 5,000 | 5,000 | 5,000 | 5,000 |
| Total expenses | 74,356 | 74,356 | 74,356 | 74,356 | 74,356 |

Note:
(A) - Formation fees do not cover captive operating expenses.
(B) - Insurance management fees and pooling fees start on the requested licensing date. In practice, these fees are deducted from the premium when it is received. The full fee is deducted in advance. Management Fees are inclusive of actuary, audit, legal, registered agent, tax filing and domicile licensing fees.
(C) Claims may be payable to the parent and vary as made.

# Blue Print for Captives-Rent- A- Center v. Commissioner 2014

The recent U.S. Tax Court case Rent-A –Center gives a blueprint on Captive Insurance Companies. Currently most fortune 400 companies operate captives, however the opportunities are for installation in the mid- size and small companies-even micro 831(b) captives.

The Rent A Center case also had dissents which were well written. Although the majority ruled in favor of the corporation, there could be future cases where the court does not see a risk shift operation. This becomes a tax risk which is difficult to quantify and insure. One potential argument for the captive is to allow a corporation to become more solvent as the captive operates as a form of reserves for the main company.
This argument would look to congressional intent in establishing a tax favored entity which encourages stability.

The argument from the IRS was clear-the parent was funding the guaranteed benefits for the sub which insured the parent. This circular transfer of funds allowed tax benefits which all inured to the "economic family".

The argument of the taxpayer is they were separate entities and the funding by the parent who may benefit should be ignored.

The Court was divided-however the majority allowed the tax benefits to stand which has opened up an entire industry of captive insurance companies for small and mid-size business entities which look for tax deductions and risk mitigation.

142 T.C. No. 1
UNITED STATES TAX COURT
RENT-A-CENTER, INC. AND AFFILIATED SUBSIDIARIES, Petitioners
v.
COMMISSIONER OF INTERNAL REVENUE, Respondent
Docket Nos. 8320-09, 6909-10, Filed January 14, 2014.
21627-10.

P, a domestic corporation, is the parent of numerous wholly owned subsidiaries including L, a Bermudian corporation. P conducted its business through stores owned and operated by its subsidiaries. The other subsidiaries and L entered into contracts pursuant to which each subsidiary paid L an amount, determined by actuarial calculations and an allocation formula, relating to workers' compensation, automobile, and general liability risks, and, in turn, L reimbursed a portion of each subsidiary's claims relating to these risks. P's subsidiaries deducted, as insurance expenses, the payments to L. In notices of deficiency issued to P, R determined that the payments were not deductible.

Held: P's subsidiaries' payments to L are deductible, pursuant to I.R.C. sec. 162, as insurance expenses.

Val J. Albright and Brent C. Gardner, Jr., for petitioners.
R. Scott Shieldes and Daniel L. Timmons, for respondent.

FOLEY, Judge: Respondent determined deficiencies of $14,931,159, $13,409,628, $7,461,039, $5,095,222, and $2,828,861 relating, respectively, to Rent-A-Center, Inc. (RAC), and its subsidiaries' 2003,[1] 2004, 2005, 2006, and 2007 (years in issue) consolidated Federal income tax returns. The issue for decision is whether payments to Legacy Insurance Co., Ltd. (Legacy), were deductible, pursuant to section 162,[2] as insurance expenses.

## FINDINGS OF FACT

RAC, a publicly traded Delaware corporation, is the parent of a group of approximately 15 affiliated subsidiaries (collectively, petitioner). During the years in issue, petitioner was the largest domestic rent-to-own company. Through stores owned and operated by RAC's subsidiaries, petitioner rented, sold, and delivered home electronics, furniture, and appliances. The stores were in all 50 States, the [1]Respondent, in his amended answer, asserted an additional $2,603,193 deficiency relating to 2003.

₂Unless otherwise indicated, all section references are to the Internal Revenue Code in effect for the years in issue, and all Rule references are to the Tax Court Rules of Practice and Procedure.

---

District of Columbia, Puerto Rico, and Canada. From 1993 through 2002, petitioner's company-owned stores increased from 27 to 2,623. During the years in issue, RAC's subsidiaries owned between 2,623 and 3,081 stores; had between 14,300 and 19,740 employees; and operated between 7,143 and 8,027 insured vehicles.

**I. Petitioner's Insurance Program**

In 2001, American Insurance Group (AIG), in response to a claim against RAC's directors and officers (D&O), withdrew a previous offer to renew RAC's D&O insurance policy. To address this problem, RAC engaged Aon Risk Consultants, Inc. (Aon), which convinced AIG to renew the policy. Impressed with Aon's insurance expertise and concerned about its growing insurance costs, petitioner engaged Aon to analyze risk management practices and to broker workers' compensation, automobile, and general liability insurance. With Aon's assistance, petitioner developed a risk management department and improved its loss prevention program.
Prior to August 2002, Travelers Insurance Co. (Travelers) provided petitioner's workers' compensation, automobile, and general liability coverage through bundled policies. Pursuant to a bundled policy, an insurer provides coverage and controls the claims administration process (i.e., investigating, evaluating, and paying claims). Travelers paid claims as they arose and withdrew amounts from petitioner's bank account to reimburse itself for any claims less than or equal to petitioner's deductible (i.e., a portion of an insured claim for which the insured is responsible). Pursuant to a predetermined formula, each store was allocated, and was responsible for paying, a portion of Travelers' premium costs.

In 2001, after receiving a $3 million invoice from Travelers for "claim handling fees", petitioner became dissatisfied with the cost and inefficiency associated with its bundled policies. On August 5, 2002, petitioner, with the assistance of Aon, obtained unbundled workers' compensation, automobile, and general liability policies from Discover Re. Pursuant to an unbundled policy, an insurer provides coverage and a third-party administrator manages the claims administration process. Discover Re underwrote the policies;

multiple insurers provided coverage;[3] and Specialty Risk Services, Inc. (SRS),[4] a third-party administrator, evaluated and paid claims. Petitioner and its staff of licensed adjusters had access to SRS' claims management system and monitored SRS to

---

[3] The following insurers provided coverage: U.S. Fidelity & Guarantee Co., Fidelity & Guaranty Insurance Co., Discover Property and Casualty Insurance Co.,
St. Paul Fire & Marine Co. of Canada, and Fidelity Guaranty Insurance Underwriters Inc.
[4] SRS was affiliated with the Hartford Insurance Co., a well-established insurer, and did not have a contract with Discover Re.

---

ensure the proper handling of claims. This arrangement gave petitioner greater control over the claims administration process.
Petitioner, pursuant to the Discover Re policies' deductibles, was liable for a specific amount of each claim against its workers' compensation, automobile, and general liability policies (e.g., pursuant to its 2002 workers' compensation policy, petitioner was liable for the first $350,000 of each claim). Petitioner's retention of a portion of the risk resulted in lower premiums.

## II. Legacy's Inception

Between 1993 and 2002, petitioner rapidly expanded and became increasingly concerned about its growing risk management costs. In 2002, after analyzing petitioner's insurance program, Aon suggested that petitioner form a wholly owned insurance company (i.e., a captive). Aon Representatives informed David Glasgow, petitioner's director of risk management, about the financial and nonfinancial benefits of forming a captive. Aon convincingly explained that a captive could help petitioner reduce its costs, improve efficiency, obtain otherwise unavailable coverage, and provide accountability and transparency. Mr. Glasgow presented the proposal to petitioner's senior management, who concurred with Mr. Glasgow's recommendation to further explore the formation of a captive. Petitioner's senior management directed Aon to conduct a feasibility study (i.e., relying on petitioner's workers' compensation, automobile, and general liability loss data) and to prepare loss forecasts and actuarial studies.

Petitioner engaged KPMG to analyze the feasibility study, review tax considerations, and prepare financial projections.

Aon, in the feasibility study, recommended that the captive be capitalized with no less than $8.8 million. Before deciding where to incorporate the captive, RAC analyzed projected financial data and reviewed multiple locations. On December 11, 2002, RAC incorporated, and capitalized with $9.9 million,[5]

Legacy, a wholly owned Bermudian subsidiary.[6] Legacy opened an account with Bank of N.T. Butterfield and Son, Ltd., and, on December 20, 2002, filed a class 1 insurance company registration application with the Bermuda Monetary Authority (BMA), which regulated Bermuda's financial services sector. A class 1 insurer may insure only the risk of its shareholders and affiliates; must be capitalized with at least $120,000; and must meet a minimum solvency margin calculated by [5]RAC contributed $9.9 million of cash and received 120,000 shares of Legacy capital stock with a par value of $1.

---

[6]Legacy elected, pursuant to sec. 953(d), to be treated as a domestic corporation for Federal income tax purposes. In addition, Legacy engaged Aon Insurance Managers (Bermuda), Ltd., to monitor Legacy's compliance with Bermudian regulations and to provide management, financial, and administrative services.

...reference to the insurer's net premiums, general business assets,[7] and general business liabilities. See Insurance Act, 1978, secs. 4B, 6, Appleby (2008) (Berm.);

Insurance Returns and Solvency Regulations, 1980, Appleby, Reg. 10(1), Schedule I, Figure B (Berm.). During the years in issue, the BMA had the authority to modify prescribed requirements through both prospective and retroactive directives for special allowances. See Insurance Act, 1978, sec.

---

Legacy planned to insure petitioner's liabilities for the period beginning in 2002 and ending December 31, 2003 (proposed period). Aon informed petitioner that coverage provided by unrelated insurers would be more costly than Aon's estimate of Legacy's premiums and that some insurers would not be willing to offer coverage. In response to a quote request, Discover Re stated that it was not in the market to provide the coverage Legacy contemplated. Discover Re estimated, however, that its premium (i.e., if it were to write one relating to the proposed period) would be approximately $3 million more than Legacy's.

[7]The Bermuda Insurance Act, the Insurance Accounts Regulations, and the Insurance Returns and Solvency Regulations reference "general business", "admitted", and "relevant" assets. See Insurance Act, 1978, sec. 1, Appleby (2008) (Berm.); Insurance Accounts Regulations, 1980, Appleby, Schedule III, Pt. 1, 13 (Berm.); Insurance Returns and Solvency Regulations, 1980, Appleby, Reg. 10(3), 11(4) (Berm.). For purposes of this Opinion, there is no significant difference among these terms.

### III. Petitioner's Policies

During the years in issue, petitioner obtained unbundled workers' compensation, automobile, and general liability policies from Discover Re. Pursuant to these policies, Discover Re provided petitioner with coverage above a predetermined threshold relating to each line of coverage. In addition, Legacy wrote policies that covered petitioner's workers' compensation, automobile, and general liability claims below the Discover Re threshold. Petitioner, depending on the amount of a covered loss, could seek payment from Legacy, Discover Re, or both companies.

The annual premium Legacy charged petitioner was actuarially determined using Aon loss forecasts and was allocated to each RAC subsidiary that owned covered stores. RAC was a listed policyholder pursuant to the Legacy policies. No premium was attributable to RAC, however, because it did not own stores, have employees, or operate vehicles. RAC paid the premiums relating to each policy, estimated petitioner's t[8]otal insurance costs (i.e., Legacy policies, Discover Re policies, third-party administrator fees, overhead, etc.), and established a

---

[8]From December 31, 2002, through September 12, 2003, Legacy incurred a $4,861,828 liability relating to claim reimbursements due petitioner. This amount was netted against petitioner's September 12, 2003, premium payment (i.e., petitioner paid a net premium of $37,938,472 rather than the $42,800,300 gross premium).

monthly rate relating to each store's portion of these costs. The monthly rate was based on three factors: each store's payroll, each store's number of vehicles, and the total number of stores. At the end of each year, RAC adjusted the allocations to ensure that its subsidiaries recognized their actual insurance costs. SRS administered all claims relating to petitioner's workers' compensation, automobile, and general liability coverage. During the years in issue, the terms of Legacy's coverage varied, Legacy progressively covered greater amounts of petitioner's risk, and Legacy did not receive premiums from any unrelated entity.

From December 31, 2002, through December 30, 2007, Legacy earned net underwriting income of $28,761,402. See infra p. 16.

### A. Legacy's Deferred Tax Assets

Pursuant to the Legacy policies, coverage began on December 31 of each year. Because petitioner was a calendar year accrual method taxpayer, these policies created temporary timing differences between income recognized for tax purposes and income recognized for financial accounting (book) purposes.[9] For

---

[9]Each premium was generally paid in September of the year following the year in which the policy became effective. Use of the recurring item exception allowed petitioner to claim a premium deduction relating to the year in which the policy became effective, rather than the following year when the premium was actually paid. See sec. 461(h)(3)(A)(iii). On August 28, 2007, petitioner filed Form 3115, Application for Change in Accounting Method, requesting permission
(continued...)

---

example, on December 31, 2002, when Legacy's second policy became effective, Legacy recognized, for tax purposes, the full amount of the premium (i.e., $42,800,300) relating to the taxable year ending December 31, 2002. See sec. 832(b)(4). For book purposes, however, Legacy in 2002 recognized only 1/365 of the premium (i.e., $117,261), and the remaining $42,683,039 constituted a reserve.

This timing difference created a deferred tax asset (DTA) because in 2002 Legacy "prepaid" its tax liability relating to income it recognized, for book purposes, in 2003. Each day Legacy recognized a portion of its premium income (i.e., $117,261) for book purposes and reduced its reserve by the same amount. On December 30, 2003, the reserve was fully depleted. Upon the issuance of a new policy on December 31, 2003, a new DTA was created because Legacy recognized, for tax purposes, in 2003 the full amount of the premium; a corresponding tax liability was incurred; the premium reserve increased; and most of the premium income attributable to the 2003 policy was recognizable, for book purposes, in 2004.

---

9(...continued)
to revoke its use of the recurring item exception.

## 1. Bermuda's Minimum Solvency Margin Requirement

Pursuant to the Bermuda Insurance Act, an insurance company must maintain a minimum solvency margin. See Insurance Act, 1978, sec. 6. More specifically, a class 1 insurer's general business assets must exceed its general business liabilities by the greatest of: $120,000; 10% of the insurer's loss and loss expense provisions plus other insurance reserves; or 20% of the first $6 million of net premiums plus 10% of the net premiums which exceed $6 million. See Insurance Returns and Solvency Regulations, 1980, Appleby, Reg. 10(1), Schedule I, Figure B. DTAs generally may be treated as general business assets only with the BMA's permission.

## 2. Legacy Receives Permission To Treat DTAs as General Business Assets Through 2003

In the minimum solvency margin calculation set forth in its insurance company registration application, Legacy treated DTAs as general business assets.

On March 11, 2003, Legacy petitioned the BMA for the requisite permission to do so. The following letter from RAC accompanied the request:
We write to confirm to you that Rent-A-Center, Inc., * * * will guarantee the payment to Legacy Insurance Company, Ltd. (the "Company"), * * * of all amounts reflected on the projected balance sheets of the Company previously delivered to you as deferred tax assets arising from timing differences in the amounts of taxes payable for tax and financial accounting purposes. This guaranty of payment will take effect in the event of any change in tax laws that would require recognition of an impairment of the deferred tax asset, and will be effective to the extent of the amount of the impairment.

On March 13, 2003, the BMA granted Legacy permission to treat DTAs as general business assets on its statutory balance sheet through December 31, 2003. The BMA also i 10 nformed Legacy that from December 31, 2002, through March 13, 2003, it "wrote insurance business without being in receipt of its Certificate of Registration and was therefore in violation of the [Bermuda Insurance] Act as it engaged in insurance business without a license." Despite this violation, the BMA registered Legacy as a class 1 insurer effective December 20, 2002 (i.e., the date Legacy filed its insurance registration request and before it issued policies relating to the years in issue).

## 3. The Parental Guaranty: Facilitating the Treatment of DTAs as General Business Assets Through 2006

In response to the recurring DTA issue, Legacy requested that RAC guarantee DTAs relating to subsequent years. On September 17, 2003, RAC's board of directors authorized the execution of a guaranty of "the obligations of Legacy to comply with the laws of Bermuda." On the same day, RAC's chairman

---

[10] See infra pp. 15-16.

---

and chief executive officer executed a parental guaranty and sent it to Legacy's board of directors. The parental guaranty provided:

The undersigned, Rent-A-Center, Inc. a Delaware corporation ("Rent-A-Center") is sole owner of 100% of the issued and outstanding shares in your share capital and as such DOES HEREBY GUARANTEE financial support for you, Legacy Insurance Co., Ltd., * * * and for your business, as more particularly set out below, which is to say:

Under the [Bermuda] Insurance Act * * * and related Regulations (the "Act"), Legacy Insurance Co., Ltd., must maintain certain solvency and liquidity margins and, in order to ensure continued compliance with the Act, it is necessary to support Legacy Insurance Co., Ltd. with a guarantee of its liabilities under the Act (the "Liabilities") not to exceed Twenty-Five Million US dollars (US $25,000,000). Accordingly, Rent-A-Center DOES HEREBY GUARANTEE to you the payment in full of the Liabilities of Legacy Insurance Co., Ltd. and further to indemnify and hold harmless Legacy Insurance Co., Ltd. from the Liabilities up to the maximum dollar amount [$25,000,000] indicated in the foregoing paragraph.

Seeking regulatory approval to treat DTAs as general business assets in subsequent years, Legacy, on October 30, 2003, petitioned the BMA and attached the parental guaranty.

On November 12, 2003, the BMA issued a directive which "approved the

Parental Guarantee from Rent-A-Center, Inc. dated 17th September, 2003 up to an aggregate amount of $25,000,000 for utilization as part of * * * [Legacy]'s capitalization". This approval was granted for the years ending December 31, 2003, 2004, 2005, and 2006. Legacy used the parental guaranty only to meet the minimum solvency margin (i.e., to treat DTAs as general business assets).[11] On December 30, 2006, RAC unilaterally canceled the parental guaranty because Legacy met the minimum solvency margin without it.

### B. Legacy's Ownership of RAC Treasury Shares

Legacy purchased RAC treasury shares during 2004, 2005, and 2006. The BMA approved the purchases and allowed Legacy to treat the shares as general business assets for purposes of calculating its liquidity ratio (i.e., its ratio of general business assets to liabilities). Pursuant to Bermuda solvency regulations, an insurer fails to meet the liquidity ratio if the value of its general business assets is less than 75% of its liabilities. See Insurance Returns and Solvency Regulations, 1980, Appleby, Reg. 11(2). During the years in issue, Legacy met its liquidity ratio and did not resell the shares.

### C. Legacy's Financial Reports

For each policy period, Legacy's auditor, Arthur Morris & Co. (Arthur Morris), prepared, and provided to RAC and the BMA, reports and financial statements. In these reports and statements, Arthur Morris calculated Legacy's

---

[11] See infra pp. 15-16.

---

DTAs, minimum solvency [12] margin,[13] premium-to-surplus ratio,[14] and net underwriting income.[15] During each of the years in issue, Legacy's total statutory capital and surplus equaled or exceeded the BMA minimum solvency margin. In calculating total statutory capital and surplus, Arthur Morris took into account the following four components: contributed surplus, statutory surplus, capital stock, and other fixed capital (i.e., assets deemed to be general business assets). During 2003, 2004, and 2005, Legacy included portions of the parental guaranty as general business assets. During the years in issue, the amounts of Legacy's DTAs exceeded the portions of Legacy's parental guaranty treated as general business assets. See infra p. 16. Arthur Morris calculated Legacy's statutory surplus by
adding statutory surplus at the beginning of the year and income for the year,

subtracting dividends paid and payable, and making other adjustments relating to changes in assets.

---

[12] See supra pp. 9-10.

[13] See supra p. 11.

[14] Premium-to-surplus ratio is one measure of an insurer's economic performance. On Legacy's reports and statements, Arthur Morris referred to Legacy's premium-to-surplus ratio as the "premium to statutory capital & surplus ratio". For purposes of this Opinion, there is no significant difference between these terms.

[15] Net underwriting income equals gross premiums earned minus underwriting expenses.

---

The following table summarizes key details relating to Legacy's policies:

| Policy period | Premium | DTAs | Parental guaranty asset | Total statutory capital & surplus | Minimum solvency margin | Premium-to-surplus ratio | Net underwriting income |
|---|---|---|---|---|---|---|---|
| 2003 | $42,800,300 | $5,840,613 | $4,805,764 | $5,898,192 | $5,898,192 | 8.983:1 | $1,587,542 |
| 2004 | 50,639,000 | 6,275,326 | 4,243,823 | 7,036,573 | 7,036,572 | 7.695:1 | (982,000) |
| 2005 | 54,148,912 | 7,659,009 | 3,987,916 | 8,379,436 | 8,379,435 | 6.369:1 | 8,411,912 |
| 2006 | 53,365,926 | 8,742,425 | -0- | 10,014,206 | 9,284,601 | 6.326:1 | 8,810,926 |
| 2007 | 63,345,022 | 9,689,714 | -0- | 12,428,663 | 10,888,698 | 5.221:1 | 10,933,022 |
| 2008 | 64,884,392 | 9,607,661 | -0- | 23,712,022 | 11,278,359 | 2.538:1 | 18,391,392 |

## IV. Procedural History

Respondent sent petitioner, on January 7, 2008, a notice of deficiency relating to 2003; on December 22, 2009, a notice of deficiency relating to 2004 and 2005; and on August 5, 2010, a notice of deficiency relating to 2006 and 2007 (collectively, notices). In these notices, respondent determined that petitioner's payments to Legacy were not deductible pursuant to section 162. On April 6, 2009, March 22, 2010, and September 29, 2010, respectively, petitioner, whose principal place of business was Plano, Texas, timely filed petitions with the Court seeking redeterminations of the deficiencies set forth in the notices. After concessions, the remaining issue for decision is whether payments to Legacy were deductible.

## OPINION

In determining whether payments to Legacy were deductible, our initial inquiry is whether Legacy was a bona fide insurance company. See Harper Grp. v. Commissioner, 96 T.C. 45, 59 (1991), aff'd, 979 F.2d 1341 (9th Cir. 1992); AMERCO v. Commissioner, 96 T.C. 18, 40-41 (1991), aff'd, 979 F.2d 162 (9$^{th}$ Cir. 1992). We respect the separate taxable treatment of a captive unless there is a finding of sham or lack of business purpose. See Moline Props., Inc. v. Commissioner, 319 U.S. 436, 439 (1943); Harper Grp. v. Commissioner, 96 T.C. at 57-59. Respondent contends that Legacy was a sham entity created primarily to generate Federal income tax savings.

### I. Legacy Was Not a Sham

#### A. Legacy Was Created for Significant and Legitimate Nontax Reasons

After successfully resolving petitioner's D&O insurance problem, Aon evaluated petitioner's risk management department. Petitioner, with Aon's assistance, improved risk management practices, switched from bundled to unbundled policies, and hired SRS as a third-party administrator. Aon proposed that petitioner form a captive, and petitioner determined that a captive would allow it to reduce its insurance costs, obtain otherwise unavailable insurance coverage, formalize and more efficiently manage its insurance program, and provide accountability and transparency relating to insurance costs. Petitioner engaged KPMG to prepare financial projections and evaluate tax considerations referenced in the feasibility study. Federal income tax consequences were considered, but the formation of Legacy was not a tax-driven transaction. See Moline Props., Inc. v. Commissioner, 319 U.S. at 439; Britt v. United States, 431 F.2d 227, 235-236 (5$^{th}$ Cir. 1970); Bass v. Commissioner, 50 T.C. 595, 600 (1968). To the contrary, in forming Legacy, petitioner made a business decision premised on a myriad of significant and legitimate nontax considerations. See Jones v. Commissioner, 64 T.C. 1066, 1076 (1975) ("A corporation is not a 'sham' if it was organized for legitimate business purposes or if it engages in a substantial business activity."); Bass v. Commissioner, 50 T.C. at 600.

#### B. There Was No Impermissible Circular Flow of Funds

Respondent further contends that Legacy was "not an independent fund, but an accounting device". In support of this contention, respondent cites a purported "circular flow of funds" through Legacy, RAC, and RAC's subsidiaries.

Respondent's expert, however, readily acknowledged that he found no evidence of a circular flow of funds, nor have we. Legacy, with the approval of the BMA, purchased RAC treasury shares but did not resell them. Furthermore, petitioner established that there was nothing unusual about the manner in which premiums and claims were paid. Finally, respondent contends that the netting of premiums owed to Legacy during 2003 is evidence that Legacy was a sham. We disagree.

This netting was simply a bookkeeping measure performed as an administrative convenience.

## C. The Premium-to-Surplus Ratios Do Not Indicate That Legacy Was a Sham

Respondent emphasizes that, during the years in issue, Legacy's premium to- surplus ratios were above the ratios of U.S. property and casualty insurance companies and Bermuda class 4 insurers[16] (collectively, commercial insurance companies). On cross-examination, however, respondent's expert admitted that his analysis of commercial insurance companies contained erroneous numbers. Furthermore, he failed to properly explain the profitability data he cited and did not include relevant data relating to Legacy. Moreover, his comparison, of Legacy's premium-to-surplus ratios with the ratios of commercial insurance companies, was not instructive. Commercial insurance companies have lower premium-to-surplus ratios because they face competition and, as a result, typically price their premiums to have significant underwriting losses. They compensate for

---

[16] A class 4 insurance company may carry on insurance business, including excess liability business or property catastrophe reinsurance business. See Insurance Act, 1978, sec. 4E.

---

underwriting losses by retaining sufficient assets (i.e., more assets per dollar of premium resulting in lower premium-to-surplus ratios) to earn ample amounts of investment income. Captives in Bermuda, however, have fewer assets per dollar of premium (i.e., higher premium-to-surplus ratios) but generate significant underwriting profits because their premiums reflect the full dollar value, rather than the present value, of expected losses. Simply put, the premium-to-surplus ratios do not indicate that Legacy was a sham.

### D. Legacy Was a Bona Fide Insurance Company

Petitioner presented convincing, and essentially uncontradicted, evidence that Legacy was a bona fide insurance company. As respondent concedes, petitioner faced actual and insurable risk. Comparable coverage with other insurance companies would have been more expensive, and some insurance companies (e.g., Discover Re) would not underwrite the coverage provided by Legacy. In addition, RAC established Legacy for legitimate business reasons, including: increasing the accountability and transparency of its insurance operations, accessing new insurance markets, and reducing risk management costs.
Furthermore, Legacy entered into bona fide arm's-length contracts with petitioner; charged actuarially determined premiums; was subject to the BMA's regulatory control; met Bermuda's minimum statutory requirements; paid claims from its separately maintained account; and, as respondent's expert readily admitted, was adequately capitalized. See Humana Inc. & Subs. v. Commissioner, 881 F.2d 247, 253 (6th Cir. 1989), aff'g in part, rev'g in part and remanding 88 T.C. 197, 206 (1987); Harper Grp. v. Commissioner, 96 T.C. at 59. Moreover, the validity of claims Legacy paid was established by SRS, an independent third-party administrator, which also determined the validity of claims pursuant to the Discover Re policies. See Harper Grp. v. Commissioner, 96 T.C. at 59. Finally,
RAC's subsidiaries did not own stock in, or contribute capital to, Legacy.

## II. The Payments to Legacy Were Deductible Insurance Expenses

The Code does not define insurance. The Supreme Court, however, has established two necessary criteria: risk shifting and risk distribution. See Helvering v. Le Gierse, 312 U.S. 531, 539 (1941). In addition, the arrangement must involve insurance risk and meet commonly accepted notions of insurance.
See Harper Grp. v. Commissioner, 96 T.C. at 58; AMERCO v. Commissioner, 96 T.C. at 38. These four criteria are not independent or exclusive, but establish a framework for determining "the existence of insurance for Federal tax purposes."
See AMERCO v. Commissioner, 96 T.C. at 38. Insurance premiums may be

deductible. A taxpayer may not, however, deduct amounts set aside in its own possession to compensate itself for perils which are generally the subject of insurance. See Clougherty Packing Co. v. Commissioner, 84 T.C. 948, 958 (1985), aff'd, 811 F.2d 1297 (9th Cir. 1987). We consider all of the facts and circumstances to determine whether an arrangement qualifies as insurance. See Harper Grp. v. Commissioner, 96 T.C. at 57. Respondent contends that payments to Legacy represent amounts petitioner set aside to self-insure its risks.

## A. The Policies at Issue Involved Insurance Risk

Respondent concedes that petitioner faced insurable risk relating to all three types of risk: workers' compensation, automobile, and general liability. Petitioner entered into contracts with Legacy and Discover Re to address these three types of risk. Thus, insurance risk was present in the arrangement between petitioner and Legacy.

## B. Risk Shifting

We must now determine whether the policies at issue shifted risk between RAC's subsidiaries and Legacy. This requires a review of our cases relating to captive insurance arrangements.

### 1. Precedent Relating to Parent-Subsidiary Arrangements

In 1978, we analyzed parent-subsidiary captive arrangements for the first time. See Carnation Co. v. Commissioner, 71 T.C. 400 (1978), aff'd, 640 F.2d 1010 (9th Cir. 1981). In Carnation, the parties entered into two insurance contracts: an agreement between Carnation and an unrelated insurer, and a reinsurance agreement between the captive and the unrelated insurer. Id. at 402- 404. The unrelated insurer expressed concern to Carnation about the captive's financial stability and requested a letter of credit or other guaranty. Id. at 404. Carnation refused to issue a letter of credit or other guaranty but did execute an agreement to provide, upon demand, $2,880,000 of additional capital to the captive. Id. at 402-404. We held, relying on Le Gierse, that the parent-subsidiary arrangement was not insurance because the three agreements (i.e., the two
insurance contracts and the agreement to further capitalize the captive), when considered together, were void of insurance risk. Id. at 409. The Court of Appeals for the Ninth Circuit affirmed and concluded that our application

of Le Gierse was appropriate given the interdependence of the three agreements. See Carnation Co. v. Commissioner, 640 F.2d at 1013. Furthermore, the Court of Appeals held that "[t]he key was that * * * [the unrelated insurer] refused to enter into the reinsurance contract with * * * [the captive] unless Carnation" executed the capitalization agreement. See id.

In Clougherty, our next opportunity to analyze a parent-subsidiary captive arrangement, the parties entered into two insurance contracts: an agreement between Clougherty and an unrelated insurer, and a reinsurance agreement between the captive and the unrelated insurer. Clougherty Packing Co. v. Commissioner, 84 T.C. at 952. We concluded that "the operative facts[17] in the instant case * * * [were] indistinguishable from the facts in Carnation", analyzed Clougherty's balance sheet, and held that risk did not shift to the captive:

We found in Carnation, as we find here, that to the extent the risk was not shifted, insurance does not exist and the payments to that extent are not insurance premiums. The measure of the risk shifted is the percentage of the premium not ceded. This is nothing more than a recharacterization of the payments which petitioner seeks to deduct as insurance premiums. Id. at 956, 958-959. The Commissioner urged us to adopt his economic family theory, which posits that the insuring parent corporation and its domestic subsidiaries, and the wholly owned "insurance" subsidiary, though separate corporate entities, represent one economic family with the result that those who bear the ultimate economic burden of loss are the same persons who suffer the loss. To the extent that the risks of loss are not retained in their entirety by * * * or reinsured with * * * insurance companies that are unrelated to the economic family of insureds, there is no risk shifting or risk-distributing, and no insurance, the premiums for which are deductible under section 162 of the Code.
Rev. Rul. 77-316, 1977-2 C.B. 53, 54.

In rejecting the Commissioner's economic family theory, we emphasized that "[w]e have done nothing more in Carnation and

---

[17] Our Opinion emphasized that the "operative" facts related to the "interdependence of all of the agreements" as confirmed by the "execution dates". See Clougherty Packing Co. v. Commissioner, 84 T.C. 948, 957 (1985), aff'd, 811 F.2d 1297 (9th Cir. 1987).

here but to reclassify, as nondeductible, portions of the payments which the taxpayers deducted as insurance premiums but which were received by the taxpayer's captive insurance subsidiaries." See Clougherty Packing Co. v. Commissioner, 84 T.C. at 960.

The Court of Appeals for the Ninth Circuit affirmed our decision in Clougherty and applied a balance sheet and net worth analysis, pursuant to which a determination of whether risk has shifted depends on whether a covered loss affects the balance sheet and net worth of the insured. See Clougherty Packing Co. v. Commissioner, 811 F.2d at 1305. In defining insurance, the Court of Appeals stated that "a true insurance agreement must remove the risk of loss from the insured party." Id. at 1306. The Court of Appeals elaborated:[W]e examine the economic consequences of the captive insurance arrangement to the "insured" party to see if that party has, in fact, shifted the risk. In doing so, we look only to the insured's assets, i.e., those of Clougherty, to determine whether it has divested itself of the adverse economic consequences of a covered workers' compensation claim. Viewing only Clougherty's assets and considering only the effect of a claim on those assets, it is clear that the risk of loss has not been shifted from Clougherty.

Id. at 1305. Furthermore, the Court of Appeals explained that the balance sheet and net worth analysis does not ignore separate corporate existence: Moline Properties requires that related corporate entities be afforded separate tax status and treatment. It does not require that the Commissioner, in determining whether a corporation has shifted its risk of loss, ignore the effect of a loss upon one of the corporation's assets merely because that asset happens to be stock in a subsidiary. Because we only consider the effect of a covered claim on Clougherty's assets, our analysis in no way contravenes Moline Properties.

Id. at 1307. Finally, the Court of Appeals concluded that "[t]he parent of a captive insurer retains an economic stake in whether a covered loss occurs. Accordingly, an insurance agreement between parent and captive does not shift the parent's risk of loss and is not an agreement for 'insurance.'" Id.

## 2. Precedent Relating to Brother-Sister Arrangements

In Humana Inc. & Subs. v. Commissioner, 88 T.C. at 206, we were faced with two distinct issues: the deductibility of premiums paid by a parent to a captive (parent-subsidiary arrangement) and the deductibility of premiums paid by affiliated subsidiaries to a captive (brother-sister arrangement). Humana, Inc.

(Humana), operated a hospital network and, in 1976, was unable to renew its existing policies relating to workers' compensation, malpractice, and general liability. Id. at 200. Humana's insurance broker could not obtain comparable coverage and recommended that Humana establish a captive insurance company. Id. Humana subsequently incorporated, and capitalized with $1 million, a Colorado captive. Id. at 201-202. The captive provided coverage relating to Humana and its subsidiaries' workers' compensation, malpractice, and general liability. Id. at 202-204. Humana paid the captive a monthly premium which was allocated among itself and each operating subsidiary. Id. at 203.

We held that the parent-subsidiary premiums were not deductible because Humana did not shift risk to the captive. See id. at 206-207. The brother-sister arrangement, however, presented an issue of first impression. See id. at 208. We rejected the Commissioner's economic family theory and held "that it is more appropriate to examine all of the facts to decide whether or to what extent there has been a shifting of the risk from one entity to the captive insurance company."

See id. at 214. We extended our rationale from Carnation and Clougherty (i.e., recharacterizing a captive insurance arrangement as self-insurance) to brother sister arrangements and stated that declining to do so "would exalt form over substance and permit a taxpayer to circumvent our holdings by simple corporate structural changes." See id. at 213. The report on which we relied, prepared by Irving Plotkin, stated: "'A firm placing its risks in a captive insurance company in which it holds a sole or predominant ownership position, is not relieving itself of financial uncertainty.'" Id. at 210 (fn. ref. omitted). In addition, the report stated:

"True insurance relieves the firm's balance sheet of any
potential impact of the financial consequences of the insured peril.
For the price of the premiums, the insured rids itself of any economic
stake in whether or not the loss occurs. * * * [However] as long as the
firm deals with its captive, its balance sheet cannot be protected from
the financial vicissitudes of the insured peril."

Humana Inc. & Subs. v. Commissioner, 88 T.C. at 211-212 (alteration in original) (fn. ref. omitted). After quoting extensively from the report and analyzing the facts, "[w]e conclude[d] that there was not the necessary shifting of risk from the operating subsidiaries of Humana Inc. to * * * [the captive] and, therefore, the amounts charged by Humana Inc. to its subsidiaries did not constitute insurance."

See id. at 214.

Seven Judges concurred with the opinion of the Court's parent-subsidiary holding but disagreed with the brother-sister holding. See id. at 219 (Korner, J., concurring and dissenting). They found the opinion of the Court's rationale

"disingenuous and entirely unconvincing" and asserted that the opinion of the Court had implicitly adopted the Commissioner's "economic family" theory. Id. At 223. After emphasizing that the subsidiaries had no ownership interest in the captive, paid premiums for their own insurance, and would not be affected (i.e., their balance sheets and net worth) by the payment of an insured claim, the dissent further stated:

The theory of Helvering v. Le Gierse, 312 U.S. 531 (1941), may have been adequate to sustain the holdings in Carnation and Clougherty, where only a parent and its insurance subsidiary were involved. It cannot be stretched to cover the instant brother-sister situation, where there was nothing--equity ownership or otherwise--to offset the shifting of risk from the hospital subsidiaries to * * * [the captive]. If the majority is to accomplish the fell deed here, "a decent respect to the opinions of mankind requires that they should declare the causes which impel them" to such a result.

Id. at 224 (fn. ref. omitted).

The Court of Appeals for the Sixth Circuit affirmed our decision relating to the parent-subsidiary arrangement, but reversed our decision relating to the brother-sister arrangement.[18] See Humana Inc. & Subs. v. Commissioner, 881 F.2d at 251-252. The Court of Appeals for the Sixth Circuit adopted the Court of Appeals for the Ninth Circuit's balance sheet and net worth analysis and held that the subsidiaries' payments to the captive were deductible. Id. at 252 ("[W]e look solely to the insured's assets, * * * and consider only the effect of a claim on those assets[.]" (citing Clougherty v. Commissioner, 811 F.2d at 1305)). In rejecting our holding relating to the brother-sister arrangement, the Court of Appeals stated that

"the tax court incorrectly extended the rationale of Carnation and Clougherty in holding that the premiums paid by the subsidiaries of Humana Inc. to * * * [the captive], as charged to them by Humana Inc., did not constitute valid insurance

---

[18] We need not defer to the Court of Appeals for the Sixth Circuit's holding because this matter is appealable to the Court of Appeals for the Fifth Circuit, which has not addressed this issue. See Golsen v. Commissioner, 54 T.C. 742, 757 (1970), aff'd, 445 F.2d 985 (10th Cir. 1971).

agreements" and concluded that "[n]either Carnation nor Cloughery * * * provide a basis for denying the deductions in the brother-sister * * * [arrangement]." Id. At 252-253. In response to our rationalization that "[i]f we decline to extend our holdings in Carnation and Clougherty to the brother-sister factual pattern, we would exalt form over substance and permit a taxpayer to circumvent our holdings by simple corporate structural changes", the Court of Appeals stated:

Such an argument provides no legal justification for denying the deduction in the brother-sister context. The legal test is whether there has been risk distribution and risk shifting, not whether Humana Inc. is a common parent or whether its affiliates are in a brother-sister relationship to * * * [the captive]. We do not focus on the relationship of the parties per se or the particular structure of the corporation involved. We look to the assets of the insured. * * * If Humana changes its corporate structure and that change involves risk shifting and risk distribution, and that change is for a legitimate business purpose and is not a sham to avoid the payment of taxes, then it is irrelevant whether the changed corporate structure has the side effect of also permitting Humana Inc.'s affiliates to take advantage of the Internal Revenue Code § 162(a) (1954) and deduct payments to a captive insurance company under the control of the Humana parent as insurance premiums.

Id. at 255-256.

The Court of Appeals held that "[t]he test to determine whether a transaction under the Internal Revenue Code § 162(a) * * * is legitimate or illegitimate is not a vague and broad 'economic reality' test. The test is whether there is risk shifting and risk distribution." Humana Inc. & Subs. v. Commissioner, 881 F.2d at 255. The Court of Appeals further addressed our analysis and stated:

The tax court cannot avoid direct confrontation with the separate corporate existence doctrine of Moline Properties by claiming that its decision does not rest on "economic family" principles because it is merely reclassifying or recharacterizing the transaction as nondeductible additions to a reserve for losses. The tax court argues in its opinion that such "recharacterization" does not disregard the separate corporate status of the entities involved, but merely disregards the particular transactions between the entities in order to take into account substance over form and the "economic reality" of the transaction that no risk has shifted.

The tax court misapplies this substance over form argument.
The substance over form or economic reality argument is not a broad legal doctrine designed to distinguish between legitimate and illegitimate transactions and employed at the discretion of the tax court whenever it feels that a taxpayer is taking advantage of the tax laws to produce a favorable result for the taxpayer. * * * The substance over form analysis, rather, is a distinct and limited exception to the general rule under Moline Properties that separate entities must be respected as such for tax purposes. The substance over form doctrine applies to disregard the separate corporate entity where "Congress has evinced an intent to the contrary" * * *

Id. at 254. In short, we do not look to the parent to determine whether premiums paid by the subsidiaries to the captive are deductible. Id. at 252. The policies shifted risk because claims paid by the captive did not affect the net worth of Humana's subsidiaries. See id. at 252-253.

### 3. Brother-Sister Arrangements May Shift Risk

We find persuasive the Court of Appeals for the Sixth Circuit's critique of our analysis of the brother-sister arrangement in Humana. First, our extension of Carnation and Clougherty to brother-sister arrangements was improper. As the Court of Appeals correctly concluded: "Carnation dealt solely with the parent subsidiary issue, not the brother-sister issue. Likewise, Clougherty dealt only with the parent-subsidiary issue and not the brother-sister issue. Nothing in either Carnation or Clougherty lends support for denying the deductibility of the payments in the brother-sister context." Id. at 253-254.

Second, the opinion of the Court's extensive reliance on Plotkin's report to analyze the brother-sister arrangement was inappropriate. The report in Humana addressed parent-subsidiary, rather than brother-sister, arrangements. See Humana Inc. & Subs. v. Commissioner, 88 T.C. at 209; see also supra pp. 26-31. In the instant cases, Plotkin explicitly addressed brother-sister arrangements and stated:

Even though the brother, the captive, and the parent are in the same economic family, to the extent that a brother has no ownership interest in the captive, the results of the parent-captive analysis do not apply. It is not the presence or absence of unrelated business, nor the number of other insureds (be they affiliates or non-affiliates), but it is the absence of ownership, the captive's capital, and the number of statistically independent risks (regardless of who owns them) that enables the captive to provide the brother with true insurance as a matter of economics and finance.

We agree. Humana's subsidiaries had no ownership interest in the captive. See Humana Inc. & Subs. v. Commissioner, 88 T.C. at 201-202. Thus, the parent subsidiary analysis employed by the opinion of the Court was incorrect.

Third, we did not properly analyze the facts and circumstances. See id. at 214. The balance sheet and net worth analysis provides the proper analytical framework to determine risk shifting in brother-sister arrangements. See Humana Inc. & Subs. v. Commissioner, 881 F.2d at 252; Clougherty Packing Co. v. Commissioner, 811 F.2d at 1305. Instead, we implicitly employed a substance over- form rationale to recharacterize Humana's subsidiaries' payments as amounts set aside for self-insurance and referenced, but did not apply, the balance sheet and net worth analysis. Indeed, we did not "examine the economic consequences of the captive insurance arrangement to the 'insured' party to see if that party * * *
[had], in fact, shifted the risk." See Clougherty v. Commissioner, 811 F.2d at 1305.

## 4. The Legacy Policies Shifted Risk

In determining whether Legacy's policies shifted risk, we narrow our scrutiny to the arrangement's economic impact on RAC's subsidiaries (i.e., the insured entities). See Humana Inc. & Subs. v. Commissioner, 881 F.2d at 252- 253; Clougherty Packing Co. v. Commissioner, 811 F.2d at 1305 ("[W]e examine the economic consequences of the captive insurance arrangement to the 'insured' party to see if that party has, in fact, shifted the risk. In doing so, we look only to the insured's assets"[.]). In direct testimony respondent's expert, however, emphasized that petitioner's "captive program * * * [did] not involve risk shifting that * * * [was] comparable to that provided by a commercial insurance program."
We decline his invitation to premise our holding on a specious comparability analysis. Simply put, the risk either was, or was not, shifted.
The policies at issue shifted risk from RAC's insured subsidiaries to Legacy, which was formed for a valid business purpose; was a separate,

independent, and viable entity; was financially capable of meeting its obligations; and reimbursed RAC's subsidiaries when they suffered an insurable loss. See Sears, Roebuck & Co. v. Commissioner, 96 T.C. 61, 100-101 (1991), aff'd in part, rev'd in part, 972 F.2d 858 (7th Cir. 1992); AMERCO v. Commissioner, 96 T.C. at 41. Moreover, a payment from Legacy to RAC's subsidiaries did not reduce the net worth of RAC's subsidiaries because, unlike RAC, the subsidiaries did not own stock in Legacy. Indeed, on cross-examination, respondent's expert conceded that the balance sheets and net worth of RAC's subsidiaries were not affected by a covered loss and that the policies shifted risk:

[Petitioner's counsel:] But if the loss gets paid, whose balance sheet gets affected in that case?
[Respondent's expert:] What's hanging me up is that I don't know whether--I guess you're right, because * * * [RAC's subsidiary] will treat the payment from--the payment that it expects from Legacy as an asset, so the loss would hit Legacy's [balance sheet].
[Petitioner's counsel:] But it wouldn't hit * * * [RAC's subsidiary's] balance sheet.
[Respondent's expert:] I would think that's right. * * *
[Petitioner's counsel:] Why is that not risk-shifting?
[Respondent's expert:] That's an--why is that not risk-shifting?
[Petitioner's counsel:] Yes. Why is that not risk-shifting? Why hasn't [RAC's subsidiary] shifted its risk to Legacy? Its insurance risk--why hasn't it shifted to Legacy in that scenario?
[Respondent's expert:] I mean, I would say from an accounting perspective, it has managed to have--is it--if we're going to respect all these [corporate] forms, then it will have shifted that risk.

**5. The Parental Guaranty Did Not Vitiate Risk Shifting**

Legacy, in March 2003, petitioned the BMA and received approval, through December 31, 2003, to treat DTAs as general business assets. On September 17, 2003, RAC issued the parental guaranty to Legacy, which petitioned, and received permission from, the BMA to treat DTAs as general business assets through December 31, 2006. Respondent contends that the parental guaranty abrogated risk shifting between Legacy and RAC's subsidiaries. We disagree. First, and most importantly, the parental guaranty did not affect the balance sheets or net worth of the subsidiaries insured by Legacy.

Petitioner's expert, in response to a question the Court posed during cross-examination, convincingly countered respondent's contention:

[The Court]: * * * [W]hat impact does the corporate structure have on the effect of the parental guarantee?
[Petitioner's expert]: I think it has a great impact on it. None of the subs, as I understand it, are entering in or [are] a part of that guarantee. Only the subs are effectively insureds under the policy. They are the only ones who produce risks that could be covered. The guarantee in no way vitiates the completeness of the transfer of their uncertainty, their risk, to the insuring subsidiary.
Even if one assumes that the guarantee increases the capital that the captive could use to pay losses, none of those payments would go to the detriment of the sub as a separate legal entity.

Second, the cases upon which respondent relies are distinguishable. Respondent cites Malone & Hyde, Inc. v. Commissioner, 62 F.3d 835, 841 (6$^{th}$ Cir. 1995) (holding that a reinsurance arrangement was not bona fide because the captive was undercapitalized and the parent guaranteed the captive's obligations to an unrelated insurer), rev'g T.C. Memo. 1993-585; Carnation Co. v. Commissioner, 71 T.C. at 404, 409 (holding that a reinsurance arrangement lacked insurance risk where the captive was undercapitalized and, at the insistence of an unrelated primary insurer, the parent agreed to provide additional capital); and Kidde Indus., Inc. v. United States, 40 Fed. Cl. 42, 49-50 (1997) (holding that a reinsurance arrangement lacked risk shifting because the parent indemnified the captive's obligation to pay an unrelated primary insurer). Unlike the agreements in these cases, the parental guaranty did not shift the ultimate risk of loss; did not involve an undercapitalized captive; and was not issued to, or requested by, an unrelated insurer. Cf. Malone & Hyde, Inc. v. Commissioner, 62 F.3d at 841-843; Carnation Co. v. Commissioner, 71 T.C. at 404, 409; Kidde Indus., Inc., 40 Fed. Cl. at 49-50.
Third, RAC guaranteed Legacy's "liabilities under the Act [(i.e., the Bermuda Insurance Act and related regulations)]", pursuant to which Legacy was required to maintain "certain solvency and liquidity margins". RAC did not pay any money pursuant to the parental guaranty and Legacy's "liabilities under the Act" did not include Legacy's contractual obligations to RAC's affiliates or obligations to unrelated insurers. For purposes of calculating the minimum solvency margin, Legacy treated a portion of the parental guaranty as a general business asset. See supra pp. 15-16. In sum,

by providing the parental guaranty to the BMA, Legacy received permission to treat DTAs as general business assets and ensured its continued compliance with the BMA's solvency requirements.[19]

The parental guaranty served no other purpose and was unilaterally revoked by RAC, in 2006, when Legacy met the BMA's solvency requirements without reference to DTAs.

## C. The Legacy Policies Distributed Risk

Risk distribution occurs when an insurer pools a large enough collection of unrelated risks (i.e., risks that are generally unaffected by the same event or circumstance). See Humana Inc. & Subs. v. Commissioner, 881 F.2d at 257. "By assuming numerous relatively small, independent risks that occur randomly over time, the insurer smoothes out losses to match more closely its receipt of premiums." Clougherty Packing Co. v. Commissioner, 811 F.2d at 1300. This distribution also allows the insurer to more accurately predict expected future losses. In analyzing risk distribution, we look at the actions of the insurer because it is the insurer's, not the insured's, risk that is reduced by risk distribution. See Harper Grp. v. Commissioner, 96 T.C. at 57. A captive may achieve adequate risk distribution by insuring only subsidiaries within its affiliated group. See Humana

[19]Legacy used a portion of the parental guaranty as a general business asset. See supra pp. 15-16. Legacy's DTAs always exceeded the amount of the parental guaranty treated as a general business asset. See supra pp. 15-16.

Inc. & Subs. v. Commissioner, 881 F.2d at 257; Rev. Rul. 2002-90, 2002-2 C.B. 985.

Legacy insured three types of risk: workers' compensation, automobile, and general liability. During the years in issue, RAC's subsidiaries owned between 2,623 and 3,081 stores; had between 14,300 and 19,740 employees; and operated between 7,143 and 8,027 insured vehicles. RAC's subsidiaries operated stores in all 50 States, the District of Columbia, Puerto Rico, and Canada. RAC's subsidiaries had a sufficient number of statistically independent risks. Thus, by insuring RAC's subsidiaries, Legacy achieved adequate risk distribution. See Humana Inc. & Subs. v. Commissioner, 881 F.2d at 257.

## D. The Arrangement Constituted Insurance in the Commonly Accepted Sense

Legacy was adequately capitalized, regulated by the BMA, and organized

and operated as an insurance company. Furthermore, Legacy issued valid and binding policies, charged and received actuarially determined premiums, and paid claims. In short, the arrangement between RAC's subsidiaries and Legacy constituted insurance in the commonly accepted sense. See Harper Grp. v. Commissioner, 96 T.C. at 60.

**Conclusion**

The payments by RAC's subsidiaries to Legacy are, pursuant to section 162, deductible as insurance expenses.

Contentions we have not addressed are irrelevant, moot, or meritless.

To reflect the foregoing,

Decisions will be entered under

Rule 155.

Reviewed by the Court.

THORNTON, VASQUEZ, WHERRY, HOLMES, BUCH, and NEGA, JJ., agree with this opinion of the Court.

GOEKE, J., did not participate in the consideration of this opinion.

BUCH, J., concurring: To the extent respondent is arguing that a captive insurance arrangement between brother-sister corporations cannot be insurance as a matter of law, we need not reach that issue. In Rev. Rul. 2001-31, 2001-1 C.B. 1348, 1348, the Internal Revenue Service stated that it would "no longer invoke the economic family theory with respect to captive insurance transactions." And in Rauenhorst v. Commissioner, 119 T.C. 157, 173 (2002), we held that we may treat as a concession a position taken by the IRS in a revenue ruling that has not been revoked. Because Rev. Rul. 2001-31 has not been revoked, we could treat the economic family argument as conceded.

At the same time the IRS abandoned the economic family theory, it made clear that it would "continue to challenge certain captive insurance transactions based on the facts and circumstances of each case." Rev. Rul. 2001-31, 2001-1 C.B. at 1348. Then, in a series of revenue rulings, the IRS shed light on the facts and circumstances it deemed relevant. See Rev. Rul. 2005-40, 2005-2 C.B. 4; Rev. Rul. 2002-91, 2002-2 C.B. 991; Rev. Rul. 2002-90, 2002-2 C.B. 985; Rev. Rul. 2002-89, 2002-2 C.B. 984.

The concise opinion of the Court sets forth facts and circumstances supporting its conclusion. I write separately to respond to points made in Judge Lauber's dissent.

**I. Legacy's Policies**

Taking into account the nature of risks that Legacy insured, Legacy was sufficiently capitalized.

### A. Long-Tail Coverage

During each of the years in issue Legacy insured three types of risk: workers' compensation, automobile, and general liability. Policies relating to these risks are generally referred to as long-tail coverage because "claims may involve damages that are not readily observable or injuries that are difficult to ascertain." See Acuity v. Commissioner, T.C. Memo. 2013-209, at *8-*9.

Workers' compensation insurance, which generated between 66% and 73% of Legacy's premiums during t₁he years in issue, "is generally long tail coverage because of the inherent uncertainty in determining the extent of an injured worker's need for medical treatment and loss of wages for time off work." Id. An insurer pays out claims relating to long-tail coverage over an extended period.

### B. Rent-A-Center's Insurance Program

Rent-A-Center did not obtain insurance solely from Legacy; Rent-A-Center also obtained insurance from multiple unrelated third parties. Legacy was

---

₁Legacy's premiums attributable to workers' compensation liability were $28,586,597 in 2003; $35,392,000 in 2004; $36,463,579 in 2005; $39,086,374 in
2006; and $45,425,032 in 2007.

---

responsible for only a portion of each claim (e.g., the first $350,000 of each workers' compensation claim during 2003). To the extent that a claim exceeded Legacy's coverage, a third-party insurer was responsible for paying the excess amount. Rent-A-Center obtained coverage from unrelated third-party insurers for claims of up to approximately $75 million. Therefore, extraordinary losses would not affect Legacy's ability to pay claims because they would be covered by unrelated third parties.

### C. Allocation Formula

Premiums were actuarially determined. At trial respondent conceded that Aon "produced reliable and professionally produced and competent actuarial studies." Legacy relied on these studies to set premiums. Once Legacy determined the premium, Rent-A-Center allocated it to each operating subsidiary in the same manner that it allocated premiums relating to unrelated insurers. In a captive arrangement, a parent may allocate a premium among its subsidiaries. See Humana Inc. & Subs. v. Commissioner, 881 F.2d 247, 248 (6th Cir. 1989) ("Humana Inc. allocated and charged to the subsidiaries portions of the amounts paid representing the share each bore for the hospitals each operated."), aff'g in part, rev'g in part and remanding 88 T.C. 197 (1987); Kidde Indus., Inc. v. United States, 40 Fed. Cl. 42, 45 (1997) ("National determined the premiums that it charged Kidde based in part on underwriting data supplied by Kidde's divisions and subsidiaries * * * Kidde used these same data to allocate the total premiums among its divisions and subsidiaries.").

## II. The Parental Guaranty

Citing a footnote in Humana, Judge Lauber's dissenting opinion asserts that the existence of a parental guaranty is enough to justify disregarding the captive insurance arrangement. That footnote, however, addresses only situations in which there is both inadequate capitalization and a parental guaranty, concluding:
"These weaknesses alone provided a sufficient basis from which to find no risk shifting and to decide the cases in favor of the Commissioner." Humana Inc. & Subs. v. Commissioner, 881 F.2d at 254 n.2 (emphasis added). Here, the fact finder did not find inadequate capitalization. And the mere existence of a parental guaranty is not enough for us to disregard the captive insurer; we must look to the substance of that guaranty.
As the opinion of the Court finds, the parental guaranty was created to convert deferred tax assets into general business assets for regulatory purposes. See op. Ct. p. 35. The circumstances relating to its issuance, including that the parental guaranty was issued to Legacy and that it was limited to $25 million--or, less than 10% of the total premiums paid to Legacy--support the conclusion that it was created solely to encourage the Bermuda Monetary Authority to allow Legacy to treat DTAs as general business assets. In contrast, the cases that have found that a parental guaranty eliminates any risk shifting involved either a blanket indemnity or a capitalization agreement that resulted in a capital infusion in excess of premiums received. And even then, the indemnity or capitalization agreement was coupled with an undercapitalized captive. Accordingly, those cases are distinguishable from the situation presented here.

Malone & Hyde, Inc. v. Commissioner, 62 F.3d 835 (6th Cir. 1995), rev'g T.C. Memo. 1993-585, involved an insurance subsidiary established to provide reinsurance for the parent and its subsidiaries. After incorporating the captive, Malone & Hyde entered into an agreement with a third-party insurer to insure both its own and its subsidiaries' risks. Id. at 836. The third-party insurer then reinsured the first $150,000 of coverage per claim with the captive. Id. Because the captive was thinly capitalized--it had no assets other than $120,000 of paid-in capital--Malone & Hyde executed "hold harmless" agreements in favor of the third-party insurer. Id. These agreements provided that if the captive defaulted on its obligations as reinsurer, then Malone & Hyde would completely shield the third-party insurer from liability. Id. In deciding whether the risk had shifted, the court held that "[w]hen the entire scheme involves either undercapitalization or indemnification of the primary insurer by the taxpayer claiming the deduction, or both, these facts alone disqualify the premium payments from being treated as ordinary and necessary business expenses to the extent such payments are ceded by the primary insurer to the captive insurance subsidiary." Id. at 842-843. In short, Malone & Hyde, Inc. had a thinly capitalized captive insurer and a blanket indemnity. Here, neither of those facts is present.

The facts in Kidde Indus., Inc. are quite similar to those in Malone & Hyde, Inc. Kidde incorporated a captive and entered into an insurance agreement with a third-party insurer who in turn entered into a reinsurance agreement with the captive. Kidde Indus., Inc., 40 Fed. Cl. at 45. As in Malone & Hyde, Inc., the captive was significantly undercapitalized, and Kidde executed an indemnification agreement to provide the third-party insurer with the "level of comfort" needed before it would issue the policies. Id. at 48. Again, the court held that Kidde retained the risk of loss and could not deduct the premiums. Id. Carnation Co. v. Commissioner, 71 T.C. 400 (1978), aff'd, 640 F.2d 1010 (9th Cir. 1981), involved slightly different facts. A captive reinsured 90% of the third-party insurer's liabilities under Carnation's policy. Id. at 403. As part of this arrangement, the third-party insurer ceded 90% of the premiums to the captive and the captive paid the third-party insurer a 5% commission based on the net premiums ceded. Id. Carnation provided $3 million of capital to the captive--an
amount that was well in excess of the total annual premiums paid to the captive-- because the third-party insurer had concerns about the captive's capitalization. Id.
at 404. The Court held that the reinsurance agreement and the agreement to

provide additional capital counteracted each other and voided any insurance risk.
Id. at 409. In affirming the Tax Court, the Court of Appeals for the Ninth Circuit held that, in considering whether the risk had shifted, the key was that the third party insurer would not have issued the policies without the capitalization agreement. Carnation Co. v. Commissioner, 640 F.2d at 1013. Those cases are distinguishable because they all involved undercapitalized captives. As explained previously, the opinion of the Court found that Legacy was adequately capitalized. Further, in each of the three cases above, the parent provided either indemnification or additional capitalization in order to persuade a third-policy insurer to issue insurance policies. Here, Discover Re provided insurance before Legacy's inception and continued providing coverage after Legacy was formed. The parental guaranty was issued to Legacy for the singular purpose of allowing Legacy to treat the DTAs as general business assets.

Additionally, the guaranty amounted to only $25 million. This small fraction of the $264 million in premiums for policies written by Legacy during the years in issue does not rise to the level of protection provided by the total indemnities in Malone & Hyde, Inc. and Kidde Indus., Inc.

When we consider the totality of the facts, the parental guaranty appears to have been immaterial. This conclusion is bolstered by the facts that the parental guaranty was unilaterally withdrawn by Rent-A-Center in 2006 and that Rent-A Center never contributed any funds to Legacy pursuant to that parental guaranty.

## III. Consolidated Groups

Judge Lauber's dissent refers to a hodgepodge of facts about how Rent-A Center operated its consolidated group as evidence that Legacy's status as a separate entity should be disregarded. Examples of the facts cited in that dissent are that Legacy had no employees and that payments between it and other members of the Rent-A-Center consolidated group were handled through journal entries.

In the real world of large corporations, these practices are commonplace. For ease of operations, including running payroll, companies create a staff leasing subsidiary and lease employees companywide. Or they hire outside consultants to handle the operations of a specialty business such as a captive insurer. Legacy, like Humana, hired an outside management company to handle its business operations. Compare op. Ct. p. 6 n.6 (Legacy engaged Aon to provide management services) with Humana Inc. & Subs. v. Commissioner, 88 T.C. at 205 (Humana engaged Marsh & McLennan to

provide management services). And it is unrealistic to expect members of a consolidated group to cut checks to each other. Rent-A-Center and Legacy did what is commonplace--they kept track of the flow of funds through journal entries. So long as complete and accurate records are maintained, the commingling of funds is not enough to require the disregarding of a separate business. See, e.g., Kahle v. Commissioner, T.C. Memo. 1991-203 (finding that the taxpayer "maintained complete and accurate records" notwithstanding the commingling of business and personal funds). Corporations filing consolidated returns are to be treated as separate entities, unless otherwise mandated. Gottesman & Co. v. Commissioner, 77 T.C. 1149, 1156 (1981). It may be advantageous for a corporation to operate through various subsidiaries for a multitude of reasons. These reasons may include State law implications, creditor demands, or simply convenience, but "so long as that purpose is the equivalent of business activity or is followed by the carrying on of business by the corporation, the corporation remains a separate taxable entity."
Moline Props., Inc. v. Commissioner, 319 U.S. 436, 438-439 (1943). Even the consolidated return regulations make clear that an insurance company that is part of a consolidated group is treated separately. See sec. 1.1502-13(e)(2)(ii)(A), Income Tax Regs. ("If a member provides insurance to another member in an intercompany transaction, the transaction is taken into account by both members on a separate entity basis."). Thus, if a corporation gives due regard to the separate corporate structure, we should do the same.

## IV. Conclusion

The issue presented in these cases is ultimately a matter of when, not whether, Rent-A-Center is entitled to a deduction relating to workers' compensation, automobile, and general liability losses.[2] Because the IRS has conceded in its rulings that insurance premiums paid between brother-sister corporations may be insurance and the Court determined that, under the facts and circumstances of these cases as found by the Judge who presided at trial, the policies at issue are insurance, Rent-A-Center is entitled to deduct the premiums as reported on its returns. See op. Ct. pp. 21-40.
FOLEY, GUSTAFSON, PARIS, and KERRIGAN, JJ., agree with this concurring opinion.

[2] If the Court had determined that the policies were not insurance, then Rent-A-Center would nevertheless have been entitled to deduct the losses as they were

paid or incurred. See sec. 162. By forming Legacy and giving due regard to its separate structure, Rent-A-Center achieved some acceleration of deductions relating to losses that would otherwise be deductible, along with other nontax benefits. See op. Ct. pp. 17-18.

**HALPERN, J., dissenting**:

"'The principle of judicial parsimony' (L. Hand, J., in Pressed Steel Car Co. v. Union Pacific Railroad Co., * * * [240 F. 135, 137 (S.D.N.Y. 1917)]), if nothing more, condemns a useless remedy." Sinclair Ref. Co. v. Jenkins Petroleum Process Co., 289 U.S. 689, 694 (1933). While usually invoked by a court to justify a stay in discovery on other issues when one issue is dispositive of a case, 8A Charles Allen Wright, Arthur R. Miller & Richard L. Marcus, Federal Practice and Procedure, sec. 2040, at 198 n.7 (3d ed. 2010), I think the principle should guide us in declining to overrule Humana Inc. & Subs. v. Commissioner, 88 T.C. 197 (1987), aff'd in part, rev'd in part and remanded, 881 F.2d 247 (6th Cir. 1989), to the extent that it holds that a captive insurance arrangement between brother sister corporations cannot be insurance as a matter of law. These cases are before the Court Conference for review, see sec. 7460(b), because we perceive that Judge Foley's report is in part overruling Humana, although Judge Foley does not in so many words say so. He says: "We find persuasive the Court of Appeals for the Sixth Circuit's critique of our analysis the brother-sister arrangement in Humana." The Court of Appeals said: "We reverse the tax court on * * * the brother-sister issue." Humana Inc. & Subs v. Commissioner, 881 F.2d at 257. Under our Conference procedures, the Conference may not adopt a report overruling a prior report of the Court absent the affirmative vote of a majority of the Judges entitled to vote on the case. Six of the sixteen Judges entitled to vote on these cases join Judge Foley, for a total of seven clearly affirmative votes. Six Judges voted "no". Three Judges voted "concur in result", and those votes, under our procedures, are counted as affirmative votes.

Whether the Court has in fact overruled a portion of Humana undoubtedly will be unclear to many readers of this report. The resulting confusion is unnecessary.

Moreover, by putting his report overruling Humana before the Conference, Judge Foley has put before the Conference his subsidiary findings of fact and his ultimate finding that the brother-sister payments were correctly characterized as insurance premiums. That has attracted two side opinions, one characterizing Judge Foley's opinion as "concise" (Judge Buch) and emphasizing evidence in the record that supports his findings and the other characterizing his ultimate findings as "conclusory" (Judge Lauber) and contending "the undisputed facts of the entire record warrant the opposite conclusion * * *, [that] the Rent-A-Center arrangements do not constitute 'insurance' for Federal income tax purposes." Whether I describe Judge Foley's analysis as concise or as conclusory, simply put, there is insufficient depth to it to persuade me to join his findings (i.e., that there is risk shifting, that there is risk distribution, and, in general, that there is a bona fide insurance arrangement). I do agree with Judge Lauber that "[w]hether the facts and circumstances, evaluated in the aggregate, give rise to 'insurance' presents a question of proper characterization. It is thus a mixed question of fact and law." Nevertheless, had Judge Foley steered clear of Humana, I believe that we could have avoided Conference consideration and have left it to the appellate process (if invoked) to determine whether Judge Foley's findings are persuasive.

And I believe that Judge Foley could have steered clear of Humana. As both Judges Buch and Lauber point out, the Commissioner has given up on arguing that captive insurance arrangement between brother-sister corporations cannot be insurance as a matter of law. See, e.g., Rev. Rul. 2001-31, 2001 C.B. 1348. Judge Foley ignores that ruling and its progeny when, pursuant to Rauenhorst v. Commissioner, 119 T.C. 157, 173 (2002), he could have relied on the Commissioner's concessions to steer clear of revisiting Humana. I agree with Judge Foley that Humana is not dispositive of the brother-sister insurance question in these cases, but not because I would overrule Humana on that issue; rather, I see no reason to address Humana in the light of the Commissioner's present administrative position. While I agree with Judge Foley that the facts and circumstances test provides the proper analytical framework, I otherwise dissent from his opinion.

**LAUBER, J., agrees with this dissent.**

LAUBER, J., dissenting: These cases, like Humana Inc. & Subs. v. Commissioner, 88 T.C. 197 (1987), aff'd in part, rev'd in part and remanded, 881 F.2d 247 (6th Cir. 1989), involve what I will refer to as a "classic" captive insurance company. In these cases, as in Humana, the captive has no outside owners and insures no outside risks. Rather, it is wholly owned by the parent of the affiliated group and it "insures" risks only of the parent and the operating subsidiaries, which stand in a brother-sister relationship to it. In Humana we held that purported "insurance" premiums paid to a captive by other members of its affiliated group--whether by the parent or by the sister corporations--were not deductible for Federal income tax purposes. An essential requirement of "insurance" is the shifting of risk from insured to insurer. Helvering v. LeGierse, 312 U.S. 531, 539 (1941). We held in Humana that "there was not the necessary shifting of risk" from the operating subsidiaries to the captive, and hence that none of the purported "premiums" constituted amounts paid for "insurance." 88 T.C. at 214. The Court of Appeals for the Sixth Circuit affirmed as to amounts paid to the captive by the parent, but reversed as to amounts paid to the captive by the sister corporations. 881 F.2d at 257.

The opinion of the Court (majority) adopts the reasoning and result of the Sixth Circuit, overrules Humana in part, and holds that amounts charged to the captive's sister corporations constitute deductible "insurance premiums." I dissent both from the majority's decision to overrule Humana and from its holding that amounts charged to the sister corporations constituted payments for "insurance" under the totality of the facts and circumstances.

## I. Background

The captive insurance issue has a rich history to which the majority refers only episodically. It has been clear from the outset of our tax law that taxpayers (other than insurance companies) cannot deduct contributions to an insurance reserve. Steere Tank Lines, Inc. v. United States, 577 F.2d 279, 280 (5th Cir. 1978); Spring Canyon Coal Co. v. Commissioner, 43 F.2d 78, 80 (10th Cir. 1930).

Thus, if a unitary operating company maintains a reserve for self-insurance, amounts it places in that reserve are not deductible as "insurance premiums." One strategy by which taxpayers sought to avoid this nondeductibility rule was to place their self-insurance reserve into a captive insurance company. In cases involving "classic" captives--i.e., captives that have no outside owners and insure no outside risks--the courts have uniformly held that this strategy does not work. Employing various legal theories, every court to consider the question has held that amounts paid by a parent to a classic captive do not constitute "insurance premiums."[1]

Insurance and tax advisers soon devised an alternative strategy for avoiding the bar against deduction of contributions to a self-insurance reserve-- namely, adoption of or conversion to a holding company structure. In essence, an operating company would drop its self-insurance reserve into a captive; drop its operations into one or more operating subsidiaries; and have the purported "premiums" paid to the captive by the sister companies instead of by the parent.

In Humana, we held that this strategy did not work either, reasoning that "we would exalt form over substance and permit a taxpayer to circumvent our holdings

---

[1] See Beech Aircraft Corp. v. United States, 797 F.2d 920 (10th Cir. 1986); Stearns-Roger Corp. v. United States, 774 F.2d 414, 415-416 (10th Cir. 1985); Humana Inc. & Subs. v. Commissioner, 88 T.C. 197, 207 (1987), aff'd in part, rev'd in part and remanded, 881 F.2d 247 (6th Cir. 1989); Clougherty Packing Co. v. Commissioner, 84 T.C. 948 (1985), aff'd, 811 F.2d 1297, 1307 (9th Cir. 1987); Carnation Co. v. Commissioner, 71 T.C. 400 (1978), aff'd, 640 F.2d 1010, 1013 (9th Cir. 1981). On the other hand, the courts have held that parent-captive payments may constitute "insurance premiums" where the captive has a sufficient percentage of outside owners or insures a sufficient percentage of outside risks.
See, e.g., Sears, Roebuck & Co. v. Commissioner, 96 T.C. 61 (1991) (approximately 99.75% of insured risks were outside risks), supplemented by 96 T.C. 671 (1991), aff'd in part and rev'd in part, 972 F.2d 858 (7th Cir. 1992); Harper Grp. v. Commissioner, 96 T.C. 45 (1991) (approximately 30% of insured risks were outside risks), aff'd, 979 F.2d 1341 (9th Cir. 1992); AMERCO v. Commissioner, 96 T.C. 18 (1991) (between 52% and 74% of insured risks were outside risks), aff'd, 979 F.2d 162 (9th Cir. 1992).

---

[involving parent-captive payments] by simple corporate structural changes." 88 T.C. at 213. In effect, we concluded in Humana that conversion to a holding company structure--without more--should not enable a taxpayer to accomplish indirectly what it cannot accomplish directly, achieving a radically different and more beneficial tax result when there has been absolutely no change in the underlying economic reality.
While the Commissioner had success litigating the parent-captive pattern, he had surprisingly poor luck litigating the brother-sister scenario. The Tenth Circuit, like our Court, agreed that brother-sister payments to a classic captive are not deductible as "insurance premiums."[2] By contrast, the Sixth Circuit in Humana reversed our holding to this effect. And after some initial ambivalence, the Court of Federal Claims appears to have concluded that brother-sister "premium" payments are deductible.[3]

---

[2] See Beech Aircraft Corp., 797 F.2d at 922; Stearns-Roger Corp., 774 F.2d at 415-416.
[3] Compare Mobil Oil Corp. v. United States, 8 Cl. Ct. 555, 566 (1985) ("[B]y deducting the premiums on its tax returns, [the affiliated group] achieved indirectly that which it could not do directly. It is well settled that tax

consequences must turn upon the economic substance of a transaction[.]"), with Kidde Indus., Inc. v. United States, 40 Fed. Cl. 42 (1997) (brother-sister payments deductible for years for which parent did not provide indemnity agreement). See generally Ocean Drilling & Exploration Co. v. United States, 988 F.2d 1135, 1153 (Fed. Cir. 1993) (continued...)

---

The Commissioner had even less success persuading courts to adopt the "single economic family" theory enunciated in Rev. Rul. 77-316, 1977-2 C.B. 53, upon which his litigating position was initially based. That theory was approved by the Tenth Circuit [4] and found some favor in the Ninth Circuit.[5] But it was rejected by our Court[6] as well as by the Sixth and Federal Circuits.[7] Assessing this track record, the Commissioner made a strategic retreat. In 2001 the IRS announced that it "will no longer invoke the economic family theory

---

[3](...continued)
(1991) (brother-sister payments deductible where captive insured significant outside risks).
[4]See Beech Aircraft Corp., 797 F.2d 920; Stearns-Roger Corp., 774 F.2d at 415-416. See generally Humana, 881 F.2d at 251 ("Stearns-Roger, Mobil Oil, and Beech Aircraft * * * each explicitly or implicitly adopted the economic family concept.").
[5]See Clougherty Packing, 811 F.2d at 1304 ("[W]e seriously doubt that the use of an economic family concept in defining insurance runs afoul of the Supreme Court's holding in Moline Properties."); id. at 1305 (finding "considerable merit in the Commissioner's [economic family] argument" but finding it unnecessary to rely on that theory); Carnation Co., 640 F.2d at 1013.
[6]See Humana, 88 T.C. at 214 (rejecting the Commissioner's "economic family" concept); Clougherty Packing, 84 T.C. at 956 (same); Carnation Co., 71 T.C. at 413 (same).
[7]See Malone & Hyde, Inc. v. Commissioner, 62 F.3d 835 (6th Cir. 1995) (rejecting "economic family" theory but ruling against deductibility of payments to captive based on facts and circumstances), rev'g T.C. Memo. 1993-585; Ocean Drilling & Exploration Co., 988 F.2d at 1150-1151; Humana, 881 F.2d at 251.

with respect to captive insurance transactions." Rev. Rul. 2001-31, 2001-1 C.B. 1348, 1348. In 2002 the IRS likewise abandoned its position that there is a per se rule against the deductibility of brother-sister "premiums," concluding that the characterization of such payments as "insurance premiums" should be governed, not by a per se rule, but by the facts and circumstances of the particular case. Rev. Rul. 2002-90, 2002-2 C.B. 985; accord Rev. Rul 2001-31, 2001-1 C.B. at 1348 ("The Service may * * * continue to challenge certain captive insurance transactions based on the facts and circumstances of each case.").

## II. Overruling Humana

We decided Humana against a legal backdrop very different from that which we confront today. The Commissioner in Humana urged a per se rule, predicated on his "single economic family" theory, against the deductibility of brother-sister "insurance premiums." The Commissioner has long since abandoned both that per se rule and the theory on which it was based. Given this change in the legal environment, I see no need for the Court to reconsider Humana, which in a practical sense may be water under the bridge.

Respondent's position in the instant cases is consistent with the ruling position the IRS has maintained for the past 12 years--namely, that characterization of intragroup payments as "insurance premiums" should be determined on the basis of the facts and circumstances of the particular case. See Rev. Rul. 2001-31, 2001-1 C.B. at 1348. The majority adopts this approach as the framework for its legal analysis. See op. Ct. p. 22 ("We consider all of the facts and circumstances to determine whether an arrangement qualifies as insurance."). The Court need not overrule Humana to decide (erroneously in my view) that respondent should lose under the facts-and-circumstances approach that respondent is now advancing. In Humana, "we emphasize[d] that our holding * * * [was] based upon the factual pattern presented in * * * [that] case," noting that in other cases "factual patterns may differ." 88 T.C. at 208. That being so, the Court today could rule for petitioners on the basis of what the majority believes to be the controlling "facts and circumstances," distinguishing Humana rather than overruling it. Principles of judicial restraint counsel that courts should decide cases on the narrowest possible ground.

## III. The "Facts and Circumstances" Approach

Although I do not believe it necessary or proper to overrule Humana, the continuing vitality of that precedent does not control the outcome. These cases can and should be decided in respondent's favor under the "facts and circumstances" approach that he is currently advancing. In Rev. Rul. 2002-90, 2002-2 C.B. at 985, the IRS concluded that brother-sister payments were correctly characterized as "insurance premiums" where the assumed facts included the following (P = parent and S = captive):

P provides S adequate capital * * *. S charges the 12 [operating] subsidiaries arms-length premiums, which are established according to customary industry rating formulas. * * * There are no parental (or other related party) guarantees of any kind made in favor of S. * * * In all respects, the parties conduct themselves in a manner consistent with the standards applicable to an insurance arrangement between unrelated parties. The facts of the instant cases, concerning both "risk shifting" and conformity to arm's-length insurance standards, differ substantially from the facts assumed in Rev. Rul. 2002-90, supra. The instant facts also differ substantially from the facts determined in judicial precedents that have characterized intragroup payments as "insurance premiums." Whether the facts and circumstances, evaluated in the aggregate, give rise to "insurance" presents a question of proper characterization. It is thus a mixed question of fact and law. The majority makes certain findings of basic fact, which I accept for purposes of this dissenting opinion. In many instances, however, the majority makes no findings of basic fact to support its conclusory findings of ultimate fact. In other instances, the majority does not mention facts that tend to undermine its ultimate conclusions. In my view, the undisputed facts of the entire record warrant the opposite conclusion from that reached by the majority and justify a ruling that the Rent-A-Center arrangements do not constitute "insurance" for Federal income tax purposes.

## A. Risk Shifting

### 1. Parental Guaranty

Rent-A-Center, the parent, issued two types of guaranties to Legacy, its captive. First, it guaranteed the multimillion-dollar "deferred tax asset" (DTA) on Legacy's balance sheet, which arose from timing differences between the captive's fiscal year and the parent's calendar year. Normally, a DTA cannot be counted as an "asset" for purposes of the (rather modest) minimum solvency requirements of Bermuda insurance law. The parent's guaranty was essential in order for Legacy to secure an exception from this rule.

Second, the parent subsequently issued an all-purpose guaranty by which it agreed to hold Legacy harmless for its liabilities under the Bermuda Insurance Act up to $25 million. These liabilities necessarily included Legacy's liabilities to pay loss claims of its sister corporations. This all-purpose $25 million guaranty was eliminated at year-end 2006, but it was in existence for the first three tax years at issue.

When approving the brother-sister premiums in Rev. Rul. 2002-90, 2002-2 C.B. at 985, the IRS explicitly excluded from the hypothesized facts the existence of any parental or related-party guaranty executed in favor of the captive.

Numerous courts have likewise ruled that the existence of a parental guaranty, indemnification agreement, or similar instrument may negate the existence of "insurance" purportedly supplied by a captive. See, e.g., Malone & Hyde, 62 F.3d 835, 842-843 (6th Cir. 1995) (finding no "insurance" where parent guaranteed captive's liabilities), rev'g T.C. Memo. 1993-585; Humana, 881 F.2d at 254 n.2 (presence of parental indemnification or recapitalization agreement may provide a sufficient basis on which to find no "risk shifting"); Carnation Co., 71 T.C. 400, 402, 409 (1978) (finding no "insurance" where parent agreed to supply captive with additional capital), aff'd, 640 F.2d 1010 (9th Cir. 1981); Kidde Indus., Inc. v. United States, 40 Fed. Cl. 42, 50 (1997) (finding no "insurance" where parent issued indemnification letter).

By guaranteeing Legacy's liabilities, Rent-A-Center agreed to step into Legacy's shoes to pay its affiliates' loss claims. In effect, the parent thus became an "insurer" of its subsidiaries' risks. The majority cites no authority, and I know of none, for the proposition that a holding company can "insure" the risks of its wholly owned subsidiaries. The presence of this parental guaranty argues strongly against the existence of "risk shifting" here.

The majority asserts that Rent-A-Center's parental guaranty "did not vitiate risk shifting" and offers three rationales for this conclusion. See op. Ct. pp. 35-38.

None of these rationales is convincing. The majority notes that the parent "did not pay any money pursuant to the parental guaranty" and suggests that the guaranty was really designed only to make sure that Legacy's DTAs were counted in calculating its Bermuda minimum solvency margin. See id. pp. 37-38. The fact that the parent was never required to pay on the guaranty is irrelevant; it is the existence of a parental guaranty that matters in determining whether a captive is truly providing "insurance." And whatever may have prompted the issuance of the guaranty, the fact is that it literally covers all of Legacy's liabilities up to $25 million. The DTAs never got above $9 million during 2003-06. See id. p. 16. Legacy's "liabilities" obviously included Legacy's liability to pay the insurance claims of its sister companies.

The majority contends that the judicial precedents cited above "are distinguishable" because the guaranty issued by Rent-A-Center "did not shift the ultimate risk of loss; did not involve an undercapitalized captive; and was not issued to, or requested by, an unrelated insurer." See op. Ct. pp. 36-37. The majority's first asserted distinction begs the question because it assumes that risk has been shifted to Legacy, which is the proposition that must be proved. The majority's second asserted distinction is a play on words. While Legacy for most of the period at issue was not "undercapitalized" from the standpoint of Bermuda's
(modest) minimum solvency rules, it was very poorly capitalized in comparison with real insurance companies. See infra pp. 67-70. Moreover, the Court of Appeals for the Sixth Circuit in Humana indicated that a parental guaranty alone, without regard to the captive's capitalization, can "provide[] a sufficient basis from which to find no risk shifting." 881 F.2d at 245 n.2. The majority's third asserted distinction is a distinction without a difference. While Rent-A-Center's guaranty was not requested by "an unrelated insurer," it was demanded by Legacy's nominal insurance regulator as a condition of meeting Bermuda's minimum solvency requirements.

As the "most important[]" ground for deeming the guaranty irrelevant, the majority asserts that the parental guaranty "did not affect the balance sheets or net worth of the subsidiaries insured by Legacy." See op. Ct. p. 36. The majority here reprises its argument that the "net worth and balance sheet analysis" must be conducted at the level of the operating subsidiaries. See id. pp. 25, 33. Whatever the merit of that argument generally, as applied to the guaranty it clearly proves too much. A parental guaranty of a captive's liabilities will never affect the balance sheet or net worth of the sister company that is allegedly "insured." But the Sixth Circuit, the Federal Circuit, and this Court have all held that the existence of a
parental guaranty may negate the existence of "insurance" within an affiliated group.

## 2. Inadequate Capitalization

When blessing the brother-sister premium payments in Rev. Rul. 2002-90, supra, the Commissioner hypothesized that the parent had supplied the captive with "adequate capital." Numerous judicial opinions have likewise held that risk cannot be "shifted" to a captive unless the captive is sufficiently capitalized to absorb the risk. See, e.g., Beech Aircraft, 797 F.2d at 922 n.1 (no "insurance" where captive was undercapitalized); Carnation Co., 71 T.C. at 409 (same).

The majority bases its conclusion that Legacy was "adequately capitalized" on the fact that Legacy "met Bermuda's minimum statutory requirements" once the parental guaranty of the DTA is counted. See op. Ct. pp. 20-21. The fact that a captive meets the minimum capital requirements of an offshore financial center is not dispositive as to whether the arrangements constitute "insurance" for Federal income tax purposes. Indeed, the Sixth Circuit in Malone & Hyde held that intragroup payments were not "insurance premiums" even though the captive met "the extremely thin minimum capitalization required by Bermuda law." 62 F.3d at 841.

In fact, Legacy's capital structure was extremely questionable during 2003-06. The only way that Legacy was able to meet Bermuda's extremely thin minimum capitalization requirement was by counting as general business assets its DTAs, and those DTAs could be counted only after Rent-A-Center issued its parental guaranty. The DTAs were essentially a bookkeeping entry. Without treating that bookkeeping entry as an "asset," Legacy would have been undercapitalized even by Bermuda's lax standards.

The extent of Legacy's undercapitalization is evidenced by its premium-to-surplus ratio, which was wildly out of line with the ratios of real insurance companies.

The premium-to-surplus ratio provides a good benchmark of an insurer's ability to absorb risk by drawing on its surplus to pay incurred losses. In this ratio, "premiums written" serves as a proxy for the losses to which the insurer is exposed.

Expert testimony in these cases indicated that U.S. property/casualty insurance companies, on average, have something like a 1:1 premium-to-surplus ratio. In other words, their surplus roughly equals the annual premiums for policies they write. By contrast, Legacy's premium-to-surplus ratio--ignoring the parental guaranty of its DTA--was 48:1 in 2003, 19:1 in 2004, 11:1 in 2005, and in excess of 5:1 in 2006 and 2007. In other words, Legacy's surplus covered only 2% of premiums for policies written in 2003 and only 5% of premiums for policies written in 2004, whereas commercial insurance companies have surplus coverage in the range of 100%. Even if we allow the parental guaranty to count toward Legacy's surplus, its premium-to-surplus ratio was never better than 5:1.

Legacy's assets were undiversified and modest. It had a money market fund into which it placed the supposed "premiums" received from its parent. This fund was in no sense "surplus"; it was a mere holding tank for cash used to pay "claims." Apart from this money-market fund, Legacy appears to have had no assets during the tax years at issue except the following: (a) the guaranties issued by its parent; (b) the DTA reflected on its balance sheet; and (c) Rent-A-Center treasury stock that Legacy purchased from its parent. For Federal tax purposes, the parental guaranties cannot count as "assets" in determining whether Legacy was adequately capitalized. They point in the precisely opposite direction.

The DTA and treasury stock have in common several features that make them poor forms of insurance capital. First, neither yields income. The DTA was an accounting entry that by definition cannot yield income, and the Rent-A-Center treasury stock paid no dividends. No true insurance company would invest 100% of its "reserves" in non-income-producing assets. With no potential to earn income, the "reserves" could not grow to afford a cushion against risk. Moreover, neither the DTA nor the treasury stock was readily convertible into cash. The DTA had no cash value. The treasury stock by its terms could not be sold or alienated, although the parent agreed to buy it back at its issue price. In effect, Legacy relied on the availability of cash from its parent, via repurchase of treasury shares, to pay claims in the event of voluminous losses.[8] Finally, Legacy's assets were, to a large degree, negatively correlated with its insurance risks. During 2004-06, Legacy purchased $108 million of Rent-A Center treasury stock, while "insuring" solely Rent-A-Center risks. Thus, if outsized losses occurred, those losses would simultaneously increase Legacy's liabilities and reduce the value of the Rent-A-Center stock that was Legacy's principal asset. No true insurance company invests its reserves in assets that are both undiversified and negatively correlated to the risks that it is insuring.

In sum, when one combines the existence of the parental guaranty, Legacy's extremely weak premium-to-surplus ratio, the speculative nature and poor quality of the assets in Legacy's "insurance reserves," and the fact that Legacy without the parental guaranty would not even have met "the extremely thin minimum capi-

---

Because Legacy [8] "insured" losses only below a defined threshold, there was

a cap on the size of any individual loss that it might have to pay. See op. Ct. p. 8. However, the number of individual loss events within that tranche could exceed expectations.

---

talization required by Bermuda law," Malone & Hyde, 62 F.3d at 841, the absence of "risk shifting" seems clear. Under the totality of the facts and circumstances, I conclude that there has been no transfer of risk to the captive and hence that the
Rent-A-Center arrangements do not constitute "insurance" for Federal income tax purposes.

## B. Conformity to Insurance Industry Standards

When blessing the brother-sister premiums in Rev. Rul. 2002-90, supra, the IRS hypothesized that "the parties [had] conduct[ed] themselves in a manner consistent with the standards applicable to an insurance arrangement between unrelated parties." Our Court has similarly ruled that transactions in a captive insurance context must comport with "commonly accepted notions of insurance."
Harper Grp. v. Commissioner, 96 T.C. 45, 58 (1991), aff'd, 979 F.2d 1341 (9th Cir. 1992). Because risk shifting is essential to "insurance," Helvering v. LeGierse, 312 U.S. at 539, the absence of risk shifting alone would dictate that the Rent-A-Center payments are not deductible as "insurance premiums." However, there are a number of respects in which Rent-A-Center, its captive, and the allegedly "insured" subsidiaries did not conduct themselves in a manner consistent with accepted insurance industry norms. These facts provide additional support for concluding that these arrangements did not constitute "insurance." Several facts discussed above in connection with "risk shifting" show that the Rent-A-Center arrangements do not comport with normal insurance industry practice. These include the facts that Legacy was poorly capitalized; that its premium-to-surplus ratio was way out of line with the ratios of true insurance companies; and that is "reserves" consisted of assets that were non-income producing, illiquid, undiversified, and negatively correlated to the risks it was supposedly "insuring." No true insurance company would act this way.
It appears that Legacy had no actual employees during the tax years at issue. It had no outside directors, and it had no officers apart from people who were also officers of Rent-A-Center, its parent. Legacy's "operations" appear to have been conducted by David Glasgow, an employee of Rent-A-Center, its parent. "Premium payments" and "loss reimbursements" were

effected through bookkeeping entries made by accountants at Rent-A-Center's corporate headquarters.

Legacy was in practical effect an incorporated pocketbook that served as a repository for what had been, until 2003, Rent-A-Center's self-insurance reserve. Legacy issued its first two "insurance policies" before receiving a certificate of registration from Bermuda insurance authorities. According to those authorities, Legacy was therefore in violation of Bermuda law and "engaged in the insurance business without a license." (Bermuda evidently agreed to let petitioners fix this problem retroactively.) For the first three months of its existence, Legacy was in violation of Bermuda's minimum capital rules because the DTA was not cognizable in determining capital adequacy. Only upon the issuance of the parental guaranty in March 2003, and the acceptance of this guaranty by Bermuda authorities, was Legacy able to pass Bermuda's capital adequacy test.

There was no actuarial determination of the premium payable to Legacy by each operating subsidiary based on the specific subsidiary's risk profile. Rather, an outside insurance adviser estimated the future loss exposure of the affiliated group, and Rent-A-Center, the parent, determined an aggregate "premium" using that estimate. The parent paid this "premium" annually to Legacy. The parent's accounting department subsequently charged portions of this "premium" to each subsidiary, in the same manner as self-insurance costs had been charged to those subsidiaries before Legacy was created. In other words, in contrast to the facts assumed in Rev. Rul. 2002-90, supra, there was in these cases no determination of "arms-length premiums * * * established according to customary industry rating formulas." To the contrary, the entire arrangement was orchestrated exactly as it had been orchestrated before 2003, when the Rent-A-Center group maintained a self-insurance reserve for the tranche of risks purportedly "insured" by Legacy.

From Legacy's inception in December 2002 through May 2004, Legacy did not actually pay "loss claims" submitted by the supposed "insureds." Rather, the parent's accounting department netted "loss reimbursements" due to the subsidiaries from Legacy against "premium payments" due to Legacy from the parent. Beginning in July 2004, the parent withdrew a fixed, preset amount of cash via weekly bank wire from Legacy's money-market account. These weekly withdrawals depleted Legacy's money-market account to near zero just before the next annual "premium" was due. This modus operandi shows that Rent-A-Center regarded Legacy not as an insurer operating at arm's length but as a bank account into which it made deposits and from which it made withdrawals.

These facts, considered in their totality, lead me to disagree with the majority's conclusory assertions that "Legacy entered into bona fide arm's-length contracts with [Rent-A-Center]"; that Legacy "charged actuarially determined premiums"; that Legacy "paid claims from its separately maintained account"; and that Legacy "was adequately capitalized." See op. Ct. pp. 20-21. In my view, the totality of the facts and circumstances could warrant the conclusion that Legacy was a sham. At the very least, the totality of the facts and circumstances makes clear that the arrangements here did not comport with "commonly accepted notions of insurance," Harper Grp., 96 T.C. at 58, and that the Rent-A-Center group of companies did not "conduct themselves in a manner consistent with the standards applicable to an insurance arrangement between unrelated parties," Rev. Rul. 2002- 90, 2001-2 C.B. at 985. The departures from accepted insurance industry practice, combined with the absence of risk shifting to the captive from the alleged "insureds," confirms that these arrangements did not constitute "insurance" for Federal income tax purposes.
COLVIN, GALE, KROUPA, and MORRISON, JJ., agree with this dissent.

**For Immediate Release**
**Date:** August 11, 2014
**Contact:** Richard Smith, President, Vermont Captive Insurance Association / smith@vcia.com

**Captive Insurance Coalition Praises New Federal Legislation**

Washington, DC -- New legislation to clarify the Non-Admitted Reinsurance Reform Act (NRRA) as it pertains to captive insurance was introduced by Senator Patrick Leahy (D-VT) and Senator Lindsay Graham (R-SC) in the U.S. Senate. A companion bill was introduced by Congressman Peter Welch (D-VT) in the U.S. House of Representatives. Efforts to clarify the law have been a priority of the Coalition for Captive Insurance Clarity (CCIC) and were met with praise by coalition members.

"We're delighted that this bi-partisan bill will continue the progress being made to clear up unintended consequences and inaccurate representations regarding the applicability of the NRRA to captive insurers," said Rich Smith, president of the Vermont Captive Insurance Association (VCIA). "I would also like to thank the members of the Coalition for their hard work and support over the past several months."

"The board of the South Carolina Captive Insurance Association (SCCIA) representing the state's captive insurance industry fully supports the NRRA Technical Corrections bill," said Andrea Bartlett, Chairman of the SCCIA.

"It is our belief that the clarifying language of this bill will eliminate current misinterpretations of the intent of the NRRA and will allow organizations to select captive domiciles that provide the best options for their risk management programs."

The original NRRA legislation created considerable confusion and inadvertently upended one of the organizing principles of the captive insurance industry – regulation and taxation by the captive's domicile.

"Congress never intended the NRRA to include captive insurers, and the legislation I have introduced with Senator Graham would simply clarify congressional intent," said Senator Patrick Leahy. "It is a straightforward, commonsense clarification that will give needed assurance to the captive insurance industries in Vermont, South Carolina, and across the country."

"This is an important issue for South Carolina," stated Senator Lindsay Graham. "The legislation I have introduced with Senator Leahy will enable organizations to have a choice in where they domicile their captive. Our legislative fix will create opportunities for this emerging industry and I hope Congress will push it into law."

"This important legislation clarifies a provision within NRRA to ensure that captives in Vermont and around the country continue to operate in the same responsible way that they have for decades," said Congressman Peter Welch. "I am pleased to work with Senators Leahy and Graham on this practical fix to an unintended consequence."

A coalition comprised of the captive insurance industry, the Coalition for Captive Insurance Clarity was formed under the leadership of the Vermont Captive Insurance Association to push for clarity that may include legislative language that would reaffirm that the intent of the new federal NRRA was never intended to apply to captive insurance. # # #

## L. IRC 501(c)(15) - SMALL INSURANCE COMPANIES OR ASSOCIATIONS

1. <u>Introduction</u> The purpose of this section is to provide some background and an update in the area of IRC 501(c)(15) insurance companies or associations. No prior ATRI or CPE text has included a topic in this area.

## 2. Exemption Provisions

### A. Background

The typical insurance company or association recognized as exempt under IRC 501(c)(15) is a mutual organization which provides its members with property damage coverage. Membership is often limited by the organization to residents of a particular county. Burial and funeral benefit companies providing their benefits in the form of supplies and services may also qualify under IRC 501(c)(15). If benefits are paid in cash upon the death of the insured, the organization is deemed a life insurance company and exemption is not appropriate under IRC 501(c)(15), but may be considered under IRC 501(c)(12) as a local benevolent life insurance association. As noted below, exemption under IRC 501(c)(15) was recently extended to include marine insurance companies.

### B. Exemption Provisions Prior to Tax Reform Act of 1986

(1) Prior to the enactment of the Tax Reform Act of 1986 ("the Act"), IRC 501(c)(15) provided that a mutual insurance company or association (other than life or marine) or a mutual interinsurer or reciprocal underwriter (other than life or marine) could be exempt under IRC 501(a) if the gross amount received from certain items during the taxable year did not exceed $150,000. These items of income consisted of:

(a) Premiums, including deposits and assessments;

(b) Interest, dividends, rents and royalties;

(c) Amounts received for entering into leases, mortgages, or other instruments or agreements from which the company or association may receive interest, rents or royalties;

(d) Amounts received for altering or terminating instruments oragreements of the type described in (3); and

(e) Gross income from a business (other than the insurance business) carried on by the company or association or by a partnership of which the company or association is a member.

(2) Although neither IRC 501(c)(15) nor the underlying regulations discuss the concept of mutuality, Rev. Rul. 74-196, 1974-1 C.B. 140, provides that the following characteristics, while not alone conclusive, must be present:

(a) **Control by members** - Membership must be limited to policyholders and all policyholders must be members. Furthermore, all policyholders must have the right to choose the management of the organization.

(b) **Providing insurance at cost** - The company must provide insurance at substantially its cost, allowing for reasonable reserves against its policy obligations and operational expenses. An unreasonable accumulation suggests that the company is not providing insurance to its members substantially at cost. Reserves maintained for business expansion would not be considered appropriate.

(c) **The right of members to excess premiums** - The excess of the premium over actual cost and reserves, as later ascertained, must be returned to the policyholder. This may take the form of a reduction in renewal premiums or the payment of dividends on the policies.

(d) **Common equitable ownership of assets by members** - This is evidenced by the right of members to receive the company's net assets in the event the members vote to wind up and dissolve the company.

C. Exemption Provisions Pursuant to the Act

The Act amended IRC 501(c)(15) with respect to taxable years beginning after December 31, 1986. The changes pertain to:

(1) **Operation as a mutual organization** - An exempt insurance company or association is no longer required to operate on a mutual basis. It may now operate on a stock basis or a mutual basis.

(2) **Coverage** - An exempt insurance company or association may now issue marine coverage. Life insurance coverage remains a prohibited activity.

(3) **Nature of receipts and ceiling** - An insurance company or association may qualify as exempt if its net written premiums (or, if greater, direct written premiums) for the taxable year do not exceed $350,000. The items of income discussed above in 2.B.(1) (other than premiums) are not taken into account for purposes of this test.

The legislation did not define "net written premiums" or "direct written premiums." However, a manual published by the National Association of Insurance Commissioners provides some guidance in this area. Direct written premiums include premiums arising from policies issued by the company acting as the primary insurance carrier. Net written premiums are equal to direct premiums plus the reinsurance assumed premiums, less the reinsurance ceded premiums.

D. Legislative History Regarding the Act

The portion of Conference Report No. 99-841, 1986-3 C.B. II 370, Vol. 4, regarding the changes discussed above follows:

7. Special exemptions, rates, and deductions of small companies

*Present Law*

Under present law, mutual property and casualty companies are classified into three categories depending upon the amounts of the gross receipts. Mutual companies with certain gross receipts not in excess of $ 150,000 are tax-exempt (sec. 501(c)(15)). Companies whose gross receipts exceed $ 150,000 but do not exceed $ 500,000 are "small mutuals" and generally are taxed solely on investment income. This provision does not apply to any mutual company that has a balance in its PAL account, or that, pursuant to a special election, chooses to be taxed on both its underwriting and investment income. Additionally, small mutuals which are subject to tax because their gross receipts exceed $ 150,000 may claim the benefit of a special rule which phases in the regular tax on investment income as gross receipts increase from $ 150,000 to $ 250,000. Companies whose gross receipts exceed $ 500,000 are ordinary mutuals taxed on both investment and underwriting income. Mutual reciprocal underwriters or interinsurers are generally taxed as mutual insurance companies, subject to special rules (sec. 826).

Like stock companies, ordinary mutuals generally are subject to the regular corporate income tax rates. Mutuals whose taxable income does not exceed $ 12,000 pay tax at a lower rate. No tax is imposed on the first $ 6,000 of taxable income, and a tax of 30 percent is imposed on the next $ 6,000 of taxable income. For small mutual companies which are taxable on investment income, no tax is imposed on the first $ 3,000 of taxable investment income, and a tax of 30 percent is imposed on taxable investment income between $3,000 and $6,000.

Mutual companies that receive a gross amount from premiums and certain investment income of less than $ 1,100,000 are allowed a special deduction against their underwriting income (if it is subject to tax). The maximum amount of the deduction is $ 6,000, and the deduction phases out as the gross amount increases from $500,000 to $1,100,000.

*House Bill*

The House bill provides that mutual and stock property and casualty companies are eligible for exemption from tax if their net written premiums or direct written premiums (whichever is greater) do not exceed $500,000.

In addition, the House bill repeals the special rates, deductions and exemptions for small mutual companies and substitutes a single provision (sec. 847 of the Code). The new provision allows mutual and stock companies with net written premiums or direct written premiums (whichever is greater) in excess of $ 500,000 but less than $ 2 million to elect to be taxed only on taxable investment income. To determine the amount of direct or net written premiums of a member of a controlled group of corporations, the direct or net written premiums of all members of the controlled group are aggregated.

The provisions are effective for taxable years beginning after December 31, 1985.

*Senate Amendment*

The Senate amendment is the same as the House bill, except that the $ 500,000 threshold is reduced to $ 350,000 and the $ 2 million threshold is reduced to $ 1,200,000. The provisions are effective for taxable years beginning after December 31, 1986.

*Conference Agreement*

The conference agreement follows the Senate amendment, effective for taxable year beginning after December 31, 1986, with the modification that, in determining whether a taxpayer is a member of a controlled group of corporations for purposes of eligibility for the provision, a 50 percent ownership test applies.

Parts II and III of Subchapter L of the Code are consolidated into Part II, under the conference agreement. Part II of Subchapter L relates generally to taxation of property and casualty insurance companies.

## 3. Current Topic of Interest

As discussed above, the Act has significantly changed IRC 501(c)(15) with respect to the nature of receipts which must be considered for purposes of the newly-defined ceiling which was itself increased to $350,000. The result is that this ceiling takes into account only net written premiums (or, if greater, direct written premiums). Premiums collected in a prior year, although they pertain to coverage in the current year, are not considered for purposes of the current year's ceiling amount. In addition, income from sources other than insurance activity is no longer taken into account for purposes of the ceiling.

These changes in the law can cause a dramatic change in the federal income tax liability faced by an insurance company. To illustrate, assume that an insurance company realized net written premiums of $500,000 in 1986 and $350,000 in 1987 and that all premiums came from policies which provide two years coverage. Assume further, underwriting expenses of $50,000 each year, interest income of $50,000 each year and that the company delays its sale of an investment from which a gain of $1,000,000 is realized from 1986 to 1987.

|  | 1986 | 1987 |
|---|---|---|
| Net written premiums | $ 500,000 | $ 350,000 |
| Amortization of unearned premium | -250,000 | -175,000 |
| Recognition of earned premium | | |

|  |  |  |
|---|---:|---:|
| from prior year | +250,000 |  |
| **Earned premiums** | **$ 250,000** | **$ 425,000** |
| Underwriting expense | - 50,000 | - 50,000 |
| Net Underwriting income | $ 200,000 | $ 375,000 |
| Investment income | + 50,000 | +1,050.000 |
| **Net income** | **$ 250,000** | **$ 1,425,000** |

# ASSET PROTECTION PLANNING

Asset protection has been around for thousands of years. Since the 1980s, a "cottage industry" has been built around asset protection planning with several law firms offering a boutique version of asset protection. Attorneys such s Barry Engel of Engel and Reiman, Jay Adkisson of Riser Adkisson and Howard Rosen of Donlevy-Rosen work diligently in the Asset protection area. Many of these attorney's devote 100% of their time to asset protection issues. During these challenging economic times, more and more clients will ask about the asset protection devices. Should your client place all their liquid assets into an S.A. and then lie about ownership? What are the ethical and legal challenges of asset protection planning? Most people who engage in asset protection planning are encouraged to keep a "low profile" as the discovery by a judgment creditor can lead to attachment and garnishment. What about the court system? What happens if a judge on summary judgment makes a mistake which cost your client a fortune or their entire savings? What are your legal and ethical responsibilities?

Asset Protection in its simplest form is used every day where you lock your door before you go to sleep at night; you lock your car when you leave your car at work. In a legal sense, it is protecting the assets tangible or intangible from legal threats, real or imagined from legal process by the state or a private party. Historically assets have been seized by a nation state for various reasons, such as assets confiscated by the Germans, in the United states, Indian lands were seized by the U.S. Government, in war, the spoils would go to the victor. Whether these acts were just or unjust is up to historians which generally are the victors. In a legal case, justice is supposed to prevail, but in some cases the system fails. An arbitrator lies on his application and takes a case where his client is one of the parties. A judge rules in favor of his favorite attorney without carefully reviewing the facts or the law. A judgment is procured against your client by surreptitious means and he or she is faced with losing her house, savings, means of support or any future that the term "life liberty or pursuit of happiness" will have any meaning other than empty words written in the constitution. Today, a student can run up student loans into the hundreds of thousands of dollars which cannot be discharged in Bankruptcy due to the "Bankruptcy Abuse Prevention and Consumer Protection Act of 2005". An unsuspecting victim of credit card debt can also have hundreds of thousands of dollars in debt by a bank which charges 32% interest or more and no way out as the debt will not be discharged in Bankruptcy. A person can have mortgage interest debt with credit card and student loans with no possibility of paying any of these debts back as they lost their job and cannot obtain any job that would give them a chance at repayment.

They are in need of asset protection, but cannot afford even the basic advice. The general client who seeks asset protection has signed a note perhaps as a guarantor of one to 5 million and cannot sleep at night if the loan goes into default. A physician is afraid that all that he or she has earned will be lost in a late in life malpractice suit. A real estate investor has millions in assets or millions in liabilities depending on how you value the assets. What form of asset protection is available?

## *Cutting off Liability using the Statute of Limitations*

SUMMARY OF ARGUMENT

The Employee Retirement Income Security Act (ERISA), 29 U.S.C. § 1001 et seq., requires a plan fiduciary to: discharge his duties with respect to a plan solely in the interest of the participants and beneficiaries and . . . with the care, skill, prudence, and diligence under the circumstances then prevailing that a prudent man acting in a like capacity and familiar with such matters would use in the conduct of an enterprise of a like character and with like aims. ERISA § 404(a)(1)(A), (B), 29 U.S.C. § 1104(a)(1)(A), ERISA § 404(a)(1)(A), (B), 29 U.S.C. § 1104(a)(1)(A), (B).

ERISA includes a limitations period which states,

in relevant part:

No action may be commenced under this subchapter with respect to a fiduciary's breach . . . after the earlier of—

(1) six years after

(A) the date of the last action which constituted a part of the breach or violation, or

(B) in the case of an omission the latest date on which the fiduciary could have cured the breach or violation. . . . ERISA § 413, 29 U.S.C. § 1113.

This case concerns the application of those sections of ERISA to the selection and monitoring of the menu of investment choices offered to participants in a defined contribution plan. 4

The Court of Appeals for the Ninth Circuit held that, although fiduciaries breached their duty of prudence by offering higher-cost retail-class mutual funds to plan participants when identical lower-cost institutional-class mutual funds were available, the claim was barred by ERISA Section 413(1), 29 U.S.C. § 1113(1), because fiduciaries initially chose the higher cost mutual funds as plan investments more than six years before the claim was filed. In reaching this decision, the Ninth Circuit appears to have confused two distinct requirements imposed by ERISA's duty of prudent investing: the duty to be prudent in the selection of plan investment options, and the duty thereafter prudently to monitor the selected investment options, to ensure that those options remain prudent choices. The court measured the limitations period from the date of the initial investment selection, rather than from the last date the imprudent investments could have been removed from the plan—the latter constituting the last date on which the fiduciary breach could have been corrected through diligent monitoring. Contrary to congressional intent, this interpretation of ERISA's six-year statute of limitations insulates fiduciaries from liability for imprudent behavior—namely, omitting to provide prudent monitoring—with regard to ongoing plan investment options, as long as that imprudent behavior occurs more than six years after the initial investment selection.

Petitioners' claims should not be barred by the statute of limitations. The law of trusts—upon which 5 ERISA is based—makes clear that fiduciaries have an ongoing duty to monitor investments, as frequently as is appropriate for the particular trust. Participants and beneficiaries are not precluded from bringing an action to challenge the prudence of an investment decision— either an act or an omission that breaches this ongoing duty—as long as the action is filed within the earlier of (1) six years after the date of the last action that constituted a breach or (2) in the event of an omission, within six years of the last date the fiduciary could have cured such a breach. That is, in the context of this case, (1) six years after the last decision to keep an imprudent investment in breach of the ongoing duty to monitor or (2) six years after the last date the fiduciary could have removed an imprudent investment.

---------------------------------- ☐ -------------------

Today, this world can be divided between Domestic and International Asset protection. For the U.S. citizen, I generally advise them to do everything they can domestically before they look internationally for relief. Domestic Protection varies from State to State as the laws are different, in some cases radically different from state to state. Also there is a federal aspect to protecting assets as some assets are 'exempt" from creditors and bankruptcy proceedings such as assets held in retirement plans.

Law 101-102-103

Law 101 is the statutory law which will be examined using the Florida Statutes. Other statutory law will also be examined including Delaware, Nevada, Alaska, Wyoming and other states which compete in the asset protection arena. The statutes of the domiciliary company must be examined as well as the statutes of where the action took place as the entity may have to be registered as a foreign entity doing business in a particular state.

Law 102 is the case law which is how the judges interpret statutes. The statutes in many cases can be overruled by common law exceptions and "judicial law". In Washington, a case was sent to arbitration where the arbitrator "made up" the rules to favor one particular individual. The arbitrator had an undisclosed conflict and created the law of "exigent circumstances" in denying a board member a seat on a board of directors. This rule does not exist in corporate law, but the arbitrator "made it up".

Law 103. Practical planning. Ralph Reed made this a comment, "it is not so important what you are saying but who you are saying it to". Basically, who is hearing the claim, what is the political aspects of the hearing. For example, is your opposing counsel a person with a "close relationship" to the presiding officer? Does the person listening to your side of the story have a son who works for the law firm that is presenting the "other side of the story"? This part of planning is not taught in law schools. When is it time to move assets outside of the U.S. Jurisdiction to allow a foreign court which may not be as receptive to the U.S. claim to hear or even recognize the foreign judgment. As a practical matter, it is best to do asset protection.

---

Five courts of appeals have agreed with the Tenth Circuit that Section 206(d)(1) does not prevent the attachment or garnishment of funds after a pension plan has paid them to retirees.... One has held that Section 206(d)(1) shields pensions from creditors even after distribution. United States v. Smith, 47 F.3d 681 (4th Cir. 1995). We agree with the majority -- and because we are the seventh court of appeals to reach this conclusion we can be brief." [NLRB v. HH3 Trucking Inc., Nos. 05-1362, 05-4075 (7th Cir. June 13, 2014)]

# ENTERPRISE RISK MANAGEMENT- CHOICE OF BUSINESS ENTITY AND ITS IMPLICATIONS

## UNITED STATES v. BESTFOODS

**Syllabus**

UNITED STATES v. BESTFOODS ( No. 97-454 )
113 F. 3d 572, vacated and remanded.

*certiorari to the united states court of appeals for the sixth circuit*

No. 97–454. Argued March 24, 1998—Decided June 8, 1998

The United States brought this action under §107(a)(2) of the Comprehensive Environmental Response, Compensation, and Liability Act of 1980 (CERCLA) against, among others, respondent CPC International Inc., the parent corporation of the defunct Ott Chemical Co. (Ott II), for the costs of cleaning up industrial waste generated by Ott II's chemical plant. Section 107(a)(2) authorizes suits against, among others, "any person who at the time of disposal of any hazardous substance owned or operated any facility." The trial focused on whether CPC, as a parent corporation, had "owned or operated" Ott II's plant within the meaning of §107(a)(2). The District Court said that operator liability may attach to a parent corporation both indirectly, when the corporate veil can be pierced under state law, and directly, when the parent has exerted power or influence over its subsidiary by actively participating in, and exercising control over, the subsidiary's business during a period of hazardous waste disposal. Applying that test, the court held CPC liable because CPC had selected Ott II's board of directors and populated its executive ranks with CPC officials, and another CPC official had played a significant role in shaping Ott II's environmental compliance policy. The Sixth Circuit reversed. Although recognizing that a parent company might be held directly liable under §107(a)(2) if it actually operated its subsidiary's facility in the stead of the subsidiary, or alongside of it as a joint venturer, that court refused to go further. Rejecting the District Court's analysis, the Sixth Circuit explained that a parent corporation's liability for operating a facility ostensibly operated by its subsidiary depends on whether the degree to which the parent controls the subsidiary and the extent and manner of its involvement with the facility amount to the abuse of the corporate form that will warrant piercing the corporate veil and disregarding the separate corporate entities of the parent and subsidiary. Applying Michigan veil-piercing law, the court decided that CPC was not liable for controlling Ott II's actions, since the two corporations maintained separate personalities and CPC did not utilize the subsidiary form to perpetrate fraud or subvert justice.

Held:

1. When (but only when) the corporate veil may be pierced, a parent corporation may be charged with derivative CERCLA liability for its subsidiary's actions in operating a polluting facility. It is a general principle of corporate law that a parent corporation (so-called because of control through ownership of another corporation's stock) is not liable for the acts of its subsidiaries. CERCLA does not purport to reject this bedrock principle, and the Government has indeed made no claim that a corporate parent is liable as an owner or an operator under §107(a)(2) simply because its subsidiary owns or operates a polluting facility. But there is an equally

fundamental principle of corporate law, applicable to the parent-subsidiary relationship as well as generally, that the corporate veil may be pierced and the shareholder held liable for the corporation's conduct when, *inter alia*, the corporate form would otherwise be misused to accomplish certain wrongful purposes, most notably fraud, on the shareholder's behalf. CERCLA does not purport to rewrite this well-settled rule, either, and against this venerable common-law backdrop, the congressional silence is audible. Cf. *Edmonds* v. *Compagnie Generale Transatlantique,* 443 U. S. 256. CERCLA's failure to speak to a matter as fundamental as the liability implications of corporate ownership demands application of the rule that, to abrogate a common-law principle, a statute must speak directly to the question addressed by the common law. *United States* v. *Texas,* 507 U. S. 529. Pp. 7–10.

2. A corporate parent that actively participated in, and exercised control over, the operations of its subsidiary's facility may be held directly liable in its own right under §107(a)(2) as an operator of the facility. Pp. 11–20.

(a) Derivative liability aside, CERCLA does not bar a parent corporation from direct liability for its own actions. Under the plain language of §107(a)(2), any person who operates a polluting facility is directly liable for the costs of cleaning up the pollution, and this is so even if that person is the parent corporation of the facility's owner. Because the statute does not define the term "operate," however, it is difficult to define actions sufficient to constitute direct parental "operation." In the organizational sense obviously intended by CERCLA, to "operate" a facility ordinarily means to direct the workings of, manage, or conduct the affairs of the facility. To sharpen the definition for purposes of CERCLA's concern with environmental contamination, an operator must manage, direct, or conduct operations specifically related to the leakage or disposal of hazardous waste, or decisions about compliance with environmental regulations. Pp. 11–13.

(b) The Sixth Circuit correctly rejected the direct liability analysis of the District Court, which mistakenly focused on the relationship between parent and subsidiary, and premised liability on little more than CPC's ownership of Ott II and its majority control over Ott II's board of directors. Because direct liability for the parent's operation of the facility must be kept distinct from derivative liability for the subsidiary's operation of the facility, the analysis should instead have focused on the relationship between CPC and the facility itself, *i.e.,* on whether CPC "operated" the facility, as evidenced by its direct participation in the facility's activities. That error was compounded by the District Court's erroneous assumption that actions of the joint officers and directors were necessarily attributable to CPC, rather than Ott II, contrary to time-honored common-law principles. The District Court's focus on the relationship between parent and subsidiary (rather than parent and facility), combined with its automatic attribution of the actions of dual officers and directors to CPC, erroneously, even if unintentionally, treated CERCLA as though it displaced or fundamentally altered common-law standards of limited liability. The District Court's analysis created what is in essence a relaxed, CERCLA-specific rule of derivative liability that would banish traditional standards and expectations from the law of CERCLA liability. Such a rule does not arise from congressional silence, and CERCLA's silence is dispositive. Pp. 13–18.

(c) Nonetheless, the Sixth Circuit erred in limiting direct liability under CERCLA to a parent's sole or joint venture operation, so as to eliminate any possible finding that CPC is liable as an operator on the facts of this case. The ordinary meaning of the word "operate" in the organizational sense is not limited to those two parental actions, but extends also to situations in which, *e.g.,* joint officers or directors conduct the affairs of the facility on behalf of the parent, or agents of the parent with no position in the subsidiary manage or direct activities at the subsidiary's facility. Norms of corporate behavior (undisturbed by any CERCLA provision) are crucial reference points, both for determining whether a dual officer or director has served the parent in conducting operations at the facility, and for distinguishing a parental officer's oversight of a subsidiary from his control over the operation of the subsidiary's facility. There is, in fact, some evidence that an agent of CPC alone engaged in activities at Ott II's plant that were eccentric under accepted norms of parental oversight of a subsidiary's facility: The District Court's opinion speaks of such an agent who played a conspicuous part in dealing with the toxic risks emanating from the plant's operation. The findings in this regard are enough to raise an issue of CPC's operation of the facility, though this Court draws no ultimate conclusion, leaving the issue for the lower courts to reevaluate and resolve in the first instance. Pp. 18–20.

113 F. 3d 572, vacated and remanded.

Souter, J., delivered the opinion for a unanimous Court.

There are many ways to start up and operate a business. The easy way is to have a "Sole Proprietorship".

## SOLE PROPRIETOR

The problem is liability. A Sole Proprietorship creates unlimited liability to the operator. If taxes are not paid, he is liable. If an employee cause's harm to another, he is liable personally. Liability is endless and in every direction. Many businesses begin as a sole proprietor, however once they hire their first employee, this form of operation breaks down. In fact if they can afford to hire an employee, they can afford to create legal protection offered by a corporation or other legal entity before they hire their first employee.

## CORPORATION

A shareholder is not responsible for the debts of the corporation. In many cases, an officer is not responsible for the acts of the corporation even though the officer was engaged in the acts. A shareholder is not liable for the acts of the employees of the corporation. There is no question that a corporation offers protection from unknown and unwanted risk. In the traditional sense, a corporation is a legal entity, a creature of the state, a "person" which is divided between ownership or shareholders, a board of directors who are responsible for the direction of the company and the officers which implement the wishes of the board, generally to make profits for the shareholders and themselves. In a small company, the board, officers and shareholders are all the same people. When a company increases in size, the shareholders may be completely different then the board and the board may be completely different than the officers. The state grants protection to the shareholders and the risk is limited to the value of their shares. The officers may also be immune from negligent acts or in some cases even intentional acts if they are operating on behalf of the corporation. The State does not offer this protection for free. There are filing fees to the division of Corporations annually. Annual reports must also be submitted. In many states there is a corporate income tax which today range from 0% in Nevada, Washington and Wyoming to 9.975% in the District of Columbia and 8.84% in California.

Corporate Formalities must also be observed to maintain the protection of the corporate form. A corporation must generally file:

A. Articles of Incorporation with the Secretary of State or Division of Corporations.
B. Create Bylaws that govern the corporation
C. Issue shares to the owners of the corporation.

Each state has their individual corporate statutes. It is best to engage an attorney licensed in that state to work on setting up the corporate structure, bylaws and issuing of shares. The attorney can also give you guidance as to the best and most favorable entity that should be set up in their jurisdiction. Is the Corporation the most favorable form of entity to conduct business, or is it a partnership, or another entity such as an LLC or LLP. Some states have LLLP statues.

**BRIEF HISTORY OF CORPORATION LAW**

The history of Corporations can date back to the Code of Hammurabi in 2083 B.C. where references were made to 'societies". Under later Roman law, the *Populous Romanus* or *Senatus Populusque Romanus* S.P.Q.R. became the original corporation. These groups were formed with and by imperial fiat assuring government control over the entity. Fast forward to England where Sir William Blackstone Commentaries on English company law in 1765 discussed extensively the law of corporations. Limited liability of the shareholder was illusory because the corporation could make calls or assessments on its shareholders to pay liabilities and creditors could assert this power on a derivative basis. In 1720 until its repeal in 1825, England had the Bubble Act of 1720 which governed corporations. During this time the United States was formed. Under the Articles of Confederation, the federal government had no power to create corporations. James Madison twice proposed a federal charter at the constitutional convention in 1787, and was twice defeated. Even today, the federal government has no incorporation powers and as a result, practically all corporations are organized under state law. In 1795 North Carolina pass a corporation statute, followed by Massachusetts in 1799, and New York in 1811. The New York statute was the first to allow any person who complied with the statute to create a corporation, however the total capital could not exceed 4,100,000 and the life was limited to 20 years. In 1888 New Jersey passed a law that allowed a corporation to own shares of another corporation creating the first "holding" company. Delaware and other states soon followed. In 1896, New Jersey passed a law that provided protection against liability for directors and managers. In 1913, the Governor of New Jersey, Woodrow Wilson caused the state to amend its permissive statute. Delaware which had copied New Jersey was now able to seize the opportunity to become a leader in corporate formation and organization. Competition between the states took place and became so intense that a Uniform Business Corporation Act was recommended by the National Conference of Commissioners on Uniform state laws in 1928. However only a few sates adopted the statute. Federal intervention only took place in the way of regulations such as antitrust and trade, labor laws and securities as well as income tax regulations concerning corporations. The Model Business Corporation Act first appeared in completed form in 1950. The model Act was a drafting guide for the various states. This Act was revised in 1984 known as the Revised Model Business Corporation Act of 1984. Once again, the states could adopt some all or none of the model which creates a patchwork of laws that exist and differ from state to state.

Today the Federal Government has <u>no legislation</u> dealing with the formation of business associations. The Federal government only has "implied powers" to regulate "interstate commerce".

Corporation asset protection varies by statute and by common law. Today states compete for asset protection status to encourage companies to file articles of incorporation using their state as the state of domicile. The two states which compete in this area are Delaware and Nevada. Recently Wyoming has joined in this competition for "asset protection". The problem with filing articles in a state such as Nevada, it does not necessarily mean that you would escape liability. For example, if the action occurred in Florida and you do business in Florida, you would have to file as a foreign corporation doing business in the State of Florida and Florida law would apply. The Judgment in Florida could attach assets in Florida and theoretically, Delaware or Nevada would have to give reciprocity to the Florida judgment based upon the "full faith and credit" clause of the constitution.

**Florida Corporation Statute:**

**607.0120**   Filing requirements.—

(1) A document must satisfy the requirements of this section and of any other section that adds to or varies these requirements to be entitled to filing by the Department of State.

(2) This act must require or permit filing the document in the office of the Department of State.

(3) The document must contain the information required by this act. It may contain other information as well.

(4) The document must be typewritten or printed, or, if electronically transmitted, the document must be in a format that can be retrieved or reproduced in typewritten or printed form, and must be legible.

(5) The document must be in the English language. A corporate name need not be in English if written in English letters or Arabic or Roman numerals, and the certificate of status required of foreign corporations need not be in English if accompanied by a reasonably authenticated English translation.

(6) The document must be executed:

    (a) By a director of a domestic or foreign corporation, or by its president or by another of its officers;

    (b) If directors or officers have not been selected or the corporation has not been formed, by an incorporator; or

    (c) If the corporation is in the hands of a receiver, trustee, or other court-appointed fiduciary, by that fiduciary.

(7) The person executing the document shall sign it and state beneath or opposite his or her signature his or her name and the capacity in which he or she signs. The document may, but need not, contain the corporate seal, an attestation, an acknowledgment, or verification.

(8) If the Department of State has prescribed a mandatory form for the document under s. 607.0121, the document must be in or on the prescribed form.

(9) The document must be delivered to the office of the Department of State for filing. Delivery may be made by electronic transmission if and to the extent permitted by the Department of State. If it is filed in typewritten or printed form and not transmitted electronically, the Department of State may require one exact or conformed copy, to be delivered with the document, (except as provided in s. 607.1509).

(10) When the document is delivered to the Department of State for filing, the correct filing fee, and any other tax, license fee, or penalty required to be paid by this act or other law shall be paid or provision for payment made in a manner permitted by the Department of State.

**607.0121** Forms.—

(1) The Department of State may prescribe and furnish on request forms for:

    (a) An application for certificate of status,

    (b) A foreign corporation's application for certificate of authority to transact business in the state,

    (c) A foreign corporation's application for certificate of withdrawal, and

    (d) The annual report, for which the department may prescribe the use of the uniform business report, pursuant to s. 606.06.

If the Department of State so requires, the use of these forms shall be mandatory.

(2) The Department of State may prescribe and furnish on request forms for other documents required or permitted to be filed by this act, but their use shall not be mandatory.

Florida has liability provisions in the statues, but not as comprehensive as Delaware.

**607.0204** Liability for pre-incorporation transactions.—All persons purporting to act as or on behalf of a corporation, having actual knowledge that there was no incorporation under this chapter, are jointly and severally liable for all liabilities created while so acting except for any liability to any person who also had actual knowledge that there was no incorporation

**607.0622** Liability for shares issued before payment.—
(1) A holder of, or subscriber to, shares of a corporation shall be under no obligation to the corporation or its creditors with respect to such shares other than the obligation to pay to the corporation the full consideration for which such shares were issued or to be issued. Such an obligation may be enforced by the corporation and its successors or assigns; by a shareholder suing derivatively on behalf of the corporation; by a receiver, liquidator, or trustee in bankruptcy of the corporation; or by another person having the legal right to marshal the assets of such corporation.
(2) Any person becoming an assignee or transferee of shares, or of a subscription for shares, in good faith and without knowledge or notice that the full consideration therefor has not been paid shall not be personally liable to the corporation or its creditors for any unpaid portion of such

consideration, but the assignor or transferor shall continue to be liable therefor.

(3) No pledgee or other holder of shares as collateral security shall be personally liable as a shareholder, but the pledgor or other person transferring such shares as collateral shall be considered the holder thereof for purposes of liability under this section.

(4) An executor, administrator, conservator, guardian, trustee, assignee for the benefit of creditors, receiver, or other fiduciary shall not be personally liable to the corporation as a holder of, or subscriber to, shares of a corporation, but the estate and funds in her or his hands shall be so liable.

(5) No liability under this section may be asserted more than 5 years after the earlier of:

    (a) The issuance of the stock, or

    (b) The date of the subscription upon which the assessment is sought.


**Delaware has a special statute not found in Florida law concerning lawsuits:**

Subchapter XIII. Suits against Corporations, Directors, Officers or Stockholders

§ 321. Service of process on corporations.

(a) Service of legal process upon any corporation of this State shall be made by delivering a copy personally to any officer or director of the corporation in this State, or the registered agent of the corporation in this State, or by leaving it at the dwelling house or usual place of abode in this State of any officer, director or registered agent (if the registered agent be an individual), or at the registered office or other place of business of the corporation in this State. If the registered agent be a corporation, service of process upon it as such agent may be made by serving, in this State, a copy thereof on the president, vice-president, secretary, assistant secretary or any director of the corporate registered agent. Service by copy left at the dwelling house or usual place of abode of any officer, director or registered agent, or at the registered office or other place of business of the corporation in this State, to be effective must be delivered thereat at least 6 days before the return date of the process, and in the presence of an adult person, and the officer serving the process shall distinctly state the manner of service in such person's return thereto. Process returnable forthwith must be delivered personally to the officer, director or registered agent.

(b) In case the officer whose duty it is to serve legal process cannot by due diligence serve the process in any manner provided for by subsection (a) of this section, it shall be lawful to serve the process against the corporation upon the Secretary of State, and such service shall be as effectual for all intents and purposes as if made in any of the ways provided for in subsection (a) of this section. Process may be served upon the Secretary of State under this subsection by means of electronic transmission but only as prescribed by the Secretary of State. The Secretary of State is authorized to issue such rules and regulations with respect to such service as the Secretary of State deems necessary or appropriate. In the event that service is effected through the Secretary of State in accordance with this subsection, the Secretary of State shall forthwith notify the corporation by letter, directed to the corporation at its principal place of business as it appears on the records relating to such corporation on file with the Secretary of State or, if no such address appears, at its last registered office. Such letter shall be sent by a mail or courier service that includes a record of mailing or deposit with the courier and a record of delivery evidenced by the signature of the recipient. Such letter shall enclose a copy of the process and any other papers served on the Secretary of State pursuant to this subsection. It shall be the duty of the plaintiff in the event of such service to serve process and any other papers in duplicate, to notify the Secretary of State that service is being effected pursuant to this subsection, and to pay the Secretary of State the sum of $50 for the use of the State, which sum shall be taxed as part of the costs in the proceeding if the plaintiff shall prevail therein. The Secretary of State shall maintain an alphabetical record of any such service setting forth the name of the plaintiff and defendant, the title, docket number and nature of the proceeding in which process has been served upon the Secretary of State, the fact that service has been effected pursuant to this subsection, the return date thereof, and the day and hour when the service was made. The Secretary of State shall not be required to retain such information for a period longer than 5 years from receipt of the service of process.

(c) Service upon corporations may also be made in accordance with § 3111 of Title 10 or any other statute or rule of court.

**§ 322**. Failure of corporation to obey order of court; appointment of receiver.

Whenever any corporation shall refuse, fail or neglect to obey any order or decree of any court of this State within the time fixed by the court for its observance, such refusal, failure or neglect shall be a sufficient ground for the appointment of a receiver of the corporation by the Court of Chancery. If the corporation be a foreign corporation, such refusal, failure or neglect shall be a sufficient ground for the appointment of a receiver of the assets of the corporation within this State.

8 Del. C. 1953, § 322; 56 Del. Laws, c. 50.;

**§ 323.** Failure of corporation to obey writ of mandamus; quo warranto proceedings for forfeiture of charter.

If any corporation fails to obey the mandate of any peremptory writ of mandamus issued by a court of competent jurisdiction of this State for a period of 30 days after the serving of the writ upon the corporation in any manner as provided by the laws of this State for the service of writs, any party in interest in the proceeding in which the writ of mandamus issued may file a statement of such fact prepared by such party or such party's attorney with the Attorney General of this State, and it shall thereupon be the duty of the Attorney General to forthwith commence proceedings of quo warranto against the corporation in a court of competent jurisdiction, and the court, upon competent proof of such state of facts and proper proceedings had in such proceeding in quo warranto, shall decree the charter of the corporation forfeited.

**§ 324.** Attachment of shares of stock or any option, right or interest therein; procedure; sale; title upon sale; proceeds.

(a) <u>The shares of any person in any corporation with all the rights thereto belonging, or any person's option to acquire the shares, or such person's right or interest in the shares, may be attached under this section for debt, or other demands, if such person appears on the books of the corporation to hold or own such shares, option, right or interest.</u> So many of the shares, or so much of the option, right or interest therein may be sold at public sale to the highest bidder, as shall be sufficient to satisfy the debt, or other demand, interest and costs, upon an order issued therefor by the court from which the attachment process issued, and after such notice as is required for sales upon execution process. Except as to an uncertificated security as defined in § 8-102 of Title 6, the attachment is not laid and no order of sale shall issue unless § 8-112 of Title 6 has been satisfied. No order of sale shall be issued until after final judgment shall have been rendered in any case. If the debtor lives out of the county, a copy of the order shall be sent by registered or certified mail, return receipt requested, to such debtor's last known address, and shall also be published in a newspaper published in the county of such debtor's last known residence, if there be any, 10 days before the sale; and if the debtor be a nonresident of this State shall be mailed as aforesaid and published at least twice for 2 successive weeks, the last publication to be at least 10 days before the sale, in a newspaper published in the county where the attachment process issued. If the shares of stock or any of them or the option to acquire shares or any such right or interest in shares, or any part of them, be so sold, any assignment, or transfer thereof, by the debtor, after attachment, shall be void.

(b) When attachment process issues for shares of stock, or any option to acquire such or any right or interest in such, a certified copy of the process shall be left in this State with any officer or director, or with the registered agent of the corporation. Within 20 days after service of the process, the corporation shall serve upon the plaintiff a certificate of the number of shares held or owned by the debtor in the corporation, with the number or other marks distinguishing the same, or in the case the debtor appears on the books of the corporation to have an option to acquire shares of stock or any right or interest in any shares of stock of the corporation, there shall be served upon the plaintiff within 20 days after service of the process a certificate setting forth any such option, right or interest in the shares of the corporation in the language and form in which the option, right or interest appears on the books of the corporation, anything in the certificate of incorporation or bylaws of the corporation to the contrary notwithstanding. Service upon a corporate registered agent may be made in the manner provided in § 321 of this title.

(c) If, after sale made and confirmed, a certified copy of the order of sale and return and the stock certificate, if any, be left with any officer or director or with the registered agent of the corporation, the purchaser shall be thereby entitled to the shares or any option to acquire shares or any right or interest in shares so purchased, and all income, or dividends which may have been declared, or become payable thereon since the attachment laid. Such sale, returned and confirmed, shall transfer the shares or the option to acquire shares or any right or interest in shares sold to the purchaser, as fully as if the debtor, or defendant, had transferred the same to such purchaser according to the certificate of incorporation or bylaws of the corporation, anything in the certificate of incorporation or bylaws to the contrary notwithstanding. The court which issued the levy and confirmed the sale shall have the power to make an order compelling the corporation, the shares of which were sold, to issue new certificates or uncertificated shares to the purchaser at the sale and to cancel the registration of the shares attached on the books of the corporation upon the giving of an open end bond by such purchaser adequate to protect such corporation.

(d) The money arising from the sale of the shares or from the sale of the option or right or interest shall be applied and paid, by the public official receiving the same, as by

§ 325. Actions against officers, directors or stockholders to enforce liability of corporation; unsatisfied judgment against corporation.

(a) When the officers, directors or stockholders of any corporation shall be liable by the provisions of this chapter to pay the debts of the corporation, or any part thereof, any person to whom they are liable may have an action, at law or in equity, against any 1 or more of them, and the complaint shall state the claim against the corporation, and the ground on which the plaintiff expects to charge the defendants personally.

(b) No suit shall be brought against any officer, director or stockholder for any debt of a corporation of which such person is an officer, director or stockholder, until judgment be obtained therefor against the corporation and execution thereon returned unsatisfied.

§ 326. Action by officer, director or stockholder against corporation for corporate debt paid.

When any officer, director or stockholder shall pay any debt of a corporation for which such person is made liable by the provisions of this chapter, such person may recover the amount so paid in an action against the corporation for money paid for its use, and in such action only the property of the corporation shall be liable to be taken, and not the property of any stockholder.

**§ 327.** Stockholder's derivative action; allegation of stock ownership.

In any derivative suit instituted by a stockholder of a corporation, it shall be averred in the complaint that the plaintiff was a stockholder of the corporation at the time of the transaction of which such stockholder complains or that such stockholder's stock thereafter devolved upon such stockholder by operation of law.;

**§ 328.** Effect of liability of corporation on impairment of certain transactions.

The liability of a corporation of this State, or the stockholders, directors or officers thereof, or the rights or remedies of the creditors thereof, or of persons doing or transacting business with the corporation, shall not in any way be lessened or impaired by the sale of its assets, or by the increase or decrease in the capital stock of the corporation, or by its merger or consolidation with 1 or more corporations or by any change or amendment in its certificate of incorporation.

**§ 329.** Defective organization of corporation as defense.

(a) No corporation of this State and no person sued by any such corporation shall be permitted to assert the want of legal organization as a defense to any claim.

(b) This section shall not be construed to prevent judicial inquiry into the regularity or validity of the organization of a corporation, or its lawful possession of any corporate power it may assert in any other suit or proceeding where its corporate existence or the power to exercise the corporate rights it asserts is challenged, and evidence tending to sustain the challenge shall be admissible in any such suit or proceeding.

**§ 330**. Usury; pleading by corporation.

No corporation shall plead any statute against usury in any court of law or equity in any suit instituted to enforce the payment of any bond, note or other evidence of indebtedness issued or assumed by it.

**Nevada also has special statutory language not found in Delaware or Florida.**

Nevada has a statute that allows the stock to be charged with the payment of an unsatisfied judgment. However NRS 78,747 limits the liability of officers unless the officer is the alter ego of the corporation. According to the statute, the decision is judicial and a matter of law, not for the jury to decide.

NRS 78.746 Action against stockholder by judgment creditor; limitations.
   1. <u>On application to a court of competent jurisdiction by a judgment creditor of a stockholder, the court may charge the stockholder's stock with payment of the unsatisfied amount of the judgment with interest</u>. To the extent so charged, the judgment creditor has only the rights of an assignee of the stockholder's stock.
   2. This section:
   (a) Applies only to a corporation that:
      (1) Has more than 1 but fewer than 100 stockholders of record at any time.

(2) Is not a subsidiary of a publicly traded corporation, either in whole or in part.

(3) Is not a professional corporation as defined in NRS 89.020.

(b) Does not apply to any liability of a stockholder that exists as the result of an action filed before July 1, 2007.

(c) Provides the exclusive remedy by which a judgment creditor of a stockholder or an assignee of a stockholder may satisfy a judgment out of the stockholder's stock of the corporation.

(d) Does not deprive any stockholder of the benefit of any exemption applicable to the stockholder's stock.

(e) Does not supersede any private agreement between a stockholder and a creditor if the private agreement does not conflict with the corporation's articles of incorporation, bylaws or any shareholder agreement to which the stockholder is a party.

3. As used in this section, "rights of an assignee" means the rights to receive the share of the distributions or dividends paid by the corporation to which the judgment debtor would otherwise be entitled. The term does not include the rights to participate in the management of the business or affairs of the corporation or to become a director of the corporation.

(Added to NRS by 2007, 2639; A 2009, 2829)

**NRS 78.747** Liability of stockholder, director or officer for debt or liability of corporation.

1. Except as otherwise provided by specific statute, no stockholder, director or officer of a corporation is individually liable for a debt or liability of the corporation, unless the stockholder, director or officer acts as the alter ego of the corporation.

2. A stockholder, director or officer acts as the alter ego of a corporation if:

(a) The corporation is influenced and governed by the stockholder, director or officer;

(b) There is such unity of interest and ownership that the corporation and the stockholder, director or officer are inseparable from each other; and

(c) Adherence to the corporate fiction of a separate entity would sanction fraud or promote a manifest injustice.

3. The question of whether a stockholder, director or officer acts as the alter ego of a corporation **must be determined by the court as a matter of law.**

## LIMITED PARTNERSHIP

Limited Partnerships also provide statutory protection from creditors as to the interest of the limited partner. The limited partners' liability is limited to the assets within the partnership. The general partner, however has unlimited liability. The rise of the Limited Liability Company or LLC is due primarily to the asset protection defect of Partnerships where to limit the general partner's liability in many cases the general partner would have to incorporate. This created a two tiered entity of a limited partnership controlled by a corporate general partner.

**620.1303**

No liability as limited partner for limited partnership obligations.—An obligation of a limited partnership, whether arising in contract, tort, or otherwise, is not the obligation of a limited partner. A limited partner is not personally liable, directly or indirectly, by way of contribution or otherwise, for an obligation of the limited partnership solely by reason of being a limited partner, even if the limited partner participates in the management and control of the limited partnership. History.—s. 17, ch. 2005-267.

**620.1404** General partner's liability.—

(1) Except as otherwise provided in subsections (2) and (3), all general partners are liable jointly and severally for all obligations of the limited partnership unless otherwise agreed by the claimant or provided by law.

(2) A person that becomes a general partner of an existing limited partnership is not personally liable for an obligation of a limited partnership incurred before the person became a general partner.

(3) An obligation of a limited partnership incurred while the limited partnership is a limited liability limited partnership, whether arising in contract, tort, or otherwise, is solely the obligation of the limited partnership. A general partner is not personally liable, directly or indirectly, by way of contribution or otherwise, for such an obligation solely by reason of being or acting as a general partner. This subsection applies despite anything inconsistent in the partnership agreement that existed immediately before the consent required to become a limited liability limited partnership

**Limited Partnership Interest**

In many cases, a client will transfer assets to the limited partnership whereupon they will receive limited partnership certificates. The assets are held by the partnership, preventing a creditor from reaching the assets and can only have a "charging order" against the limited partnership certificates.

**620.1703** Rights of creditor of partner or transferee.—

(1) On application to a court of competent jurisdiction by any judgment creditor of a partner or transferee, the court may charge the partnership interest of the partner or transferable interest of a transferee with payment of the unsatisfied amount of the judgment with interest. <u>To the extent so charged, the judgment creditor has only the rights of a transferee of the partnership interest.</u>

(2) This act shall not deprive any partner or transferee of the benefit of an exemption law applicable to the partner's partnership or transferee's transferable interest.

(3) <u>This section provides the exclusive remedy which a judgment creditor of a partner or transferee may use to satisfy a judgment out of the judgment debtor's interest in the limited partnership or transferable interest. Other remedies, including foreclosure on the partner's interest in the limited partnership or a transferee's transferable interest and a court order for directions, accounts, and inquiries that the debtor general or limited partner might have made, are not available to the judgment creditor attempting to satisfy the judgment out of the judgment debtor's interest in the limited partnership and may not be ordered by a court.</u>

This concept would work in a corporation as well if assets are transferred to a corporation and minority shares are issued. A judgment creditor may be entitled to the shares, but cannot reach the assets in the corporation. The problem in a corporation solution is when distributions are made they must be made in accordance with the shareholders interest.

## UNIFORM LIMITED PARTNERSHIP ACT (1976)

## § 703. RIGHTS OF CREDITOR.

On application to a court of competent jurisdiction by any judgment creditor of a partner, the court may charge the partnership interest of the partner with payment of the unsatisfied amount of the judgment with interest. To the extent so charged, the judgment creditor has only the rights of an assignee of the partnership interest. This [Act] does not deprive any partner of the benefit of any exemption laws applicable to his [or her] partnership interest.

### The Uniform Limited Partnership Act of 2001
### §703. RIGHTS OF CREDITOR

(a) On application to a court of competent jurisdiction by any judgment creditor
of a partner or transferee, the court may charge the transferable interest of the judgment
debtor with payment of the unsatisfied amount of the judgment with interest. To the
extent so charged, the judgment creditor has only the rights of a transferee.

The court may appoint a receiver of the share of the distributions due or to become due to the judgment debtor in respect of the partnership and make all other orders, directions, accounts, and inquiries the judgment debtor might have made or which the circumstances of the case may require to give effect to the charging order.

(b) <u>A charging order constitutes a lien on the judgment debtor's transferable interest. The court may order a foreclosure upon the interest subject to the charging order</u>

(c) At any time before foreclosure, an interest charged may be redeemed: at any time. The purchaser at the foreclosure sale has the rights of a transferee.

    (1) by the judgment debtor;

    (2) with property other than limited partnership property, by one or more of the other partners; or

    (3) with limited partnership property, by the limited partnership with the consent of all partners whose interests are not so charged.

(d) This [Act] does not deprive any partner or transferee of the benefit of any exemption laws applicable to the partner's or transferee's transferable interest.

(e) This section provides the exclusive remedy by which a judgment creditor of a partner or transferee may satisfy a judgment out of the judgment debtor's transferable

interest.

Comment

Source – RUPA Section 504 and ULLCA Section 504.

This section balances the needs of a judgment creditor of a partner or transferee with the needs of the limited partnership and non-debtor partners and transferees. The section achieves that balance by allowing the judgment creditor to collect on the judgment through the transferable interest of the judgment debtor while prohibiting interference in the management and activities of the limited partnership.

Under this section, the judgment creditor of a partner or transferee is entitled to a charging order against the relevant transferable interest. While in effect, that order entitles the judgment creditor to whatever distributions would otherwise be due to the partner or transferee whose interest is subject to the order. The creditor has no say in the timing or amount of those distributions. The charging order does not entitle the creditor to accelerate any distributions or to otherwise interfere with the management and activities of the limited partnership.

<u>Foreclosure of a charging order effects a permanent transfer of the charged transferable interest to the purchaser. The foreclosure does not, however, create any rights to participate in the management and conduct of the limited partnership's activities.</u>
The purchaser obtains nothing more than the status of a transferee.
Subsection (a) – The court's power to appoint a receiver and "make all other

orders, directions, accounts, and inquiries the judgment debtor might have made or which the circumstances of the case may require" must be understood in the context of the balance described above. In particular, the court's power to make orders "which the circumstances may require" is limited to "giv[ing] effect to the charging order."

Example: A judgment creditor with a charging order believes that the limited partnership should invest less of its surplus in operations, leaving more funds for distributions. The creditor moves the court for an order directing the general partners to restrict re-investment. This section does not authorize the court to grant the motion.

Example: A judgment creditor with a judgment for $10,000 against a partner obtains a charging order against the partner's transferable interest. The limited partnership is duly served with the order. However, the limited partnership subsequently fails to comply with the order and makes a $3000 distribution to the partner. The court has the power to order the limited partnership to turn over $3000 to the judgment creditor to "give effect to the charging order."

The court also has the power to decide whether a particular payment is a distribution, because this decision determines whether the payment is part of a transferable interest subject to a charging order. (To the extent a payment is not a distribution, it is not part of the transferable interest and is not subject to subsection (e).

The payment is therefore subject to whatever other creditor remedies may apply.) Subsection (c)(3) – This provision requires the consent of all the limited as well as general partners.

**Hellman v. Anderson (1991) 233 Cal.App.3d 840, Cal.Rptr. 830**

[No. C008611. Third Dist. Aug 20, 1991.]

FRED N. HELLMAN et al., Plaintiffs and Respondents, v. JOHN B. ANDERSON, Defendant and Appellant; EUREKA FEDERAL SAVINGS AND LOAN ASSOCIATION, Interveners and Appellants.

(Superior Court of Yolo County, No. 52196, Frank D. Francis, Judge.)

(Opinion by Sims, J., with Sparks, Acting P. J., and Davis, J., concurring.)

## COUNSEL

Calfee & Young, Kent N. Calfee and Christopher J. Konwinski for Defendant and Appellant.

Steefel, Levitt & Weiss, Michael J. Lawson, Leonard H. Watkins, Hansen, Boyd, Culhane & Watson, Kevin R. Culhane and Betsy S. Kimball for Interveners and Appellants.

Reuben, Quint & Valkevich, Matthew F. Quint and Jeffrey S. Rosen for Plaintiffs and Respondents.

## OPINION

SIMS, J.

In this case, we hold that a judgment debtor's interest in a partnership (meaning the right to share in the profits and surplus) may be foreclosed upon and sold, even though other partners do not consent to the sale, provided the foreclosure does not unduly interfere with the partnership business.

Judgment debtor John B. Anderson (Anderson) appeals from the trial court's order authorizing the foreclosure and sale of Anderson's interest in a California general partnership known as Rancho Murieta Investors (RMI). The foreclosure and sale was requested to enforce a money judgment against Anderson in his individual capacity by judgment creditors Fred N. Hellman, **[233 Cal.App.3d 843]** Peter N. Hellman, Lesleigh A. Hellman, Judith S. Johnson, and D. James Fajack (hereafter collectively referred to as Hellman). Interveners Eureka Federal Savings and Loan Association (Eureka) and Eric J. Tallstrom (Tallstrom) have also appealed the trial court's order. Eureka is Anderson's largest creditor. Tallstrom is Anderson's partner in RMI.

Appellants contend (1) the foreclosure sale is not authorized by law where the partnership is not the judgment debtor and (2) sale cannot be ordered where, as here, the "innocent" partner does not consent. Anderson additionally argues the trial court abused its discretion in ordering foreclosure in this case. We will conclude that such foreclosure is authorized by law and, while consent of nondebtor partners is not an inflexible requirement, the trial court should consider whether foreclosure of a charged partnership interest will unduly interfere with partnership business before the court exercises its equitable powers to order foreclosure. Because the parties in this case relied on authority requiring nondebtor partner consent, no evidentiary showing was made on the effect of foreclosure on partnership business. We therefore reverse the trial court's order directing foreclosure and remand for the trial court to make a finding whether foreclosure will unduly interfere with partnership business.

**Factual and Procedural Background**

In 1985 and 1986, Hellman filed lawsuits against Anderson for accounting, breach of contract, breach of fiduciary duty, mandatory injunction, rescission, and fraud. In 1987, Anderson and Hellman settled the suits. Anderson failed to make any of the payments required by the settlement agreements, and in October 1987, stipulated judgments totaling more than $440,000 were entered against Anderson and in favor of Hellman.

In July 1988, after various unsuccessful attempts to enforce the judgments, Hellman obtained an "Order Charging Debtor John B. Anderson's Partnership Interest" in RMI pursuant to Corporations Code section 15028.fn. 1 Anderson owns 80 percent of RMI; Tallstrom owns the other 20 percent and is the managing partner of RMI. The charging order stated that Anderson's interest in RMI was charged with the unsatisfied judgment in the amount of $494,885 plus interest. Thus, all profits or other monies due Anderson by virtue of the charged partnership interest were thereafter to be conveyed to Hellman.

Despite the above orders, Hellman has not received any monies in satisfaction of the judgments. Anderson testified in an October 1988 debtor's **[233 Cal.App.3d 844]** examination that RMI had not generated profits and was not expected to do so in the near future.

In December 1988, Hellman filed a motion for an order authorizing and directing a foreclosure sale of Anderson's charged partnership interest in

RMI, based on the unlikelihood that the charging order would result in satisfaction of the judgment within a reasonable time. On December 15, 1989, the trial court ordered that the interest of the judgment debtor in the profits and surplus of RMI would be sold at a public sale by the Sheriff of Yolo County. The trial court retained jurisdiction over all phases of the sale.

[1] (See fn. 2.) All appellants assign error to the trial court's order directing foreclosure and sale of the partnership interest. fn. 2

**Discussion**

I. California's Uniform Partnership Act (? 15001 et seq.) Authorizes Foreclosure of a Partner's Charged Interest Without the Consent of the Other Partners

Appellants contend foreclosure of Anderson's charged interest in RMI is contrary to law. Anderson argues foreclosure was improper because a partnership interest is statutorily exempt from execution. All appellants argue that the trial court cannot order foreclosure unless the nondebtor partners consent.

A. The applicable statutes authorize the foreclosure of a charged partnership interest.

In Crocker Nat. Bank v. Perroton (1989) 208 Cal.App.3d 1 [255 Cal.Rptr. 794],fn. 3 the First District recently addressed the question whether a charged partnership interest was subject to foreclosure and sale. Crocker's analysis **[233 Cal.App.3d 845]** begins with a summary of the background of the adoption of relevant provisions of the Uniform Partnership Act:

" 'A creditor with a judgment against a partner but not against the partnership ordinarily cannot execute directly on partnership assets or on the partner's interest in the partnership.' (Advising California Partnerships 2d (Cont.Ed.Bar 1988) ? 6.88, p. 428, citing Code Civ. Proc., ? 699.720; see also Corp. Code, ? 15025, subd. (2)(c).) The reasons for the rule were discussed at some length in Taylor v. S & M Lamp Co. [(1961)] 190 Cal.App.2d 700, 707-708 [12 Cal.Rptr. 323]: 'Prior to California's adoption of the Uniform Partnership Act (Corp. Code, ? 15001 et seq.) a judgment creditor of a partner whose personal debt, as distinguished from partnership debt, gave rise to the judgment, could cause a sale at execution of partnership assets, including specific items of partnership property, to satisfy his judgment. [Citation.]fn. [4]

" 'Lord Justice Lindley gave the following reason for the English rule forbidding execution sale of a partner's interest in the partnership to satisfy his nonpartnership debt:

" ' "When a creditor obtained a judgment against one partner and he wanted to obtain the benefit of that judgment against the share of that partner in the firm, the first thing was to issue a fi. fa. ['fieri facias'-term used to describe writ of execution commanding the sheriff to levy on goods and chattels], and the sheriff went down to the partnership place of business, seized everything, stopped the business, drove the solvent partners wild, and caused the execution creditor to bring an action in Chancery in order to get an injunction to take an account and pay over that which was due the execution debtor. A more clumsy method of proceeding could hardly have grown up." (28 Wash.L.Rev. 1; see also 9 Cal.L.Rev. 117.)

" 'It was to prevent such "hold up" of the partnership business and the consequent injustice done the other partners resulting from execution against partnership property that the quoted code sections and their counterparts in the Uniform Partnership Act and the English Partnership Act of 1890 were [233 Cal.App.3d 846] adopted. As we view those code sections they are not intended to protect a debtor partner against claims of his judgment creditors where no legitimate interest of the partnership, or of the remaining or former partners is to be served.'

"Therefore, a judgment creditor must seek a charging order to reach the debtor partner's interest in the partnership. (See Corp. Code, ?? 15028, 15522, 15673; Code Civ. Proc., ?? 699.720, 708.310-708.320; Advising California Partnership, supra, ? 6.88, pp. 428-429.) Through a charging order, the court may charge the debtor's interest in the partnership with payment of the unsatisfied judgment, plus interest. The court may also appoint a receiver of subsequent profits or other money due to the debtor partner. (Corp. Code, ? 15028, subd. (1).)" (Crocker, supra, 208 Cal.App.3d at pp. 5-6, fns. omitted.)

Crocker concluded the trial court could order the "sale of a judgment debtor partner's partnership interest as distinct from the property of the [] partnership, where the creditor has shown that it was unable to obtain satisfaction of the debt under the charging order, and where the remaining partner [] has consented to the sale." (208 Cal.App.3d at p. 7.)

[2a] Crocker's requirement of nondebtor partner consent will be discussed below. Before reaching that question, we must reexamine another question resolved in Crocker: whether foreclosure is authorized at all. Our

reexamination is necessary because appellants tender some statutory arguments not considered by Crocker. We therefore begin with the basics, discuss the applicable statutes, and conclude Crocker correctly decided that court-ordered foreclosure and sale of a charged partnership interest is statutorily authorized.

First, we clarify the nature of the property interest at issue in this case, i.e., Anderson's interest in the partnership, not in the partnership property.

"A partner's right in specific partnership property is not subject to enforcement of a money judgment, except on a claim against the partnership. ..." (? 15025, subd. (2)(c).)

However, a partner's right in specific partnership property is different from his interest in the partnership. "The property rights of a partner are (1) his rights in specific partnership property, (2) his interest in the partnership, and (3) his right to participate in the management." (? 15024, italics added.) "A partner's interest in the partnership is his share of the profits and surplus, and the same is personal property." (? 15026.) [233 Cal.App.3d 847]

Code of Civil Procedure section 708.310 provides: "If a money judgment is rendered against a partner but not against the partnership, the judgment debtor's interest in the partnership may be applied toward the satisfaction of the judgment by an order charging the judgment debtor's interest pursuant to Section 15028 [general partnership] or 15673 [limited partnership] of the Corporations Code."

Section 15028 fn. 5 authorizes a charging order on the debtor partner's partnership interest and further allows the trial court to "make all other orders ... which the circumstances of the case may require." (? 15028, subd. (1); see also 6 West's U.Laws Ann. (1969) Uniform Partnership Act, ? 28.) The statute clearly implies judicial authority to order foreclosure and sale of the charged interest because it further says the interest charged may be redeemed "at any time before foreclosure, or in case of a sale being directed by the court" may be purchased by nondebtor partners without causing a dissolution of the partnership. (? 15028, subd. (2), italics added.) [3] "It is a settled axiom of statutory construction that significance should be attributed to every word and phrase of a statute, and a construction making some words surplusage should be avoided." (People v. Woodhead (1987) 43 Cal.3d 1002, 1010 [239 Cal.Rptr. 656, 741 P.2d 154].) [2b] We cannot imagine why the statute would give advice about redemption prior to foreclosure and sale unless foreclosure and sale were contemplated.

Foreclosure sales of charged partnership interests are also implicitly recognized in section 15032 fn. 6 which deals with partnership dissolutions and makes reference to "the purchaser" of a partner's interest under section 15028. **[233 Cal.App.3d 848]**

Anderson contends foreclosure is contrary to law because Code of Civil Procedure section 699.720, subdivision (a) fn. 7 says a partnership interest is not subject to execution where the partnership is not a judgment debtor. Anderson notes that section 15028, subdivision (3) (fn. 5, ante), specifies the charging order statute does not affect a partner's right under the exemption laws.

However, contrary to Anderson's argument, "the exemption laws" do not exempt a partnership interest from enforcement of judgment. Those exemptions which protect property from enforcement of judgment are found in article 3 "Exempt Property" (Code Civ. Proc., ?? 704.010- 704.210) of chapter 4 "Exemptions" (Code Civ. Proc., ? 703.010 et seq.) of division 2 ("Enforcement of Money Judgments") of title 9 ("Enforcement of Judgments") of the Code of Civil Procedure. Partnership interests are not listed as exempt property under article 3. (Code Civ. Proc., ?? 704.010-704.210.)

Subdivision (a) of Code of Civil Procedure section 699.720, on which Anderson relies, protects a partnership interest only from execution, not from enforcement of judgment. Thus, subdivision (b) of section 699.720 of the Code of Civil Procedure provides: "Nothing in subdivision (a) affects or limits the right of the judgment creditor to apply property to the satisfaction of a money judgment pursuant to any applicable procedure other than execution." As we shall explain, foreclosure of a statutory charging order is a "procedure other than execution."

Code of Civil Procedure section 699.720 is found in chapter 3 ("Execution"-? 699.010 et seq.) of division 2 ("Enforcement of Money Judgments"-? 695.010 et seq.) of title 9 ("Enforcement of Judgments"-? 680.010 et seq.).

As we have noted, charging orders are authorized under Code of Civil Procedure section 708.310. That section is part of chapter 6-"Miscellaneous Creditors' Remedies" (Code Civ. Proc. 708.010 et seq.).

[4] There is a difference between an execution sale (pursuant to a writ of execution) and a foreclosure sale (of a debtor partner's charged interest). Code of Civil Procedure section 699.510 provides in part that, with

exceptions inapplicable here, "after entry of a money judgment, a writ of execution [233 Cal.App.3d 849] shall be issued by the clerk of the court upon application of the judgment creditor and shall be directed to the levying officer in the county where the levy is to be made and to any registered process server." Thus, in ordinary civil actions, after entry of a money judgment and upon the judgment creditor's application, the court clerk acts in a ministerial capacity and has no discretion to refuse issuance of a writ of execution. (In re Marriage of Farner (1989) 216 Cal.App.3d 1370 [265 Cal.Rptr. 531].) The levying officer then executes the writ in accordance with written instructions of the judgment creditor. (Code Civ. Proc., ? 699.530.) No court intervention is required.

In contrast, a court-ordered sale to foreclose the lien fn. 8 created by a charging order on a partnership interest involves judicial supervision. The charging order procedure has replaced levies of execution as the remedy for reaching partnership interests. (Baum v. Baum (1959) 51 Cal.2d 610, 612-613 [335 P.2d 481].)

[2c] Thus, Code of Civil Procedure section 699.720, subdivision (a) on which Anderson relies, is inapplicable because Hellman seeks to foreclose on the charging order, not to proceed by writ of execution.

As we have mentioned, the statutory authority for the sale of a partnership interest in satisfaction of a debt of an individual partner was recognized in Crocker Nat. Bank v. Perroton, supra, 208 Cal.App.3d 1. Courts from other jurisdictions have agreed that the charging order provision of the Uniform Partnership Act authorizes sale of a charged partnership interest. (FDIC v. Birchwood Builders (1990) 240 N.J.Super. 260 [573 A.2d 182]; Wills v.

Wills (Mo.App. 1988) 750 S.W.2d 567; Bohonus v. Amerco (1979) 124 Ariz. 88 [602 P.2d 469]; Tupper v. Kroc (1972) 88 Nev. 146 [494 P.2d 1275]; Beckley v. Speaks (1963) 39 Misc.2d 241 [240 N.Y.S.2d 553]; see First Nat. Bank of Denver v. District Court (Colo. 1982) 652 P.2d 613.) In Tupper v. Kroc, supra, the Nevada Supreme Court affirmed denial of a motion to set aside a court-ordered sale of a charged partnership interest. The Nevada statute, just as California's, authorized the trial court to make all orders and directions as the case required, and this, said the court, included sale of the charged interest. (494 P.2d at p. 1278.) Bohonus v. Amerco, supra, emphasized the distinction between a partnership "interest" and partnership "property," the latter of which may not be sold. (602 P.2d at p. 471.) **[233 Cal.App.3d 850]**

Anderson attempts to distinguish cases from other jurisdictions by referring to the California rule that a partnership interest is not subject to execution. (Code. Civ. Proc., ? 699.720, subd. (a), fn. 7, ante.) However, as we have discussed, that statute is not implicated in court-ordered foreclosures.

Eureka mentions Georgia law as precluding a forced sale; however, the cited law review article merely indicates that Georgia's statute, by not providing for foreclosure, differs from the Uniform Partnership Act. (Ribstein, An Analysis of Georgia's New Partnership Law (1985) 36 Mercer L.Rev. 443, 490.) The Georgia statute says a charged interest "is not liable to be seized and sold by the judgment creditor under execution." (Ga. Code Ann. 14-8-28, subd. (b).) We are presented with no persuasive authority or argument that the Georgia statute compels a prohibition against foreclosure and sale otherwise authorized in California by section 15028.

Other commentators, though cited by Eureka, support Hellman's position that the Uniform Partnership Act's charging order provision is widely accepted as authorizing the sale of the charged partnership interest. (Gose, The Charging Order Under the Uniform Partnership Act (1953) 28 Wash.L.Rev. 1, 6-7, 10-12, 16 [partnership interest may be sold if charging order ineffectual]; Lewis, The Uniform Partnership Act (1915) 24 Yale L.J. 617, 634 [charging order avoids undue interference with rights in partnership business and property].)

Anderson is concerned that the sale will detrimentally affect his other creditors, whose interests are subordinate to Hellman. However, the priority of creditors' interests is not a legitimate concern. Creditors with subordinate interests are always subject to the interests of prior creditors.

We conclude section 15028 authorized the trial court's order directing foreclosure and sale of the charged partnership interest. (Crocker, supra, 208 Cal.App.3d at pp. 8-9.)

**B. The consent of non-debtor partners is not invariably required.**

In Crocker, the non-debtor partner effectively consented to the foreclosure and sale of a limited partnership interest. Crocker concluded a trial court "may authorize sale of the debtor partner's partnership interest even in the absence of fraud, where three conditions are met: first, the creditor has previously obtained a charging order; second, the judgment nevertheless remains unsatisfied; and third, all partners other than the debtor have consented to the sale of the interest." (Crocker, supra, 208 Cal.App.3d at p. 9.) **[233 Cal.App.3d 851]**

Appellants contend Crocker requires that nondebtor partners consent to foreclosure and that the trial court here erred in deciding Crocker's statement was mere dictum. Hellman considers the consent requirement in Crocker to be dictum because the nondebtor partner in that case had effectively consented to the sale and therefore the issue of partner consent was never raised. While we agree Crocker's consent requirement was not dictum, we disagree with Crocker's requirement that other partners must invariably consent to a foreclosure sale. fn. 9

[5] The *ratio decidendi*, as opposed to dictum, is the "principle or rule which constitutes the ground of the decision, and it is this principle or rule which has the effect of a precedent. It is therefore necessary to read the language of an opinion in the light of its facts and the issues raised, to determine (a) which statements of law were necessary to the decision, and therefore binding precedents, and (b) which were arguments and general observations, unnecessary to the decision, i.e., dicta, with no force as precedents." (9 Witkin, Cal. Procedure (3d ed. 1985) Appeal, ? 783, p. 753.)

[2d] There can be no dispute that the partner consent requirement was necessary to the Crocker decision. The court said so. That consent was given in that case does not mean the issue was not raised; it merely means the requirement imposed by the court was met.

Nevertheless, we respectfully disagree with that requirement.

First, the statutes do not say that nondebtor partner consent is required for foreclosure on a charging order. Yet section 15028, subdivision (2)(b) (fn. 5, ante) expressly requires the consent of nondebtor partners before partnership property may be used to redeem the charged interest. Plainly, if the Legislature wants to make partner consent a condition, it knows how to do so. Thus, the very code provision authorizing foreclosure expressly requires consent of nondebtor partners in connection with redemption but is silent on the question of nondebtor partner consent in connection with foreclosure. [6] "[W]hen the drafters of a statute have employed a term in one place and omitted it in another, it should not be inferred where it has been excluded." (People v. Woodhead, supra, 43 Cal.3d at p. 1010.)

[2e] A second consideration is the policy underlying the Uniform Partnership Act of avoiding undue interference with partnership business. [233 Cal.App.3d 852] (Crocker, supra, 208 Cal.App.3d at p. 9.) However, we do not think that foreclosure of a partner's interest will always unduly interfere with the business of the partnership. This is because the statutory scheme itself limits the interest subject to foreclosure and sale. As we have mentioned, a partner's "interest in the partnership" is a personal property right separate and distinct from the partner's (1) rights in specific partnership property and (2) right to participate in management. The "interest in the partnership" means only the partner's share of profits and surplus. Foreclosure entails no execution upon partnership assets, and the interest acquired by foreclosure does not include the right to participate in management.

The limited nature of the interest being sold was emphasized in Beckley v. Speaks, supra, 240 N.Y.S.2d 553. That case held that, under the Uniform Partnership Act provisions, the purchaser of a charged liquor store partnership interest acquired only the debtor partner's share of profits and surplus and did not acquire any interest in specific partnership property or any right to participate as partner in applying for renewal of the liquor license. (Id. at pp. 556-557.)

We conclude that since the interest acquired by the purchaser of a partnership interest is limited by operation of law to the partner's share of profits and surpluses, with no acquisition of interest in partnership property or management participation, the foreclosure and sale of the partnership interest will not always unduly interfere with the partnership business to the extent of requiring consent of the nondebtor partners. In some cases, foreclosure might cause a partner with essential managerial skills to abandon the partnership. In other cases, foreclosure would appear to have no appreciable effect on the conduct of partnership business. Thus, the effect of foreclosure on the partnership fn. 10 should be evaluated on a case-by-case basis by the trial court in connection with its equitable power to order a foreclosure.

Because we believe the effect of foreclosure on the partnership should be determined on a case-by-case basis, we respectfully disagree with Crocker's inflexible requirement of partners' consent in order for the court to authorize a sale of a charged partnership interest. fn. 11 [233 Cal.App.3d 853]

In this case, we are not satisfied that a full record was made on the effect of foreclosure on the partnership, because appellants apparently relied on the consent requirement found in Crocker, supra, 208 Cal.App.3d 1. Therefore, no evidentiary showing of the effect on partnership business was made. The trial court rejected Crocker's consent requirement as dictum and found, in line with the other two requirements set forth in Crocker, that: "Judgment creditors have received nothing from their Charging Order. It is unlikely that the Judgment will be satisfied within a reasonable time." Thus, we cannot infer that the trial court considered the effect on partnership business before granting the equitable relief sought by Hellman.

Since we disagree with Crocker's consent requirement, remand is required in order for the trial court to make a finding, upon such evidence as may be presented by the parties, on the question whether foreclosure in this case will unduly interfere with partnership business of the nondebtor partnership.

On remand, the burden of proving undue interference with partnership business will be upon defendant and appellant Anderson. Evidence Code section 500 provides, "Except as otherwise provided by law, a party has the burden of proof as to each fact the existence or nonexistence of which is essential to the claim for relief or defense that he is asserting." (Italics added.) "The general rule allocating the burden of proof applies 'except as otherwise provided by law.' The exception is included in recognition of the fact that the burden of proof is sometimes allocated in a manner that is at variance with the general rule. In determining whether the normal allocation of the burden of proof should be altered, the courts consider a number of factors: the knowledge of the parties concerning the particular fact, the availability of the evidence to the parties, the most desirable result in terms of public policy and the absence of proof of the particular fact, and the probability of the existence or nonexistence of the fact." (Cal. Law Revision Com. com., 29B West's Ann. Evid. Code, 500 (1966 ed.), p. 430, Deering's Ann. Evid. Code, 500 (1986 ed.) p. 215; see 1 Witkin, Cal. Evidence (3d ed. 1986) Burden of Proof and Presumptions, 136-138, pp. 119-121.) Here, because knowledge about (and evidence of) the effect of foreclosure upon the partnership is peculiarily known to defendant and appellant Anderson, in his capacity as a partner, the burden of proving undue interference as a consequence of foreclosure is properly placed upon him.

Since we conclude remand is necessary, we need not address appellants' other contentions that the trial court abused its discretion. [233 Cal.App.3d 854]

**Disposition**

The order of December 15, 1989, is reversed and the matter remanded to the trial court for further proceedings consistent with this opinion. The parties will bear their own costs on appeal.

Sparks, Acting P. J., and Davis, J., concurred.

Judge of the Nevada Superior Court sitting under assignment by the Chairperson of the Judicial Council.

FN 1. Undesignated statutory references are to the Corporations Code.

FN 2. All appellants filed notice of appeal from the December 15, 1989, order directing foreclosure of the partnership interest. Additionally, Anderson appeals from the trial court's March 2, 1990, denial of a motion for new trial and Eureka appeals from a denial of a motion for reconsideration on the same date. However, denial of a motion for new trial is not an appealable order. (Rodriguez v. Barnett (1959) 52 Cal.2d 154, 156 [338 P.2d 907].) Anderson's appeal from this nonappealable order is dismissed. Assuming denial of the motion for reconsideration is an appealable order (but see Rojes v. Riverside General Hospital (1988) 203 Cal.App.3d 1151, 1160-1161 [250 Cal.Rptr. 435], overruled by the same court on other grounds in Passavanti v. Williams (1990) 225 Cal.App.3d 1602, 1607 [275 Cal.Rptr. 887]), Eureka raises no issues as to the merits of the ruling on reconsideration.

FN 3. Appellants originally cited this case by the caption under which it appeared in the advance sheets-Centurion Corp. v. Crocker National Bank.

FN [4]. Section 15028, as part of the Uniform Partnership Act, was adopted in 1949. (Stats. 1949, ch. 383, 1.) We note, however, the same provisions regarding partnership interests and charging orders were previously contained in Civil Code sections 2418 to 2422. (Stats. 1929, ch. 864, pp. 1903-1904.) Sherwood v. Jackson (1932) 121 Cal.App. 354 [8 P.2d 943] held a creditor could not properly proceed by execution sale pursuant to an ex parte order to levy execution on the debtor's partnership interest. The creditor's remedy was through the charging order procedure. (Id. at pp. 356-357.)

FN 5. Section 15028 provides: "(1) On due application to a competent court by any judgment creditor of a partner, the court which entered the judgment, order, or decree, or any other court, may charge the interest of the debtor partner with payment of the unsatisfied amount of such judgment debt with the interest thereon; and may then or later appoint a receiver of his share of the profits, and of any other money due or to fall due to him in respect of the partnership, and make all other orders, directions, accounts, and inquiries which the debtor partner might have made, or which the circumstances of the case may require.

"(2) The interest charged may be redeemed at any time before foreclosure, or in case of a sale being directed by the court may be purchased without thereby causing a dissolution:

"(a) With separate property, by any one or more of the partners, or

"(b) With partnership property, by any one or more of the partners with the consent of all the partners whose interests are not so charged or sold.

"(3) Nothing in this act shall be held to deprive a partner of his right, if any, under the exemption laws, as regards his interest in the partnership." (Italics added.)

FN 6. Section 15032 provides in part:

"(2) On the application of the purchaser of a partner's interest under Sections 15027 [conveyance of partnership interest] and 15028 [fn. 5, ante] [the court shall decree a dissolution]:

"(a) After the termination of the specified term or particular undertaking,

"(b) At any time if the partnership was a partnership at will when the interest was assigned or when the charging order was issued."

FN 7. Code of Civil Procedure section 699.720 provides in part: "(a) The following types of property are not subject to execution: ... (2) The interest of a partner in a partnership where the partnership is not a judgment debtor. ...(b) Nothing in subdivision (a) affects or limits the right of the judgment creditor to apply property to the satisfaction of a money judgment pursuant to any applicable procedure other than execution."

FN 8. Code of Civil Procedure section 708.320 provides: "(a) Service of a notice of motion for a charging order on the judgment debtor and on the other partners or the partnership creates a lien on the judgment debtor's interest in the partnership. [?] (b) If a charging order is issued, the lien created pursuant to subdivision (a) continues under the terms of the order. If issuance of the charging order is denied, the lien is extinguished."

FN 9. It is undisputed in this case that the nondebtor partner, Tallstrom, does not consent. We agree with appellants that Tallstrom's prior consent to Anderson's assignment of his interest to Eureka as collateral has no bearing on the question of consent in the context of this dispute. Nor do we consider it relevant that Tallstrom did not seek to oppose the order imposing the charging order in the first place. On the other hand, we do not consider Tallstrom's consent compelled by the trial court's rulings (1) that Tallstrom was entitled to notice of the foreclosure motion, or (2) that Tallstrom be permitted to intervene.

FN 10. Eureka contends the trial court failed to consider its interests as senior lienholder. However, the interest at issue is the effect of the court's order on the partnership, not upon other creditors.

FN 11. The parties do not challenge the other two prerequisites to foreclosure that (1) the creditor previously obtained a charging order, and (2) the judgment nevertheless remained unsatisfied. (Crocker, supra, 208 Cal.App.3d at p. 9.) The first condition seems obvious-obtaining a charging order is a prerequisite to foreclosing on the charging order. The second condition-that the charging order be unsuccessful-is, we believe, implied in the statute, which authorizes "all other orders ... which the circumstances of the case may require." (15028, subd. (1), fn. 5, ante.)

## LIMITED LIABILITY COMPANY (LLC)

A Limited Liability Company (LLC) is a business structure allowed by state statute. LLCs are popular because, similar to a corporation, owners have limited personal liability for the debts and actions of the LLC. Other features of LLCs are more like a partnership, providing management flexibility and the benefit of pass-through taxation.

Owners of an LLC are called members. Since most states do not restrict ownership, members may include individuals, corporations, other LLCs and foreign entities. There is no maximum number of members. Most states also permit "single member" LLCs, those having only one owner.

A few types of businesses generally cannot be LLCs, such as banks and insurance companies. Check your state's requirements and the federal tax regulations for further information. There are special rules for foreign LLCs.

### Classifications

The federal government does not recognize an LLC as a classification for federal tax purposes. An LLC business entity must file a corporation, partnership or sole proprietorship tax return.

An LLC that is not automatically classified as a corporation can file Form 8832 to elect their business entity classification. A business with at least 2 members can choose to be classified as an association taxable as a corporation or a partnership, and a business entity with a single member can choose to be classified as either an association taxable as a corporation or disregarded as an entity separate from its owner, a "disregarded entity." Form 8832 is also filed to change the LLC's classification.

**Effective Date of Election**

The election to be taxed as the new entity will be in effect on the date the LLC enters on line 8 of Form 8832. However, if the LLC does not enter a date, the election will be in effect as of the form's filing date. The election cannot take place more than 75 days prior to the date that the LLC files Form 8832 and the LLC cannot make the election effective for a date that is more than 12 months after it files Form 8832. However, if the election is the "initial classification election," and not a request to change the entity classification, there is relief available for a late election (more than 75 days before the filing of the Form 8832)

**Single Member Limited Liability Companies**

Over the years, there has been confusion regarding Single Member Limited Liability Companies in general and specifically, how they can report and pay employment taxes.

An LLC is an entity created by state statute. The IRS uses tax entity classification, which allows the LLC to be taxed as a corporation, partnership, or sole proprietor, depending on elections made by the LLC and the number of members. An LLC is always classified under federal law as one of these types of taxable entities.

A multi-member LLC can be either a partnership or a corporation, including an S corporation. To be treated as a corporation, an LLC has to file Form Form 8832, Entity Classification Election , and elect to be taxed as a corporation. A multi-member LLC that does not so elect will be classified under federal law as a partnership.

A single member LLC (SMLLC) can be either a corporation or a single member "disregarded entity". Again, to be treated under federal law as a corporation, the SMLLC has to file Form 8832 and elect to be classified as a corporation. An SMLLC that does not elect to be a corporation will be classified by the existing federal guidance as a "disregarded entity" which is taxed as a sole proprietor for income tax purposes.

Employment tax and certain excise tax requirements for an SMLLC that is a disregarded entity have changed over the past few years. In August, 2007, final regulations (T.D. 9356) were issued requiring disregarded single member LLCs to be treated as the taxpayer for certain excise taxes accruing on or after January 1, 2008 and employment taxes accruing on or after January 1, 2009.

SMLLC's will continue to be disregarded for other federal tax purposes.

For employment taxes, prior to the regulation changes, the single member owner of a disregarded SMLLC was responsible for reporting and paying employment taxes. Before January 1, 2009 the single member owner could file using either the name and EIN assigned to the SMLLC, or the name and EIN of the single member owner. Even if the pre-January 1, 2009 employment tax obligations were reported using the disregarded SMLLC's name and employer identification number, the single member owner retains ultimate responsibility for collecting, reporting and paying over employment taxes for those periods.

As of January 1, 2009, Notice 99-6 is obsolete and the SMLLC will be responsible for collecting, reporting and paying over employment tax and excise tax obligations using the name and EIN assigned to the LLC.

An LLC applies for an EIN by filing Form SS-4, Application for Employer Identification Number, and completing lines 8 a, b, and c. An SMLLC that is a disregarded entity that does not have employees and does not have an excise tax liability does not need an EIN. It should use the name and TIN of the single member owner for federal tax purposes. However, if a SMLLC, whose taxable income and loss will be reported by the single member owner, nevertheless needs an EIN to open a bank account or if state tax law requires the SMLLC to have a federal EIN, then the SMLLC can apply for and obtain an EIN.

**LLC Filing as a Corporation or Partnership**

The LLC structure is not recognized by federal law and therefore their filing status is determined by the Entity Classification Rules. Form 8832 is used for this purpose. Pursuant to the entity classification rules, LLCs with multiple owners that do not elect to be taxed as a corporation are taxed as a partnership.

## Classification

The Entity Classification rules classify certain LLC business entities as Corporations:

- A business entity formed under a Federal or State statute or under a statute of a federally recognized Indian tribe if the statute describes or refers to the entity as incorporated or as a corporation, body corporate, or body politic.
- An Association under Regulations section 301.7701-3.
- A business entity formed under a Federal or State statute if the statute describes or refers to the entity as a joint stock association.
- A state chartered business entity conducting banking activities if any of its deposits are insured by the FDIC.
- A business entity wholly owned by a state of political subdivision thereof, or a business entity wholly owned by a foreign government or other entity described in Regulations section 1.892.2-T.
- A business entity taxable as a corporation under a provision of the code other than section 7701.(a)(3).
- Certain foreign entities (see Form 8832 instructions).
- Insurance Company

An LLC that is not automatically classified as a corporation can file Form 8832 to elect their business entity classification. A business with at least 2 members can choose to be classified as an association taxable as a corporation or a partnership, and a business entity with a single member can choose to be classified as either an association taxable as a corporation or disregarded as an entity separate from its owner, a "disregarded entity." The Form 8832 is also filed to change the LLC's classification.

**Filing**

If the LLC is a partnership, it should file a Form 1065, U.S. Return of Partnership Income. Each owner should show their pro-rata share of partnership income (reduced by any tax the partnership paid on the income), credits and deductions on Schedule K-1 (1065), Partner's Share of Income, Deductions, Credits, etc.

If the LLC is a corporation, it should file a Form 1120, U.S. Corporation Income Tax Return. The 1120 is the corporate income tax return, and there are no flow-through items to a 1040 from a corporate return. However, if the LLC filed as an S Corporation, it should file a Form 1120S, U.S. Income Tax Return for an S Corporation and each owner reports their pro-rata share of corporate income, credits and deductions on Schedule K-1 (Form 1120).

## OFFSHORE, THE "SOCIEDAD ANONIMA"

What can be better and more dangerous than corporations that have "bearer shares". When shares are paid to the "bearer", you own the shares if you hold them in your hands. Nearly 25 years ago, there were U.S. tax free municipal bonds that were issued to the "bearer". These were known as "Bearer Bonds". One of our clients gave $800,000 of these bonds to his trusted financial advisor to distribute to his family while he was on his deathbed. This was his plan to avoid the Federal estate tax which was back then had high rates and a low exemption. Fortunately, he recovered from the 'deathbed' and asked for his money back. Unfortunately, the stockbroker/financial advisor said, they are mine now- you gave them to me and kept them. We ended up suing the stockbroker/financial advisor and were able to settle the case and receive the funds back at the time we were engaged in jury selection. We were able to identify the original purchaser using CUSIP numbers.

In Costa Rica, one of our clients had a Sociedad Anonima. Two miles of beachfront property was held in the S.A. along with other assets. The danger in this case was not losing the shares as they kept the shares under lock and key. The danger was the peonies or squatters who set up residence on his property. Asset protection can have a "physical" as well as "intangible" nature in some cases.

This creature, the S.A. can be created offering "bearer shares" to the stockholders. This form of doing business is found in many Latin American countries.

**S.A.** generally designates corporations in various countries, mostly those employing the civil law. It originated in Spain during the 16th century. Though literally translated as *anonymous society*, *anonymous company*, *anonymous partnership*, or *share company*, it is known more commonly in Spanish by the abbreviation, **S.A.** and in English as a public limited company. It can be differentiated from partnerships and limited liability companies. In American English, they are called joint-stock-companies.

**PERSONAL RISK MANAGEMENT-ASSET PROTECTION**

**HOMESTEAD OR STATE LAW EXEMPTIONS**

The first part of a good asset protection plan is to look at the state law exemptions from creditor claims. Each state will have a different law and different amounts that are exempt from legal process. This creates a patchwork of 50 different possibilities of creditor protection depending where the domicile of the actor or principal resides. The two states which have the highest degree of asset protection under their homestead acts are Florida and Texas. Most of the southern states will have added protection as these laws were designed to prevent the scalawags and carpetbaggers from the north seizing property in the south after the civil war. Part of good asset protection planning is to re-domicile the actor to a jurisdiction which is more user friendly to the actor. For example, the CEO of Enron took up residence in Florida as well as O.J. Simpson and many others which looked to shelter assets knowing they were in a high risk situation.

The state patchwork of laws creates 50 different scenarios depending on the domicile of the actor. Once the actor looks worldwide to asset protection, the scenarios increase to another 108 jurisdictions and 108 different possibilities in asset protection.

Jay Adkisson has published a great book on asset protection which includes he creditor debtor chart on the following pages and more material to create a good asset protection plan. Jay is one of the "asset protection mavens" and is a specialist in the area of asset protection planning.

The matrix that follows changes all the time as various states adopt legislation which may change the amount you can protect under the homestead and other acts. Hence-you must research your own state laws. This "matrix" is designed to give the reader an "example" of the variance in state laws.

## CREDITOR-DEBTOR STATE EXEMPTION CHART

The All-Time Asset Protection Bestseller

The following table is the result of exhaustive research by Chris Riser. It is current as of May, 2007. **Very important: See the explanations at the bottom of the chart.** This chart is meant to provide a *starting* place for research; it is not intended to provide any definitive answer on the subject. This chart is certainly not any substitute for the advice and counsel of a licensed attorney in the relevant state. **General rules are generally inapplicable!** In each state, there are likely cases that carve out exceptions to these exemptions, such as for alimony, proceeds of crime, and child support, etc. Federal tax liens are often not subject to state exemptions. **For all these reasons, this chart should not be used as any basis for any legal decisions or to advise clients.** Further research into the source materials and any court opinions that identify "exceptions to the exemptions" is required.

"Asset Protection: Concepts & Strategies" by Jay D. Adkissonv and Christopher M. Riser, published by McGraw-Hill & Co.

Available Immediately Online at: Amazon.com or Barnesandnoble.com

| State[1] (opt out of federal exemptions in bankruptcy) | Exemption for Tax-Qualified Retirement Plans, IRAs & Roth IRAs[2] | Homestead Exemption[3] | Exemption for Life Insurance Cash Value from Claims of Policyowner's Creditors[4] | Exemption for (Non-IRA / Non-ERISA) Annuity Cash Value and Payments from Claims of Owner's Creditors[5] |
|---|---|---|---|---|
| FED[1] BKRP | 100% exclusion for ERISA qualified plans. 100% exemption for SEP-IRA and SIMPLE IRA with no cap. 100% exemption for IRAs and Roth IRAs with $1MM cap (cap does not apply to rollover IRAs). 11 U.S.C. § 522(d)(12) | $20,200 11 U.S.C. § 522(d)(1) | $10,775 11 U.S.C. § 522(d)(8) | Payments from an annuity on account of illness, disability, death, age, or length of service are exempt to the extent reasonably necessary for the support of the debtor and dependents. 11 U.S.C. § 522(d)(10)(E) |
| AL opt out | 100% for assets held in "qualified trust" as defined in IRC § 401(a). No Roth IRA protection. Ala. Code § 19-3-1. | $5,000 / $10,000 Ala. Code § 6-10-2, 27-14-29 | 100% for insurance on self or spouse payable to self, spouse or children. Ala. Code §§ 6-10-8, 27-14-29, 27-14-30 | $250/mo annuity payments in the aggregate. Ala. Code §§ 27-14-30, 27-14-32 |
| AK | 100% Alaska Stat. § 09.38.017 | $67,500 Alaska Stat. § 09.38.010 | $12,500 Alaska Stat. § 09.38.017 | $12,500 cash value. Alaska Stat. § 09.38.017 |
| AZ | 100% Ariz. Rev. Stat. Ann. § 33-1126C | $150,000 Ariz. Rev. Stat. § 33-1101A | 100% Ariz. Rev. Stat. § 33-1126A6 | 100% Ariz. Rev. Stat. § 33-1126A7 |
| AR | IRA protection limited to $20,000. Ark. Code Ann. § 16-66-220. However, see *In re Holt*, 894 F.2d 1005 (8th Cir. 1990) holding that Arkansas statutory exemptions are invalid as they violate the Arkansas Constitution. | Unlimited for married and head-of-household residents (but once homestead attaches, not destroyed by death, divorce, or dependents' emancipation) Ark. Const. art. 4 | None | None |
| CA opt out | SEPs and IRAs are limited to to the extent reasonably necessary for support. Profit-sharing and non-qualified plans may be exempt. Cal. Civ. Proc. Code § 704.115 | $50,000 single / $75,000 head of household / $150,000 over 65 or disabled. Cal. Civ. Proc. Code § 704.730 | $9,700 single / $19,400 married. Cal. Civ. Proc. Code § 704.100 | Same as life insurance if annuity contract considered "life insurance" and not "investment." *In re Payne*, 323 B.R. 723 (9th Cir. BAP 2005) |

Reprinted with permission from Jay Akisson

| State | | | | |
|---|---|---|---|---|
| CO<br>opt out | 100%<br>Colo. Rev. Stat. § 13-54-102(1)(s) | $45,000<br>Colo. Rev. Stat. § 38-41-201 | $50,000<br>Colo. Rev. Stat. § 13-54-102(1)(l)(I)(A) | None<br>Annuity not "life insurance." *In re Raymond*, 132 Bankr. 53 (Bankr. D. Colo. 1991). |
| CT | 100%<br>Conn. Gen. Stat. § 52-321a | $75,000<br>Conn. Gen. Stat. § 52-352b(t) | $4,000<br>Conn. Gen. Stat. § 52-352b(s) | None |
| DE<br>opt out | 100%<br>Del Code Ann. § 10-4915 | $50,000<br>10 Del Code Ann. § 4914 (c)(1) | None | $350/mo, plus amount needed for reasonable requirements of debtor and dependents.<br>18 Del Code Ann. § 6708 |
| DC | 100%<br>D.C. Code § 15-501(a)(9) & (10) | Unlimited<br>D.C. Code § 15-501(a)(14) | None (except for group life - 100%) | $200/mo for prior two months |
| FL<br>opt out | 100%<br>Fla. Stat. Ann. §§ 121.131, 222.21 | Unlimited for 160 acres rural or 1/2 acre urban.<br>Fla. Stat. Ann. §§ 222.01, 222.02, Fla. Const. Art. X, § 4. | 100%<br>Fla. Stat. Ann. §222.14 | 100% for beneficiary (including owner-beneficiary).<br>Fla. Stat. Ann. §222.14 |
| GA<br>opt out | 100% for undistributed interests; Georgia Code Ann. § 18-4-22<br>Distributions exempt to the extent reasonably necessary for support; No Roth IRA protection. Georgia Code Ann. § 44-13-100(a)(2.1). | $10,000 single / $20,000 married<br>Georgia Code Ann. § 44-13-100(a)(1). *Note: S.B. 133, which would raise the exemption to $50,000 / $100,000, was reported favorably by the Senate Judiciary Committee on 3/1/07.* | $2,000<br>Georgia Code Ann. § 44-13-100(a)(9). Additionally, § 33-25-11 provides that cash values are protected from creditors of insured, without specifying whether this includes owner-insured | ?<br>Georgia Code Ann. § 33-28-7 provides that annuity proceeds are protected from creditors of beneficiary, without specifying whether this includes owner-beneficiary |
| HI | 100% for funds deposited at least 3 years prior.<br>Hawaii Rev. Stat. § 651-124 | $20,000 / $30,000 for head of household or over 65.<br>Hawaii Rev. Stat. § 651-92(a) | 100%<br>Hawaii Rev. Stat. § 431-10-232 | 100%<br>Hawaii Rev. Stat. § 431-10-232 |
| ID<br>opt out | 100%<br>Idaho Code §§ 11-604A, 55-1011 | $100,000<br>Idaho Code § 50-1003 | Beneficiary's right to proceeds and avails protected from insured's creditors<br>Idaho Code § 41-1833 | $1,250/month<br>Idaho Code § 41-1836 |
| IL<br>opt out | 100%<br>I.L.C.S. § 5/12-1006 | $15,000<br>I.L.C.S. §§ 5/12-901; 5/12-906 | 100% for policy payable to dependent<br>I.L.C.S. § 5/12-1001(f) | 100% for annuity payable to dependent<br>I.L.C.S. § 5/12-1001(f) |
| IN<br>opt out | 100%<br>Ind. Code Ann. § 55-10-2(c)(6) | $15,000<br>Ind. Code Ann. § 34-55-10-2(b)(1) | 100% for policy payable to spouse, child, dependent or creditor.<br>Ind. Code Ann. § 27-1-12-14(e) | 100% for policy payable to spouse, child, dependent or creditor.<br>Ind. Code Ann. § 27-2-5-1(b) |

Advanced Risk Management

| State | | | | |
|---|---|---|---|---|
| IA opt out | 100% Iowa Code Ann. § 627.6 (8)(e), (f) | Unlimited for 40 acres rural, 1/2 acre urban. Iowa Code Ann. § 561.16 | 100% for policy payable to spouse, child, dependent or creditor, but protection for policy acquired within 2 years or increases in value within 2 years limited to $10,000. Iowa Code Ann. § 627.6 (6) | None. In re Huebner, 986 F.2d 1222 (8th Cir. 1993), cert. denied, 510 U.S. 900. |
| KS opt out | 100% for principal. Kan. Stat. Ann. § 60-2308. No exemption for distributions. In re Moore, 214 B.R. 628 (Bankr.D.Kan. 1997) | Unlimited for 160 acres rural or 1 acre urban. Kan. Stat. Ann. § 60-2301 | 100% if policy held for more than 1 year. Kan. Stat. Ann. §§ 60-2313(a)(7), 40-414. In re Hodes, 308 B.R. 61 (10th Cir. BAP 2004) | 100% if policy held for more than 1 year. Kan. Stat. Ann. §§ 60-2313(a)(7), 40-414. |
| KY | 100% Ky. Rev. Stat. Ann. § 427.150(2)(f) | $5,000 Ky. Rev. Stat. Ann. § 427.060 | 100% 304.14.300. In re Worthington, 28 B.R. 736 (Bankr. W.D. Ky, 1983) | $350/month Ky. Rev. Stat. Ann. § 304.14-330 |
| LA opt out | 100% La. Rev. Stat. Ann. §§ 20:33(1), 13:3881(D) for funds deposited at least 1 year prior | $25,000 La. Rev. Stat. Ann. § 20:1. La. Const. Art. 12:9 | Interest of beneficiary in proceeds and avails 100% protected. La. Rev. Stat Ann. § 22:647(A). Limited to $35,000 if issued within 9 months. | 100% protected. La. Rev. Stat Ann. § 22:647(B). Limited to $35,000 if issued within 9 months. |
| ME opt out | Limited to to the extent reasonably necessary for support. Me. Rev. Stat. Ann. Tit. 14, § 4422(13)(E) | $35,000 / $70,000 if minor dependents. 14 Me. Rev. Stat. Ann. § 4422(1) | Interest of beneficiary in proceeds and avails 100% protected. Interest of owner protected up to $4,000. 14 Me. Rev. Stat. Ann. §§ 4422(10) and (11) | $450/month 24-A Me. Rev. Stat. Ann. §§ 2428 and 2431 |
| MD opt out | 100%. Md. Code Ann. Cts. & Jud. Proc. § 11-504(h)(1) | None | 100% Md. Code Ann. Ins. § 16-111(a) | 100% Md. Code Ann. Ins. § 16-111(a) |
| MA | Limited to deposits equal to 7% of debtor's total income in preceding 5 years (though limitation likely not applicable to rollover IRAs). Mass. Gen. L. Ch. 235 § 34A; 236 § 28 | $500,000 and $500,000 for each age 62+ or disabled person. Mass. Gen. L. Ch. 188 §§ 1, 1A | Interest of original beneficiary in proceeds 100% protected. Mass. Gen. L. Ch. 175 § 125. Protection exempts cash value from claims of owner's creditors if beneficiary unchanged since issuance. In re Sloss, 279 B.R. 6 (Bankr. D. Mass 2002) | None. |
| MI | 100% Mich. Comp. Laws Ann. §§ 600.5451(1), 600.6023(1)(k). No protection for non-ERISA qualified plans. | $30,000 / $45,000 if 65+ or disabled. Mich. Comp. Laws Ann. § 600.5451(n) | 100% Mich. Comp. Laws Ann. § 500.2207 | 100% Mich. Comp. Laws Ann. § 500.2207 |

| State | | | | |
|---|---|---|---|---|
| MS opt out | 100% Miss. Code Ann. § 85-3-1(e) | $75,000 for 160 acres Miss. Code Ann. § 85-3-21 | Interest of beneficiary in proceeds and avails 100% protected Miss. Code Ann. § 85-3-11. Limited to $50,000 if issued within 12 months | None |
| MO opt out | Limited to to the extent reasonably necessary for support. Mo. Ann. Stat. § 513.430.1(10)(e) and (f) | $15,000 Mo. Ann. Stat. § 513.475 | $150,000 Mo. Ann. Stat. § 513.430(8) | None In re Stover, 332 B.R. 400 (Bankr. W.D. Mo 2005) |
| MT opt out | 100% Mont. Code Ann. §§ 19-2-1004, 25-13-608, 31-2-106 | $100,000 Mont. Code Ann. § 70-32-104 | $4,000 Mont. Code Ann. § 25-13-609(4) | None |
| NE opt out | Limited to to the extent reasonably necessary for support Neb. Rev. Stat. § 25-1563.01 | $12,500, limited to head of household Neb. Rev. Stat. §§ 40-101 to -108 | $100,000 for cash value attributable to premiums paid at least three years prior Neb. Rev. Stat. § 44-371 | $100,000 for cash value attributable to premiums paid at least three years prior Neb. Rev. Stat. § 44-371 |
| NV opt out | Limited to a present value of $500,000 Nev. Rev. Stat. § 21.090(1)(q) | $350,000 Nev. Rev. Stat. § 21.090(1)(l) | All cash value attributable to premiums not exceeding $15,000/yr in the aggregate. Nev. Rev. Stat. § 21.090(1)(k) | $350/month Nev. Rev. Stat. § 687B.290 |
| NH | 100% N.H. Code Ann. § 511:2, XIX. Statute applies only to extensions of credit and debts arising after 1/1/1999. However, see In re Stewart, 246 B.R. 134 (Bankr. D.N.H. 2000), holding that post-1/1/99 provision preempted by 11 U.S.C.A. § 522(c). | $100,000 N.H. Code Ann. § 480:1 | None In re Monahan, 171 B.R. 710 (Bankr. D.N.H. 1994) | None |
| NJ | 100% N.J. Stat. Ann. § 25:2-1(b) | None | None | $500/month N.J. Stat. Ann. § 17B-24-7 |
| NM | 100% N.M. Stat. Ann. §§ 42-10-1, 42-10-2 | $60,000 N.M. Stat. Ann. § 42-10-9 | 100% N.M. Stat. Ann. § 42-10-3 | 100% N.M. Stat. Ann. § 42-10-3 |
| MN | IRA protection limited to $60,000 (adjusts for inflation) Minn. Rev. Stat. Ann. § 550.37(24) | Up to 160 acres $750,000 rural $300,000 urban Minn. Rev. Stat. Ann. § 510.01 | $7,600 Minn. Rev. Stat. Ann. § 550.37(23) | Interest of beneficiary in proceeds 100% protected Minn. Rev. Stat. Ann. § 61A.12 |
| NY opt out | 100% N.Y. Civ. Prac. L. and R. § 5205(c) | $50,000 N.Y. Civ. Prac. L. and R. § 5206(a) | 100% N.Y. Ins. Law § 3212(b). In re Mesinger, 29 F.2d 158 (2nd Cir. 1928) | 100%, however, court may order that debtor pay creditor "just and proper amount" with "due regard for the reasonable requirements" of the debtor and dependents. N.Y. Ins. Law § 3212(d) |

| State | | | | |
|---|---|---|---|---|
| NC opt out | 100% N.C. Gen. Stat. § 1C-1601 (a)(9) | $18,500 / $37,500 married N.C. Gen. Stat. § 1C-1601 (a)(1) | 100% for insurance payable to spouse and/or children N.C. Const. Art. X § 5, N.C. Gen. Stat. § 1C-1601 (a)(6) | None |
| ND opt out | $100,000 per account / $200,000 max. unless reasonably necessary for support. N.D. Cent. Code § 28-22-03.1(3) | $80,000 N.D. Cent. Code §§ 47-18-01, 28-22-02(7) | $100,000 per policy / $200,000 max. for policies payable to a dependent and which have been in effect for at least one year N.D. Cent. Code § 28-22-04.1(3) | $100,000 per policy / $200,000 max. for contracts payable to a dependent and which have been in effect for at least one year N.D. Cent. Code § 28-22-04.1(3) |
| OH opt out | Limited to to the extent reasonably necessary for support Ohio Rev. Code Ann. § 2329.66(A)(10)(b) and (c) SEP-IRA not protected. In re Rayl, 299 B.R. 465 | $5,000 Ohio Rev. Code Ann. § 2329.66(A)(1) | 100% for policies payable to spouse, children or dependent Ohio Rev. Code Ann. §§ 2329.66(A)(6)(b), 3911.10 | 100% for contracts payable to spouse, children or dependent Ohio Rev. Code Ann. §§ 2329.66(A)(6)(b), 3911.10 |
| OK opt out | 100% 31 Okla. St. Ann. § 1(A)(20) | Unlimited for 160 acres rural, 1 acre urban 31 Okla. St. Ann. § 2 | 100% 36 Okla. St. Ann. § 3631.1 | 100% 36 Okla. St. Ann. § 3631.1 |
| OR opt out | 100% Ore. Rev. Stat. § 18.358 | $39,600 Or. Rev. Stat. § 18.395 | 100% so long as owner's estate is not beneficiary. Ore. Rev. Stat. § 743.046 | $500/mo aggregate Ore. Rev. Stat. § 743.049 |
| PA | 100%, except for amounts (1) contributed within 1 year (not including rollovers), (2) contributed in excess of $15,000 in a one-year period, or (3) deemed to be fraudulent conveyances. 42 Pa. C.S. §§ 8124(b)(1)(vii), (viii), (ix) | None | Income or return of $100/month 42 Pa. C.S. § 8124(c)(3) | $100/month 42 Pa. C.S. § 8124(c)(3) |
| PR | No statutory exemption. | $15,000 31 P.R. Laws Ann. §§ 1851 to 1857 | 100% if beneficiary is spouse legal representative of insured. 32 P.R. Laws Ann. § 1130 (9). | $250/month 26 P.R. Laws Ann. § 1135 |
| RI | 100% R.I. Gen. Laws § 9-26-4 (11), (12). No protection for non-ERISA qualified plans. | $300,000 R.I. Gen. Laws § 9-26-4.1 | Non-owner, non-insured beneficiary's right to proceeds and avails protected from insured's creditors. R.I. Gen. Laws §§ 27-4-12, 27-18-24 | None |
| SC opt out | IRA exemption limited to to the extent reasonably necessary for support. S.C. Code Ann. § 15-41-30(12) | $50,000 per owner; $100,000 maximum (adjusted for inflation each July starting July 2007) S.C. Code Ann. § 15-41-30(1) | $4,000 S.C. Code Ann. § 15-41-30(8) | None |
| SD | Limited to $250,000 S.D. Cod. Laws §§ 43-45-16, 17 | Unlimited for 160 acres rural, 1 acre urban S.D. Cod. Laws § 43-45-3 | $20,000 S.D. Cod. Laws § 58-12-4 | $250/month S.D. Cod. Laws § 58-12-8 |

| | | | | |
|---|---|---|---|---|
| **TN** opt out | Principal 100% exempt. Tenn. Code Ann. § 26-2-105. Distributions 100% exempt to the extent they are on account of age, death, or length of service and debtor has no right or option to receive other than periodic payments at or after age 58 | $7,500 unmarried / $12,500 unmarried 62+ / $20,000 married and one spouse 62+ / $25,000 married and both spouses 62+ Tenn. Code Ann. § 26-2-301 | 100% for insurance payable to spouse, child or dependents Tenn. Code Ann. § 56-7-203 In re Huffines, 57 B.R. 740 (Bankr. M.D. Tenn. 1985) | 100% for net amounts payable to spouse, child or dependents Tenn. Code Ann. § 56-7-203 |
| **TX** | 100% Tex. Prop. Code § 42.0021 | Unlimited for 100 acres rural (single) / 200 acres rural (family), 1 acre urban Tex. Const. Art. XVI, §§ 50, 51, Tex. Prop. Code §§ 41.001 to 002 | 100% Tex. Ins. Code § 1108.051 | 100% Tex. Ins. Code § 1108.051 |
| **UT** opt out | 100% except for amounts contributed within 1 year Utah Code Ann. § 78-23-5 (1)(a)(xiv) | $20,000 / $40,000 married Utah Code Ann. § 78-23-3 | 100% for the proceeds and avails, excluding any payments made on the contract during previous year. Utah Code Ann. § 78-23-5 (1)(a)(xii) | None |
| **VT** | 100% except for amounts contributed to self-directed plans within 1 year. 12 Vt. Stat. Ann. § 2740 (16) | $75,000 12 Vt. Stat. Ann. § 2740 (19)(D) | 100% 12. Vt. Stat. Ann. § 2740 (18), 8 Vt. Stat. Ann. § 3706. In re Gabelhart, 138 B.R. 425 (Bankr. D. Vt. 1992) | $350/month 8 Vt. Stat. Ann. §3709 |
| **VI** | No statutory exemption. | $30,000 5 V.I. Code § 478(a) | None | None |
| **VA** opt out | Limited to interest in one or more plans sufficient to produce annual benefit of up to $25,000 (pursuant to actuarial table in statute). Va. Code Ann. § 34-34 | $5,000 Va. Code Ann. § 34-4 | 100% for policies payable to others. Va. Code Ann. § 38.2-3122 | None |
| **WA** | 100% Wash. Rev. Code § 6.15.020 | $125,000 Wash. Rev. Code § 6.13.030 | 100% for policies payable to others. Wash. Rev. Code § 48.18.410 | $2,500/month Wash. Rev. Code § 48.18.430 |
| **WV** opt out | Principal 100% protected. Exemption for distributions limited to to the extent reasonably necessary for support. W. Va. Code § 38-10-4(j)(5). No Roth IRA protection. | $25,000 W. Va. Code § 38-10-4(a) | $8,000 W. Va. Code § 38-10-4(h) | None |
| **WY** opt out | 100% exemption for qualified retirement plans. Wy. Stat. Ann § 1-20-110 (a)(i), (ii). No statutory exemption for IRAs. | $20,000 Wy. Stat. Ann. § 1-20-101 | 100% Wy. Stat. Ann. § 26-15-129. In re Vigil, 74 Fed.Appx. 19 (10th Cir. 2003) | $350/month Wy. Stat. Ann. § 15-5-132 (a) |

This section is provided by Barry Nelson, Adjunct Professor at the University of Miami School of Law. Professor Nelson is one of the "Asset Protection Mavens" in the U.S.

The Homestead Act of 1862 was signed by President Lincoln to encourage settlement in the West. The Southern Homestead Act of 1866 was signed by Andrew Jackson to encourage and reward loyal southerners.

As the Florida Supreme Court noted in *Snyder v. Davis*, 699 So.2d 999, 1001-02 (Fla.1997), there are three kinds of homestead with one purpose: preserving the family home for its owner and heirs. The first kind, unrelated to this case, provides homestead with an exemption from taxes. See Art. VII, § 6, Fla. Const. The second protects homestead from forced sale by creditors. Art. X, §§ 4(a)-(b), Fla. Const. The third delineates the restrictions a homestead owner faces when attempting to alienate or devise homestead property. Art. X, § 4(c), Fla. Const. This case involves the second of these protections. The specific homestead protection at issue in this case is protection against forced transfer for use by an estate after the death of a decedent. Art. X, § 4(b), Fla. Const. To clearly distinguish this particular protection in the Florida Probate Code from other forms of homestead, the Legislature has denominated it as "protected homestead." See § 731.201(29), Fla. Stat. (2003) (defining "protected homestead as [that] property described in s. 4(a) (1), Art. X of the State Constitution on which at the death of the owner the exemption inures to the owner's surviving spouse or heirs under s. 4(b), Art X of the State Constitution").FN3

As previously stated, Edward contests Cynthia's claim that her mother's residence was "protected homestead" under Article X, section 4(b) of the Florida Constitution because, at the time of her death, title resided in an irrevocable trust. Edward further contends that even if the property was homestead in his mother when she died, nevertheless her residuary direction that the homestead abate equally, if necessary, to pay estate expenses controls. We consider each of these contentions in turn.

A. Was Edith's Property "Protected Homestead" At The Time of Her Death?

## Florida Constitution

Art. X, [section] 4 of the Florida Constitution sets forth the homestead exemption. It states:

(a) There shall be exempt from forced sale under process of any court, and no judgment, decree or execution shall be a lien thereon, except for the payment of taxes and assessments thereon, obligations contracted for the purchase, improvement or repair thereof, or obligations contracted for house, field or other labor performed on the realty, the following property owned by a natural person:

(1) a homestead, if located outside a municipality, to the extent of 160 acres of contiguous land and improvements thereon, which shall not be reduced without the owner's consent by reason of subsequent inclusion in a municipality; or if located within a municipality, to the extent of one-half acre of contiguous land, upon which the exemption shall be limited to the residence of the owner or the owner's family.

There are thus three significant requirements that the courts must consider in order to determine whether a debtor's homestead qualities for Florida's constitutional exemption from forced sale: 1) acreage limitations, 2) residency requirements, and 3) ownership requirements. Of course, to be eligible for protection from creditors, the property must be located in the State of Florida. (4) Furthermore, for policy reasons, homestead laws are applied liberally in favor of the homeowner.

## Policy Behind the Homestead Exemption

Because the purpose of the unlimited exemption is to protect families from misfortune, the burden is on the creditor to argue against homestead protection. (5) In Public Health Trust v. Lopez, 531 So. 2d, 946, 948 (Fla. 1988), aff'g, 509 So. 2d 1286 (Fla. 3d DCA 1987), the court stated that the purpose of the homestead law is to promote the stability and welfare of the state by securing to the householder a home, so that the homeowner may live beyond the reach of financial misfortune. Similarly, in Orange Brevard Plumbing & Heating Co. v. La Croix, 137 So. 2d 201, 204 (Fla. 1962), the court said that the purpose of the homestead law "is to benefit the debtor by securing his or her homestead beyond all liability from forced sale under process of any court." Such cases reflect that courts apply the homestead exemption laws liberally so that families will have shelter and will not be reduced to absolute destitution.

**Acreage Limitations**

Whether the residence is within or without a municipality is of critical importance in determining the portion of the debtor's homestead that will be protected. As stated above, Florida's constitutional protection is generally limited to the extent of one-half acre if the residence is within a municipality. Until 1997 when the U.S. Supreme Court denied cert in the case In re Englander, 520 U.S. 1186 (1997), thereby letting stand the decision of the 11th Circuit Court of Appeals, (6) the extent to which homestead protection was available for a residence on more than one-half acre within a municipality was uncertain. The debtor in Englander owned a home on approximately one acre within a municipality, and the property could not be legally subdivided due to local zoning regulations. The debtor claimed a homestead exemption for a portion of the property that surrounded the nonexempt portion, eliminating any reasonable access to the nonexempt portion and rendering it valueless. The court, in reaching its conclusion that the homestead designation sought for a portion of the property was improper, stated that the debtor's "attempt at homestead exemption `gerrymandering' was clearly in bad faith." (8) The bankruptcy court granted the debtor an exemption in a portion of the proceeds to be derived from the sale of the property equal to the value of one-half acre. (9) The court of appeals reasoned that a sale and apportionment of the sales proceeds is an equitable solution that allows for the appropriate recognition of the debtor's homestead and affords creditors some satisfaction of their claims.

The 11th Circuit Court of Appeals reinforced Englander when given an opportunity with In re Kellogg, 197 F.3d 1116 (1999). There, the debtor, who owned a 1.3 acre oceanfront home in Palm Beach, argued his home should not be sold to pay creditors. Instead, the debtor reasoned, he should be able to remain in his residence and surrounding property to the extent of one-half acre; the remaining acreage could be assigned to creditors. The court found that Palm Beach's zoning laws required a minimum parcel size that could not be maintained after subdivision. As a result, relying on Englander, the court ordered the sale of the homestead property and an allocation of the proceeds, with the proceeds which exceeded those attributable to one-half acre being made available to creditors.

As shown by the Englander and Kellogg decisions, courts can order the sale of a homestead when such property exceeds the constitutional size limitations set forth in the Florida Constitution and when the property cannot be practically or legally subdivided. Consequently, it may be advisable for individuals concerned about retaining protection for all of their homestead real estate to either purchase a residence outside a municipality on 160 acres or less or to purchase a residence within a municipality located on no more than one-half acre. Alternatively, a would-be debtor could purchase a condominium, which could be fully protected by the exemption.

As noted above, Art. X, [section] 4(a)(1) of Florida's Constitution provides that the acreage limitation may not be reduced without the owner's consent by reason of subsequent inclusion in a municipality. Thus, assuming the size of the homestead does not exceed 160 acres, homeowners need not be concerned whether they will lose their homestead protection if they live in a home that exceeds one-half acre within an unincorporated area that later becomes a municipality. For example, four municipalities in South Florida have incorporated since 1990: Aventura, Key Biscayne, Pinecrest, and Sunny Isles Beach. Persons owning homes in these or other new municipalities on more than one-half acre (but on no more than 160 acres) before the date of the municipal incorporation will continue to benefit from the 160-acre limitation for as long as their homes continue as their homestead. Accordingly, certain homes within new municipalities are effectively "grandfathered" for homestead protection while those purchased after becoming a municipality are subject to the usual one-half-acre limitation. This distinction causes a potential trap for those advisors who simply apply the one-half-acre rule without questioning the date of incorporation of a municipality and the date that home was purchased.

**Residence Limitations**

To obtain the benefits of the homestead exemption for asset protection, the debtor must be a resident in Florida. In order to be a resident of Florida, the debtor must have a residence in the state as well as the actual intent to reside in Florida permanently. (10) An alien debtor can only satisfy the permanent residency requirement if the debtor is granted a permanent visa or "green card." (11) The bankruptcy court in In re Bermudez, 1992 Bankr. LEXIS 547, at *4 (Bankr. S.D. Fla. 1992), citing In re Gilman, 68 Bankr. 374, 375-376 (Bankr. S.D. Fla. 1986), and In re Cooke, 412 So. 2d 340, 342 (Fla. 1982), reasoned that "unless the debtor is issued such permanent status, the alien debtor cannot legally formulate the requisite intent to make the house the family's permanent residence, regardless of the debtor's subjective intention to remain indefinitely." Accordingly, in In re Boone, 134 B.R. 979 (Bankr. M.D, Fla. 1991), the bankruptcy court held that a noncitizen of the U.S., who had failed to maintain her U.S. visa status and had lost the right to remain in the U.S. at the time she filed for bankruptcy, was not a resident of Florida for purposes of the homestead forced sale exemption.

If the court finds that the owner of an otherwise qualified homestead has formed the requisite intent to obtain a homestead in Florida, the results can be quite advantageous for debtors who are new Florida residents if another potential obstacle is overcome. Under existing bankruptcy laws, prior to obtaining creditor protection, debtors must be Florida residents or domiciliary for the greater portion of the 180 days prior to filing for federal bankruptcy protection. (12) F.S. [section] 222.17 instructs individuals on how to establish domicile for purposes of being eligible for the homestead exemption. It states that any person who has a domicile in Florida simply needs to file a sworn statement with the clerk of the county in which such person resides stating that "he or she resides in and maintains a place of abode in that county which he or she recognizes and intends as his or her permanent home." (13) If the individual also has a domicile in another state, the sworn statement must indicate that "his or her place of abode in Florida constitutes his or her predominant and principal home, and that he or she intends to continue it permanently as such." (14) Under Florida law, "where a good faith intention is coupled with an actual removal evidenced by positive overt acts, then the change of residence is accomplished and becomes effective." (15) However, even if such a statement is filed, unless a person actually spends more time in Florida than elsewhere and holds himself or herself out as a Florida resident, the statement by itself is likely to have no benefit to establishing such person's Florida domicile. (16) F.S. [section] 222.01 provides a form for notice of homestead that responds to a certified judgment filed in the public records. The notice of homestead states that the property is homestead and that the judgment does not contain a valid lien and provides 45 days for the holder of the judgment to file a claim for a declaratory judgment to determine the constitutional homestead status of the property.

Assuming the residency/domiciliary requirement is satisfied, separated married couples may find themselves in the situation of benefiting from two homestead exemptions. The U.S. Court of Appeals in In re Colwell, 196 F.3d 1225 (11th Cir. 1999), held that a married couple living in separate residences for over three years prior to the filing of their respective bankruptcy petitions qualified for homestead protection for each residence because there was no showing of fraudulent intent behind their marital separation. Similarly, a bankruptcy court held that, after a separation by two spouses, each would be able to claim a homestead in a home even though the net effect would be to exempt two homesteads where both had filed separate bankruptcies. (17)

**Ownership Requirements**

Once debtors have established a Florida residence on the requisite acreage, in order to obtain protection they must also meet ownership requirements. The identity of the legal owner of the homestead can have dramatic impact on the availability of the exemption. In a December 2001 decision that is likely to be controversial, the bankruptcy court held a debtor could not claim the homestead exemption from forced sale for a personal residence she owned not in her individual capacity, but as trustee of the revocable trust into which she had conveyed the homestead. Crews v. Bosonetto (In re Bosonetto), 271 B.R. 403 (Bankr. M.D. Fla. 2001). The court in Bosonetto reasoned the homestead exemption from forced sale can only be claimed for property owned by a natural person. If homestead protection for asset protection purposes is an objective, the safest manner in which to hold title is in an individual capacity or as tenants by the entirety for a husband and wife, and not through a trust, corporation, partnership, LLC, or other business entity.

This section was provided by:

Barry A. Nelson the founder of the law offices of Nelson & Levine, P.A. and The Victory School For Children with Autism, both in North Miami Beach. He is board certified in both taxation and wills, trusts and estates. Mr. Nelson is an adjunct professor at the University of Miami School of Law graduate tax program and a member of the American College of Trusts and Estates Counsel. He received his LL.M and J.D., cum laude, from the University of Miami School of Law.

Kevin E. Packman is an associate with the law offices of Nelson & Levine, P.A. He is a graduate of the Washington University School of Law (J.D.) and the University of Miami School of Law where he earned a masters in estate planning.

**Florida Homestead Act**

222.01   Designation of homestead by owner before levy.—
(1)   Whenever any natural person residing in this state desires to avail himself or herself of the benefit of the provisions of the constitution and laws exempting property as a homestead from forced sale under any process of law, he or she may make a statement, in writing, **containing a description of the real property, mobile home, or modular home claimed to be exempt** and declaring that the real property, mobile home, or modular home is the homestead of the party in whose behalf such claim is being made. Such statement shall be signed by the person making it and shall be recorded in the circuit court.
(2)   When a certified copy of a judgment has been filed in the public records of a county pursuant to chapter 55, a person who is entitled to the benefit of the provisions of the State Constitution exempting real property as homestead and who has a contract to sell or a commitment from a lender for a mortgage on the homestead may file a notice of homestead in the public records of the county in which the homestead property is located in substantially the following form:

**Example**

NOTICE OF HOMESTEAD

To: (Name and address of judgment creditor as shown on recorded judgment and name and address of any other person shown in the recorded judgment to receive a copy of the Notice of Homestead).

You are notified that the undersigned claims as homestead exempt from levy and execution under Section 4, Article X of the State Constitution, the following described property:

(Legal description)

The undersigned certifies, under oath, that he or she has applied for and received the homestead tax exemption as to the above-described property, that ____ is the tax identification parcel number of this property, and that the undersigned has resided on this property continuously and uninterruptedly from (date) to the date of this Notice of Homestead. Further, the undersigned will either convey or mortgage the above-described property pursuant to the following:

(Describe the contract of sale or loan commitment by date, names of parties, date of anticipated closing, and amount. The name, address, and telephone number of the person conducting the anticipated closing must be set forth.)

The undersigned also certifies, under oath, that the judgment lien filed by you on (date) and recorded in Official Records Book ____, Page ____, of the Public Records of _____ County, Florida, does not constitute a valid lien on the described property.

YOU ARE FURTHER NOTIFIED, PURSUANT TO SECTION 222.01 ET SEQ., FLORIDA STATUTES, THAT WITHIN 45 DAYS AFTER THE MAILING OF THIS NOTICE YOU MUST FILE AN ACTION IN THE CIRCUIT COURT OF _____ COUNTY, FLORIDA, FOR A DECLARATORY JUDGMENT TO DETERMINE THE CONSTITUTIONAL HOMESTEAD STATUS OF THE SUBJECT PROPERTY OR TO FORECLOSE YOUR JUDGMENT LIEN ON THE PROPERTY AND RECORD A LIS PENDENS IN THE PUBLIC RECORDS OF THE COUNTY WHERE THE HOMESTEAD IS LOCATED. YOUR FAILURE TO SO ACT WILL RESULT IN ANY BUYER OR LENDER, OR HIS OR HER SUCCESSORS AND ASSIGNS, UNDER THE ABOVE-DESCRIBED CONTRACT OF SALE OR LOAN COMMITMENT TO TAKE FREE AND CLEAR OF ANY JUDGMENT LIEN YOU MAY HAVE ON THE PROPERTY.

This ____ day of _____, 2____.

_____

_____

(Signature of Owner)

_____

(Printed Name of Owner)

_____

(Owner's Address)

Sworn to and subscribed before me by _____ who is personally known to me or produced _____ as identification, this ____ day of _____, 2____.

_____

Notary Public

(3)  The clerk shall mail a copy of the notice of homestead to the judgment lienor, by certified mail, return receipt requested, at the address shown in the most recent recorded judgment or accompanying affidavit, and to any other person designated in the most recent recorded judgment or accompanying affidavit to receive the notice of homestead, and shall certify to such service on the face of such notice and record the notice. Notwithstanding the use of certified mail, return receipt requested, service shall be deemed complete upon mailing.

(4)  A lien pursuant to chapter 55 of any lienor upon whom such notice is served, who fails to institute an action for a declaratory judgment to determine the constitutional homestead status of the property described in the notice of homestead or to file an action to foreclose the judgment lien, together with the filing of a lis pendens in the public records of the county in which the homestead is located, within 45 days after service of such notice shall be deemed as not attaching to the property by virtue of its status as homestead property as to the interest of any buyer or lender, or his or her successors or assigns, who takes under the contract of sale or loan commitment described above within 180 days after the filing in the public records of the notice of homestead. This subsection shall not act to prohibit a lien from attaching to the real property described in the notice of homestead at such time as the property loses its homestead status.

(5) As provided in s. 4, Art. X of the State Constitution, this subsection shall not apply to:

(a) Liens and judgments for the payment of taxes and assessments on real property.

(b) Liens and judgments for obligations contracted for the purchase of real property.

(c) Liens and judgments for labor, services, or materials furnished to repair or improve real property.

(d) Liens and judgments for other obligations contracted for house, field, or other labor performed on real property.

History.—s. 1, ch. 1715, 1869; RS 1998; GS 2520; RGS 3875; CGL 5782; s. 20, ch. 73-334; s. 2, ch. 77-299; s. 1, ch. 83-40; s. 1195, ch. 95-147; s. 25, ch. 2000-258; s. 17, ch. 2005-241.

222.02 Designation of homestead after levy.—Whenever a levy is made upon the lands, tenements, mobile home, or modular home of such person whose homestead has not been set apart and selected, such person, or the person's agent or attorney, may in writing notify the officer making such levy, by notice under oath made before any officer of this state duly authorized to administer oaths, at any time before the day appointed for the sale thereof, of what such person regards as his or her homestead, with a description thereof; and the remainder only shall be subject to sale under such levy.

**Method of exempting personal property; inventory.—**

(1) When a levy is made by writ of execution, writ of attachment, or writ of garnishment upon personal property which is allowed by law or by the State Constitution to be exempt from levy and sale, the debtor may claim such personal property to be exempt from sale by making, within 15 days after the date of the levy, an inventory of his or her personal property. The inventory shall show the fair market valuation of the property listed and shall have an affidavit attached certifying that the inventory contains a correct list of all personal property owned by the debtor in this state and that the value shown is the fair market value of the property. The debtor shall designate the property listed in the schedule which he or she claims to be exempt from levy and sale.

(2) The original inventory and affidavit shall be filed with the court which issued the writ. The debtor, by mail or hand delivery, shall promptly serve one copy on the judgment creditor and furnish one copy to the sheriff who executed the writ. If the creditor desires to object to the inventory, he or she shall file an objection with the court which issued the writ within 5 days after service of the inventory, or he or she shall be deemed to admit the inventory as true. If the creditor does not file an objection, the clerk of the court shall immediately send the case file to the court issuing the writ, and the court shall promptly issue an order exempting the items claimed. Such order shall be sent by the court to the sheriff directing him or her to promptly redeliver to the debtor any exempt property under the levy and to sell any nonexempt property under the levy according to law.

(3) If the creditor files an objection, he or she shall promptly serve, by mail or hand delivery, one copy on the debtor and furnish one copy to the sheriff who executed the writ. Upon the filing of an objection, the clerk shall immediately send the case file to the court issuing the writ, and the court shall automatically schedule a prompt evidentiary hearing to determine the validity of the objection and shall enter its order therein describing the exempt and nonexempt property. Upon its issuance, the order shall be sent by the court to the sheriff directing him or her to promptly redeliver to the debtor any exempt property under the levy and to sell the nonexempt property under the levy according to law.

(4) The court shall appoint a disinterested appraiser to assist in its evidentiary hearing unless the debtor and creditor mutually waive the appointment of such appraiser. The appraiser shall take and file an oath that he or she will faithfully appraise the property at its fair market value and that he or she will file a signed and sworn appraisal with the court as required by law. Notice of the time and place of the inspection of the property for the purpose of its appraisal shall be given by the appraiser to the debtor, creditor, and sheriff, at least 24 hours before the inspection is made. The appraiser shall be entitled to a reasonable fee as determined by the court for his or her services. The appraiser's fee shall be taxed as costs, but no costs shall be assessed against the debtor for the proceedings under this section if the debtor prevails on his or her claim of exemption. The court may

require the creditor to deposit a cash bond, a surety bond, or other security, conditioned on the creditor's obligation to pay reasonable appraisal expenses, not to exceed $100.

(5) During the pendency of proceedings under this section, the sheriff shall safeguard the property seized under the writ, and the creditor shall deposit sufficient moneys with the sheriff to pay the cost of such safeguarding until the property is sold or redelivered to the debtor. When the sheriff receives a copy of a court order identifying which property has been declared exempt and which property has been declared not exempt and ordering the sale of the property not exempt from levy, he or she shall sell the property.

(6) The party who successfully maintains his or her claim at the time of the evidentiary hearing may be entitled to reasonable attorney's fees and shall be entitled to costs. The costs shall include, but not be limited to, appraisal fees, storage fees, and such other costs incurred as a result of the levy.

(7) No inventory or schedule to exempt personal property from sale shall be accepted prior to a levy on the property.

**222.11** Exemption of wages from garnishment.—

(1) As used in this section, the term:

(a) "Earnings" includes compensation paid or payable, in money of a sum certain, for personal services or labor whether denominated as wages, salary, commission, or bonus.

(b) "Disposable earnings" means that part of the earnings of any head of family remaining after the deduction from those earnings of any amounts required by law to be withheld.

(c) "Head of family" includes any natural person who is providing more than one-half of the support for a child or other dependent.

(2)(a) All of the disposable earnings of a head of family whose disposable earnings are less than or equal to **$750 a week** are exempt from attachment or garnishment.

(b) Disposable earnings of a head of a family, which are greater than $750 a week, may not be attached or garnished unless such person has agreed otherwise in writing. The agreement to waive the protection provided by this paragraph must:

1. Be written in the same language as the contract or agreement to which the waiver relates;

2. Be contained in a separate document attached to the contract or agreement; and

3. Be in substantially the following form in at least 14-point type:

IF YOU PROVIDE MORE THAN ONE-HALF OF THE SUPPORT FOR A CHILD OR OTHER DEPENDENT, ALL OR PART OF YOUR INCOME IS EXEMPT FROM GARNISHMENT UNDER FLORIDA LAW. YOU CAN WAIVE THIS PROTECTION ONLY BY SIGNING THIS DOCUMENT. BY SIGNING BELOW, YOU AGREE TO WAIVE THE PROTECTION FROM GARNISHMENT.

(Consumer's Signature)   (Date Signed)

I have fully explained this document to the consumer.

(Creditor's Signature)   (Date Signed)

The amount attached or garnished may not exceed the amount allowed under the Consumer Credit Protection Act, 15 U.S.C. s. 1673.

(c) Disposable earnings of a person other than a head of family may not be attached or garnished in excess of the amount allowed under the Consumer Credit Protection Act, 15 U.S.C. s. 1673.

(3) Earnings that are exempt under subsection (2) and are credited or deposited in any financial institution are exempt from attachment or garnishment for 6 months after the earnings are received by the financial institution if the funds can be traced and properly identified as earnings. Commingling of earnings with other funds does not by itself defeat the ability of a head of family to trace earnings.

**222.14 Exemption of cash surrender value of life insurance policies and annuity contracts from legal process.**—The cash surrender values of life insurance policies issued upon the lives of citizens or residents of the state and the proceeds of annuity contracts issued to citizens or residents of the state, upon whatever form, shall not in any case be liable to attachment, garnishment or legal process in favor of any creditor of the person whose life is so insured or of any creditor of the person who is the beneficiary of such annuity contract, unless the insurance policy or annuity contract was effected for the benefit of such creditor.

**222.16** Wages or unemployment compensation payments so paid not subject to administration.—Any wages, travel expenses, or unemployment compensation payments so paid under the authority of s. 222.15 shall not be considered as assets of the estate and subject to administration; provided, however, that the travel expenses so exempted from administration shall not exceed the sum of $300.

**222.18** Exempting disability income benefits from legal processes.—Disability income benefits under any policy or contract of life, health, accident, or other insurance of whatever form, shall not in any case be liable to attachment, garnishment, or legal process in the state, in favor of any creditor or creditors of the recipient of such disability income benefits, unless such policy or contract of insurance was effected for the benefit of such creditor or creditors.

**222.21** Exemption of pension money and certain tax-exempt funds or accounts from legal processes.—

(1) Money received by any debtor as pensioner of the United States within 3 months next preceding the issuing of an execution, attachment, or garnishment process may not be applied to the payment of the debts of the pensioner when it is made to appear by the affidavit of the debtor or otherwise that the pension money is necessary for the maintenance of the debtor's support or a family supported wholly or in part by the pension money. The filing of the affidavit by the debtor, or the making of such proof by the debtor, is prima facie evidence; and it is the duty of the court in which the proceeding is pending to release all pension moneys held by such attachment or garnishment process, immediately, upon the filing of such affidavit or the making of such proof.

(2)(a) Except as provided in paragraph (d), any money or other assets payable to an owner, a participant, or a beneficiary from, or any interest of any owner, participant, or beneficiary in, a fund or account is exempt from all claims of creditors of the owner, beneficiary, or participant if the fund or account is:

1. Maintained in accordance with a master plan, volume submitter plan, prototype plan, or any other plan or governing instrument that has been preapproved by the Internal Revenue Service as exempt from taxation under s. 401(a), s. 403(a), s. 403(b), s. 408, s. 408A, s. 409, s. 414, s. 457(b), or s. 501(a) of the Internal Revenue Code of 1986, as amended, unless it has been subsequently determined that the plan or governing instrument is not exempt from taxation in a proceeding that has become final and nonappealable;

2. Maintained in accordance with a plan or governing instrument that has been determined by the Internal Revenue Service to be exempt from taxation under s. 401(a), s. 403(a), s. 403(b), s. 408, s. 408A, s. 409, s. 414, s. 457(b), or s. 501(a) of the Internal Revenue Code of 1986, as amended, unless it has been subsequently determined that the plan or governing instrument is not exempt from taxation in a proceeding that has become final and nonappealable; or

3. Not maintained in accordance with a plan or governing instrument described in subparagraph 1. or subparagraph 2. if the person claiming exemption under this paragraph proves by a preponderance of the evidence that the fund or account is maintained in accordance with a plan or governing instrument that:

a. Is in substantial compliance with the applicable requirements for tax exemption under s. 401(a), s. 403(a), s. 403(b), s. 408, s. 408A, s. 409, s. 414, s. 457(b), or s. 501(a) of the Internal Revenue Code of 1986, as amended; or

b. Would have been in substantial compliance with the applicable requirements for tax exemption under s. 401(a), s. 403(a), s. 403(b), s. 408, s. 408A, s. 409, s. 414, s. 457(b), or s. 501(a) of the Internal Revenue Code of 1986, as amended, but for the negligent or wrongful conduct of a person or persons other than the person who is claiming the exemption under this section.

(b) It is not necessary that a fund or account that is described in paragraph (a) be maintained in accordance with a plan or governing instrument that is covered by any part of the Employee Retirement Income Security Act for money or assets payable from or any interest in that fund or account to be exempt from claims of creditors under that paragraph.

(c) Any money or other assets that are exempt from claims of creditors under paragraph (a) do not cease to qualify for exemption by reason of a direct transfer or eligible rollover that is excluded from gross income under s. 402(c) of the Internal Revenue Code of 1986.

(d) Any fund or account described in paragraph (a) is not exempt from the claims of an alternate payee under a qualified domestic relations order or from the claims of a surviving spouse pursuant to an order determining the amount of elective share and contribution as provided in part II of chapter 732. However, the interest of any alternate payee under a qualified domestic relations order is exempt from all claims of any creditor, other than the Department of Revenue, of the alternate payee. As used in this paragraph, the terms "alternate payee" and "qualified domestic relations order" have the meanings ascribed to them in s. 414(p) of the Internal Revenue Code of 1986.

(e) This subsection applies to any proceeding that is filed on or after the effective date of this act.

**222.22** Exemption of assets in qualified tuition programs, medical savings accounts, Coverdell education savings accounts, and hurricane savings accounts from legal process.—

(1) Moneys paid into or out of, the assets of, and the income of any validly existing qualified tuition program authorized by s. 529 of the Internal Revenue Code of 1986, as amended, including, but not limited to, the Florida Prepaid College Trust Fund advance payment contracts under s. 1009.98 and Florida Prepaid College Trust Fund participation agreements under s. 1009.981, are not liable to attachment, levy, garnishment, or legal process in the state in favor of any creditor of or claimant against any program participant, purchaser, owner or contributor, or program beneficiary.

(2) Moneys paid into or out of, the assets of, and the income of a health savings account or medical savings account authorized under ss. 220 and 223 of the Internal Revenue Code of 1986, as amended, are not liable to attachment, levy, garnishment, or legal process in this state in favor of any creditor of or claimant against any account participant, purchaser, owner or contributor, or account beneficiary.

(3) Moneys paid into or out of, the assets of, and the income of any Coverdell education savings account, also known as an educational IRA, established or existing in accordance

with s. 530 of the Internal Revenue Code of 1986, as amended, are not liable to attachment, levy, garnishment, or legal process in this state in favor of any creditor of or claimant against any account participant, purchaser, owner or contributor, or account beneficiary.

(4)(a) Moneys paid into or out of, the assets of, and the income of any hurricane savings account established by an insurance policyholder for residential property in this state equal to twice the deductible sum of such insurance to cover an insurance deductible or other uninsured portion of the risks of loss from a hurricane, rising flood waters, or other catastrophic windstorm event are not liable to attachment, levy, garnishment, or legal process in this state in favor of any creditor of or claimant against any account participant, purchaser, owner or contributor, or account beneficiary.

(b) As used in this subsection, the term "hurricane savings account" means an account established by the owner of residential real estate in this state, which meets the requirements of homestead exemption under s. 4, Art. X of the State Constitution, who specifies that the purpose of the account is to cover the amount of insurance deductibles and other uninsured portions of risks of loss from hurricanes, rising flood waters, or other catastrophic windstorm events.

(c) This subsection shall take effect only when the federal government provides tax-exempt or tax-deferred status to a hurricane savings account, disaster savings account, or other similar account created to cover an insurance deductible or other uninsured portion of the risks of loss from a hurricane, rising flood waters, or other catastrophic windstorm event.

**222.25** Other individual property of natural persons exempt from legal process.—The following property is exempt from attachment, garnishment, or other legal process:

(1) A debtor's interest, not to exceed $1,000 in value, in a single motor vehicle as defined in s. 320.01.

(2) A debtor's interest in any professionally prescribed health aids for the debtor or a dependent of the debtor.

(3) A debtor's interest in a refund or a credit received or to be received, or the traceable deposits in a financial institution of a debtor's interest in a refund or credit, pursuant to s.

32 of the Internal Revenue Code of 1986, as amended. This exemption does not apply to a debt owed for child support or spousal support.

(4) A debtor's interest in personal property, not to exceed $4,000, if the debtor does not claim or receive the benefits of a homestead exemption under s. 4, Art. X of the State Constitution. This exemption does not apply to a debt owed for child support or spousal support.

222.29 No exemption for fraudulent transfers.—An exemption from attachment, garnishment, or legal process provided by this chapter is not effective if it results from a fraudulent transfer or conveyance as provided in chapter 726.

**222.30** Fraudulent asset conversions.—

(1) As used in this section, "conversion" means every mode, direct or indirect, absolute or conditional, of changing or disposing of an asset, such that the products or proceeds of the asset become immune or exempt by law from claims of creditors of the debtor and the products or proceeds of the asset remain property of the debtor. The definitions of chapter 726 apply to this section unless the application of a definition would be unreasonable.

(2) Any conversion by a debtor of an asset that results in the proceeds of the asset becoming exempt by law from the claims of a creditor of the debtor is a fraudulent asset conversion as to the creditor, whether the creditor's claim to the asset arose before or after the conversion of the asset, if the debtor made the conversion with the intent to hinder, delay, or defraud the creditor.

(3) In an action for relief against a fraudulent asset conversion, a creditor may obtain:

(a) Avoidance of the fraudulent asset conversion to the extent necessary to satisfy the creditor's claim.

(b) An attachment or other provisional remedy against the asset converted in accordance with applicable law.

(c) Subject to applicable principles of equity and in accordance with applicable rules of civil procedure:

1. An injunction against further conversion by the debtor of the asset or of other property.

2. Any other relief the circumstances may require.

(4) If a creditor has obtained a judgment on a claim against the debtor, the creditor, if the court so orders, may levy execution on the asset converted or its proceeds.

(5) A cause of action with respect to a fraudulent asset conversion is extinguished unless an action is brought within 4 years after the fraudulent asset conversion was made.

(6) If an asset is converted and the converted asset is subsequently transferred to a third party, the provisions of chapter 726 apply to the transfer to the third party.

**726.105** Transfers fraudulent as to present and future creditors.—

(1) A transfer made or obligation incurred by a debtor is fraudulent as to a creditor, whether the creditor's claim arose before or after the transfer was made or the obligation was incurred, if the debtor made the transfer or incurred the obligation:

(a) With actual intent to hinder, delay, or defraud any creditor of the debtor; or

(b) Without receiving a reasonably equivalent value in exchange for the transfer or obligation, and the debtor:

1. Was engaged or was about to engage in a business or a transaction for which the remaining assets of the debtor were unreasonably small in relation to the business or transaction; or

2. Intended to incur, or believed or reasonably should have believed that he or she would incur, debts beyond his or her ability to pay as they became due.

(2) In determining actual intent under paragraph (1)(a), consideration may be given, among other factors, to whether:

(a) The transfer or obligation was to an insider.

(b) The debtor retained possession or control of the property transferred after the transfer.

(c) The transfer or obligation was disclosed or concealed.

(d) Before the transfer was made or obligation was incurred, the debtor had been sued or threatened with suit.

(e) The transfer was of substantially all the debtor's assets.

(f) The debtor absconded.

(g) The debtor removed or concealed assets.

(h) The value of the consideration received by the debtor was reasonably equivalent to the value of the asset transferred or the amount of the obligation incurred.

(i) The debtor was insolvent or became insolvent shortly after the transfer was made or the obligation was incurred.

(j) The transfer occurred shortly before or shortly after a substantial debt was incurred.

(k) The debtor transferred the essential assets of the business to a lienor who transferred the assets to an insider of the debtor.

**Texas Homestead Act**

Texas along with Florida are the two best states to domicile for asset protection both having strong homestead acts. Florida gets the "nod" according to one study as the protection occurs even if a criminal act takes place. Is it any wonder O.J. Simpson moved to Florida not Texas.

TITLE 5. EXEMPT PROPERTY AND LIENS

SUBTITLE A. PROPERTY EXEMPT FROM CREDITORS' CLAIMS

CHAPTER 41. INTERESTS IN LAND

SUBCHAPTER A. EXEMPTIONS IN LAND DEFINED

Sec. 41.001. INTERESTS IN LAND EXEMPT FROM SEIZURE. (a) A homestead and one or more lots used for a place of burial of the dead are exempt from seizure for the claims of creditors except for encumbrances properly fixed on homestead property.

(b) Encumbrances may be properly fixed on homestead property for:

(1) purchase money;

(2) taxes on the property;

(3) work and material used in constructing improvements on the property if contracted for in writing as provided by Sections 53.254(a), (b), and (c);

(4) an owelty of partition imposed against the entirety of the property by a court order or by a written agreement of the parties to the partition, including a debt of one spouse in favor of the other spouse resulting from a division or an award of a family homestead in a divorce proceeding;

(5) the refinance of a lien against a homestead, including a federal tax lien resulting from the tax debt of both spouses, if the homestead is a family homestead, or from the tax debt of the owner;

(6) an extension of credit that meets the requirements of Section 50(a)(6), Article XVI, Texas Constitution; or

(7) a reverse mortgage that meets the requirements of Sections 50(k)-(p), Article XVI, Texas Constitution.

(c) The homestead claimant's proceeds of a sale of a homestead are not subject to seizure for a creditor's claim for six months after the date of sale.

Sec. 41.002. DEFINITION OF HOMESTEAD. (a) If used for the purposes of an urban home or as both an urban home and a place to exercise a calling or business, the homestead of a family or a single, adult person, not otherwise entitled to a homestead, shall consist of not more than 10 acres of land which may be in one or more contiguous lots, together with any improvements thereon.

(b) If used for the purposes of a rural home, the homestead shall consist of:

(1) for a family, not more than 200 acres, which may be in one or more parcels, with the improvements thereon; or

(2) for a single, adult person, not otherwise entitled to a homestead, not more than 100 acres, which may be in one or more parcels, with the improvements thereon.

(c) A homestead is considered to be urban if, at the time the designation is made, the property is:

(1) located within the limits of a municipality or its extraterritorial jurisdiction or a platted subdivision; and

(2) served by police protection, paid or volunteer fire protection, and at least three of the following services provided by a municipality or under contract to a municipality:

 (A) electric;

 (B) natural gas;

 (C) sewer;

 (D) storm sewer; and

 (E) water.

(d) The definition of a homestead as provided in this section applies to all homesteads in this state whenever created.

Sec. 41.0021. HOMESTEAD IN QUALIFYING TRUST. (a) In this section, "qualifying trust" means an express trust:

(1) in which the instrument or court order creating the express trust provides that a settlor or beneficiary of the trust has the right to:

 (A) revoke the trust without the consent of another person;

 (B) exercise an inter vivos general power of appointment over the property that qualifies for the homestead exemption; or

 (C) use and occupy the residential property as the settlor's or beneficiary's principal residence at no cost to the settlor or beneficiary, other than payment of taxes and other costs and expenses specified in the instrument or court order:

  (i) for the life of the settlor or beneficiary;

  (ii) for the shorter of the life of the settlor or beneficiary or a term of years specified in the instrument or court order; or

  (iii) until the date the trust is revoked or terminated by an instrument or court order recorded in the real property records of the county in which the property is located and that describes the property with sufficient certainty to identify the property; and

(2) the trustee of which acquires the property in an instrument of title or under a court order that:

(A) describes the property with sufficient certainty to identify the property and the interest acquired; and

(B) is recorded in the real property records of the county in which the property is located.

(b) Property that a settlor or beneficiary occupies and uses in a manner described by this subchapter and in which the settlor or beneficiary owns a beneficial interest through a qualifying trust is considered the homestead of the settlor or beneficiary under Section 50, Article XVI, Texas Constitution, and Section 41.001.

(c) A married person who transfers property to the trustee of a qualifying trust must comply with the requirements relating to the joinder of the person's spouse as provided by Chapter 5, Family Code.

(d) A trustee may sell, convey, or encumber property transferred as described by Subsection (c) without the joinder of either spouse unless expressly prohibited by the instrument or court order creating the trust.

(e) This section does not affect the rights of a surviving spouse or surviving children under Section 52, Article XVI, Texas Constitution, or Part 3, Chapter VIII, Texas Probate Code.

Sec. 41.003. TEMPORARY RENTING OF A HOMESTEAD. Temporary renting of a homestead does not change its homestead character if the homestead claimant has not acquired another homestead.

Sec. 41.004. ABANDONMENT OF A HOMESTEAD. If a homestead claimant is married, a homestead cannot be abandoned without the consent of the claimant's

Sec. 41.005. VOLUNTARY DESIGNATION OF HOMESTEAD. (a) If a rural homestead of a family is part of one or more parcels containing a total of more than 200 acres, the head of the family and, if married, that person's spouse may voluntarily designate not more than 200 acres of the property as the homestead. If a rural homestead of a single adult person, not otherwise entitled to a homestead, is part of one or more parcels containing a total of more than 100 acres, the person may voluntarily designate not more than 100 acres of the property as the homestead.

(b) If an urban homestead of a family, or an urban homestead of a single adult person not otherwise entitled to a homestead, is part of one or more contiguous lots containing a total of more than 10 acres, the head of the family and, if married, that person's spouse or the single adult person, as applicable, may voluntarily designate not more than 10 acres of the property as the homestead.

(c) Except as provided by Subsection (e) or Subchapter B, to designate property as a homestead, a person or persons, as applicable, must make the designation in an instrument that is signed and acknowledged or proved in the manner required for the recording of other instruments. The person or persons must file the designation with the county clerk of the county in which all or part of the property is located. The clerk shall record the designation in the county deed records. The designation must contain:

(1) a description sufficient to identify the property designated;

(2) a statement by the person or persons who executed the instrument that the property is designated as the homestead of the person's family or as the homestead of a single adult person not otherwise entitled to a homestead;

(3) the name of the current record title holder of the property; and

(4) for a rural homestead, the number of acres designated and, if there is more than one survey, the number of acres in each.

(d) A person or persons, as applicable, may change the boundaries of a homestead designated under Subsection (c) by executing and recording an instrument in the manner required for a voluntary designation under that subsection. A change under this subsection does not impair rights acquired by a party before the change.

(e) Except as otherwise provided by this subsection, property on which a person receives an exemption from taxation under Section 11.43, Tax Code, is considered to have been designated as the person's homestead for purposes of this subchapter if the property is listed as the person's residence homestead on the most recent appraisal roll for the appraisal district established for the county in which the property is located. If a person designates property as a homestead under Subsection (c) or Subchapter B and a different property is considered to have been designated as the person's homestead under this subsection, the designation under Subsection (c) or Subchapter B, as applicable, prevails for purposes of this chapter.

(f) If a person or persons, as applicable, have not made a voluntary designation of a homestead under this section as of the time a writ of execution is issued against the person, any designation of the person's or persons' homestead must be made in accordance with Subchapter B.

(g) An instrument that made a voluntary designation of a homestead in accordance with prior law and that is on file with the county clerk on September 1, 1987, is considered a voluntary designation of a homestead under this section.

Sec. 41.0051. DISCLAIMER AND DISCLOSURE REQUIRED. (a) A person may not deliver a written advertisement offering, for a fee, to designate property as a homestead as provided by Section 41.005 unless there is a disclaimer on the advertisement that is conspicuous and printed in 14-point boldface type or 14-point uppercase typewritten letters that makes the following statement or a substantially similar statement:

(b) A person who solicits solely by mail or by telephone a homeowner to pay a fee for the service of applying for a property tax refund from a tax appraisal district or other governmental body on behalf of the homeowner shall, before accepting money from the homeowner or signing a contract with the homeowner for the person's services, disclose to the homeowner the name of the tax appraisal district or other governmental body that owes the homeowner a refund.

(c) A person's failure to provide a disclaimer on an advertisement as required by Subsection (a) or to provide the disclosure required by Subsection (b) is considered a false, misleading, or deceptive act or practice for purposes of Section 17.46(a), Business & Commerce Code, and is subject to action by the consumer protection division of the attorney general's office as provided by Section 17.46(a), Business & Commerce Code.

Sec. 41.006. CERTAIN SALES OF HOMESTEAD. (a) Except as provided by Subsection (c), any sale or purported sale in whole or in part of a homestead at a fixed purchase price that is less than the appraised fair market value of the property at the time of the sale or purported sale, and in connection with which the buyer of the property executes a lease of the property to the seller at lease payments that exceed the fair rental value of the property, is considered to be a loan with all payments made from the seller to the buyer in excess of the sales price considered to be interest subject to Title 4, Finance Code.

(b) The taking of any deed in connection with a transaction described by this section is a deceptive trade practice under Subchapter E, Chapter 17, Business & Commerce Code, and the deed is void and no lien attaches to the homestead property as a result of the purported sale.

(c) This section does not apply to the sale of a family homestead to a parent, stepparent, grandparent, child, stepchild, brother, half brother, sister, half-sister, or grandchild of an adult member of the family.

Sec. 41.007. HOME IMPROVEMENT CONTRACT. (a) A contract for improvements to an existing residence described by Section 41.001(b)(3) must contain:

(1) the contractor's certificate of registration number from the Texas Residential Construction Commission if the contractor is required to register as a builder with the commission;

(2) the address and telephone number at which the owner may file a complaint with the Texas Residential Construction Commission about the conduct of the contractor if the contractor is required to register as a builder with the commission; and

(3) the following warning conspicuously printed, stamped, or typed in a size equal to at least 10-point bold type or computer equivalent:

"IMPORTANT NOTICE: You and your contractor are responsible for meeting the terms and conditions of this contract. If you sign this contract and you fail to meet the terms and conditions of this contract, you may lose your legal ownership rights in your home. KNOW YOUR RIGHTS AND DUTIES UNDER THE LAW."

(b) A violation of Subsection (a) of this section is a false, misleading, or deceptive act or practice within the meaning of Section 17.46, Business & Commerce Code, and is actionable in a public or private suit brought under the provisions of the

Deceptive Trade Practices-Consumer Protection Act (Subchapter E, Chapter 17, Business & Commerce Code).

(c) A provision of a contract for improvements to an existing residence described by Section 41.001(b)(3) that requires the parties to submit a dispute arising under the contract to binding arbitration must be conspicuously printed or typed in a size equal to at least 10-point bold type or the computer equivalent.

(d) A provision described by Subsection (c) is not enforceable against the owner unless the requirements of Subsection (c) are met.

Sec. 41.008. CONFLICT WITH FEDERAL LAW. To the extent of any conflict between this subchapter and any federal law that imposes an upper limit on the amount, including the monetary amount or acreage amount, of homestead property a person may exempt from seizure, this subchapter prevails to the extent allowed under federal law.

## SUBCHAPTER B. DESIGNATION OF A HOMESTEAD IN AID OF ENFORCEMENT OF A JUDGMENT DEBT

Sec. 41.021. NOTICE TO DESIGNATE. If an execution is issued against a holder of an interest in land of which a homestead may be a part and the judgment debtor has not made a voluntary designation of a homestead under Section 41.005, the judgment creditor may give the judgment debtor notice to designate the homestead as defined in Section 41.002. The notice shall state that if the judgment debtor fails to designate the homestead within the time allowed by Section 41.022, the court will appoint a commissioner to make the designation at the expense of the judgment debtor.

Sec. 41.022. DESIGNATION BY HOMESTEAD CLAIMANT. At any time before 10 a.m. on the Monday next after the expiration of 20 days after the date of service of the notice to designate, the judgment debtor may designate the homestead as defined in Section 41.002 by filing a written designation, signed by the judgment debtor, with the justice or clerk of the court from which the writ of execution was issued, together with a plat of the area designated.

Sec. 41.023. DESIGNATION BY COMMISSIONER. (a) If a judgment debtor who has not made a voluntary designation of a homestead under Section 41.005 does not designate a homestead as provided in Section 41.022, on motion of the judgment creditor, filed within 90 days after the issuance of the writ of execution, the court from which the writ of execution issued shall appoint a commissioner to designate the judgment debtor's homestead. The court may appoint a surveyor and others as may be necessary to assist the commissioner. The commissioner shall file his designation of the judgment debtor's homestead in a written report, together with a plat of the area designated, with the justice or clerk of the court not more than 60 days after the order of appointment is signed or within such time as the court may allow.

(b) Within 10 days after the commissioner's report is filed, the judgment debtor or the judgment creditor may request a hearing on the issue of whether the report should be confirmed, rejected, or modified as may be deemed appropriate in the particular circumstances of the case. The commissioner's report may be contradicted by evidence from either party, when exceptions to it or any item thereof have been filed before the hearing, but not otherwise. After the hearing, or if there is no hearing requested, the court shall designate the homestead as deemed appropriate and order sale of the excess.

(c) The commissioner, a surveyor, and others appointed to assist the commissioner are entitled to such fees and expenses as are deemed reasonable by the court. The court shall tax these fees and expenses against the judgment debtor as part of the costs of execution.

Sec. 41.024. SALE OF EXCESS. An officer holding an execution sale of property of a judgment debtor whose homestead has been designated under this chapter may sell the excess of the judgment debtor's interest in land not included in the homestead.

**Other State Considerations**

Different jurisdictions provide different degrees of protection under homestead exemption laws. Some only protect property up to a certain value, while others are limited by acreage limitations. If homesteads exceeds these limits creditors may still force the sale while the homesteader may keep a certain amount of the proceeds of the sale.

California - Protects up to $75,000 for single people, $100,000 for married couples, and $175,000 for people over 65 or legally disabled.

Texas, Florida, Iowa, Kansas, and Oklahoma have some of the broadest homestead protections in the U.S., in terms of the value of property that can be protected.

Texas's homestead exemption has no dollar value limit and has a 10 acres (4.0 hectares) exemption limit for homesteads inside of a municipality (urban homestead) and 100 acres (40 hectares) for those outside of a municipality (rural homestead). The rural acre allotment is doubled for a family: 200 acres (81 hectares) can be shielded from creditors in Texas for a rural homestead.[1]

Both the Kansas and Oklahoma exemptions protect 160 acres (65 hectares) of land of any value outside of a municipality's corporate limits and 1 acre (0.40 hectares) of land of any value within a municipality's corporate limits. Most homestead exemptions cover the land including fixtures and improvements to it, such as buildings, timber, and landscaping.

New Mexico has a $60,000 exemption.[2] Alaska has a $54,000 exemption.

In most instances, the exemptions do not protect against the value of a loan made in order to purchase the home (purchase money security interest).

In the majority of states, the real dollar value of "protection" provided by these laws has diminished as exemption dollar amounts are seldom adjusted for inflation. The protective intent of such laws, with some notable exceptions stated above, has been eroded in most states.

See In The News > Florida v. Texas: Which State Has Best Homestead Protection
Posted on June 9, 2004 by Jonathan Alper

**Florida v. Texas: Which State Has Best Homestead Protection**

The Spring 2004 edition of the American Bar Association Real Property Journal included an interesting comparison of homestead laws of different states. It is well known that Florida and Texas have the most protective homestead provisions in their state constitutions. Both states protect unlimited value of homestead property, and the courts of both states have liberally construed these homestead protections in favor of debtors. Texas protects homesteads of unlimited value up to 200 acres in size, and Florida protects homesteads of unlimited value up to 160 acres in a county and ½ acre within a municipality. So, which state has the best protection?

Texas courts have refused to extend homestead protection to protect criminal conduct. The Florida Supreme Court, in a 1992 decision, said that the Florida Constitution does not exempt from homestead protection the proceeds of criminal activity. In addition, the Florida Supreme Court in 2001 case of Havoco v. Hill stated that homestead protections supersede fraudulent conveyance claims. The lack of any exception from criminal proceeds under Florida case law is one reason why people such as Dennis Kozlowski (Tyco), Scott Sullivan (Worldcom) and O.J. Simpson have moved to Florida and built very expensive homes. It is fair to say that why the Constitutional homestead provisions of Florida and Texas are similar, the Florida courts have made Florida's homestead protections most attractive to those seeking shelter from liability.

## Fraudulent Transfers

- Fraudulent transfer
    o Creditors can reach trust's assets if trust is set up fraudulently, meaning that the "transfer with actual intent to hinder, delay, or defraud" a creditor
    o Uniform Fraudulent Transfer Act (below)
    o DAPT: can help taxation of estate at death and is meant to keep assets out of reach of creditors while allowing the opportunity for the settlor to be the beneficiary if funds are needed in the future.

*Fraud vs. Fraudulent Transfer*

The term "fraud" is distinct from the term "fraudulent conveyance." As applicable under the ethical rules, the term fraud is defined under the law of deceit as applicable to the conduct of a lawyer to a third party. The term "deceit" refers to actual fraud.93 It does not include, for ethical rule purposes, a "fraudulent conveyance" or "fraudulent transfer." Those terms are defined under specified remedy statutes. They are not defined under the common law of deceit. As to the clients' conduct, the conveyance of property which may later be subject to an action under the Uniform Fraudulent Conveyance Act or the Uniform Fraudulent Transfer Act or a similar statute in not unlawful nor is it tortious. A

---

# Uniform Fraudulent Transfer Act

**SECTION 4.**
(a) A transfer made or obligation incurred by a debtor is fraudulent as to a creditor, whether the creditor's claim arose before or after the transfer was made or the obligation was incurred, if the debtor made the transfer or incurred the obligation:
(1) with actual intent to hinder, delay, or defraud any creditor of the debtor; or
(2) without receiving a reasonably equivalent value in exchange for the transfer or obligation, and the debtor:
(i) was engaged or was about to engage in a business or a transaction for which the remaining assets of the debtor were unreasonably small in relation to the business or transaction; or
(ii) Intended to incur, or believed or reasonably should have believed that he [or she] would incur, debts beyond his [or her] ability to pay as they became due.
(b) In determining actual intent under subsection (a)(1), consideration may be given, among other factors, to whether:
(1) the transfer or obligation was to an insider;
(2) the debtor retained possession or control of the property transferred after the transfer;
(3) the transfer or obligation was disclosed or concealed;
(4) before the transfer was made or obligation was incurred, the debtor had been sued or threatened with suit;
(5) the transfer was of substantially all the debtor's assets;
(6) the debtor absconded;
(7) the debtor removed or concealed assets;
(8) the value of the consideration received by the debtor was reasonably equivalent to the value of the asset transferred or the amount of the obligation incurred;
(9) the debtor was insolvent or became insolvent shortly after the transfer was made or the obligation was incurred;
(10) the transfer occurred shortly before or shortly after a substantial debt was incurred; and
(11) the debtor transferred the essential assets of the business to a lienor who transferred the assets to an insider of the debtor.

creditor has no cognizable interest in the property mof a debtor prior to judgment. The transfer of freely alienable property by a debtor to avoid a creditor is "entirely proper" and "entirely predictable" as specifically enunciated in *Grupo Mexicano.* The attorney providing related legal services has no ethical duty to a third party nonclient when providing those services to his or her client. There is no common law tort of aiding and abetting. There is no common law tort of conspiracy. There is no common law tort of fraudulent conveyance. These are unknown under the tort law of the United States. The term "fraud" for purposes of Model Rule 1.2(d) and 8.4(c) does not include conduct maunder the statutory remedy commonly known as fraudulent conveyance or transfer law. Perhaps the ethical resolution of these issues has been best summed up by Professor Wolfram: "To this point, the focus has been upon client conduct that is criminal, fraudulent or contrary to a direct rule of a court. Are the considerations different if the clients' conduct is not of this description but violates other law? For example, what if the client wishes to pursue a course of conduct which is unconscionable under applicable law but is not criminal, fraudulent or in violation of a court order? What if client conduct violates the law of torts, contracts, property or some other noncriminal law that does not deal with fraud? ……….. Under the Model Rules a lawyer who assists the conduct described definitely commits no professional offense."94

A period of time exists after transfer made when creditors from past can still rear their head and reach assets. The US legal system allows protection from unforeseeable future creditors. A DAPT offers no protection from current or foreseeable creditors
It is best to protect assets when the skies are blue and no clouds in sight. Better safe than sorry.

**Domestic Asset Protection Trusts**

The surge of interest in asset protection tools can be attributed to a variety of factors, including bankruptcy reforms and the perception of a growing risk of liability, whether from tort, contract, or professional conduct. One viable option for clients seeking to place assets beyond the reach of future creditors consists of the asset protection trust. In addition to traditional asset protection techniques, like limited liability companies, family limited partnerships, and offshore asset protection trusts, estate planners may now consider the use of domestic asset protection trusts.

The DAPT was created mainly as a marketing tool in an attempt to exploit the growing market for the Foreign Asset Protection Trust (FAPT). However, the FAPT went out of vogue, and many planners now advocate the use of DAPTs as primary asset protection planning vehicles for clients. However, as with the FAPT before it, the benefits of the DAPT are mostly theoretical, and, thus far, there have been no significant court cases which have validated the benefits of DAPTs in tough debtor-creditor situations. At the same time, the false hype of FAPT promoters, who claimed that an Anderson- or Lawrence case-type situation could "never occur," are all too fresh in memory and similar claims are being made by some DAPT promoters. Therefore, it is a laudable goal to attempt to evaluate how the DAPT might fare in certain scenarios, including scenarios having already occurred with the very similar FAPT.

Advocates of APTs and legislators responsible for asset protection trust legislation may rationalize that wealthy individuals will always engage in transfers to protect their assets from future creditors in any event, so why not keep the money in the United States and available for domestic investment.

**Effective Trust Structures**

**Irrevocable Trust**

The assets are not controlled by the settlor. The trust maker makes the decisions in regard to the trust. In few states now the DAPT allows the settlor to be one of the beneficiaries. This is a great benefit because assets are protected better and the assets can still be enjoyed by the settlor. A revocable trust will not provide asset protection because and to the extent of the settlor's power to revoke

**Spendthrift**

A spendthrift provision is a clause in a legal document, typically a trust that limits the beneficiary's ability to transfer, assign or otherwise dispose of his interest in the trust. A spendthrift provision is often required to create a spendthrift trust, where an independent trustee decides how to spend the trust funds for the beneficiary's benefit. The purpose of a spendthrift provision is to prevent wasteful, extravagant and otherwise unwise spending by the beneficiary. The provision protects the trust by prohibiting its use as a security and preventing the beneficiary's creditors from attaching to her interest. Normally the provision only covers the future interest in the trust. Its protection does not extend to the money already distributed to the beneficiary. Additionally, the trust is subject to applicable state statutes. Some states will disregard the provision to fulfill child support and alimony obligations and satisfy debt for essential living expenses like food and shelter. Other states might either limit the protection to the amount necessary to support the beneficiary or disallow spendthrift trusts altogether.

**Not effective: Grantor Trust**

Too much control that a judge can order you to repay your creditors and you will be responsible for reaching into the trust to repay liability.

**Trust Situs Considerations**

The following other states now have a DAPT statute: Alaska, Delaware, Nevada, South Dakota, Wyoming, Tennessee, Utah, Oklahoma, Colorado, Missouri, Rhode Island, and New Hampshire.

Where the settlor lives influences where he may create a trust. Each state varies in DAPT provisions and the three more beneficial states to build a trust in are Alaska, Delaware, and Nevada. Attractive provisions include self-settled spendthrift trusts, shortened statutes of limitations, and conservative fraudulent transfer standards.

The trustee may prefer to create a trust in his home state because his state's laws are much more familiar to him than another state's.

Where beneficiaries live may affect the tax implications of the disbursement of the trust's funds in the future.

- Where income producing property is an influence
- Duration: trust may face limitations state to state
- Privacy: trust become public document?
- Convenience: close by or far away state?

**ALASKA**

A lack of control with an irrevocable and spendthrift may not protect your assets if one of the following circumstances exists:

- the settlor intended the transfer in trust to defraud creditors
- the settlor executed the transfer when in default, by a certain period of time, on an order for the payment of child support; or
- the settlor retained a power to revoke or terminate the trust without the consent of an adverse party who had a substantial trust interest. Alaska Stat. § 34.40.11(b)(1)-(4) (1997).

Certain characteristics must exist for Alaska's laws to be applicable:

- At least some of the trust assets must be deposited and administered within Alaska. *Id.* § 13.36.035(c)(1). "Deposited" includes assets being held in a checking account, certificate of deposit, brokerage account or trust fiduciary account in the state. *Id.*
- At least one of the trustees must be a "qualified person," a term that includes an individual residing in the state, a bank formed under Alaska law and an Alaska based trust company. *Id.* § 13.36.390(1)(A)-(C). If a trust meets these requirements, then settlors may designate Alaska law as the law to apply in case of a dispute, including disputes that may arise with creditors regarding the

effectiveness of a spendthrift clause. Hogan at 29. Effective October 8, 2003, Alaska trust law was revised, allowing third-party beneficiary trusts and self-settled trusts greater protection from creditors. *Lawyers Weekly*, USA (August 18, 2003). Even if a beneficiary is named the sole trustee or co-trustee of a trust, spendthrift protection is valid under the new statute. Alaska Stat. § 34.40.110(a). Further, under the revised statute, a non-resident beneficiary (a person who moves from or who never resided in Alaska) can be named a co-trustee, with distribution authority, without losing creditor protection. In the case of a nonresident beneficiary, distribution authority is limited to the beneficiary's health, education, maintenance, or support. Alaska Stat. § 13.36.320. Another provision of the revised statute allows trust assets, consisting of real property and tangible personal property, to be used by a beneficiary without being considered a distribution. This provision serves to prevent creditors from asserting an interest in property that is intended for the beneficiary. Alaska Stat. § 34.40.110. Previously, nothing in Alaska's trust law prevented a court from ordering the trustee to make a distribution to the beneficiary, which could then be attacked by a creditor. Pursuant to the new statute, creditors cannot attach trust assets as long as the assets remain in the trust, and courts cannot order distributions. *Id*. Under the new law, a beneficiary would have more control over trust assets without losing creditor protection.

### *Alaska Statute: AS 34.40.110. Restricting Transfers of Trust Interests*

**(a)** A person who in writing transfers property in trust may provide that the interest of a beneficiary of the trust, including a beneficiary who is the settlor of the trust, may not be either voluntarily or involuntarily transferred before payment or delivery of the interest to the beneficiary by the trustee. Payment or delivery of the interest to the beneficiary does not include a beneficiary's use or occupancy of real property or tangible personal property owned by the trust if the use or occupancy is in accordance with the trustee's discretionary authority under the trust instrument. A provision in a trust instrument that provides the restrictions described in this subsection is considered to be a restriction that is a restriction on the transfer of the transferor's beneficial interest in the trust and that is enforceable under applicable nonbankruptcy law within the meaning of 11 U.S.C. 541(c)(2) (Bankruptcy Code), as that paragraph reads on September 15, 2004, or as it may be amended in the future. In this subsection,

**(1)** "property" includes real property, personal property, and interests in real or personal property;

**(2)** "transfer" means any form of transfer, including deed, conveyance, or assignment.

**(b)** If a trust contains a transfer restriction allowed under (a) of this section, the transfer restriction prevents a creditor existing when the trust is created or a person who subsequently becomes a creditor from satisfying a claim out of the beneficiary's interest in the trust, unless the creditor is a creditor of the settlor and

**(1)** the settlor's transfer of property in trust was made with the intent to defraud that creditor, and a cause of action or claim for relief with respect to the fraudulent transfer complies with the requirements of (d) of this section;

**(2)** the trust, except for an eligible individual retirement account trust, provides that the settlor may revoke or terminate all or part of the trust without the consent of a person who has a substantial beneficial interest in the trust and the interest would be adversely affected by the exercise of the power held by the settlor to revoke or terminate all or part of the trust; in this paragraph, "revoke or terminate" does not include a power to veto a distribution from the trust, a testamentary nongeneral power of appointment or similar power, or the right to receive a distribution of income, principal, or both in the discretion of a person, including a trustee, other than the settlor, or a right to receive a distribution of income or principal under (3)(A), (B), (C), or (D) of this subsection;

**(3)** the trust, except for an eligible individual retirement account trust, requires that all or a part of the trust's income or principal, or both, must be distributed to the settlor; however, this paragraph does not apply to a settlor's right to receive the following types of distributions, which remain subject to the restriction provided by (a) of this section until the distributions occur:

(A) income or principal from a charitable remainder annuity trust or charitable remainder unitrust; in this subparagraph, "charitable remainder annuity trust" and "charitable remainder unitrust" have the meanings given in 26 U.S.C. 664 (Internal Revenue Code) as that section reads on October 8, 2003, and as it may be amended;

(B) a percentage of the value of the trust each year as determined from time to time under the trust instrument, but not exceeding the amount that may be defined as income under AS 13.38 or under 26 U.S.C. 643(b) (Internal Revenue Code) as that subsection reads on October 8, 2003, and as it may be amended;

(C) the transferor's potential or actual use of real property held under a qualified personal residence trust within the meaning of 26 U.S.C. 2702(c) (Internal Revenue Code) as that subsection reads on September 15, 2004, or as it may be amended in the future; or

(D) income or principal from a grantor retained annuity trust or grantor retained unitrust that is allowed under 26 U.S.C. 2702 (Internal Revenue Code) as that section reads on September 15, 2004, or as it may be amended in the future; or

(4) at the time of the transfer, the settlor is in default by 30 or more days of making a payment due under a child support judgment or order.

(c) The satisfaction of a claim under (b)(1) - (4) of this section is limited to that part of the trust for which a transfer restriction is not allowed under (b)(1) - (4) of this section, and an attachment or other order may not be made against the trustee with respect to a beneficiary's interest in the trust or against property that is subject to a transfer restriction, except to the extent that a transfer restriction is determined not to be allowed under (b)(1) - (4) of this section.

(d) A cause of action or claim for relief with respect to a fraudulent transfer of a settlor's assets under (b)(1) of this section is extinguished unless the action under (b)(1) of this section is brought by a creditor of the settlor who

(1) is a creditor of the settlor before the settlor's assets are transferred to the trust, and the action under (b)(1) of this section is brought within the later of

    (A) four years after the transfer is made; or

    (B) one year after the transfer is or reasonably could have been discovered by the creditor if the creditor

        (i) can demonstrate, by a preponderance of the evidence, that the creditor asserted a specific claim against the settlor before the transfer; or

        (ii) files another action, other than an action under (b)(1) of this section, against the settlor that asserts a claim based on an act or omission of the settlor that occurred before the transfer, and the action described in this sub-subparagraph is filed within four years after the transfer; or

(2) becomes a creditor subsequent to the transfer into trust, and the action under (b)(1) of this section is brought within four years after the transfer is made.

(e) If a trust contains a transfer restriction allowed under (a) of this section, the transfer restriction prevents a creditor existing when the trust is created, a person who subsequently becomes a creditor, or another person from asserting any cause of action or claim for relief against a trustee of the trust or against others involved in the preparation or funding of the trust for conspiracy to commit fraudulent conveyance, aiding and abetting a fraudulent conveyance, or participation in the trust transaction. Preparation or funding of the trust includes the preparation and funding of a limited partnership or a limited liability company if interests in the limited partnership or limited liability company are subsequently transferred to the trust. The creditor and other person prevented from asserting a cause of action or claim for relief are limited to recourse against the trust assets and the settlor to the extent allowed under AS 34.40.010.

(f) A transfer restriction allowed under (a) of this section and enforceable under (b) of this section applies to a settlor who is also a beneficiary of the trust even if the settlor serves as a co-trustee or as an advisor to the trustee under AS 13.36.375 if the settlor does not have a trustee power over discretionary distributions.

**(g)** A transfer restriction allowed under (a) of this section and enforceable under (b) of this section applies to a beneficiary who is not the settlor of the trust, whether or not the beneficiary serves as a sole trustee, a co-trustee, or an advisor to the trustee under AS 13.36.375.

**(h)** A transfer restriction is allowed under (a) of this section and is enforceable under (b) of this section even if a settlor has the authority under the terms of the trust instrument to appoint a trust protector under AS 13.36.370 or an advisor to the trustee under AS 13.36.375.

**(i)** A settlor whose beneficial interest in a trust is subject to a transfer restriction that is allowed under (a) of this section may not benefit from, direct a distribution of, or use trust property except as may be stated in the trust instrument. An agreement or understanding, express or implied, between the settlor and the trustee that attempts to grant or permit the retention of greater rights or authority than is stated in the trust instrument is void.

**(j)** A settlor who creates a trust that names the settlor as a beneficiary and whose beneficial interest is subject to a transfer restriction allowed under (a) of this section shall sign a sworn affidavit before the settlor transfers assets to the trust. The affidavit must state that

   **(1)** the settlor has full right, title, and authority to transfer the assets to the trust;
   **(2)** the transfer of the assets to the trust will not render the settlor insolvent;
   **(3)** the settlor does not intend to defraud a creditor by transferring the assets to the trust;
   **(4)** the settlor does not have any pending or threatened court actions against the settlor, except for those court actions identified by the settlor on an attachment to the affidavit;

(5) the settlor is not involved in any administrative proceedings, except for those administrative proceedings identified on an attachment to the affidavit;

(6) at the time of the transfer of the assets to the trust, the settlor is not currently in default of a child support obligation by more than 30 days;

(7) the settlor does not contemplate filing for relief under the provisions of 11 U.S.C. (Bankruptcy Code); and

(8) the assets being transferred to the trust were not derived from unlawful activities.

(k) Notwithstanding another provision of the law of this state, an action, including an action to enforce a judgment entered by a court or other body having adjudicative authority, may not be brought at law or in equity for an attachment or other provisional remedy against property of a trust subject to this section or to avoid a transfer of property to a trust that is the subject of this section unless the action is brought under (b)(1) of this section and within the limitations period of (d) of this section. A court of this state has exclusive jurisdiction over an action brought under a cause of action or claim for relief that is based on a transfer of property to a trust that is the subject of this section.

(l) If a trust has a transfer restriction allowed under (a) of this section, in the event of the divorce or dissolution of the marriage of a beneficiary of the trust, the beneficiary's interest in the trust is not considered property subject to division under AS 25.24.160 or 25.24.230 or a part of a property division under AS 25.24.160 or 25.24.230. Unless otherwise agreed to in writing by the parties to the marriage, this subsection does not apply to a settlor's interest in a self-settled trust with respect to assets transferred to the trust

(1) after the settlor's marriage; or

(2) within 30 days before the settlor's marriage unless the settlor gives written notice to the other party to the marriage of the transfer.

(m) In this section,

**(1)** "eligible individual retirement account trust" means an individual retirement account under 26 U.S.C. 408(a) or an individual retirement plan under 26 U.S.C. 408A(b)(Internal Revenue Code), as those sections read on the effective date of this paragraph or as they may be amended in the future, that is in the form of a trust, if a trust company or bank with its principal place of business in this state is the trustee or custodian;

**(2)** "settlor" means a person who transfers real property, personal property, or an interest in real or personal property, in trust.

*Delaware Statute*

The Delaware trust statute contains similar protections as the Alaska statute without the detailed conflict of law provisions. Passed in response to the Alaska statute, the Delaware statute offers settlors a similar opportunity to create self-settled spendthrift trusts. ["Under § 3571 of the Delaware statute, a spendthrift clause may protect the settlor's interest in trust if the interest is discretionary and the trustees sufficiently independent.]. As with the Alaska statute, a trust formed to take advantage of Delaware's trust laws must meet certain requirements.

- The trustee must be a state resident or an entity authorized to act as a trustee in Delaware. Del. Code Ann. Tit. 12, § 3570(8)a (1998).
- The trustee must also "materially participate" in the trust administration. *Id.*, § 3570(8)b.
- The trust instrument itself must adopt Delaware law as the governing law. *Id.* § 3570(9)a.
- The instrument must be irrevocable. *Id.* § 3570(9)b.
- The instrument must contain a spendthrift provision protecting the interest of all the trust beneficiaries. *Id.* § 3570(9)c.

Unlike the Alaska statute, Delaware's statute permits not only child support claimants to reach the settlor's interest, but other claimants as well. The additional claimants include alimony and marital property settlement claimants, creditors who relied on a writing stating that the trust property was subject to any debt that the settlor incurred, and parties to whom the settlor became liable, after forming the trust, for death, personal injury or property damage. *Id.* § 3573(1)-(2). Delaware enacted several laws in 1998 to fine tune its trust laws. In general, Amendments to Title 12 of the Delaware Code (the 1997 "Qualified Dispositions in Trust Act") increase trust protection against creditors. The definition of "disposition" was amended to exclude the release or relinquishment of an interest in property under certain specific situations, permitting a transfer or to release a special power of appointment without causing the limitations period to start again. 12 Del. C. 3570 (4). The fraudulent transfer provisions were amended to add a new subsection, which provides that the original transfer to the trustee marks the start of the limitations period where a qualified disposition is thereafter made by a transferor who is a trustee. 12 Del. C. 3572(c).

Under Delaware's original Qualified Dispositions In Trust Act, a transferor's protections "do not apply to debts that a transferor may have to a spouse or former spouse." 12 Del. C. 3573. With the enactment of Senate Bill 67, the legislature broadened the protections of a transferor by clearly providing that the exemptions do not apply to a spouse or former spouse who marries the transferor after the qualified disposition has occurred. *Id.* In June, 2000, Delaware's Qualified Dispositions In Trust Act, 12 Del. C § 3572 and § 3574(b)(2), and Delaware Code (Fraudulent Transfers), 6 Del. C § 1307 were amended to allow additional protection for professionals and advisors.

## TITLE 12

Decedents' Estates and Fiduciary Relations

Fiduciary Relations CHAPTER 35. TRUSTS

Subchapter VI. Qualified Dispositions in Trust § 3570. Definitions.

As used in this subchapter:

(1) "Claim" means a right to payment, whether or not the right is reduced to judgment, liquidated, unliquidated, fixed, contingent, matured, unmatured, disputed, undisputed, legal, equitable, secured or unsecured.

(2) "Creditor" means, with respect to a transferor, a person who has a claim.

(3) "Debt" means liability on a claim.

(4) "Disposition" means a transfer, conveyance or assignment of property (including a change in the legal ownership of property occurring upon the substitution of 1 trustee for another or the addition of 1 or more new trustees), or the exercise of a power so as to cause a transfer of property, to a trustee or trustees, but shall not include the release or relinquishment of an interest in property that theretofore was the subject of a qualified disposition.

(5) "Person" has the meaning ascribed to it in § 302(16) of Title 1.

(6) "Property" includes real property, personal property, and interests in real or personal property.

(7) "Qualified disposition" means a disposition by or from a transferor (or multiple transferors in the case of property in which each such transferor owns an undivided interest) to 1 or more trustees, at least 1 of which is a qualified trustee, with or without consideration, by means of a trust instrument.

(8) "Qualified trustee" means a person who:

a. In the case of a natural person, is a resident of this State other than the transferor or, in all other cases, is authorized by the law of this State to act as a trustee and whose activities are subject to supervision by the Bank Commissioner of the State, the Federal Deposit Insurance Corporation, the Comptroller of the Currency, or the Office of Thrift Supervision or any successor thereto; and

b. Maintains or arranges for custody in this State of some or all of the property that is the subject of the qualified disposition, maintains records for the trust on an exclusive or nonexclusive basis, prepares or arranges for the preparation of fiduciary income tax returns for the trust, or otherwise materially participates in the administration of the trust.

c. For purposes of this subchapter, neither the transferor nor any other natural person who is a nonresident of this State nor an entity that is not authorized by the law of this State to act as a trustee or whose activities are not subject to supervision as provided in paragraph (8)a. of this section shall be considered a qualified trustee; however, nothing in this subchapter shall preclude a transferor from appointing one or more advisers, including but not limited to:

1. Advisers who have authority under the terms of the trust instrument to remove and appoint qualified trustees or trust advisers;

2. Advisers who have authority under the terms of the trust instrument to direct, consent to or disapprove distributions from the trust; and

3. Advisers described in § 3313 of this title, whether or not such advisers would meet the requirements imposed by paragraphs a. and b. of this subsection.

For purposes of this subsection, the term "adviser" includes a trust "protector" or any other person who, in addition to a qualified trustee, holds 1 or more trust powers.

d. A person may serve as an investment adviser described in § 3313 of this title, notwithstanding that such person is the transferor of the qualified disposition, but such a person may not otherwise serve as adviser of a trust that is a qualified disposition although such person may retain any of the powers and rights described in paragraph (11)b. of this section.

e. In the event that a qualified trustee of a trust ceases to meet the requirements of paragraph (8)a. of this section, and there remains no trustee that meets such requirements, such qualified trustee shall be deemed to have resigned as of the time of such cessation, and thereupon the successor qualified trustee provided for in the trust instrument shall become a qualified trustee of the trust, or in the absence of any successor qualified trustee provided for in the trust instrument, the Court of Chancery shall, upon application of any interested party, appoint a successor qualified trustee.

f. In the case of a disposition to more than 1 trustee, a disposition that is otherwise a qualified disposition shall not be treated as other than a qualified disposition solely because not all of the trustees are qualified trustees.

(9) "Spouse" and "former spouse" means only persons to whom the transferor was married at, or before, the time the qualified disposition is made.

(10) "Transferor" means a person who, as an owner of property, as a holder of a power of appointment which authorizes the holder to appoint in favor of the holder, the holder's creditors, the holder's estate or the creditors of the holder's estate, or as a trustee, directly or indirectly makes a disposition or causes a disposition to be made.

(11) "Trust instrument" means an instrument appointing a qualified trustee or qualified trustees for the property that is the subject of a disposition, which instrument:

a. Expressly incorporates the law of this State to govern the validity, construction and administration of the trust;

b. Is irrevocable, but a trust instrument shall not be deemed revocable on account of its inclusion of 1 or more of the following:

1. A transferor's power to veto a distribution from the trust;

2. Except as otherwise provided in paragraph (11)b.10. of this section, a power of appointment (other than a power to appoint to the transferor, the transferor's creditors, the transferor's estate or the creditors of the transferor's estate) exercisable by will or other written instrument of the transferor effective only upon the transferor's death;

3. The transferor's potential or actual receipt of income, including rights to such income retained in the trust instrument;

4. The transferor's potential or actual receipt of income or principal from a charitable remainder unitrust or charitable remainder annuity trust as such terms are defined in § 664 of the Internal Revenue Code of 1986 [26 U.S.C. § 664] and any successor provision thereto; and the transferor's right, at any time and from time to time by written instrument delivered to the trustee, to release such transferor's retained interest in such a trust, in whole or in part, in favor of a charitable organization that has or charitable organizations that have a succeeding beneficial interest in such trust;

5. The transferor's potential or actual receipt of income or principal from a grantor-retained annuity trust or grantor-retained unitrust as such terms are defined in § 2702 of the Internal Revenue Code of 1986 (26 U.S.C. § 2702) and any successor provision thereto or the transferor's receipt each year of a percentage (not to exceed 5 percent) specified in the governing instrument of the initial value of the trust assets (which may be described either as a percentage or a fixed amount) or their value determined from time to time pursuant to the governing instrument.

6. The transferor's potential or actual receipt or use of principal if such potential or actual receipt or use of principal would be the result of a trustee's acting:

A. In such trustee's discretion;

B. Pursuant to a standard that governs the distribution of principal and does not confer upon the transferor a substantially unfettered right to the receipt or use of the principal; or

C. At the direction of an adviser described in paragraph (8)c. of this section who is acting: I. In such adviser's discretion; or II. Pursuant to a standard that governs the distribution of principal and does not confer upon the transferor a substantially unfettered right to the receipt of or use of principal;

For purposes of this paragraph, a trustee is presumed to have discretion with respect to the distribution of principal unless such discretion is expressly denied to such trustee by the terms of the trust instrument.

7. The transferor's right to remove a trustee or adviser and to appoint a new trustee or adviser;

8. The transferor's potential or actual use of real property held under a qualified personal residence trust within the meaning of such term as described in § 2702(c) of the Internal Revenue Code of 1986 [26 U.S.C. § 2702(c)] and any successor provision thereto or the transferor's possession and enjoyment of a qualified annuity interest within the meaning of such term as described in Treasury Regulation § 25.2702-5(c)(8) [26 C.F.R. 25.2702-5(c)(8)] and any successor provision thereto;

9. The transferor's potential or actual receipt of income or principal to pay, in whole or in part, income taxes due on income of the trust if such potential or actual receipt of income or principal is pursuant to a provision in the trust instrument that expressly provides for the payment of such taxes and if such potential or actual receipt of income or principal would be the result of a qualified trustee's or qualified trustees' acting:

A. In such qualified trustee's or qualified trustees' discretion or pursuant to a mandatory direction in the trust instrument; or

B. At the direction of an adviser described in paragraph (8)c. of this section who is acting in such adviser's discretion; and

10. The ability, whether pursuant to discretion, direction or the grantor's exercise of a testamentary power of appointment, of a qualified trustee to pay, after the death of the transferor, all or any part of the debts of the transferor outstanding at the time of the transferor's death, the expenses of administering the transferor's estate, or any estate or inheritance tax imposed on or with respect to the transferor's estate; and

c. Provides that the interest of the transferor or other beneficiary in the trust property or the income therefrom may not be transferred, assigned, pledged or mortgaged, whether voluntarily or involuntarily, before the trustee or trustees actually distribute the property or income therefrom to the beneficiary, and such provision of the trust instrument shall be deemed to be a restriction on the transfer of the transferor's beneficial interest in the trust that is enforceable under applicable nonbankruptcy law within the meaning of § 541(c)(2) of the Bankruptcy Code (11 U.S.C. § 541(c)(2)) or any successor provision thereto.

d. [Repealed.]

A disposition by a trustee that is not a qualified trustee to a trustee that is a qualified trustee shall not be treated as other than a qualified disposition solely because the trust instrument fails to meet the requirements of paragraph (11)a. of this section. Distributions to pay income taxes made under a discretionary or mandatory provision included in a governing instrument pursuant to paragraph (11)b.3., paragraph (11)b.6., or paragraph (11)b.9. of this section may be made by direct payment to the taxing authorities.

§ 3571. Retained interests of transferor.

A qualified disposition shall be subject to § 3572 of this title notwithstanding a transferor's retention of any or all of the powers and rights described in § 3570(11)b. of this title and the transferor's service as investment adviser pursuant to § 3570(8)d. of this title. The transferor shall have only such powers and rights as are conferred by the trust instrument. Except as permitted by §§ 3570(8)d. and 3570(11)b. of this title, a transferor shall have no rights or authority with respect to the property that is the subject of a qualified disposition or the income therefrom, and any agreement or understanding purporting to grant or permit the retention of any greater rights or authority shall be void.

§ 3572. Avoidance of qualified dispositions.

(a) Notwithstanding any other provision of this Code, no action of any kind, including, without limitation, an action to enforce a judgment entered by a court or other body having adjudicative authority, shall be brought at law or in equity for an attachment or other provisional remedy against property that is the subject of a qualified disposition or for avoidance of a qualified disposition unless such action shall be brought pursuant to the provisions of § 1304 or § 1305 of Title 6 and, in the case of a creditor whose claim arose after a qualified disposition, unless the qualified disposition was made with actual intent to defraud such creditor. The Court of Chancery shall have exclusive jurisdiction over any action brought with respect to a qualified disposition.

(b) A creditor's claim under subsection (a) of this section shall be extinguished unless:

(1) The creditor's claim arose before the qualified disposition was made, and the action is brought within the limitations of § 1309 of Title 6 in effect on the later of the date of the qualified disposition or August 1, 2000; or

(2) Notwithstanding the provisions of § 1309 of Title 6, the creditor's claim arose concurrent with or subsequent to the qualified disposition and the action is brought within 4 years after the qualified disposition is made.

In any action described in subsection (a) of this section, the burden to prove the matter by clear and convincing evidence shall be upon the creditor.

(c) For purposes of this subchapter, a qualified disposition that is made by means of a disposition by a transferor who is a trustee shall be deemed to have been made as of the time (whether before, on or after July 1, 1997) the property that is the subject of the qualified disposition was originally transferred to the transferor (or any predecessor trustee) making the qualified disposition in a form that meets the requirements of § 3570(11)b. and c. of this title. If a trustee of an existing trust proposes to make a qualified disposition pursuant to the provisions of this subsection (c) of this section but the trust would not conform to the requirements of § 3570(11)b.2. of this title as a result of the original transferor's nonconforming powers of appointment, then, upon the trustee's delivery to the qualified trustee of an irrevocable written election to have this subsection apply to the trust, the nonconforming powers of appointment shall be deemed modified to the extent necessary to conform with § 3570(11)b.2. of this title. For purposes of this subchapter, the irrevocable written election shall include a description of the original transferor's powers of appointment as modified together with the original transferor's written consent thereto, but no such consent of the original transferor shall be considered a disposition within the meaning of § 3570(4) of this title.

(d) Notwithstanding any law to the contrary, a creditor, including a creditor whose claim arose before or after a qualified disposition, or any other person shall have only such rights with respect to a qualified disposition as are provided in this section and §§ 3573 and 3574 of this title, and no such creditor nor any other person shall have any claim or cause of action against the trustee, or advisor described in § 3570(8)c. of this title, of a trust that is the subject of a qualified disposition, or against any person involved in the counseling, drafting, preparation, execution or funding of a trust that is the subject of a qualified disposition.

(e) Notwithstanding any other provision of law, no action of any kind, including, without limitation, an action to enforce a judgment entered by a court or other body having adjudicative authority, shall be brought at law or in equity against the trustee, or advisor described in § 3570(8)c. of this title, of a trust that is the subject of a qualified disposition, or against any person involved in the counseling, drafting, preparation, execution or funding of a trust that is the subject of a qualified disposition, if, as of the date such action is brought, an action by a creditor with respect to such qualified disposition would be barred under this section.

(f) In circumstances where more than 1 qualified disposition is made by means of the same trust instrument, then:

(1) The making of a subsequent qualified disposition shall be disregarded in determining whether a creditor's claim with respect to a prior qualified disposition is extinguished as provided in subsection (b) of this section; and

(2) Any distribution to a beneficiary shall be deemed to have been made from the latest such qualified disposition.

(g) If, in any action brought against a trustee of a trust that is the result of a qualified disposition, a court takes any action whereby such court declines to apply the law of this State in determining the validity, construction or administration of such trust, or the effect of a spendthrift provision thereof, such trustee shall immediately upon such court's action and without the further order of any court, cease in all respects to be trustee of such trust and a successor trustee shall thereupon succeed as trustee in accordance with the terms of the trust instrument or, if the trust instrument does not provide for a successor trustee and the trust would otherwise be without a trustee, the Court of Chancery, upon the application of any beneficiary of such trust, shall appoint a successor trustee upon such terms and conditions as it determines to be consistent with the purposes of such trust and this statute. Upon such trustee's ceasing to be trustee, such trustee shall have no power or authority other than to convey the trust property to the successor trustee named in the trust instrument or appointed by the Court of Chancery in accordance with

§ 3573. Limitations on qualified dispositions.

With respect to the limitations imposed by § 3572 of this title, those limitations on actions by creditors to avoid a qualified disposition shall not apply:

(1) To any person to whom the transferor is indebted on account of an agreement or order of court for the payment of support or alimony in favor of such transferor's spouse, former spouse or children, or for a division or distribution of property incident to a separation or divorce proceeding in favor of such transferor's spouse or former spouse, but only to the extent of such debt; or

(2) To any person who suffers death, personal injury or property damage on or before the date of a qualified disposition by a transferor, which death, personal injury or property damage is at any time determined to have been caused in whole or in part by the tortious act or omission of either such transferor or by another person for whom such transferor is or was vicariously liable but only to the extent of such claim against such transferor or other person for whom such transferor is or was vicariously liable.

Paragraph (1) of this section shall not apply to any claim for forced heirship, legitimate or elective share.

§ 3574. Effect of avoidance of qualified dispositions.

(a) After making any payments from the trust required under subsection (b) of this section, a qualified disposition shall be avoided only to the extent necessary to satisfy the transferor's debt to the creditor at whose instance the disposition had been avoided, together with such costs, including attorneys' fees, as the court may allow.

(b) In the event any qualified disposition shall be avoided as provided in subsection (a) of this section, then:

(1) If the court is satisfied that a trustee has not acted in bad faith in accepting or administering the property that is the subject of the qualified disposition:

a. Such trustee shall have a first and paramount lien against the property that is the subject of the qualified disposition in an amount equal to the entire cost, including attorneys' fees, properly incurred by such trustee in the defense of the action or proceedings to avoid the qualified disposition;

b. The qualified disposition shall be avoided subject to the proper fees, costs, preexisting rights, claims and interests of such trustee (and of any predecessor trustee that has not acted in bad faith); and

c. For purposes of this paragraph (1) of this subsection, it shall be presumed that such trustee did not act in bad faith merely by accepting such property; and

(2) If the court is satisfied that a beneficiary of a trust has not acted in bad faith, the avoidance of the qualified disposition shall be subject to the right of such beneficiary to retain any distribution made prior to the creditor's commencement of an action to avoid the qualified disposition. For purposes of this subdivision, it shall be presumed that the beneficiary, including a beneficiary who is also a transferor of the trust, did not act in bad

faith merely by creating the trust or by accepting a distribution made in accordance with the terms of the trust.

(c) <u>A creditor shall have the burden of proving that a trustee or beneficiary acted in bad faith as required under subsection (b) of this section by clear and convincing evidence except that, in the case of a beneficiary who is also the transferor, the burden on the creditor shall be to prove that the transferor-beneficiary acted in bad faith by a preponderance of the evidence. The preceding sentence provides substantive not procedural rights under Delaware law.</u>

(d) For purposes of this subchapter, attachment, garnishment, sequestration, or other legal or equitable process shall be permitted only in those circumstances permitted by the express terms of this subchapter.

(e) Notwithstanding any other provision of this subchapter, a creditor shall have no right against the interest of a beneficiary in a trust solely because such beneficiary has the right to authorize or direct the trustee to pay all or part of the trust property in satisfaction of estate or inheritance taxes imposed upon or with respect to the beneficiary's estate, or the debts of the beneficiary's estate, or the expenses of administering the beneficiary's estate unless such beneficiary actually directs the payment of such taxes, debts or expenses and then only to the extent of such direction.

(f) Where a husband and wife make a qualified disposition of property to 1 or more trusts and, immediately before such qualified disposition, such property or any part thereof or any accumulation thereto was, pursuant to applicable law, owned by them as tenants by the entireties, then notwithstanding such qualified disposition and except where the provisions of the trust instrument may expressly provide to the contrary, that property and any accumulation thereto shall, while held in trust during the lifetime of both spouses, be treated as though it were tenancy by the entireties property to the extent that, in any action concerning whether a creditor of either or both spouses may recover the debt from the trust, upon avoidance of the qualified disposition, the sole remedy available to the creditor with respect to trust property that is treated as though it were tenancy by the entireties property shall be an order directing the trustee to transfer the property to both spouses as tenants by the entireties.

(g) Subject to all of the foregoing provisions of this section, and except as otherwise expressly provided in subsection (f) of this section, upon avoidance of a qualified disposition to the extent permitted under subsection (a) of this section, the sole remedy available to the creditor shall be an order directing the trustee to transfer to the transferor such amount as is necessary to satisfy the transferor's debt to the creditor at whose instance the disposition has been avoided.

**Nevada**

Nevada has the most favorable self-settled spendthrift trust laws largely because of its much shorter statute of limitations period, and is often the jurisdiction of choice for asset protection trusts. The advantage of a Nevada asset protection trust lies in the shorter period of time required under Nevada's law between the date an asset is transferred to the trust and the date the asset is protected from the creditors of the settlor. On October 1, 1999, major changes to Chapter 166 of the Nevada Revised Statutes, otherwise known as "The Spendthrift Trust Act of Nevada," went into effect. A.B.469, 70th Leg. (Nev. Oct. 1, 1999). The most significant change is that now settlor (the creator or grantor of a trust) can obtain protection from potential creditor's claims on assets transferred to a qualified spendthrift trust, even though the settlor remains a trustee and beneficiary of the trust. Previously, a Nevada spendthrift trust could only be executed for the benefit of someone other than the settlor.

Protection of a spendthrift trust is extended to a settlor as long as:
- the trust is irrevocable
- income or principal distributions to the settlor are in the discretion of a third party (not mandatory)
- the trust is not intended to hinder, delay, or defraud known creditors.
  Nev. Rev. Stat. § 166.040 (Supp. 1999).

The revised Nevada statute's two-year statute of limitations provides that a person may not bring an action with respect to a transfer of property to a Nevada spendthrift trust (1) if he is a creditor when the transfer is made, unless the action is commenced within (a) two years after the transfer is made, or (b) six months after the creditor discovers or reasonably should have discovered the transfer, whichever is later; or (2) if he becomes a creditor *after* the transfer is made, unless the action is commenced within two years after the transfer is made. Nev. Rev. Stat. § 166.70. Nevada's revised statute also provides favorable choice of law provisions, with the following conditions:

- At least one trustee is a Nevada resident, or a bank or trust company maintaining a Nevada office
- Some portion of the trust property is located in Nevada
- The trustor is domiciled in Nevada
- The trust was created in Nevada
- Records are maintained for the trust
- At least part of the trust is administered in Nevada

**Nevada Statute § 166.015**

## GENERAL PROVISIONS

**NRS 166.010 Short title.** This chapter may be referred to by the short title of Spendthrift Trust Act of Nevada, and such reference will be sufficient for all purposes.

[7:86:1939; 1931 NCL § 6880.06]

**NRS 166.015 Applicability of chapter; requirement of trustee if settlor is beneficiary of trust.**

1. Unless the writing declares to the contrary, expressly, this chapter governs the construction, operation and enforcement, in this State, of all spendthrift trusts created in or outside this State if:

(a) All or part of the land, rents, issues or profits affected are in this State;

(b) All or part of the personal property, interest of money, dividends upon stock and other produce thereof, affected, are in this State;

(c) The declared domicile of the creator of a spendthrift trust affecting personal property is in this State; or

(d) At least one trustee qualified under subsection 2 has powers that include maintaining records and preparing income tax returns for the trust, and all or part of the administration of the trust is performed in this State.

2. If the settlor is a beneficiary of the trust, at least one trustee of a spendthrift trust must be:

(a) A natural person who resides and has his or her domicile in this State;

(b) A trust company that:

(1) Is organized under federal law or under the laws of this State or another state; and

(2) Maintains an office in this State for the transaction of business; or

(c) A bank that:

(1) Is organized under federal law or under the laws of this State or another state;

(2) Maintains an office in this State for the transaction of business; and

(3) Possesses and exercises trust powers.

3. Except as otherwise provided in subsection 1, this chapter also governs the construction, operation and enforcement, outside of this State, of all spendthrift trusts created in this State, except so far as prohibited by valid laws of other states. Unless the writing declares to the contrary, expressly, it shall be deemed to be made in the light of this chapter and all other acts relating to spendthrift trusts enacted in this State.

[4:86:1939; 1931 NCL § 6880.03]—(NRS A 1999, 1236)—(Substituted in revision for NRS 166.060)

**NRS 166.020 "Spendthrift trust" defined.** For the purposes of this chapter, a spendthrift trust is defined to be a trust in which by the terms thereof a valid restraint on the voluntary and involuntary transfer of the interest of the beneficiary is imposed. It is an active trust not governed or executed by any use or rule of law of uses.

[1:86:1939; 1931 NCL § 6880]

**NRS 166.025 Terms: "Writing" or "written."** As used in this chapter, unless the context otherwise requires, when the term "writing" or "written" is used in reference to a will, trust or instrument, the term includes an electronic will as defined in NRS 132.119 and an electronic trust as defined in NRS 163.0015.

(Added to NRS by 2001, 2353)

## CREATION OF SPENDTHRIFT TRUSTS

**NRS 166.040  Competency of settlor; writing required; settlor's ability to hold other powers.**

1. Any person competent by law to execute a will or deed may, by writing only, duly executed, by will, conveyance or other writing, create a spendthrift trust in real, personal or mixed property for the benefit of:

(a) A person other than the settlor;

(b) The settlor if the writing is irrevocable, does not require that any part of the income or principal of the trust be distributed to the settlor, and was not intended to hinder, delay or defraud known creditors; or

(c) Both the settlor and another person if the writing meets the requirements of paragraph (b).

2. For the purposes of this section, a writing:

(a) Is "irrevocable" even if the settlor may prevent a distribution from the trust or holds a testamentary special power of appointment or similar power.

(b) Does not "require" a distribution to the settlor if the trust instrument provides that the settlor may receive it only in the discretion of another person.

3. Except for the power of the settlor to make distributions to himself or herself without the consent of another person, the provisions of this section shall not be construed to prohibit the settlor of a spendthrift trust from holding other powers under the trust, whether or not the settlor is a cotrustee, including, without limitation, the power to remove and replace a trustee, direct trust investments and execute other management powers.

[2:86:1939; 1931 NCL § 6880.01]—(NRS A 1999, 1236; 2007, 894; 2009, 801)

**NRS 166.050  No specific language necessary for creation of trust.**  No specific language is necessary for the creation of a spendthrift trust. It is sufficient if by the terms of the writing (construed in the light of this chapter if necessary) the creator manifests an intention to create such a trust.

[3:86:1939; 1931 NCL § 6880.02]

## PRINCIPLES GOVERNING CONSTRUCTION

**NRS 166.070 Principles enumerated in NRS 166.080 to 166.150, inclusive.** Unless the writing shall declare to the contrary, expressly, the construction, operation and enforcement of all spendthrift trusts, heretofore or hereafter created in this state, shall be governed by the principles stated in NRS 166.080 to 166.150, inclusive, to the same effect as if they were written therein.

[Part 5:86:1939; 1931 NCL § 6880.04]

**NRS 166.080 Beneficiaries to be named.** The beneficiary or beneficiaries of such trust shall be named or clearly referred to in the writing. No spouse, former spouse, child or dependent shall be a beneficiary unless named or clearly referred to as a beneficiary in the writing.

[Part 5:86:1939; 1931 NCL § 6880.04]

**NRS 166.090 Provision for support.**

1. Provision for the beneficiary will be for the support, education, maintenance and benefit of the beneficiary alone, and without reference to or limitation by the beneficiary's needs, station in life, or mode of life, or the needs of any other person, whether dependent upon the beneficiary or not.

2. The existence of a spendthrift trust does not depend on the character, capacity, incapacity, competency or incompetency of the beneficiary.

[Part 5:86:1939; 1931 NCL § 6880.04]

**NRS 166.100 Income.** Provision for the beneficiary will extend to all of the income from the trust estate, devoted for that purpose by the creator of the trust, without exception or deduction, other than for:

1. Costs or fees regularly earned, paid or incurred by the trustee for administration of or protection of the trust estate;

2. Taxes on the same; or

3. Taxes on the interest of the beneficiary thereof.

[Part 5:86:1939; 1931 NCL § 6880.04]

**NRS 166.110  Discretion of trustee.**

1. In all cases where the creator of a spendthrift trust shall indicate the sum to be applied for or paid to the beneficiary or shall make the application or payment of sums or further sums for or to the beneficiary discretionary with the trustee, or shall make the amount thereof discretionary with the trustee, or shall give the trustee discretion to pay all or any part of the income to any one or more of the beneficiaries, such discretionary power shall be absolute, whether any valid provision for the accumulation of income is made or not and whether it relates to the income from real or personal property.

2. Such discretion shall never be interfered with for any consideration of the needs, station in life or mode of life of the beneficiary, or for uncertainty, or on any pretext whatever.

3. The giving of any such discretion does not invalidate any spendthrift trust.

[Part 5:86:1939; 1931 NCL § 6880.04]

**NRS 166.120  Restraints on alienation; exclusive jurisdiction of court.**

1. A spendthrift trust as defined in this chapter restrains and prohibits generally the assignment, alienation, acceleration and anticipation of any interest of the beneficiary under the trust by the voluntary or involuntary act of the beneficiary, or by operation of law or any process or at all. The trust estate, or corpus or capital thereof, shall never be assigned, aliened, diminished or impaired by any alienation, transfer or seizure so as to cut off or diminish the payments, or the rents, profits, earnings or income of the trust estate that would otherwise be currently available for the benefit of the beneficiary.

2. Payments by the trustee to the beneficiary, whether such payments are mandatory or discretionary, must be made only to or for the benefit of the beneficiary and not by way of acceleration or anticipation, nor to any assignee of the beneficiary, nor to or upon any order, written or oral, given by the beneficiary, whether such assignment or order be the voluntary contractual act of the beneficiary or be made pursuant to or by virtue of any legal process in judgment, execution, attachment, garnishment, bankruptcy or otherwise, or whether it be in connection with any contract, tort or duty. Any action to enforce the

beneficiary's rights, to determine if the beneficiary's rights are subject to execution, to levy an attachment or for any other remedy must be made only in a proceeding commenced pursuant to chapter 153 of NRS, if against a testamentary trust, or NRS 164.010, if against a nontestamentary trust. A court has exclusive jurisdiction over any proceeding pursuant to this section.

   3. The beneficiary shall have no power or capacity to make any disposition whatever of any of the income by his or her order, voluntary or involuntary, and whether made upon the order or direction of any court or courts, whether of bankruptcy or otherwise; nor shall the interest of the beneficiary be subject to any process of attachment issued against the beneficiary, or to be taken in execution under any form of legal process directed against the beneficiary or against the trustee, or the trust estate, or any part of the income thereof, but the whole of the trust estate and the income of the trust estate shall go to and be applied by the trustee solely for the benefit of the beneficiary, free, clear, and discharged of and from any and all obligations of the beneficiary whatsoever and of all responsibility therefor.

   4. The trustee of a spendthrift trust is required to disregard and defeat every assignment or other act, voluntary or involuntary, that is attempted contrary to the provisions of this chapter.
   [Part 5:86:1939; 1931 NCL § 6880.04]—(NRS A 2009, 802)

   **NRS 166.130  Legal estate of beneficiary in corpus.**  A beneficiary of a spendthrift trust has no legal estate in the capital, principal or corpus of the trust estate unless under the terms of the trust the beneficiary or one deriving title from him or her is entitled to have it conveyed or transferred to him or her immediately or after a term of years or after a life, and in the meantime the income from the corpus is not to be paid to him or her or any other beneficiary.
   [Part 5:86:1939; 1931 NCL § 6880.04]

   **NRS 166.140  Perpetuities.**  A spendthrift trust may not continue for a period longer than that allowed under NRS 111.103 to 111.1039, inclusive. The free alienation of the legal estate by the trustee may not be suspended for a period exceeding the limit prescribed in any constitutional or statutory prohibition against perpetuities existing in this State or in the state where the lands affected by the trust are situate, but a contingent remainder in fee may be created on a prior remainder in fee, to take effect if the persons to whom the first remainder is limited die under the age of 21 years, or upon any other contingency by which the estate of those persons may be determined before they attain that age.

[Part 5:86:1939; 1931 NCL § 6880.04]—(NRS A 1999, 1237)

**NRS 166.150  Accumulation of income.** An accumulation of the income of trust property may be directed in the will or other writing creating a spendthrift trust, for the benefit of one or more beneficiaries, to commence within the time permitted for the vesting of future interests and not to extend beyond the period limiting the time within which the absolute power of alienation of property may be suspended. If the direction is for a longer term than is permitted by law, it is void only as to the excess time, whether the direction be separable from the other clauses in the trust or not, and in such cases of invalidity the income may be paid and distributed to the next succeeding beneficiary in interest.

[Part 5:86:1939; 1931 NCL § 6880.04]

**NRS 166.160  Settlor may make different provisions.** The principles stated in NRS 166.080 to 166.150, inclusive, shall not prevent the creator of any spendthrift trust, by will or other writing, from making other or different provisions provided he or she uses express, specific language to that end.

[Part 5:86:1939; 1931 NCL § 6880.04]

## MISCELLANEOUS PROVISIONS

**NRS 166.170  Limitation of actions with respect to transfer of property to trust; certain transfers of property disregarded; limitation of actions against advisers to settlors or trustees.**

1. A person may not bring an action with respect to a transfer of property to a spendthrift trust:

(a) If the person is a creditor when the transfer is made, unless the action is commenced within:

(1) Two years after the transfer is made; or

(2) Six months after the person discovers or reasonably should have discovered the transfer,

☐ whichever is later.

(b) If the person becomes a creditor after the transfer is made, unless the action is commenced within 2 years after the transfer is made.

2. A person shall be deemed to have discovered a transfer at the time a public record is made of the transfer, including, without limitation, the conveyance of real property that is recorded in the office of the county recorder of the county in which the property is located or the filing of a financing statement pursuant to chapter 104 of NRS.

3. A creditor may not bring an action with respect to transfer of property to a spendthrift trust unless a creditor can prove that the transfer of property was a fraudulent transfer pursuant to chapter 112 of NRS or was otherwise wrongful as to the creditor. In the absence of such proof, the property transferred is not subject to the claims of the creditor. Proof by one creditor that a transfer of property was fraudulent or wrongful does not constitute proof as to any other creditor and proof of a fraudulent or wrongful transfer of property as to one creditor shall not invalidate any other transfer of property.

4. If property transferred to a spendthrift trust is conveyed to the settlor or to a beneficiary for the purpose of obtaining a loan secured by a mortgage or deed of trust on the property and then reconveyed to the trust, for the purpose of subsection 1, the transfer is disregarded and the reconveyance relates back to the date the property was originally transferred to the trust. The mortgage or deed of trust on the property shall be enforceable against the trust.

5. A person may not bring a claim against an adviser to the settlor or trustee of a spendthrift trust unless the person can show by clear and convincing evidence that the adviser acted in violation of the laws of this State, knowingly and in bad faith, and the adviser's actions directly caused the damages suffered by the person.

6. As used in this section:

(a) "Adviser" means any person, including, without limitation, an accountant, attorney or investment adviser, who gives advice concerning or was involved in the creation of, transfer of property to, or administration of the spendthrift trust or who participated in the preparation of accountings, tax returns or other reports related to the trust.

(b) "Creditor" has the meaning ascribed to it in subsection 4 of NRS 112.150.

(Added to NRS by 1999, 1236; A 2007, 894; 2009, 803)

## SOUTH DAKOTA

**South Dakota** has enacted legislation establishing disinterested third party "trust protectors." S.D. § 55-1B. The trust protectors' powers may include the power to modify or amend the trust to obtain favorable tax status, to increase or decrease the interests of any named beneficiary, and to modify the terms of any power of appointment granted within the trust. *Id.*A trust protector may not grant a beneficial interest to anyone not specifically provided for in the trust instrument. Under the South Dakota law, by becoming a trust protector, that individual is subject to the jurisdiction of South Dakota courts. *Id.* Idaho "trust protector" law has gone a step further by enumerating specific powers the trust protector may hold, thereby giving the protector more flexibility which may afford additional value to the trust but may also make the protector's powers exclusionary. S.B. 1078 enacted March 24, 1999. For example, although a trust protector may have the power to increase or decrease the interests of trust beneficiaries, effectively "deleting" a beneficiary by deleting his/her interest to zero, the trust protector may not add a new beneficiary. Idaho law also provides for a "trust advisor" who is nominated for the sole purpose of making investment decisions for the trust to the exclusion of all others. Under this provision, the settlor of the trust may be a trust advisor. *Id.* Although variations exist among state trust statutes, they are all substantially similar in that they are all irrevocable and that at least one of the trustees must be local. The statutes all prohibit a trustor (settlor) from having a right to distributions, and all require that payments to beneficiaries be discretionary with the trustee. Definitions of "fraudulent conveyance" differ, in that, some states require a showing of actual intent to defraud for a creditor to be successful in its challenge to the trust, (i.e., Alaska), while other states require only a showing of constructive fraud (i.e.,

Delaware, Nevada, Rhode Island). Regardless of the differences in the trust statutes of the participating states, the statutes were all designed to validate the self-settled spendthrift trust.

## *DAPT Concerns*

### Trustee is subject to U.S. jurisdiction

If a U.S. court ordered an offshore trustee to do something, he could simply ignore it since he is not bound by U.S. court decisions. However, a U.S. trustee can be compelled (by being thrown in jail for contempt of court) to do what the U.S. court wants. Almost as bad is the fact that the U.S. trustee is vulnerable to a civil lawsuit, as well as available to law enforcement authorities that could bring money laundering charges, etc., to coerce the trustee to cooperate. This defect alone guts the alleged protection of the DAPT.

### Full Faith and Credit

One of the best things about offshore trusts was that the offshore jurisdiction wouldn't recognize a U.S. judgment, meaning that a creditor would have to start over and start the trial process all over again, bringing in witnesses, evidence, etc., from the U.S., all of which is very expensive and time-consuming, and is huge deterrent to creditors. This is not true for a DAPT. No matter which state the trust is formed in, that state is required by the "full faith and credit" clause of the U.S. Constitution to recognize the judgment of other states. This means that all a creditor has to do is take its judgment and register the judgment without having to retry the case, and presto the creditor is knocking at your door again.

Constitution Article 4 sections 1 and 2:
Full Faith and Credit shall be given in each State to the public Acts, Records, and judicial Proceedings of every other State. And the Congress may by general Laws prescribe the Manner in which such Acts, Records and Proceedings shall be proved, and the Effect thereof.
The Citizens of each State shall be entitled to all Privileges and Immunities of Citizens in the several States.

Does **Full Faith and Credit,** as it applies to states, apply to federal law?

From the beginning of US history the courts have interpreted Article IV to require that the judgments of federal courts sitting in a state be accorded, in state courts, the same effect that would be accorded to a judgment of a state court of equal authority. *Hancock Nat'l Bank v. Farnum, 176 U.S. 640, 645 (1900); Pendleton v. Russell, 144 U.S. 640, 644 (1892).*

The history of **Full Faith and Credit** is convincing enough to make the point that asset protection plans are prudent tools used to protect assets from unforeseen circumstances and the decisions of courts anywhere in the United States, which are not necessarily unfair to one party but not necessarily just too both parties.

There is another aspect that is clearly defined in the **United States Constitution in the Full Faith and Credit Clause**. The forefathers of this country intended that no person shall be able to dodge their obligations in the United States by just moving to another jurisdiction within the United States.

## Attempting to "import" law or to make a "choice of law" favoring the laws of Alaska, Delaware, or Nevada will fail

If you think you can get an Indiana judge to apply Alaska law in favor of an Indiana resident against an Indiana judgment held by an Indiana creditor which involves Indiana property? Well, you can just forget about that sort of thing happening. And if the trial judge rules against you, then you (and not the creditor) will wind up fighting an uphill battle in a vain attempt to get the decision reversed on appeal, while in the meantime the creditor gets your assets. Even if you win the appeal, there is a chance that you might not get them back.

**Federal Courts ignore state law**

Because of the Supremacy Clause of the U.S. Constitution, federal courts are not necessarily bound by state law, which is really vile when you consider that most nightmare cases are as often federal cases, or worse, defenses against federal administrative actions.

Supremacy clause: Constitution article 6 clause 2:

This Constitution, and the Laws of the United States which shall be made in Pursuance thereof; and all Treaties made, or which shall be made, under the Authority of the United States, shall be the supreme Law of the Land; and the Judges in every State shall be bound thereby, any Thing in the Constitution or Laws of any State to the Contrary notwithstanding.

US law rules state law= federal bankruptcy or suit by federal government can reach assets in DAPT.

*The "supremacy clause" is the most important guarantor of national union. It assures that the Constitution and federal laws and treaties take precedence over state law and binds all judges to adhere to that principle in their courts.* - **United States Senate**[1]

**No secrecy**

Because the trustee resides in the U.S., he will be subject to discovery order and subpoenas, and as each state applies its own procedure (as opposed to substantive law) without regard to the other states' procedure, while the federal courts follow their own procedure, it means that any secrecy protections of the laws of the state where the trust is formed will wind up being totally irrelevant and ineffective.

*Trustee Designation and Replacement*

Good idea to allow provision for beneficiaries to be able to fire the trustee. Below is the Alaska Statute which allows reappointment of the trustee.

Alaska: Sec. 13.36.076. Removal of trustee.

(a) A trustee may be removed from office

(1) by the decision of a trust protector under AS 13.36.370 (b)(1);

(2) by the decision of another person specified in the trust instrument;

(3) under a procedure specified in the trust instrument;

(4) by a court on petition by the settlor, a co-trustee, a qualified beneficiary, or the court on its own initiative, if

(A) the court finds there is a basis for removal under (b) of this section, there is not a trust protector or another specified person who is currently acting and who may be contacted by the settlor, trustee, or qualified beneficiary in person, by mail, electronically, or by another means, and there is not a procedure for removal specified in the trust instrument; or

(B) notwithstanding the appointment of a trust protector under AS 13.36.370 or the existence of a procedure for trustee removal specified in the trust instrument, there has been a serious breach of trust as specified under (b)(1) of this section.

(b) A trustee may be removed from office under (a)(4) of this section if the court finds that removal would be in the best interests of all the beneficiaries and,

(1) for (a)(4)(A) or (B) of this section, the trustee has committed a serious breach of trust under the terms of the trust and AS 13.36.070 - 13.36.290; or

(2) for (a)(4)(A) of this section,

(A) lack of cooperation among co-trustees substantially impairs the administration of the trust;

(B) a trustee is unfit, is unwilling, or persistently fails to administer the trust effectively; or

(C) there has been a substantial change of circumstances not anticipated by the settlor, removal is requested by all of the qualified beneficiaries, the court finds that removal of the trustee best serves the interests of all of the beneficiaries and is not inconsistent with a material purpose of the trust, and a suitable co-trustee or successor trustee is available.

(c) When appointing a successor trustee, the court shall first consider the successor trustees named in the trust or, if the trust is a testamentary trust, in the testator's will, or, if a successor is not named, another procedure contained in the instrument for the appointment of a successor. When selecting a successor trustee, the court shall also consider the tax, creditor liability, and similar consequences of selecting a certain individual or institution.

(d) Pending a final decision on a petition to remove a trustee, or instead of or in addition to removing a trustee, the court may order relief that is appropriate and necessary to protect the trust property or the interest of the beneficiaries.

(e) A qualified beneficiary who may be represented and bound by another person under AS 13.06.120 may have the qualified beneficiary's consent to the removal of a trustee as specified in this section given by the person who may represent the qualified beneficiary under AS 13.06.120.

A protector is assigned by the settlor to oversee the trustee. It is important to include this cause as to not leave all the power with the trustee.

**Trustee Successor in Alaska**

AK Sec. 13.36.073. Vacancy in trusteeship; appointment of successor.

(a) Except as otherwise provided in the trust instrument, a vacancy in a trusteeship occurs if

(1) a person designated as a trustee rejects the trusteeship or is considered to have rejected the trusteeship under AS 13.36.071 ;

(2) a person designated as a trustee cannot be identified or does not exist;

(3) a trustee resigns;

(4) a trustee is disqualified or removed under AS 13.36.076 ;

(5) a trustee dies;

(6) a guardian or conservator is appointed for an individual serving as a trustee.

(b) Except as otherwise provided in the trust instrument, if one or more co-trustees remain in office, it is not necessary to fill a vacancy in a trusteeship, but a vacancy in a trusteeship shall be filled if the trust does not have a remaining trustee.

(c) A vacancy in a trusteeship of a noncharitable trust that is required to be filled shall be filled in the following order of priority:

(1) under the terms of the trust;

(2) by a person, other than a beneficiary, appointed by unanimous agreement of the qualified beneficiaries; or

(3) by a person appointed by the court.

(d) A vacancy in a trusteeship of an exclusively charitable trust that is required to be filled shall be filled in the following order of priority:

(1) under the terms of the trust;

(2) by a person selected by the unanimous consent of the charitable organizations expressly designated to receive distributions under the terms of the trust; or

(3) by a person appointed by the court.

(e) Except as otherwise provided in the trust instrument, a qualified beneficiary who may be represented and bound by another person under AS 13.06.120 may have the qualified beneficiary's consent to the appointment of a trustee as specified in this section given by the person who may represent the qualified beneficiary under AS 13.06.120.

**In any event, the Federal Courts did not recognize the Alaska Statute when it came to Bankruptcy Proceeding before an Article I Judge.**

UNITED STATES BANKRUPTCY COURT
FOR THE DISTRICT OF ALASKA

| | |
|---|---|
| In re: Case No. A09-00565-DMD<br><br>THOMAS WILLIAM MORTENSEN,<br><br>Debtor. | Chapter 7 |
| KENNETH BATTLEY,<br><br>Plaintiff,<br><br>v.<br><br>ERIC J. MORTENSEN, ROBIN MARIE MULLINS, MARY MARGARET MORTENSEN-BELOUD, in their capacities as trustees of the Mortensen Seldovia Trust, and THOMAS W. MORTENSEN, in his individual capacity,<br><br>Defendants. | Adv. No. A09-90036 |

# MEMORANDUM DECISION

Kenneth Battley, chapter 7 trustee, has brought this adversary proceeding to set aside a transfer of real property as a fraudulent conveyance. It is a core proceeding under 28 U.S.C. § 157(b)(2)(H). Jurisdiction arises under 28 U.S.C. § 1334(b) and the district court's order of reference. Trial was held on March 21 - 23, 2012. I find for the plaintiff.

Factual Background

Thomas Mortensen, the debtor and one of the defendants herein, is a self-employed project manager. He has a master's degree in geology but has not worked in that field for 20 years. He manages the environmental aspects of construction projects. Mortensen has contracted with major oil companies for work in the past.

In 1994, Mortensen and his former wife purchased 1.25 acres of remote, unimproved real property located near Seldovia, Alaska.[1] They paid $50,000.00 cash for the purchase. The parties divorced in 1998. Mortensen received his former wife's interest in the property. Subsequently, improvements were made to the property. A small shed was placed on the parcel in 2000 and some other small structures were built on it from 2001 through 2004. There is power to the property along with a well and septic system. The debtor transferred the property to a self-settled trust on February 1, 2005. The transfer of this property is the focal point of the current dispute.

Mortensen's divorce was a contested proceeding. In 1998, when the court divided the parties' assets and liabilities, Mortensen argued that the Seldovia property had been purchased with an inheritance and was to remain his sole and separate property. The court rejected his argument. It found that Mortensen wasn't credible on the issue, [2] and that the property was joint marital property. [3] Nonetheless, Mortensen received the Seldovia property. He also received $61,581.00 from his wife's SBS account, another $24,000.00 in cash from the refinance of the couple's home and other miscellaneous personal property. In total, Mortensen received assets of $164,402.00 in the divorce. [4]

Mortensen was not liable for any debt arising out of the marital estate. His ex-wife received the family home. She assumed an encumbrance against the home and was obligated to remove Mortensen's name from a $78,000 obligation encumbering the home. [5] There was no credit card debt described in the courts findings and conclusions and no credit card debt was to be assumed by either party to the divorce. [6]

In June of 2004, Mortensen filed a motion to impose child support against his ex-wife. [7] Despite a joint custody arrangement, he asked for an increase in child support due to a decrease in his income. After the superior court granted his uncontested request, Mortensen's former spouse filed a Rule 60(b) motion. He filed an opposition to the motion on July 30, 2004. In his opposition, Mortensen stated:

The property settlement and other expenses of the divorce drove me deeply into debt. After the divorce my debt continued to increase due to the ongoing legal expenses and the time required from profitable work in order to respond to two more years of repeated motions from the defendant. The defendant continued with motion practice for two years after the divorce ended. The defendant did not cease the motion practice until Judge Shortell told her in 2000 that he would consider awarding me attorney's fees if she persisted in filing frivolous motions. Saddled with debt and with increasing competition in my shrinking business market I have not recovered from the financial carnage of the divorce. [8]

Mortensen's income fluctuated substantially from year to year after the divorce. His 1999 income tax return was not placed into evidence. At a hearing held in state court on December 22, 2004, Mortensen revealed his annual income from 2000 through 2004. His net income in 2000 was $32,822.00. [9] He also cashed out an annuity for $102,023.18 that year. In 2001, Mortensen had net income of $16,985.00. [10] In 2002, his annual income dipped to $3,236.00. [11] 2003 yielded income of $13,185.00. [12] Mortensen's 2004 income was "about the same" as 2003. [13] Prior to the divorce, Mortensen had averaged $50,000.00 to $60,000.00 a year in net income. [14]

Mortensen didn't reveal his interest in establishing an asset protection trust at the hearing in December of 2004. Mortensen had heard about Alaska's asset protection trust scheme in casual conversation. He researched the topic and, using a template he had found, drafted a document called the "Mortensen Seldovia Trust (An Alaska Asset Preservation Trust)." Mortensen then had the trust document reviewed by an attorney. He said only minor changes were suggested by the attorney.

The express purpose of the trust was "to maximize the protection of the trust estate or estates from creditors' claims of the Grantor or any beneficiary and to minimize all wealth transfer taxes." [15] The trust beneficiaries were Mortensen and his descendants. Mortensen had three children at the time the trust was created.

Mortensen designated two individuals, his brother and a personal friend, to serve as trustees. His mother was named as a "trust protector," and had the power to remove and appoint successor trustees and designate a successor trust protector. She could not designate herself as a trustee, however. The trustees and Mortensen's mother are named defendants in this adversary proceeding.

The trust was registered on February 1, 2005. [16] As required by AS 34.40.110(j), Mortensen also submitted an affidavit which stated that: 1) he was the owner of the property being placed into the trust, 2) he was financially solvent, 3) he had no intent to defraud creditors by creating the trust, 4) no court actions or administrative proceedings were pending or threatened against him, 5) he was not required to pay child support and was not in default on any child support obligation, 6) he was not contemplating filing for bankruptcy relief, and 7) the trust property was not derived from unlawful activities. [17]

On February 1, 2005, Mortensen quitclaimed the Seldovia property to the trust, as contemplated in the trust document. [18] Per the trust, this realty was "considered by the Grantor and the Grantor's children to be a special family place that should not be sold and should remain in the family." [19] To facilitate this purpose, the trustees of the trust were requested, but not directed, to maintain and improve the Seldovia property "in the trust for the benefit, use and enjoyment of the Grantor's descendants and beneficiaries." [20]

The Seldovia property was worth roughly $60,000.00 when it was transferred to the trust in 2005. Mortensen's mother sent him checks totaling $100,000.00 after the transfer. Mortensen claims this was part of the deal in his creation of the trust; his mother was paying him to transfer the property to the trust because she wanted to preserve it for her grandchildren. This desire is corroborated by notes his mother included with the two $50,000.00 checks she sent to him. The first check, No. 1013, was dated February 22, 2005, and referenced the Seldovia Trust, which had been registered just three weeks earlier. [21] A short, handwritten note from Mortensen's mother, bearing the same date stated:

Enclosed is my check #1013 in the amount of fifty thousand dollars, as we have discussed, to pay you for the Seldovia property that you have put into the trust for my three special "Grands"!

In the next few weeks there will be a second check mailed to you in the amount of fifty thousand dollars, making a total of $100,000.00.

What a lot of fun memories have been made there! [22]

Mortensen's mother wrote him a second check on April 8, 2005. [23] This check also referenced the Seldovia Trust. It was accompanied by a typewritten note which said, "Here we go with the second and final check for the Seldovia property in the amount of fifty thousand dollars, totaling in all $100,000.00, as we have been talking about." [24]

Mortensen says he used the money his mother sent him to pay some existing debts and also put about $80,000.00 of the funds into the trust's brokerage account as "seed money" to get the trust going and to pay trust-related expenses, such as income and property taxes. There was no promissory note for the money he lent to the trust. Mortensen said these funds were invested, some profits were made, and he was repaid "pretty much" all of the loan within about a year's time.

Mortensen says the Seldovia property is recreational property. It was used primarily by him and his three children, but other family members also used it. Before the trust was created, Mortensen had lived on the property the majority of the time, and he says he could have exempted it from creditors' claims as an Alaska homestead if he had retained it rather than placing it in the trust. In support of this contention, he has provided copies of his 2004 Alaska voter registration application, [25] his 2003 fishing certificate, [26] his 2004 Alaska PFD application (filed in 2005), [27] a January, 2005, jury summons, [28] and his Alaska driver's license, [29] which all indicate that he resided in Seldovia when the trust was created.

Mortensen's financial condition has deteriorated since the establishment of the trust. His income has been sporadic. [30] He used the cash he received from his mother and his credit cards to make speculative investments in the stock market and to pay living expenses. His credit card debt ballooned after the trust was created. In 2005, total credit card debt ranged from $50,000.00 to $85,000.00. [31] When he filed his petition in August of 2009, Mortensen had over $250,000.00 in credit card debt. The $100,000.00 he received from his mother has been lost.

Mortensen claims that he was always able to make at least the minimum monthly payment on his credit card debts until he became ill in April of 2009. He needed immediate surgery and was hospitalized for almost two weeks. His illness required a long period of convalescence. Mortensen says he tried to return to work but was on pain medication which made him "fuzzy." He lost several work contracts while he was recovering. He first considered filing bankruptcy in early August, 2009.

Mortensen filed his chapter 7 petition on August 18, 2009. He owned no real property at the time of filing, but his Schedule B itemized personal property with a value of $26,421.00. He scheduled no secured or priority claims. General unsecured claims totaled $259,450.01, consisting of $8,140.84 in medical debt and $251,309.16 in credit card debt on 12 separate credit cards. His interest in the Seldovia Trust was not scheduled, but Mortensen disclosed the creation of the trust on his statement of financial affairs. His monthly income was listed as $4,221.00, consisting of $321.00 in child support and the balance as income from the operation of his business as a geologist and permits consultant. Mortensen indicates that he expected his income to decrease due to his ongoing health issues and the increasingly unfavorable market conditions for his profession. His itemized monthly expenses totaled $5,792.00, which exceeded his income by more than $1,500.00. Expenses included $1,350.00 for rent, $600.00 for "income and FICA tax obligations, not withheld," and $1,650.00 for expenses from the operation of his business.

Analysis

The trustee alleges that Mortensen failed to establish a valid asset protection trust under Alaska's governing statutes because Mortensen was insolvent when the trust was created on February 1, 2005. Under A.S. 34.40.110(j)(2), the settlor of an Alaskan asset protection trust must file an affidavit stating that "the transfer of the assets to the trust will not render the settlor insolvent." [32] "Insolvent" is not defined in Alaska's asset protection trust statute or in any cases arising thereafter. The trustee applies the Bankruptcy Code's definition of insolvency found in 11 U.S.C. § 101(32), which provides that the term "insolvent" means:

(A) with reference to an entity other than a partnership and a municipality, financial condition such that the sum of such entity's debts is greater than all of such entity's property, at a fair evaluation, exclusive of –

(i) property transferred, concealed, or removed with intent to hinder, delay, or defraud such entity's creditors; and

(ii) property that may be exempted from property of the estate under section 522 of this title; [33]

While there is no indication that Alaska would adopt a similar definition in the trust statute, other states have adopted a similar approach. [34] I conclude that insolvency is established for purposes of Alaska's asset protection trust law if the debtor's liabilities exceed its assets, excluding the value of fraudulent conveyances and exemptions. Here, the applicable exemptions will be determined under state rather than federal law, because this court is applying Alaska law to determine if the trust was correctly established. The federal exemption statutes have no role in making that determination.

The trustee contends that the $100,000.00 received from Mortensen's mother was a gift and cannot be considered as an asset in making a determination of solvency. I respectfully disagree. Mortensen and his mother had an oral agreement for the creation of a trust for the benefit of Ms. Mortensen-Belound's grandchildren. Mortensen was to place the Seldovia property in trust and in return, his mother promised to pay him $100,000.00. Mortensen performed his end of the bargain. Based on his mother's promise, he transferred the Seldovia property to an irrevocable trust on February 1, 2005. [35] His partial performance took the agreement outside the statute of frauds. [36] As noted in § 90(1) of the *Restatement (Second) of Contracts*:

(1) A promise which the promisor should reasonably expect to induce action or forbearance on the part of the promisee or a third person and which does induce such action or forbearance is binding if injustice can be avoided only by enforcement of the promise. The remedy granted for breach may be limited as justice requires. [37]

Ms. Mortensen-Belound's promise of payment should reasonably have been expected to induce action on the part of Mortensen and it did induce such action. The promise was binding on Ms. Mortensen-Belound and the proper remedy for a breach would have been payment of $100,000.00. Justice could have been avoided only by enforcement of the promise because Mortensen's creation of the trust was irrevocable. Justice would not require limitation of a remedy for breach because the damages are clearly liquidated. It is proper to include the $100,000.00 in Mortensen's balance sheet to determine solvency as a contract right existing as of February 1, 2005.

Mortensen prepared a balance sheet on March 8, 2010, which reconstructs his financial status as of February 1, 2005. [38] This balance sheet shows that Mortensen had $153,020.00 in assets as of February 1, 2005. Some of those assets may have been exempt. He had a brokerage account designated as "ML SEP" for $3,606.00. This may be a form of pension plan that is exempt under AS 09.38.017. His other liquid assets may be exempt in the sum of $1,750.00 under A.S. 09.38.020 as it existed in 2005. The only other exemption for Mortensen would have been for an automobile in the amount of $3,750.00. After deductions for exemptions, Mortensen had assets totaling $143,914.00.

Mr. Mortensen's balance sheet lists liabilities totaling $49,711.00 as of February 1, 2005. [39] This sum may be low. At his § 341 creditors' meeting held on September 24, 2009, Mortensen testified that he owed roughly $85,000.00 on credit cards at the time the trust was created. [40] Using either figure, however, Mortensen was solvent at the time he created the trust. The trust was created in accordance with Alaska law.

Battley seeks judgment against Mortensen under 11 U.S.C. § 548(e), which contains a ten-year limitation period for setting aside a fraudulent transfer. Section 548(e) provides:

(e)(1) In addition to any transfer that the trustee may otherwise avoid, the trustee may avoid any transfer of an interest of the debtor in property that was made on or within 10 years before the date of the filing of the petition, if –

(A) such transfer was made to a self-settled trust or similar device;

(B) such transfer was by the debtor;

(C) the debtor is a beneficiary of such trust or similar device; and

(D) the debtor made such transfer with actual intent to hinder, delay, or defraud any entity to which the debtor was or became, on or after the date that such transfer was made, indebted. [41]

Section 548(e) was added to the Bankruptcy Code in 2005, as part of the Bankruptcy Abuse Prevention and Consumer Protection Act. [42] Section 548(e) "closes the self-settled trusts loophole" and was directed at the five states that permitted such trusts, including Alaska. [43] Its main function "is to provide the estate representative with an extended reachback period for certain types of transfers." [44] However, the "actual intent" requirement found in § 548(e)(1)(D) is identical to the standard found in § 548(a)(1)(A) for setting aside other fraudulent transfers and obligations. [45]

Mortensen's trust, established under AS 34.40.110, satisfies the first three subsections of § 548(e) – the Seldovia property was transferred to a self-settled trust, Mortensen made the transfer, and he is a beneficiary of the trust. The determinative issue here is whether Mortensen transferred the Seldovia property to the trust "with actual intent to hinder, delay, or defraud" his creditors. [46]

Mortensen says he did not have this intent when he created the trust and that he simply wanted to preserve the property for his children. Battley counters that Mortensen's intent is clear from the trust language itself. The trust's stated purpose was "to maximize the protection of the trust estate or estates from creditors' claims of the Grantor or any beneficiary and to minimize all wealth transfer taxes." [47] Mortensen argues that the trust language cannot be used to determine intent because Alaska law expressly prohibits it. Under Alaska law, "a settlor's expressed intention to protect trust assets from a beneficiary's potential future creditors is not evidence of an intent to defraud." [48] But is this state statutory provision determinative when applying § 548(e)(1)(D) of the Bankruptcy Code?

Ordinarily, it is state law, rather than the Bankruptcy Code, which creates and defines a debtor's interest in property. [49]

Unless some federal interest requires a different result, there is no reason why such interests should be analyzed differently simply because an interested party is involved in a bankruptcy proceeding. [50]

Here, Congress has codified a federal interest which requires a different result. Only five states allow their citizens to establish self-settled trusts. [51] Section 548(e) was enacted to close this "self-settled trust loophole." [52] As noted by Collier:

[T]he addition of section 548(e) is a reaction to state legislation overturning the common law rule that self-settled spendthrift trusts may be reached by creditors (and thus also by the bankruptcy trustee.) [53]

It would be a very odd result for a court interpreting a federal statute aimed at closing a loophole to apply the state law that permits it. I conclude that a settlor's expressed intention to protect assets placed into a self-settled trust from a beneficiary's potential future creditors can be evidence of an intent to defraud. In this bankruptcy proceeding, AS 34.40.110(b)(1) cannot compel a different conclusion.

To establish an avoidable transfer under § 548(e), the trustee must show that the debtor made the transfer with the actual intent to hinder, delay and defraud present or future creditors by a preponderance of the evidence. [54] Here, the trust's express purpose was to hinder, delay and defraud present and future creditors. However, there is additional evidence which demonstrates that Mortensen's transfer of the Seldovia property to the trust was made with the intent to hinder, delay and defraud present and future creditors.

First, Mortensen was coming off some very lean years at the time he created the trust in 2005. His earnings over the preceding four years averaged just $11,644.00 annually. [55] He had burned through a $100,000.00 annuity which he had cashed out in 2000. He had also accumulated credit card debt of between $49,711.00 to $85,000.00 at the time the trust was created. He was experiencing "financial carnage" from his divorce. Comparing his low income to his estimated overhead of $5,000.00 per month (or $60,000.00 per year), Mortensen was well "under water" when he sought to put the Seldovia property out of reach of his creditors by placing it in the trust.

Further, when Mortensen received the $100,000.00 from his mother he didn't pay off his credit cards. Rather, he transferred $80,000.00 into the trust after paying a few bills and began speculating in the stock market. He had a substantial credit card debt due to AT&T, approximately $15,200.00, [56] which was not paid in 2005. This debt had increased to $19,096.00 by the time he filed his bankruptcy petition. [57] In 2005, Mortensen also owed Capital 1 approximately $6,350.00 in credit card debt. [58] This debt had bumped up to $7,525.00 when he filed for bankruptcy. [59] He had a Discover card with a balance of $12,588.00 as of Feb. 1, 2005. [60] He owed Discover $11,905.00 when he filed bankruptcy. [61]

Mortensen claims he paid these accounts off on a number of occasions and then re-borrowed against them. I can find no evidence of such pay-offs in the documentary evidence and I don't believe Mortensen. Nor do I believe that the trust repaid Mortensen the $80,000 in 2006. If that had been the case, Mortensen wouldn't have needed to borrow another $29,000.00 on his credit cards. [62] I conclude that Mortensen's transfer of the Seldovia property and the placement of $80,000.00 into the trust constitutes persuasive evidence of an intent to hinder, delay and defraud present and future creditors.

Mortensen alleged that the purpose of the trust was to preserve the Seldovia property for his children. Yet he used the trust as a vehicle for making stock market investments. In

2005, the trust had capital gains of nearly $7,000.00. [63] In 2006, the trust had capital gains of over $26,000.00. [64] In 2007, the trust had capital gains of $6,448.00. [65] In 2008 and 2009 the trust had either no capital gain income or experienced losses. [66] The trust also made a car loan to one of Mortensen's acquaintances. These activities had no relationship to the trust's alleged purpose.

The bottom line for Mr. Mortensen is that he attempted a clever but fundamentally flawed scheme to avoid exposure to his creditors. When he created the trust in 2005, he failed to recognize the danger posed by the Bankruptcy Abuse Protection and Consumer Protection Act, which was enacted later that year. Mortensen will now pay the price for his actions. His transfer of the Seldovia property to the Mortensen Seldovia Trust will be avoided.

The trustee has asked for costs and attorney's fees. His costs will be awarded. However, under the American Rule, attorney's fees are generally not recoverable for litigating federal issues absent an agreement or specific statutory authority. [67] This avoidance action is brought under a provision of the Bankruptcy Code and raises federal issues. The trustee is not entitled an award of attorney's fees against the defendants.   Conclusion

The transfer of the Seldovia property from Thomas Mortensen to the Mortensen Seldovia trust will be avoided, pursuant to 11 U.S.C. § 548(e). The trustee will be awarded his costs but denied attorney's fees. An order and judgment will be entered consistent with this memorandum.

DATED: May 26, 2011

## DONALD MacDONALD IV

### United States Bankruptcy Judge

NOTES:

1. Mortensen testified that he accesses the property by taking a boat from Homer to Seldovia, then driving about 7 miles down an old logging road out of Seldovia and, finally, switching to a narrower footpath or ATV trail to reach the parcel.

2. Pl.'s Ex. 13 at 8, ¶ 36.

3. *Id.* at 12, ¶ 66.

4. *Id.* at 13, ¶ 17.

5. *Id.* at 14, ¶ 84.A.

6. Pl.'s Ex. 13.

7. Exhibit 12.

8. Pl.'s Ex. 9 at 15.

9. Pl.'s Ex. 4 at 24:22.

10. *Id.* at 24:20.

11. *Id.* at 24:16.

12. *Id.* at 21:25 - 22:6.

13. Pl.'s Ex. 4 at 24:25.

14. The superior court found that Mortensen earned $54,000.00 in 1994, $57,000.00 in 1995, $46,500.00 in 1996, and $62,690.00 in 1997. His estimated income for 1998 was between $53,360.00 and $69,000.00. Exhibit 13, page 5, paragraph 13.

15. Def.'s Ex. A at Mortenson 0006.

16. Def.'s Ex. B.

17. Def.'s Ex. C.

18. Def.'s Ex. D. The quitclaim deed was recorded in the Seldovia Recording District on February 3, 2005. *Id.*

19. Def.'s Ex. A at Mortensen 0009.

20. *Id.*

21. Def.'s Ex. E at Mortensen 0079.

22. *Id.* at Mortensen 0080.

23. *Id.* at Mortensen 0087.

24. *Id.* Mortensen 0088.

25. Def.'s Ex. I.

26. Def.'s Ex. J.

27. Def.'s Ex. K.

28. Def.'s Ex. L.

29. Def.'s Ex. M.

30. Mortensen had total income of $63,197.00 in 2005; $24,430,00 in 2006; $50,040.00 in 2007; $24,887 in 2008; and $6,142.00 in 2009.

31. Mortensen's statements and other evidence regarding the amount of his credit card debt at the time of the creation of the trust have been inconsistent.

32. AS 34.40.110(j)(2).

33. 11 U.S.C. § 101(32)(A).

34. *See* 37 Am.Jur. 2d *Fraudulent Conveyances and Transfers* §§ 20, 21 (1964).

35. Article 13 of the trust states that it is an irrevocable trust. *See* Def.'s Ex. A at Mortensen 0043.

36. *Martin v. Mears*, 602 P.2d 421, 428-429 (Alaska 1979).

37. *Restatement (Second) of Contracts* § 90 (1981).

38. Pl.'s Ex. 21; Def.'s Ex. G.

39. *Id.*

40. Pl.'s Ex. 2 at 6.

41. 11 U.S.C. § 548(e)(1).

42. Pub. L. No. 109-8, § 1042 (2005).

43. 5 Collier on Bankruptcy ¶ 548.10[1], [3][a] n.6 (N. Alan Resnick & Henry J. Sommer eds., 16th ed.).

44. *Id.*, ¶ 548.10[2].

45. 11 U.S.C. § 548(a)(1)(A), (e)(1)(D), *see also* 5 Collier on Bankruptcy ¶ 548.10[3][d].

46. 11 U.S.C. § 548(e)(1)(D).

47. Def.'s Ex. A at Mortenson 0006.

48. AS 34.40.110(b)(1).

49. *Butner v. United States*, 440 U.S. 48, 55 (1979).

50. *Id.*

51. In addition to Alaska, Delaware, Nevada, Rhode Island and Utah permit the creation of self-settled trusts.

52. 5 Collier on Bankruptcy ¶ 548.10[1], *citing* H.R. Rep. No. 109-31, 109th Cong., 1st Sess. 449 (2005) (statement of Rep. Cannon).

53. 5 Collier on Bankruptcy ¶ 548.10[3][a] (footnotes omitted).

54. *Consolidated Partners Inv. Co. v. Lake*, 152 B.R. 485, 488 (Bankr. N.D. Ohio 1993).

55. See the discussion herein regarding Mortensen's income during this time, at pp. 4 - 5.

56. Pl.'s Ex. 23.

57. Pl.'s Ex. 18 at 13. Citibank took over AT&T''s credit card business. It is listed as a creditor in the debtor's bankruptcy schedules for a loan with the same account number as the AT&T debt.

58. Pl.'s Ex. 24 at 12.

59. Pl.s Ex. 18 at 14.

60. Pl.'s Ex. 25.

61. Pl.'s Ex. 18 at 13.

62. Pl.'s Ex. 44 shows an increase of about $29,000.00 in credit card debt from February 1, 2005 through December 31, 2006.

63. Def.'s Ex. S.

64. Def.'s Ex. T.

65. Def.'s Ex. U.

66. Def.'s Exs. V and W.

67. *Alyeska Pipeline Service Co. v. Wilderness Society*, 421 U.S. 240 (1975).

# JURISDICTION

Scenario: Your client is a DAPT state resident (South Dakota) and wants to protect their assets to be protected from potential future creditors. You set up a DAPT for him in South Dakota. Suppose he plans on moving to Arizona upon retirement. Will his Arizona creditors be able to reach his DAPT in South Dakota?

Following the jurisdiction ruling in the 1958 case of Hanson vs. Denckla Arizona would not have jurisdiction on the South Dakota DAPT. Here is that ruling.

U.S. Supreme Court

**HANSON v. DENCKLA, 357 U.S. 235 (1958)**

**357 U.S. 235**

**HANSON, EXECUTRIX, ET AL. v. DENCKLA ET AL.**
**APPEAL FROM THE SUPREME COURT OF FLORIDA.**
No. 107.
**Argued March 10-11, 1958.**
**Decided June 23, 1958.** *

While domiciled in Pennsylvania, a woman executed in Delaware a revocable deed of trust making a Delaware trust company trustee of certain securities, reserving the income for life and providing that the remainder should be paid to such parties as she should appoint by inter vivos or testamentary instrument. Later, after becoming domiciled in Florida, where she remained until her death, she executed (1) an inter vivos instrument appointing certain beneficiaries to receive $400,000 of the trust property, and (2) a will containing a residuary clause covering, inter alia, "all property, rights and interest over which I may have power of appointment which prior to my death has not been effectively exercised." In a proceeding in which the Delaware trust company did not appear and was given notice only by mail and publication, a Florida State Court held that the trust and power of appointment were ineffective under Florida law and that the $400,000 passed under the residuary clause of the will. This ruling was sustained by the Supreme Court of Florida, which also held that the Florida court had jurisdiction over the nonresident trust company, and an appeal was taken to this Court. A Delaware court with personal jurisdiction over the trust company sustained the trust and inter vivos appointment and held that the parties designated therein were entitled to the $400,000. This decision was sustained by the Supreme Court of Delaware, and its judgment was brought here on certiorari. Both Delaware courts denied motions to give full faith and credit to the Florida decree. Held:

> 1. This Court need not determine whether Florida was bound to give full faith and credit to the Delaware decree, because that question was not seasonably presented to the Florida court. Pp. 243-244.
>
> 2. This Court is without jurisdiction of the Florida appeal, and it is dismissed; but, treating the papers whereon appeal was taken [357 U.S. 235, 236] as a petition for certiorari, 28 U.S.C. 2103, certiorari is granted. P. 244.
>
> 3. Appellants in the Florida case have standing to challenge the jurisdiction of the Florida court over the nonresident trust company which made no appearance, because they have a "direct and substantial personal interest in the outcome" of the litigation, Chicago v. Atchison, T. & S. F. R. Co., ante, p. 77, and the trustee was an indispensable party without whom a Florida court had no power to adjudicate the controversy. Pp. 244-245.
>
> 4. The Florida court did not have in rem jurisdiction over the corpus of the trust or personal jurisdiction over the trust company. without such jurisdiction it had no power under Florida law to pass on the validity of the trust. Therefore, its decree is void under the Due Process Clause of the Fourteenth Amendment, and it is reversed, not only as to the trust company but also as to the individuals over whom it did have jurisdiction. Pp. 245-254.
>
> (a) Though the property involved was intangible personal property, the settlor was domiciled in Florida at the time of her death, and Florida had jurisdiction over the probate and construction of her will, it had no in rem jurisdiction over the trust

assets, and its judgment is invalid insofar as it rests on the basis of in rem jurisdiction. Pp. 246-250.

(b) The trust company did not have sufficient affiliation with Florida to empower the Florida courts to exercise personal jurisdiction over it. McGee v. International Life Ins. Co., 355 U.S. 220 , distinguished. Pp. 250-253.

(c) Since it is the validity of the trust agreement, not the exercise of the power of appointment, that is at issue here, the execution in Florida of the power of appointment does not give Florida a substantial connection with the contract on which the suit is based nor justify the exercise of personal jurisdiction over the nonresident trustee. Pp. 253-254.

(d) That the settlor and most of the appointees and beneficiaries were domiciled in Florida does not give Florida personal jurisdiction over this nonresident trustee. P. 254.

(e) Because the Florida Supreme Court has repeatedly held that a trustee is an indispensable party without whom a Florida court has no power to adjudicate controversies affecting the validity of a trust (though it did not rule on that point in this case), the [357 U.S. 235, 237] Florida judgment must be reversed, not only as to the nonresident trustees but also as to the appellants over whom the Florida court admittedly had jurisdiction. Pp. 254-255.

5. Delaware was under no obligation to give full faith and credit to the invalid Florida judgment, and the Delaware judgment is affirmed. Pp. 255-256.

(a) Since Delaware was entitled to conclude that Florida law made the trust company an indispensable party, it was under no obligation to give the Florida judgment any faith and credit - even against parties over whom Florida's jurisdiction was unquestioned. P. 255.

(b) The Delaware case should not be held while the Florida case is remanded to give the Florida court an opportunity to determine whether the trustee is an indispensable party in the circumstances of this case, since there is ample Florida authority from which the answer to that question may be determined. Pp. 255-256.

100 So.2d 378, reversed and cause remanded. ___ Del. ___, 128 A. 2d 819, affirmed.

HANSON V. DENCKLA, 357 U. S. 235 (1958)

*Conclusion*

Though unproven, DAPT probably has a fair chance of prevailing in the following circumstances:

First, you actually live in Alaska, Delaware, Nevada or a state that has adopted a similar statute, have all of your assets there, fund the trust well in advance and follow all formalities, and avoid federal court actions.

Creditor-debtor law is dynamic and changing — particular in economically bad times where there is a lot of litigation going on and decisions coming down. Today's perfect asset protection plan may be worthless tomorrow, which is why clients need to continue to maintain a relationship with their attorney and periodically re-visit their plan to make sure that it still is sound both in design and how the client actually operates it.

Offshore Trust

*Offshore over DAPT*

Domestic asset protection trusts (DAPTs): How effective are they really? Comfort in having assets in US. Issues with jurisdiction and conflicting laws.
international structures:

- US courts have no power (not true)
- Shorter time period to protect the transferred assets
- Proof of fraudulent intent is on creditor
- Trust remains valid and remaining assets are protected despite a portion of the trust being used to satisfy a creditor
- Few contingency fees allowed internationally
- High costs to begin a lawsuit
- self-settled trusts to be available

- stable political climate and economy

ART # 2: Traditionally, the creditor can make two arguments to reach trust assets: first, he may argue that the trust is invalid because the settlor retained too many controls over the trustee or over the trust assets (hence, the assets still belong to the settlor), and/or second, the creditor may argue that the transfer of assets into the trust was a fraudulent transfer. The fraudulent transfer argument will be the most likely one to be made (although neither Alaska nor Delaware has sufficiently disposed of the retained controls/validity issue, as certain offshore jurisdictions have). If the creditor is propounding a fraudulent transfer argument, he will join the trustee (not difficult if the trustee is located in the United States) as a party (transferee) in the fraudulent transfer case. In this manner, the trust assets will be reachable because the Florida Court (example) will then have jurisdiction over the Alaska trustee, and the "full faith and credit" clause of the Constitution will require the Alaska Court to enforce the judgment of the Florida Court against the Alaska trustee. This **CANNOT HAPPEN** with a properly structured offshore trust.

Let's review and compare the domestic and offshore APT's on the "full faith and credit" issue: a creditor holding a fraudulent transfer judgment in his favor from a U.S. Court cannot hope to have the (properly selected) offshore jurisdiction enforce the judgment against the trust. The creditor must *commence a new fraudulent transfer action in the offshore jurisdiction,* and utilize a lawyer admitted to practice in that jurisdiction (not his U.S. lawyer). In most asset protection jurisdictions, lawyers cannot take cases on a contingency fee basis — this means that the creditor must make a significant personal financial commitment before his case even gets off the ground. What's next? A consideration of the legal basis for creditor's attack on the trust: if the trust situs jurisdiction has been carefully selected, its laws will preclude many conventional legal bases of attack, usually leaving as the only avenue of attack the fraudulent transfer argument. Here the creditor is faced with an insurmountable burden of proof (see below) and a severely contracted statute of limitations (in many cases, the statute of limitations will be zero). The foregoing hurdles in the legal obstacle course of attacking the offshore trust are not the end, however. If threatened with litigation in its original situs, the properly drafted offshore trust can move to another favorable offshore jurisdiction – requiring the creditor to start his litigation all over again.

How does this offshore legal obstacle course compare to that faced by a creditor attempting to reach assets held in a domestic APT? Let's see: as discussed above, a creditor, *using his U.S. lawyer*, making a fraudulent transfer attack on a domestic trust, will be able to **easily get jurisdiction** over the trustee, and if successful with his case, get the trust assets. Protection? Remember, the *foreign court will not enforce* the U.S. judgment. Compare: the foreign court "will not enforce" with the fact that the *Alaska Court will be required to enforce*….. You decide: do you want to roll the dice, or eliminate risk?

Some assets are required to remain in Alaska; a Cook Islands trust need not have any of its assets in the Cook Islands. Although not usually discussed, the trustee fees charged by the Alaska and Delaware trust companies (based upon a percentage of trust assets) are often more than twice as much as those charged by the Cook Islands trust companies (flat fees). The fraudulent transfer statute of limitations in Alaska and Delaware is four years, and may permit a subsequent creditor to bring an action. The statute can be as short as zero in the Cook Islands and *subsequent creditors are precluded from bringing an action*. The standard of proof required to establish a fraudulent transfer in Alaska or Delaware is our usual civil standard: "preponderance of the evidence" – not a difficult standard to meet, while the Cook Islands Law requires the significantly more difficult standard of proof "beyond a reasonable doubt" – a nearly impossible standard to meet. Finally, as mentioned above, neither Alaska nor Delaware has addressed the "invalidity" basis of attack in their statutes, thus *leaving a significant avenue of attack available to a creditor*; this issue has essentially been eliminated by Cook Islands legislation. (Art # 2)

# "The" Anderson Case

*FTC v. Affordable Media, LLC,* 179 F.3d 1228 (9th Cir. 1999) (aka the Anderson case). Settlor kept too strong a control over their International Trust and were deemed able to have their offshore assets returned; the judge held them in contempt of court) (many see this case as "bad facts make bad law." [See §5:51.]

**FEDERAL TRADE COMMISSION, Plaintiff-Appellee,**

v.

**AFFORDABLE MEDIA, LLC, Defendant,**

and

**DENYSE LINDA ALYCE ANDERSON; MICHAEL K. ANDERSON, Defendants-Appellants.**

**179 F.3d 1228 (9th Cir.1999)**

Appeal No. 98-16378

Case Below: CV-98-00669-LDG (RLH)

Appeal from the United States District Court for the District of Nevada Lloyd D. George, District Judge, Presiding

Argued and Submitted January 13, 1999-San Francisco, California

Filed June 15, 1999

**JUDGES:** Charles E. Wiggins, A. Wallace Tashima, and Barry G. Silverman, Circuit Judges.

Opinion by Judge Wiggins

**COUNSEL:** Pamela J. Naughton and Michael P. McCloskey, Baker & McKenzie, San Diego, California, for the defendants-appellants.

Michael S. Fried, Federal Trade Commission, Washington, D.C., for the plaintiff-appellee.

OPINION

WIGGINS, Circuit Judge:

A husband and wife, Denyse and Michael Anderson, were involved in a telemarketing venture that offered investors the chance to participate in a project that sold such modern marvels as talking pet tags and water-filled barbells by means of late-night television. Although the promoters promised that an investment in the project would return 50 per cent in a mere 60 to 90 days, the venture in fact was a Ponzi scheme, which eventually unraveled and left thousands of investors with tremendous losses. When the Federal Trade Commission brought a complaint against the telemarketing duo, they claimed that they were simply innocent dupes rather than a modern day telephonic Bonnie and Clyde.

While the investors' money was lost in the fraudulent scheme, the Andersons' profits from their commissions remained safely tucked away across the sea in a Cook Islands trust. When the Commission brought a civil action to recover as much money as possible for the defrauded investors, the Andersons advanced two incredible propositions. First, they claimed that they should retain the 45 percent commissions they received for their role in the fraud, even though they acknowledged that the investors were defrauded. They claimed this entitlement because they merely sold the toxic investments that fueled the scheme and propped up the duplicitous house of cards. Second, the Andersons claimed that they were unable to repatriate the assets in the Cook Islands trust because they had willingly relinquished all control over the millions of dollars of commissions in order to place this money overseas in the benevolent hands of unaccountable overseers, just on the off chance that a law suit might result from their business activities. The learned district court was skeptical of both arguments and choose to grant the Commission its requested preliminary relief. An old adage warns that a fool and his money are easily parted. This case shows that the same is not true of a district court judge and his common sense. After the Andersons refused to comply with the preliminary injunction by refusing to return their illicit proceeds, the district court found the Andersons in civil contempt of court. The Andersons appealed. We have jurisdiction under 28 U.S.C. S1292(a)(1) and we affirm. fn1 fn1 We also grant the Commission's motion to strike the materials contained in the first tab of Appellants' Supplemental Excerpts of Record. These materials are declarations, executed in September 1998, months after the district court issued the preliminary injunction and found the Andersons in contempt of court. We, therefore, order these materials stricken. See *Kirshner v. Uniden Corp. of Am.*, 842 F.2d 1074, 1078 (9th Cir. 1988) (striking portions of excerpts of record that were "neither filed with the district court, considered by the court, nor even before the court when it entered the order that [appellant] now challenges on appeal").

I

Sometime after April 1997, Denyse and Michael Anderson became involved with The Sterling Group ("Sterling"). Sterling sold such imaginative products as the "Aquabell," a water-filled dumbbell, the "Talking Pet Tag," and a plastic wrap dispenser known as "KenKut" by means of late-night television commercials broadcast between the hours of 11:00 p.m. and 4:00 a.m. The Andersons formed Financial Growth Consultants, LLC ("Financial") to serve as the primary telemarketer of media units, an investment that afforded purchasers the opportunity to receive a portion of the profits generated from the sales of Sterling's outlandish products. Financial's telemarketers thereupon set about locating prospective investors in the media unit scheme.

The media units sold for $5,000. Each media unit entitled the investor to participate in the sale of Sterling's products from 201 of the late-night commercials. Each product sold for

$20.00. The investor would receive $7.50 for each product sold during his 201 commercials, up to a maximum of five products per commercial. According to Financial's telemarketers, the investors would likely receive $37.50 per commercial (from five products sold during each commercial) for a total of $7,537.50—an astronomical fifty percent return in sixty to ninety days. Financial, for its part, would receive forty-five percent of the investor's $5,000.00 investment, an amount that the Andersons assert is the industry standard.

It appears that Financial's telemarketers were especially skilled at marketing the media units. Financial may have raised at least $13,000,000 from investors in the media-unit scheme, retaining an estimated $6,300,000 in commissions for itself. Perhaps unsurprisingly to those not involved in the media-unit project, it turned out that Sterling could not sell enough Talking Pet Tags and Aquabells to return the promised yields to the media-unit investors. Instead, it appears that Sterling used later investors' investments to pay the promised yields to earlier investors—a classic Ponzi scheme.

On April 23, 1998, the Federal Trade Commission (the "Commission") filed a complaint in the United States District Court for the District of Nevada, charging the Andersons, Financial, and others with violations of the Federal Trade Commission Act (the "Act") and the Telemarketing Sales Rule for their participation in a scheme to telemarket fraudulent investments to consumers. Upon motion by the Commission, the district court issued an ex parte temporary restraining order against the defendants.fn2 After hearings on April 30 and May 8, 1998, the district court entered a preliminary injunction against the defendants, which incorporated the provisions of the temporary restraining order. Both the temporary restraining order and the preliminary injunction required the Andersons to repatriate any assets held for their benefit outside of the United States.

fn2 The temporary restraining order prohibited the Andersons, the other defendants, and their agents from making false or misleading statements in connection with the marketing of investments or destroying or otherwise failing to maintain their business records. It also froze the defendants' assets and required the defendants to provide a financial statement to the Commission's counsel. In addition, it required any financial institutions in possession of the defendants' assets to preserve the assets and provide the Commission's counsel information about the assets. Finally, it required the defendants to repatriate all assets outside of the United States to the territory of the United States.

In July, 1995, the Andersons had created an irrevocable trust under the law of the Cook Islands. The Andersons were named as co-trustees of the trust, together with AsiaCiti Trust Limited ("AsiaCiti"), a company licensed to conduct trustee services under Cook Islands law. Apparently, the Andersons created the trust in an effort to protect their assets from business risks and liabilities by placing the assets beyond the jurisdiction of the United States courts. As discussed more fully below, the provisions of the trust were intended to frustrate the operation of domestic courts, by removing the Andersons as trustees and preventing AsiaCiti from repatriating any of the trust assets to the United States if a so-called "event of duress" occurred.

In response to the preliminary injunction, the Andersons faxed a letter to AsiaCiti on May 12, 1998, instructing AsiaCiti to provide an accounting of the assets held in the trust and to repatriate the assets to the United States to be held under the control of the district court. AsiaCiti thereupon notified the Andersons that the temporary restraining order was an event of duress under the trust, removed the Andersons as cotrustees under the trust because of the event of duress, and refused to provide an accounting or repatriation of the assets. The trust assets were therefore not repatriated to the United States and the Andersons have provided only limited information to the district court and the Commission regarding the trust assets.

On May 7, 1998, the Commission moved the district court to find the Andersons in civil contempt for their failure to comply with the temporary restraining order's requirements that they submit an accounting of their foreign assets to the Commission and to repatriate all assets located abroad. At a hearing on June 4, 1998, the district court found the Andersons in civil contempt of court for failing to repatriate the trust assets to the United States and failing to provide an accounting of the trust's assets. The district court, however, continued the hearing until June 9, then until June 11, and finally until June 17, in an effort to allow the Andersons to purge themselves of their contempt. In attempting to purge themselves of their contempt, the Andersons attempted to appoint their children as trustees of the trust, but AsiaCiti removed them from acting as trustees because the event of duress was continuing. At the June 17 hearing, the district court indicated that it believed that the Andersons remained in control of the trust and rejected their assertion that compliance with the repatriation provisions of the trust was impossible. At the close of the June 17 hearing, the district judge ordered the Andersons taken into custody because they had not purged themselves of their contempt. The Andersons timely appealed the district court's issuance of the preliminary injunction and finding them in contempt. We affirm the district court.fn3

fn3 Subsequent to the Andersons' appeal to this court, but prior to oral argument, the district court ordered the Andersons released from custody. In its Release Order, filed December 22, 1998, the district court ordered the Andersons released but found that they remain in contempt of court. Because they remain in contempt, their appeal of the court's order finding them in contempt has not been rendered moot, even though they are no longer in custody.

II

The first issue in the Anderson's appeal concerns the district court's issuance of the preliminary injunction. This court only subjects a district court's order regarding preliminary injunctive relief to "limited review." *Does 1-5 v. Chandler*, 83 F.3d 1150, 1152 (9th Cir. 1996). We will reverse a district court's issuance of a preliminary injunction only if the district court abused its discretion by basing its decision on an erroneous legal standard or on clearly erroneous factual findings. See id. Based on the record, we find that the district court did not abuse its discretion in issuing the preliminary injunction.

Section 13(b) of the Act allows a district court to grant the Commission a preliminary injunction "[u]pon a proper showing that, weighing the equities and considering the Commission's likelihood of ultimate success, such action would be in the public interest." 15 U.S.C. S 53(b). Section 13(b), therefore, "places a lighter burden on the Commission than that imposed on private litigants by the traditional equity standard; the Commission need not show irreparable harm to obtain a preliminary injunction." *FTC v. Warner Communications, Inc.*, 742 F.2d 1156, 1159 (9th Cir. 1984). Under this more lenient standard, "a court must 1) determine the likelihood that the Commission will ultimately succeed on the merits and 2) balance the equities." Id. at 1160.

A. Likelihood of Success on the Merits

In its complaint, the Commission alleged that: (1) the Andersons and Financial violated Section 5(a) of the Act by representing that consumers were highly likely to earn returns of 25 percent or more on their investments within a period of 90 days even though these consumers were not likely to earn such returns; and (2) the Andersons and Financial violated Section 310.3 of the Telemarketing Sales Rule, 16 C.F.R. S 310.3(a)(2)(vi), by misrepresenting a material aspect of the investors' investment opportunity by misrepresenting the return the investors were likely to earn. In granting the preliminary injunction, the district court found a "substantial likelihood that the Commission will ultimately succeed" in establishing that the Andersons and their company had violated these provisions and were likely to violate these provisions in the future. Preliminary Injunction, entered and served May 22, 1998, at 2. The Andersons do not deny that the Sterling enterprise was a Ponzi scheme. Instead, the Andersons challenge the district court's order by claiming that the Commission will not succeed in holding them personally liable for their involvement in the scheme. This contention lacks merit; the Commission has made a sufficient showing to justify preliminary injunctive relief.

The Andersons claim that the Commission will not succeed on the merits in holding them personally liable for restitution for any deceptive practices of Financial. Their contention reveals a crucial misunderstanding regarding the requisite factual showing in order to obtain preliminary, as compared to permanent, injunctive relief. Once the correct standard is applied, it becomes abundantly clear that the district court did not abuse its discretion in finding that the Commission had made a sufficient showing that it will likely succeed in holding the Andersons personally liable for Financial's misconduct.

Individuals are personally liable for restitution for corporate misconduct if they "had knowledge that the corporation or one of its agents engaged in dishonest or fraudulent conduct, that the misrepresentations were the type upon which a reasonable and prudent person would rely, and that consumer injury resulted." *FTC v. Publishing Clearing House, Inc.*, 104 F.3d 1168, 1171 (9th Cir. 1996). The knowledge requirement can be satisfied by showing that the individuals

had actual knowledge of material misrepresentations,[were] recklessly indifferent to the truth or falsity of a misrepresentation, or had an awareness of a high probability of fraud along with an intentional avoidance of the truth.

*Id.*fn4 The Commission, however, "is not required to show that a defendant intended to defraud consumers in order to hold that individual personally liable." Id.

> fn4 The Commission claims that knowledge or reckless indifference is not necessary for disgorgement, as compared to restitution. The Commission bases this claim upon cases dealing with the Commodity Futures Trading Commission. This argument has been proffered by the Commission before and this Circuit has declined to reach the issue. See, e.g., *FTC v. Pantron I Corporation*, 33 F.3d 1088, 1103 (9th Cir. 1994). We will not decide today whether the Act allows the Commission to obtain disgorgement, without regard to the defendant's mental state, because we believe that the Commission has made a sufficient showing of reckless indifference to obtain preliminary injunctive relief.

The Andersons concede that reckless indifference is legally sufficient to impose personal liability on principals for corporate wrongdoing. Instead of challenging the legal standard applied by the district court, they challenge the court's factual findings. In its preliminary injunction, the district court found "substantial evidence that [the Andersons] were at least recklessly indifferent to the deceptive profit representations of the telemarketers" who worked for Financial and its independent sales offices. Preliminary Injunction, entered and served May 22, 1998, at 2. The Andersons assert that the district court's "finding of reckless indifference is based on clearly erroneous findings of fact." Appellants' Opening Brief at 27. In making this assertion, the Andersons reveal a fundamental misunderstanding of the factual showing necessary to support a district court's preliminary injunction (as compared to a permanent injunction) as well as confusion regarding the appropriate legal standards for imposing personal liability on principals for corporate misconduct.

In reviewing a preliminary injunction, our review is significantly constrained because of the state of the record available for our review. This constraint is especially limiting when we are asked to review the district court's factual findings that serve as the basis for a preliminary injunction. We have explained these limitations in another case in which we had to review a district court's issuance of a preliminary injunction:

We begin by identifying how little we can assist in the final resolution of the critical issues before the district court. Until a permanent injunction is granted or denied, we are foreclosed from fully reviewing the important questions presented.... Review of factual findings at the preliminary injunction stage is, of course, restricted to the limited and often non- testimonial record available to the district court when it granted or denied the injunction motion. The district court's findings supporting its order granting or denying a permanent injunction may differ from its findings at the preliminary injunction stage because by then presentation of all the evidence has been completed. Then too, our determination whether its subsequent findings are clearly erroneous may differ from our view taken at the preliminary stage.

*Zepeda v. INS,* 753 F.2d 719, 723-724 (9th Cir. 1985) (emphasis added). Recognizing the limitations we face, and applying the appropriately deferential level of scrutiny to the district court's findings, the Andersons' contentions can be dealt with without any difficulty.

The Andersons claim that the district court's finding of reckless indifference was clearly erroneous because they had conducted extensive due diligence before becoming involved with Sterling. The district court was skeptical of the Andersons' claim because extensive due diligence likely would have brought to light the scheme's fraudulent nature.fn5 More importantly, the Andersons' assertion evidences a clear misunderstanding of the relevant standard for personal liability on the part of corporate principals for corporate misconduct. The extent of an individual's involvement in a fraudulent scheme alone is sufficient to establish the requisite knowledge for personal restitutionary liability. See *FTC v. Sharp*, 782 F. Supp. 1445, 1450 (D. Nev. 1991); *FTC v. Amy Travel Service, Inc.*, 875 F.2d 564, 574 (7th Cir. 1989) ("Also, the degree of participation in business affairs is probative of knowledge.") The Andersons' control of Financial, the chief telemarketer of Sterling and the media units, establishes strong evidence of the Andersons' knowledge. See *Sharp*, 782 F. Supp. at 1450 ("Here, Hall was a principal in, and president of MEHA, the chief broker of White Rock mines. Hall was deeply involved in the marketing of White Rock for around two and a half years. Thus, there is strong evidence that Hall knew his representations were false.").

> fn5 The district court found the Andersons' due diligence efforts to be extremely deficient. See Opinion and Order, entered and served May 22, 1998, at 2-3. The only reliable information concerning actual sales by Sterling was obtained five months after the Andersons began selling the media units for Sterling. Nor did the Andersons conduct continuing diligence efforts to ensure that the media units were profitable investments rather than the Ponzi scheme that they proved to be. Id. Although the Andersons emphasize what they feel were adequate due diligence efforts, they fail to respond in any way to the specific deficiencies noted by the district court. Our review of the record indicates that there is more than sufficient evidence to support the district court's findings and nothing approaching what would be necessary for us to conclude that the district court's

findings were clearly erroneous, given the level of deference afforded a district court's findings in connection with a preliminary injunction.

Even though the Andersons claim to have relied on their due diligence efforts, ample evidence, at least for preliminary injunctive relief, supports the district court's conclusion that in light of their central involvement in the media unit scheme the Andersons were at a minimum recklessly indifferent to the truth of the representations Financial was making regarding the profit potential of the media unit investments. See id; see also *Pantron I Corporation,* 33 F.3d at 1104 ("Given the overwhelming evidence that no scientific support existed for the product's efficacy claims, Lederman could not have failed to know that the scientific support claims were false unless he intentionally avoided the truth.").

The district court found that the promised yields on the media unit investments were so extraordinary that the Andersons should have been suspicious of the investment scheme. The Andersons claim that the district court miscalculated the promised yield on the media units. Instead of the 1000% annualized yield that the district court found would be necessary to earn the promised returns to the investors, they claim that under a profit-margin per-item analysis, the media units only had to yield a more modest 50% return in 60 to 90 days in order to deliver the promised yields—an annualized return of 200% to 300%. The Andersons seem to believe that these more modest returns on the media unit investments were so reasonable that they were not required to conduct more extensive due diligence. Perhaps the Andersons' telemarketers were able to convince their victims that Sterling could sell enough water-filled barbells and talking pet name tags to deliver 50% returns on their investments in 60 to 90 days, but the Andersons have failed to convince us that the district court erred in finding that experienced business persons like the Andersons should have conducted greater due diligence efforts before representing to potential investors that the investment would yield 50% returns in a mere 60 to 90 days. Consequently, we cannot conclude, at least at this preliminary stage of the proceeding, that the district court clearly erred when it found that " [t]he Andersons had experience in the investment business, and should have been highly suspect of promises of such yields [on the media unit investments]. Yet they fell woefully short in verifying the legitimacy of the venture they were promoting." Opinion and Order, entered and served May 22, 1998, at 2. Therefore, we find that the Commission has shown a sufficient likelihood of succeeding in holding the Andersons personally liable for the actions of Financial to warrant preliminary relief.

B. Balance of the Equities

The Andersons also argue that the district court ignored the hardships borne by the Andersons and Financial because of the issuance of the preliminary injunction. This argument ignores the fact that the district court released monies to pay Inter Com's operating expenses,fn6 to pay Inter Com's employees, and to pay for the Andersons' living expenses and attorneys' fees. Therefore the burden of the preliminary injunction, although not insubstantial, is not as great as the Andersons claim. We find that the district court did not clearly err in balancing the equities involved in this case.

fn6 When the temporary restraining order was granted, the Andersons had already discontinued their involvement with Sterling. They were operating a new telemarketing company, Inter Com, in the same office in which they had operated Financial.

Under this Circuit's precedents, "when a district court balances the hardships of the public interest against a private interest, the public interest should receive greater weight." *FTC v. World Wide Factors, Ltd.*, 882 F.2d 344, 347 (9th Cir. 1989); see also *Warner Communications, Inc.*, 742 F.2d at 1165. Obviously, the public interest in preserving the illicit proceeds of the media unit-scheme for restitution to the victims is great.

Incredibly, the Andersons assert that "the district court did not find that there was a likelihood of asset dissipation." Appellants' Reply Brief at 7. This astounding assertion is made even in light of the clear finding of the district court that " [t]here is a substantial likelihood that, absent the continuation of the asset freeze, the Enjoined Defendants will conceal, dissipate, or otherwise divert their assets, thereby defeating the possibility of the Court granting effective final relief in the form of equitable monetary relief for consumers." Preliminary Injunction, entered and served May 22, 1998, at 2. Given the Andersons' history of spiriting their commissions away to a Cook Islands trust, which was intentionally designed to frustrate United States courts' powers to grant effective relief to prevailing parties, the district court's finding regarding the likelihood of dissipation is far from clearly erroneous.

Based on our review of the record, the district court did not clearly err in balancing the equities in this case simply because the court concluded that the important public interest in preserving the Andersons' steep commissions from the Ponzi scheme was more important than the private interests, the harm to which was minimized by the district court's release of monies to pay particular expenses. Therefore, we find that the Commission has adequately shown that the balance of the equities warrants preliminary injunctive relief.

C. Mootness

The Andersons also contend that their cessation of sales for Sterling mooted the need for injunctive relief. In making this contention, the Andersons exhibit a startling misunderstanding of the nature of the preliminary relief that the district court actually granted. At a minimum, the Andersons' cessation of sales has no bearing on the need to repatriate the assets they have secreted off to the Cook Islands. More importantly, however, their argument mischaracterizes the law to such a degree that they are advocating a legal proposition that is precisely opposite the rule established by our precedents. As such, we conclude that the Commission's need for injunctive relief has not become moot.

The Andersons' first difficulty arises from their misunderstanding of the preliminary relief that the district court actually granted the Commission. The preliminary injunction contains both a prohibitory component and a mandatory component. In relevant part, the prohibitory component prohibited the Andersons from (1) engaging in certain types of business practices, (2) destroying any of their financial records, or (3) dissipating any of their assets. In relevant part, the mandatory component of the preliminary injunction required the Andersons to (1) prepare and deliver financial reports to the Commission's counsel, and (2) transfer to the United States all funds and assets held in foreign countries. While the Andersons' cessation of sales might possibly effect the need to restrain them from engaging in prohibited business practices, it could in no way affect the need to have the Andersons repatriate their assets from the Cook Islands. Therefore, the Andersons' cessation of sales for Sterling has not rendered moot the Commission's need for the mandatory component of the preliminary injunction.

The Andersons also appear to misunderstand the legal significance of their voluntary cessation of sales for Sterling in terms of the prohibitory aspect of the preliminary injunction. The Andersons contend that " [v]oluntary cessation of an unlawful course of conduct precludes the issuance of an injunction if there is no cognizable danger of recurrent violations." Appellants' Opening Brief at 28. Contrary to the Andersons' assertion, however, it is actually well-settled "that an action for an injunction does not become moot merely because the conduct complained of was terminated, if there is a possibility of recurrence, since otherwise the defendant's would be free to return to [their] old ways." *FTC v. American Standard Credit Systems, Inc*. 874 F. Supp. 1080, 1087 (C.D. Cal. 1994) (quoting *Allee v. Medrano*, 416 U.S. 802, 811 (1974)) (internal citations omitted) (emphasis added).

In part, the Andersons' misunderstanding may involve a misunderstanding of the difference between the effect of the perpetrator's conduct, as compared to the victim's conduct, on the need for injunctive relief. The difference is that the victim can moot her need for injunctive relief by her own conduct, but the alleged wrongdoer cannot moot the need for injunctive relief as easily. This confusion becomes apparent from the cases upon which the Andersons rely. If an employee leaves the employ of an employer, she cannot obtain injunctive relief to prevent her former employer from engaging in future retaliation in the workplace. See *Taylor v. Resolution Trust Corp.*, 56 F.3d 1497, 1502 (D.C. Cir.

1995). It would obviously be a different case if an employer claimed that an injunction to prevent future retaliation against current employees was no longer necessary because the employer had stopped retaliating against its employees in the workplace.

It is possible, of course, that a defendant's conduct can moot the need for injunctive relief, but the "test for mootness in cases such as this is a stringent one." *United States v. Concentrated Phosphate Export Ass'n., Inc.*, 393 U.S. 199, 203 (1968). The reason that the defendant's conduct, in choosing to voluntarily cease some wrongdoing, is unlikely to moot the need for injunctive relief is that the defendant could simply begin the wrongful activity again: "Mere voluntary cessation of allegedly illegal conduct does not moot a case; if it did, the courts would be compelled to leave `[t]he defendant … free to return to his old ways.' " *Id.* (quoting *United States v. W.T. Grant Co.*, 345 U.S. 629, 632 (1953)).

The Andersons contend that they have satisfied their burden because "[t]he FTC did not offer any admissible evidence that the Andersons were likely to repeat any wrongful conduct." Appellants' Opening Brief at 28. This asserted failure on the part of the Commission, however, is not sufficient to satisfy the Andersons' burden of establishing that the need for injunctive relief has become moot as a result of their own conduct.fn7 The standard for the voluntary cessation exception to mootness is "whether the defendant is free to return to its illegal action at any time." *Public Utilities Comm'n of California v. Federal Energy Regulatory Comm'n*, 100 F.3d 1451, 1460 (9th Cir. 1996). In order to meet their burden, the Andersons must show that "subsequent events [have] made it absolutely clear that the allegedly wrongful behavior cannot reasonably be expected to recur." *Norman-Bloodsaw v. Lawrence Berkeley Laboratory*, 135 F.3d 1260, 1274 (9th Cir. 1998) (internal quotation omitted); cf. *Lindquist v. Idaho State Bd. of Corrections*, 776 F.2d 851, 854 (9th Cir. 1985) (A case may become moot as a result of voluntary cessation of wrongful conduct only if "interim relief or events have completely and irrevocably eradicated the effects of the alleged violation."). The Andersons allege nothing that would suggest that it is "absolutely clear" that their wrongful activities are not reasonably likely to recur. Because they have failed to satisfy their burden, we cannot conclude that the need for injunctive relief is moot solely because of the Andersons' cessation of their unlawful conduct.

> fn7 Because the Andersons have failed to satisfy their burden of proving that they are not likely to resume engaging in illegal telemarketing activities, we do not decide today the merits of the Andersons' assertion that the Commission has failed to "offer any admissible evidence that the Andersons were likely to repeat any wrongful conduct." Nevertheless, we do note that one of the Andersons' complaints about the preliminary injunction is that it disrupted the operations of the Andersons' new telemarketing project, Inter Com. According to the Andersons, Inter Com is involved with pre-paid residential telephone service rather than the sale of media units. Inter Com apparently is involved with Tel Com Plus, which was subject to at least one state cease and desist order. At this point, the factual record is insufficient for us to decide whether the Andersons' involvement in another fraudulent telemarketing scheme could provide a sufficient independent basis for the prohibitory aspect of the preliminary injunction.

In light of our conclusions regarding the Andersons' various challenges to the propriety of the district court's granting the Commission preliminary injunctive relief, we conclude that the district court did not abuse its discretion in issuing the preliminary injunction, based on the factual record available at such a preliminary stage of the proceeding.

III

The next issue on appeal is the district court's finding the Andersons in contempt for refusing to repatriate the assets in their Cook Islands trust.fn8 We review a district court's civil contempt order for an abuse of discretion. *Hilao v. Estate of Marcos*, 103 F.3d 762, 764 (9th Cir. 1996). We review the district court's findings of fact in connection with the civil contempt adjudication for clear error. *Reliance Ins. Co. v. Mast Constr. Co.*, 84 F.3d 372, 375 (10th Cir. 1996). We review a district court's findings in connection with rejecting an impossibility defense for clear error. See *Fortin v. Commissioner of Mass. Dep't of Pub. Welfare*, 692 F.2d 790, 797 (1st Cir. 1982) (affirming contempt order when district court's finding that compliance was not impossible was not clearly erroneous). Based on the record before us, we find that the district court did not abuse its discretion in holding the Andersons in contempt.

> fn8 We have interlocutory appellate jurisdiction over the district court's adjudication of civil contempt where it is incident to an appeal from a preliminary injunction. See *Diamontiney v. Borg*, 918 F.2d 793, 796-97 (9th Cir. 1990).

The standard for finding a party in civil contempt is well settled:

The moving party has the burden of showing by clear and convincing evidence that the contemnors violated a specific and definite order of the court. The burden then shifts to the contemnors to demonstrate why they were unable to comply.

*Stone v. City and County of San Francisco*, 968 F.2d 850, 856 n.9 (9th Cir. 1992) (citations omitted).

The temporary restraining order required the Andersons, in relevant part, to "transfer to the territory of the United States all funds, documents and assets in foreign countries held either: (1) by them; (2) for their benefit; or (3) under their direct or indirect control, jointly or singly." Temporary Restraining Order, entered and served April 23, 1998, at 8. These provisions were continued in the preliminary injunction. See Preliminary Injunction, entered and served May 22, 1998, at 9. It is undisputed that the Andersons are beneficiaries of an irrevocable trust established under the laws of the Cook Islands. The Andersons do not dispute that the trust assets have not been repatriated to the United States. Instead, the Andersons claim that compliance with the temporary restraining order is impossible because the trustee, in accordance with the terms of the trust, will not repatriate the trust assets to the United States.

<u>A party's inability to comply with a judicial order constitutes a defense to a charge of civil contempt. See *United States v. Rylander*, 460 U.S. 752, 757(1983) ("While the court is bound by the enforcement order, it will not be blind to evidence that compliance is now factually impossible. Where compliance is impossible, neither the moving party nor the court has any reason to proceed with the civil contempt action."). The Andersons claim that the refusal of the foreign trustee to repatriate the trust assets to the United States, which apparently was the goal of the trust, makes their compliance with the preliminary injunction impossible.</u>

Although the Andersons assert that their "inability to comply with a judicial decree is a complete defense to a charge of civil contempt, regardless of whether the inability to comply is self-induced," Appellants' Reply Brief at 12 (emphasis added), we are not certain that the Andersons' inability to comply in this case would be a defense to a finding of contempt. It is readily apparent that the Andersons' inability to comply with the district court's repatriation order is the intended result of their own conduct—their inability to comply and the foreign trustee's refusal to comply appears to be the precise goal of the Andersons' trust.fn9 The Andersons claim that they created their trust as part of an "asset protection plan." See Appellant's Opening Brief at 36. These "[s]o called asset protection trusts are designed to shield wealth by moving it to a foreign jurisdiction that does not recognize U.S. judgments or other legal processes, such as asset freezes." Debra Baker, Island Castaway, ABA Journal, October 1998, at 55. The "asset protection" aspect of these foreign trusts arises from the ability of people, such as the Andersons, to frustrate and impede the United States courts by moving their assets beyond those courts' jurisdictions:

Perhaps most importantly, situs courts typically ignore United States courts' demands to repatriate trust assets to the United States. A situs court will not enforce a United States order from a state court compelling the turnover of trust assets to a creditor that was defrauded under United States law, or assets that were placed into a self-settled spendthrift trust.

James T. Lorenzetti, The Offshore Trust: A Contemporary Asset Protection Scheme, 102 Com. L. J. 138, 143-144 (1997). Because these asset protection trusts move the trust assets beyond the jurisdiction of domestic courts, often times all that remains within the jurisdiction is the physical person of the defendant. Because the physical person of the defendant remains subject to domestic courts' jurisdictions, courts could normally utilize their contempt powers to force a defendant to return the assets to their jurisdictions. Recognizing this risk, asset protection trusts typically are designed so that a defendant can assert that compliance with a court's order to repatriate the trust assets is impossible:

Another common issue is whether the client may someday be in the awkward position of either having to repatriate assets or else be held in contempt of court. A well-drafted [asset protection trust ] would, under such a circumstance, make it impossible for the client to repatriate assets held by the trust. Impossibility of performance is a complete defense to a civil contempt charge.

Barry S. Engel, Using Foreign Situs Trusts For Asset Protection Planning, 20 Est. Plan. 212, 218 (1993).

> fn9 The Andersons' trust created the circumstances in which a foreign trustee would refuse to repatriate assets to the United States by means of so-called duress provisions. Under the trust agreement, an event of duress includes " [t]he issuance of any order, decree or judgment of any court or tribunal in any part of the world which in the opinion of the protector will or may directly or indirectly, expropriate, sequester, levy, lien or in any way control, restrict or prevent the free disposal by a trustee of any monies, investments or property which may from time to time be included in or form part of this trust and any distributions therefrom." Trust Agreement at 3. Upon the happening of an event of duress, the trust agreement provides that the Andersons would be terminated as co-trustees, so that control over the trust assets would appear to be exclusively in the hands of a foreign trustee, beyond the jurisdiction of a United States court:

Notwithstanding any other provision contained in this deed any trustee hereof shall automatically cease to be a trustee upon the happening of an event of duress within the territory where such trustee is ... resident (in the case of an individual) and upon ceasing to be a trustee pursuant to this clause such trustee shall be divested of title to the property of this trust which shall automatically vest in the remaining or continuing trustee (if any) located in a territory not having an event of duress and the form for administration of this trust shall notwithstanding any other provision in this deed be deemed to be the place of residence or incorporation (if a corporation) of such continuing trustee.

Trust Agreement at 17 (emphasis added).

**<u>Given that these offshore trusts operate by means of frustrating domestic courts' jurisdiction, we are unsure that we would find that the Andersons' inability to comply with the district court's order is a defense to a civil contempt charge.</u>** We leave for another day the resolution of this more difficult question because we find that the Andersons have not satisfied their burden of proving that compliance with the district court's repatriation order was impossible. It is well established that a party petitioning for an adjudication that another party is in civil contempt does not have the burden of showing that the other party has the capacity to comply with the court's order. See *NLRB v. Trans Ocean Export Packing, Inc.*, 473 F.2d 612, 616 (9th Cir. 1973). Instead, the party asserting the impossibility defense must show "categorically and in detail" why he is unable to comply. Id.; See also Rylander, 460 U.S. at 757 ("It is settled, however, that in raising this defense, the defendant has a burden of production.").

In the asset protection trust context, moreover, the burden on the party asserting an impossibility defense will be particularly high because of the likelihood that any attempted compliance with the court's orders will be merely a charade rather than a good faith effort to comply. Foreign trusts are often designed to assist the settlor in avoiding being held in contempt of a domestic court while only feigning compliance with the court's orders:

Finally, the settlor should be aware that, although his trust will probably prove unassailable by domestic creditors, he may face minor hassles while defending his trust in court. In particular, if a creditor attacks an offshore trust in United States court, the settlor may face contempt of court orders during the proceedings… . [T]here is a possibility that the court will … order the settlor to collect his assets from the trust and turn them over to the court. If the settlor does not comply with these orders, a court may hold him in contempt. However, there are ways around such a conflict…. [T]he settlor could comply with the court order and 'order' his trustee to turn over the funds, knowing full well that the trustee will not comply with his request. Thereby, the settlor would technically comply with the court's orders, escape contempt of court charges, and still rest assured that his assets will remain protected.

James T. Lorenzetti, The Offshore Trust: A Contemporary Asset Protection Scheme, 102 Com. L. J. 138, 158 (1997). With foreign laws designed to frustrate the operation of domestic courts and foreign trustees acting in concert with domestic persons to thwart the United States courts, the domestic courts will have to be especially chary of accepting a defendant's assertions that repatriation or other compliance with a court's order concerning a foreign trust is impossible. Consequently, the burden on the defendant of proving impossibility as a defense to a contempt charge will be especially high.

Given these considerations, we cannot find that the district court clearly erred in finding that the Andersons' compliance with the repatriation order was not impossible because the Andersons remain in control of their Cook Islands trust. In finding the Andersons in civil contempt, the district court rejected the Andersons' impossibility defense, specifically finding that the Andersons "in the judgment of the Court [and] from the evidence that I've heard are in control of this trust." Transcript of June 17, 1998 Hearing Regarding Plaintiff's Motion for Civil Contempt, p. 30. Because we only review a district court's findings in connection with rejecting an impossibility defense for clear error, we will treat the district court's finding that the Andersons were in control of their trust as a finding of fact, subject only to the clearly erroneous standard of review. Based upon the record before us, we find that the district court's finding that compliance with the repatriation order was possible because the Andersons remain in control of their trust was not clearly erroneous.

The Andersons claim that they have "demonstrated to the district court 'categorically and in detail' that they cannot comply with the repatriation section of the preliminary injunction." Appellants' Reply Brief at 13. The district court was not convinced and neither are we. While it is possible that a rational person would send millions of dollars overseas and retain absolutely no control over the assets, we share the district court's skepticism. The district court found, notwithstanding the Andersons' protestations, that

As I look at the totality of the scheme of what I see before me at this time, I have no doubt that the Andersons can if they wish to correct this problem and provide the means of putting these funds in a position that they can be accountable if the final determination of the Court is that the funds should be returned to those who made these payments.

Transcript of June 9, 1998 Hearing Regarding Plaintiff's Motion for Civil Contempt, p. 18.

We cannot say that this finding was clearly erroneous. The Andersons had previously been able to obtain in excess of $1 million from the trust in order to pay their taxes. Given their ability to obtain, with ease, such large sums from the trust, we share the district court's skepticism regarding the Andersons' claim that they cannot make the trust assets subject to the court's jurisdiction.

Moreover, beyond this general skepticism concerning the Andersons' lack of control over their trust, the specifics of the Andersons' trust indicate that they retained control over the trust assets. These offshore trusts allow settlors, such as the Andersons, significant control over the trust assets by allowing the settlor to act as a co-trustee or "protector" of the trust. See Debra Baker, Island Castaway, ABA Journal, October 1998, at 56 ("Further, an offshore trust, may allow settlors to maintain significant control over their assets. Trusts can include co-trustees in the United States to watch over the actions of the foreign trustees, and settlors can name anyone, including themselves, as 'protectors' to oversee the trustees and veto their actions if necessary."). When the settlors retain this type of control, however, they can jeopardize the asset protection scheme because they will be subject to a U.S. court's personal jurisdiction and be forced to exercise their control to repatriate the assets. See id. ("If litigation is threatened, the protector and the co-trustee can resign so that no one within the personal jurisdiction of a federal or state court has control over the assets of the trust.").

[14] The district court's finding that the Andersons were in control of their trust is well supported by the record given that the Andersons were the protectors of their trust. A protector has significant powers to control an offshore trust. See Gideon Rothschild, "Establishing and Drafting Offshore Asset Protection Trusts," 23 Est. Plan. 65, 70 (1996) ("The use of a trust protector or advisor is common among foreign trusts. This person ... has the power to replace trustees and veto certain actions by the trustees."). A protector can be compelled to exercise control over a trust to repatriate assets if the protector's powers are not drafted solely as the negative powers to veto trustee decisions or if the protector's powers are not subject to the anti-duress provisions of the trust. See *id.* ("The protector's powers should generally be drafted as negative powers and subject to the anti-duress provisions to protect against an order compelling the protector to exercise control over the trust."). The Andersons' trust gives them affirmative powers to appoint new trustees and makes the anti-duress provisions subject to the protectors' powers, fn10 therefore; they can force the foreign trustee to repatriate the trust assets to the United States.

fn10 For example, the trust provides the protectors with discretion to conclusively determine that an event of duress has not occurred: "For the purpose of determining whether an Event of Duress has occurred pursuant to paragraph (c) and paragraph (d) of this clause (1) (a) (vi) of this Deed, the written certificate of the Protector to that effect shall be conclusive." Trust Agreement at 3 (emphasis added).

Perhaps the most telling evidence of the Andersons' control over the trust was their conduct after the district court issued its temporary restraining order ordering the repatriation of the trust funds. The Andersons sent a notice to the foreign trustee, ordering it to repatriate the trust assets because the district court had issued a temporary restraining order. The foreign trustee removed the Andersons from their positions as co-trustees and refused to comply with the repatriation order. After the Andersons claimed that compliance with the repatriation provisions of the temporary restraining order was impossible, the Commission revealed to the court that the Andersons were the protectors of the trust. The Andersons immediately attempted to resign as protectors of the trust. This attempted resignation indicates that the Andersons knew that, as the protectors of the trust, they remained in control of the trust and could force the foreign trustee to repatriate the assets.fn11

> fn11 Although we have concentrated on the Andersons' capacity as protectors of the trust to support the district court's finding that the Andersons remain in control of the trust, we have not considered whether other facts might support the Andersons' continuing control over the trust, regardless of who is the protector of the trust. The Andersons attempted to resign their position as protectors and that attempt appears to have failed. If the Andersons have in fact resigned their position as protectors, they may still remain in control of the trust. We have not resolved this issue at this time because the Andersons have conceded that they are the protectors of the trust.

The Andersons contend that even though they are the protectors of the trust, it is impossible for them to repatriate the trust assets. The Andersons' argument, that "[t]here is a misstep in the FTC's logic, "Appellants' Reply Brief at 17, ignores the fact that they bear the burden of proving impossibility, not the Commission. Their pointing to a few provisions of the trust, alone, fn12 is insufficient to carry their burden or to establish that the district court's finding that they remain in control of their trust was clearly erroneous.fn13 Because we see no clear error in the district court's finding that the Andersons remain in control of their trust and could repatriate the trust assets, the district court did not abuse its discretion in holding them in contempt. We, therefore, affirm the district court's finding the Andersons in contempt. <u>Given the nature of the Andersons' so-called "asset protection" trust, which was designed to frustrate the power of United States' courts to enforce judgments, there may be little else that a district court judge can do besides exercise its contempt powers to coerce people like the Andersons into removing the obstacles they placed in the way of a court. Given that the Andersons' trust is operating precisely as they intended, we are not overly sympathetic to their claims and would be hesitant to overly-restrict the district court's discretion, and thus legitimize what the Andersons have done.</u>

Fn12 The district court excluded evidence that the Andersons claimed supported their impossibility defense. The Andersons did not challenge this evidentiary ruling at all until their Reply Brief. Accordingly, we will not consider the propriety of the district court's exclusion of the Andersons' evidence concerning impossibility. See *All Pacific Trading, Inc. v. Vessel M/V Hanjin Yosu*, 7 F.3d 1427, 1434 (9th Cir. 1993). Moreover, what little the Andersons say in their Reply Brief cannot be considered an adequate argument challenging the district court's evidentiary ruling. From the Andersons' meager assertions, it is unclear what their challenge to the district court's ruling would be.

Fn13 The provisions of the trust also make clear that the Andersons' position as protectors gives them control over the trust. In provisions of the trust agreement that the Andersons conveniently fail to reference, the trust agreement makes clear that the Andersons, as protectors, have the power to determine whether or not an event of duress has occurred: "For the purpose of determining whether an Event of Duress has occurred pursuant to paragraph (c) and paragraph (d) of this clause (1) (a) (vi) of this Deed, the written certificate of the Protector to that effect shall be conclusive." Trust Agreement at 3 (emphasis added). Moreover, the very definition of an event of duress that the Andersons assert has occurred makes clear that whether or not an event of duress has occurred depends upon the opinion of the protector: "The issuance of any order, decree or judgment of any court or tribunal in any part of the world which in the opinion of the Protector will or may directly or indirectly, expropriate…." Trust Agreement at 3 (emphasis added). Therefore, notwithstanding the provisions of the trust agreement that the Andersons point to, it is clear that the Andersons could have ordered the trust assets repatriated simply by certifying to the foreign trustee that in their opinion, as protectors, no event of duress had occurred.

AFFIRMED.

# "The" Lawrence Case

*In re Lawrence,* 227 B.R. 907 (Bankr. S.D. Fla. (1998).

Lawrence set up and funded an IAPT weeks after an arbitration award against him for over $20m. He then filed bankruptcy. The court discredited his testimony and found that he still had control over the trust, including the power to repatriate its assets. Lawrence was held in contempt and jailed. Lawrence remained in jail for about six years, after which time he was released by the court, based on a ruling that there was no realistic possibility that Lawrence would comply with the order for repatriation. [See §5:52.]

# SAMPLE FEE AGREEMENT

**Example**

LIMITED SCOPE REPRESENTATION AGREEMENT

TO THE CLIENT: THIS IS A LEGALLY BINDING CONTRACT. PLEASE READ IT CAREFULLY AND MAKE CERTAIN THAT YOU UNDERSTAND ALL OF THE TERMS AND CONDITIONS. YOU MAY TAKE THIS CONTRACT HOME WITH YOU, REVIEW IT WITH ANOTHER ATTORNEY IF YOU WISH, AND ASK ANY QUESTIONS YOU MAY HAVE BEFORE SIGNING.

EMPLOYMENT OF A LAWYER FOR LIMITED SCOPE REPRESENTATION REQUIRES THAT THE LAWYER AND CLIENT CAREFULLY AND THOROUGHLY REVIEW THE DUTIES AND RESPONSIBILITIES EACH WILL ASSUME. ANY LIMITED REPRESENTATION AGREEMENT SHOULD DESCRIBE, IN DETAIL, THE LAWYER'S DUTIES IN THE CLIENT'S INDIVIDUAL CASE.

To help you in litigation, you and a lawyer may agree that the lawyer will represent you in the entire case, or only in certain parts of the case. "Limited representation" occurs if you retain a lawyer only for certain parts of the case. When a lawyer agrees to provide limited scope representation in litigation, the lawyer must act in your best interest and give you competent help. However, when a lawyer and you agree that the lawyer will provide only limited help,

- the lawyer DOES NOT HAVE TO GIVE MORE HELP than the lawyer and you agreed.
- the lawyer DOES NOT HAVE TO help with any other part of your case.

Date: _____

1. CLIENT,_____, retains LAWYER,_____,
to perform limited legal services only in the following matter:
_____.

2. Client seeks only the following services from Lawyer (check appropriate box):
   - ☐ Legal advice: office visits, telephone calls, fax, mail, e-mail
     - ☐ This is a one time consultation.
   - ☐ Advice about availability of alternative means of resolving the dispute, including mediation and arbitration, including helping you prepare for mediation or arbitration.
   - ☐ Evaluation of Client self-diagnosis of the case and advising Client about legal rights and responsibilities.
   - ☐ Guidance and procedural information for filing or serving court documents.
   - ☐ Review pleadings and other documents prepared by Client.
   - ☐ Review pleadings and other documents prepared by opposing party/counsel.
   - ☐ Suggest documents for you to prepare.
   - ☐ Draft pleadings, motions, and other documents.
     - List the documents to be prepared:_____

☐ Factual investigation: contacting witnesses, public record searches, in-depth interview of Client.
*If not checked, Client understands that Lawyer will not make any independent investigation of the facts and is relying entirely on Client's limited disclosure of the facts given the limited services provided.*
☐ Assistance with computer support programs.
List the programs to be used:_____
☐ Legal research and analysis.
List the issues to be researched and analyzed:_____
_____.
☐ Evaluate settlement options.
☐ Prepare discovery documents, such as interrogatories and requests for document production.
List the discovery documents to be prepared: _____
☐ Help you prepare for depositions.
☐ Planning for negotiations.
☐ Planning for court appearances.
☐ Standby telephone assistance during negotiations or settlement conferences.
☐ Referring Client to expert witnesses, other counsel, or other service providers.
☐ Counseling Client about an appeal.
☐ Procedural assistance with an appeal and assisting with substantive legal argument in an appeal.
☐ Provide preventive planning and/or schedule legal check-ups.
☐ Representing you in court but only for the following specific matters: _____
_____
____.
☐ Other:_____

3. Client shall pay the Lawyer for those limited services as follows (check agreed options):
　　☐ <u>Hourly Fee</u>. Client agrees to pay Lawyer for the agreed limited services at an hourly rate. The current hourly fee charged by Lawyer or Lawyer's law firm for services under this agreement is as follows:
　　　　i. Lawyer: $_____
　　　　ii. Associate: $_____
　　　　iii. Paralegal: $_____
　　　　iv. Law Clerk: $_____
　　Unless a different fee arrangement is established in clause "b" of this paragraph, the hourly fee shall be payable at the time of the service. Time will be charged in increments of one-tenth of an hour, rounded off for each particular activity to the nearest one-tenth of an hour.
　　☐ <u>Flat Fee</u>. Client will pay Lawyer a flat fee for the limited services listed of $____.
　　☐ <u>Retainer/Payment from Deposit</u>. Client will pay to Lawyer a retainer/deposit of $_____, to be received by Lawyer on or before_____, and to be applied against attorney fees and costs incurred by Client. This amount will be deposited by Lawyer in attorney trust account. Client authorizes Lawyer to

withdraw funds from the trust account to pay attorney fees and costs as they are incurred by Client. The deposit is refundable. If, at the termination of services under this agreement, the total amount incurred by Client for attorney fees and costs is less than the amount of the deposit, the difference will be refunded to Client. If the deposit is not enough to pay for the services provided by the attorney, Client shall pay any additional costs within thirty days of billing.

☐ Costs. Client shall pay Lawyer all out-of-pocket costs incurred in connection with this agreement, including long distance telephone and fax costs, photocopy expense, postage, filing fees, investigation fees, deposition fees, and the like unless paid directly by Client. Lawyer will not advance costs to third parties on Client's behalf and Lawyer will not pay filing fees, court costs, or other costs to any court unless specifically requested by Client and agreed upon in advance by Attorney. Advances will be repaid to Lawyer in addition to any attorney's fee charged as set forth above. Lawyer may request that the amount to be advanced or paid on behalf of Client be paid to Lawyer before any payment is made to a third party.

1. Lawyer representation begins with the signing of this Agreement and it terminated at the completion of the services requested and identified above or _____, whichever happens first.

5. Additional Services/Representation: Lawyer and Client may later determine that the Lawyer should provide additional limited services or assume full representation. Lawyer has no further obligation to Client after completing the above described limited legal services unless and until both Lawyer and Client enter into another written representation agreement. Lawyer may decline to provide additional services.

   a. If Lawyer agrees to provide additional services, those additional service should be specifically listed in an amendment to this agreement, signed and dated by both the Lawyer and Client.

   b. If Lawyer and Client agree that Lawyer will serve as Client's attorney of record on all matters related to handling Client's case, Client and Lawyer should indicate that agreement in an amendment to this agreement, signed and dated by both the Lawyer and Client.

   c. NEITHER LAWYER NOR CLIENT SHOULD RELY ON VERBAL DISCUSSIONS OR VERBAL AGREEMENTS WHEN CHANGING THE TERMS OF THE LAWYER'S RESPONSIBILITY FOR REPRESENTATION.

6. If any dispute between Client and Lawyer arises under this agreement concerning the payment of fees, Client and Lawyer will submit the dispute for fee dispute resolution.

7. Client has read this Limited Scope Representation Agreement and understands what it says. Client agrees that the legal services specified above are the only legal help Lawyer will provide. Client understands and agrees that:

- the Lawyer who is helping me with these services is not my lawyer for any other purpose and does not have to give me any more legal help;
- Lawyer is not promising any particular outcome;
- because of the limited services to be provided, Lawyer has limited his or her investigation of the facts as set out in specifically in this agreement; and
- if Lawyer goes to court with me, Lawyer does not have to help me afterwards, unless we both agree in writing.

Client understands that it is important that Lawyer, the opposing party, and the court handling my case be able to reach me at this address. I therefore agree that I will inform Lawyer or any Court and opposing party, if applicable, of any change in my permanent address or telephone number.

WE HAVE EACH READ THE ABOVE AGREEMENT BEFORE SIGNING IT.

Client:                                                Lawyer:


Printed Name: _____    Firm: _____
Address: _____    Address: _____

Phone: _____    Phone: _____

# ASSET PROTECTION "STRESS TEST"

THERE ARE BASICALLY THREE TYPES OF ASSETS THAT ARE HELD BY INDIVIDUALS THAT NEED A "STRESS TEST'- PSTR VALUES.

Stress test can perform a quantitative ranking based on how the asset is held. You can use Professor Paleveda's Stress Test Rating. PSTR value.

1. REAL ESATE: This is the most difficult asset to protect as it is not movable. Jurisdiction can be obtained over the asset where the real estate is located a/k/a "In Rem" Jurisdiction.
2. STOCKS, BONDS AND CASH: These assets are intangible asset and are portable.
3. PERSONAL RESIDENCE: This asset is difficult to move and you generally rely on your state's Homestead Act.

A Stress test will list all the assets and do an analysis of the risk of loss on these assets. In many cases, the risk of loss depends on the title as to how the assets are held. For example:
1. Stocks and bonds held in a Defined benefit plan may have a stress test value of .95. Stocks and Bonds held in your brokerage account in your name would have a stress test value of .5.

|  | PSTR Value |
|---|---|
| Cash in your name | .5 |
| Cash in joint tenancy | .7 |
| Cash in tenancy by the entireties | .8 |
| Cash in an ERISA plan | .97 |
| | |
| Real estate in your name | .5 |
| Real estate in a FLP | .7 |
| Real estate in a corporation | .7 |
| Real estate in a DFPT | .8 |
| Real estate in a FAPT | .85 |
| | |
| Personal Residence in Florida | .95 |
| Personal Residence in Texas | .91 |

Once you have listed the assets and given them weight as to the net value of the assets, you can then assign a PSTR value. A value above .9 is Grade A planning, Value at .8 is Grade B, Value at .7 is Grade C, below .7 is failing which means tremendous exposure to a lawsuit. If you would like a copy of the PTSR system, please email me nick@nationalpensions.com

It is actually a simple diagnostic system that assigns quantifiable values to a persons net worth and you can use it for all your estate planning clients. Performing an asset protection "stress test" can be a very valuable tool for an estate planning attorney and their client.

Example 1: John owns a home in Florida worth $250,000. He has $700,000 in a retirement plan and $50,000 in a bank.

| Net assets | % of net worth | Stress test factor | Stress test |
|---|---|---|---|
| 250,000.00 | .25 | .95 | 2375 |
| 700,000.00 | .70 | .97 | 6790 |
| 50,000.00 | .05 | .5 | 25 |

$1,000,000               91.70 = A

Very little of Jon's assets are exposed to creditors.

Example 2:
Mary owns $700,000 at a bank in her name. Mary owns a house in Florida worth $150,000 and an IRA worth $100,000. Mary owns a lot worth $50,000.

| Net assets | % of net worth | Stress test factor | |
|---|---|---|---|
| 700,000.00 | .7 | .5 | 3500 |
| 150,000.00 | .15 | .95 | 1425 |
| 100,000.00 | .1 | .97 | 0970 |
| 50,000.00 | .05 | .5 | 0025 |

59.20 = F

Mary can find herself in dire straits if a lawsuit was to occur. Mary fails the stress test.

Diagnostic tools can help determine exposure. They are not a substitute for an attorney's judgment. For example if Mary is retired, her exposure goes down. If Mary is a business owner her exposure increases. There is also a cost to asset protection structures. However you can integrate Estate tax planning and income tax planning by creating a pension plan to offset these cost.

## Fuel Hedging in the Airline Industry: The Case of Southwest Airlines

*David Carter*

Oklahoma State University - Stillwater - Department of Finance

*Daniel A. Rogers*

Portland State University - School of Business Administration

*Betty J. Simkins*

Oklahoma State University - Stillwater - Department of Finance

July 2004

**Abstract:**

Set in June 2001, the case places the student in the role of Scott Topping, Director of Corporate Finance at Southwest Airlines. Scott is responsible for the airline's fuel hedging program. The case describes the importance of jet fuel hedging in the airline industry, the volatility of jet fuel prices, hedging strategies available to manage jet fuel price risk, and related issues. [Note: The time period of the case allows the instructor to discuss additional issues not specifically addressed in the case such as the impact of September 11th, 2001 terror attacks on the airline's hedging strategy and the collapse of Enron (e.g., counterparty credit risk in hedging).]

Southwest Airlines has a business model based on being a low cost provider and has been very successful at offering the lowest airfares in the industry. This business strategy has effectively resulted in a consistently increasing market share over the years.

A dominant factor on the expense side of its business is the cost of fuel. Fuel is the second largest expense behind labor. Most recently, fuel costs have reached the highest annual average over the six-year period from 1994 to 2000 at $0.7869 per gallon in 2000. This fact has led to the increased importance of minimizing fuel cost for 2001 and beyond. To mitigate the sensitivity to fuel prices, Southwest has consistently hedged its fuel usage but wants to reevaluate the strategies it employs. As listed in the case, the student is asked to evaluate the following hedging strategies: (1) doing nothing, (2) hedge using plain vanilla swaps, (3) hedge using options, (4) hedge using zero cost collars, and (5) hedge using futures contracts.

The case is intended for use in an advanced corporate finance course or risk management at the graduate level. However, the case can also be used in an undergraduate risk management course.

Daniel A. Rogers
Portland State University - School of
Business Administration ( email )
P.O. Box 751
Portland, OR 97207-0751
United States

    503-725-3790 (Phone)
503-725-5850 (Fax)

Betty J. Simkins
Oklahoma State University - Stillwater -
Department of Finance ( email )
336 Business Building
Stillwater, OK 74078-4011
United States

    405-744-8625 (Phone)
405-744-5180 (Fax)
HOME PAGE:
http://spears.okstate.edu/~simkins

© 2014 Social Science Electronic Publishing, Inc. All Rights Reserved.  FAQ  Terms of Use  Privacy Policy  Copyright  Contact Us

# Credit Risk Scoring Models

*Gabriele Sabato*

Group Risk Management, RBS ; University of Rome

February 2, 2010

**Abstract:**
Credit scoring models play a fundamental role in the risk management practice at most banks. They are used to quantify credit risk at counterparty or transaction level in the different phases of the credit cycle (e.g. application, behavioural, collection models). The credit score empowers users to make quick decisions or even to automate decisions and this is extremely desirable when banks are dealing with large volumes of clients and relatively small margin of profits at individual transaction level (i.e. consumer lending, but increasingly also small business lending). In this article, we analyze the history and new developments related to credit scoring models. We find that with the new Basel Capital Accord, credit scoring models have been remotivated and given unprecedented significance. Banks, in particular, and most financial institutions worldwide, have either recently developed or modified existing internal credit risk models to conform with the new rules and best practices recently updated in the market. Moreover, we analyze the key steps of the credit scoring model's lifecycle (i.e. assessment, implementation, validation) highlighting the main requirement imposed by Basel II. We conclude that banks that are going to implement the most advanced approach to calculate their capital requirements under Basel II will need to increase their attention and consideration of credit scoring models in the next future.

# Bear Stearns and the Seeds of its Demise

*Susan Chaplinsky*

University of Virginia - Darden School of Business

*Darden Case No. UVA-F-1574*

## Abstract:

This case is suitable for courses on corporate finance at the graduate or advanced undergraduate level that cover banking, financing, security design, capital structure, or capital markets. The case covers the events that led to the collapse of Bear Stearns's (Bear's) hedge funds in July 2007 and traces management's response to the situation through January 2008. These events include macroeconomic factors that fueled the housing boom, the growth of securitization, structured products, and credit default swaps, and the maturity mismatch of financial institutions' funding strategies. The case provides a rich setting for students to understand the increasingly interrelated nature of banking activities, which poses large systemic risk to the financial sector. Two key questions are posed: "What factors were responsible for the collapse of Bear's hedge funds?" and "Was the response by Bear's management adequate in light of the collapse and the credit problems that ensued?" John Corso is a hedge fund manager with large cash balances in a prime brokerage account at Bear. In January 2008, he receives a call from a senior Bear executive reassuring him that the firm is in good hands following a shakeup of top management. The previous summer, two Bear hedge funds collapsed as a result of their investments in collateralized debt obligations (CDOs) that were backed by subprime mortgages. As a longtime client of Bear, Corso must evaluate whether the steps taken by management have been sufficient to resolve its credit problems or whether now is the time to remove his funds from the firm.

# Modern Pension Fund Diversification

*Marty Anderson-et. Al.*

Government of Arizona - Arizona Public Service Personnel Retirement System (PSPRS) Trust

April 18, 2014

## Abstract:

The risk and return characteristics of a highly diversified investment portfolio are examined in an effort to best assess its potential by means that incorporate both conventional risk estimation and performance evaluation. Estimation of performance variability and downside risk often assumes a constant, stable, average covariance matrix of asset returns and only provides an indirect gauge of capacity for the downside compensation interplay between assets. Performance measurement allows for final conclusions to be drawn, but does not capture the structural characteristics leading to results, nor does it make a distinction between chance occurrence and structural bias. The Mahalanobis distance is employed in order to quantify both aspects simultaneously and document a contemporary shift in advanced pension trust management. The asset liability structures of pension trusts allow for unusually long time-horizons and managing agencies typically possess the resources necessary to select and maintain opaquely priced investments in a controlled fashion. A particular pension fund history, involving a period of transition from a conventional, strictly US-based mix of stocks, bonds, real estate and cash, to a more diversified set of eight additional asset classes, allows for discussion of first results and assessment of the trend towards diversification.

# Why Did U.S. Banks Invest in Highly-Rated Securitization Tranches?

*Isil Erel*

Ohio State University (OSU) - Department of Finance

*Taylor Nadauld*

Brigham Young University

*Rene M. Stulz*

Ohio State University (OSU) - Department of Finance ; National Bureau of Economic Research (NBER) ; European Corporate Governance Institute (ECGI)

July 25, 2011

*Fisher College of Business Working Paper Paper No. 2011-03-016*
*Charles A. Dice Center Working Paper No. 2011-16*
*ECGI - Finance Working Paper No. 313/2011*

**Abstract:**

We estimate holdings of highly-rated tranches of mortgage securitizations of American deposit-taking banks ahead of the credit crisis and evaluate hypotheses that have been advanced to explain these holdings. We find that holdings of highly-rated tranches were economically trivial for the typical bank, but banks with greater holdings performed more poorly during the crisis. Though univariate comparisons show that banks with large trading books had greater holdings, the holdings of highly-rated tranches are not higher for banks with large trading books in regressions that control for bank size. The ratio of highly-rated tranches holdings to assets increases with bank assets, but not for banks with more than $50 billion of assets. This evidence is inconsistent with explanations for holdings of highly-rated tranches that emphasize the incentives of banks deemed "too-big-to-fail". Further, the evidence does not provide support for "bad incentives" or "bad risk management" theories of holdings of highly-rated tranches. We find, however, that banks active in securitization held more highly-rated tranches. Such a result can be consistent with regulatory arbitrage as well as with securitizing banks holding highly-rated tranches to convince investors of the quality of these securities. Our evidence is more supportive of the latter hypothesis.

# UNITED STATES
# SECURITIES AND EXCHANGE COMMISSION
Washington, D.C. 20549

## FORM 10-Q

☒ Quarterly Report Pursuant to Section 13 or 15(d) of the Securities Exchange Act of 1934

For the quarterly period ended September 30, 2014

or

☐ Transition Report Pursuant to Section 13 or 15(d) of the Securities Exchange Act of 1934

Commission File No. 001- 34280

# American National Insurance Company
(Exact name of registrant as specified in its charter)

| Texas | 74-0484030 |
|---|---|
| (State or other jurisdiction of incorporation or organization) | (I.R.S. Employer Identification No.) |

**One Moody Plaza**
**Galveston, Texas 77550-7999**
(Address of principal executive offices) (Zip Code)

**(409) 763-4661**
(Registrant's telephone number, including area code)

Indicate by check mark whether the registrant (1) has filed all reports required to be filed by Section 13 or 15(d) of the Securities Exchange Act of 1934 during the preceding 12 months (or for such shorter period that the registrant was required to file such reports), and (2) has been subject to such filing requirements for the past 90 days.  ☒ Yes  ☐ No

Indicate by check mark whether the registrant has submitted electronically and posted on its corporate Web site, if any, every Interactive Data File required to be submitted and posted pursuant to Rule 405 of Regulation S-T (§229.405 of this chapter) during the preceding 12 months (or for such shorter period that the registrant was required to submit and post such files).  ☒ Yes  ☐ No

Indicate by check mark whether the registrant is a large accelerated filer, an accelerated filer, a non-accelerated filer or a smaller reporting company. See definitions of "large accelerated filer", "accelerated filer" and "smaller reporting company" in Rule 12b-2 of the Exchange Act:

Large accelerated filer ☒                           Accelerated filer              ☐
Non-accelerated filer  ☐                           Smaller reporting company ☐

Indicate by check mark whether the registrant is a shell company (as defined in Rule 12b-2 of the Exchange Act).  ☐ Yes  ☒ No

As of October 31, 2014, there were 26,871,942 shares of the registrant's voting common stock, $1.00 par value per share, outstanding.

Table of Contents

## AMERICAN NATIONAL INSURANCE COMPANY
## TABLE OF CONTENTS

### PART I – FINANCIAL INFORMATION

| | | |
|---|---|---|
| ITEM 1. | FINANCIAL STATEMENTS (Unaudited): | 3 |
| | Consolidated Statements of Financial Position as of September 30, 2014 and December 31, 2013 | 3 |
| | Consolidated Statements of Operations for the three and nine months ended September 30, 2014 and 2013 | 4 |
| | Consolidated Statements of Comprehensive Income (Loss) for the three and nine months ended September 30, 2014 and 2013 | 5 |
| | Consolidated Statements of Changes in Stockholders' Equity for the nine months ended September 30, 2014 and 2013 | 5 |
| | Consolidated Statements of Cash Flows for the nine months ended September 30, 2014 and 2013 | 6 |
| | Notes to the Unaudited Consolidated Financial Statements | 7 |
| ITEM 2. | MANAGEMENT'S DISCUSSION AND ANALYSIS OF FINANCIAL CONDITION AND RESULTS OF OPERATIONS | 32 |
| ITEM 3. | QUANTITATIVE AND QUALITATIVE DISCLOSURES ABOUT MARKET RISK | 51 |
| ITEM 4. | CONTROLS AND PROCEDURES | 51 |

### PART II – OTHER INFORMATION

| ITEM 1. | LEGAL PROCEEDINGS | 52 |
| ITEM 1A. | RISK FACTORS | 52 |
| ITEM 2. | UNREGISTERED SALES OF EQUITY SECURITIES AND USE OF PROCEEDS | 52 |
| ITEM 3. | DEFAULTS UPON SENIOR SECURITIES | 52 |
| ITEM 4. | MINE SAFETY DISCLOSURES | 52 |
| ITEM 5. | OTHER INFORMATION | 52 |
| ITEM 6. | EXHIBIT INDEX | 53 |

Table of Contents
**PART I—FINANCIAL INFORMATION**

ITEM 1. FINANCIAL STATEMENTS

**AMERICAN NATIONAL INSURANCE COMPANY**
**CONSOLIDATED STATEMENTS OF FINANCIAL POSITION**
(Unaudited and in thousands, except for share and per share data)

|  | September 30, 2014 | December 31, 2013 |
|---|---|---|
| **ASSETS** | | |
| Fixed maturity, bonds held-to-maturity, at amortized cost (Fair Value $8,826,253 and $8,823,068) | $ 8,364,731 | $ 8,491,347 |
| Fixed maturity, bonds available-for-sale, at fair value (Amortized cost $4,700,235 and $4,456,391) | 4,926,218 | 4,599,673 |
| Equity securities, at fair value (Cost $745,733 and $741,080) | 1,494,471 | 1,410,608 |
| Mortgage loans on real estate, net of allowance | 3,318,552 | 3,299,242 |
| Policy loans | 404,705 | 397,407 |
| Investment real estate, net of accumulated depreciation of $181,125 and $211,575 | 458,116 | 507,142 |
| Short-term investments | 346,343 | 495,386 |
| Other invested assets | 202,131 | 201,442 |
| Total investments | **19,515,267** | **19,402,247** |
| Cash and cash equivalents | 136,142 | 117,946 |
| Investments in unconsolidated affiliates | 335,419 | 341,012 |
| Accrued investment income | 198,559 | 194,830 |
| Reinsurance recoverables | 410,525 | 414,743 |
| Prepaid reinsurance premiums | 55,681 | 57,869 |
| Premiums due and other receivables | 294,678 | 279,929 |
| Deferred policy acquisition costs | 1,249,704 | 1,277,733 |
| Property and equipment, net | 119,259 | 107,070 |
| Current tax receivable | 4,403 | 18,507 |
| Other assets | 148,448 | 142,043 |
| Separate account assets | 992,615 | 970,954 |
| **Total assets** | **$23,460,700** | **$23,324,883** |
| **LIABILITIES** | | |
| Future policy benefits | | |
| Life | $ 2,736,156 | $ 2,677,213 |
| Annuity | 982,720 | 903,437 |
| Accident and health | 70,699 | 71,941 |

|  | | |
|---|---:|---:|
| Policyholders' account balances | 10,893,918 | 11,181,650 |
| Policy and contract claims | 1,289,997 | 1,297,646 |
| Unearned premium reserve | 779,934 | 739,878 |
| Other policyholder funds | 332,411 | 326,885 |
| Liability for retirement benefits | 143,400 | 160,853 |
| Notes payable | 109,349 | 113,849 |
| Deferred tax liabilities, net | 286,545 | 220,428 |
| Other liabilities | 433,855 | 456,818 |
| Separate account liabilities | 992,615 | 970,954 |
| **Total liabilities** | **19,051,599** | **19,121,552** |
| **STOCKHOLDERS' EQUITY** | | |
| Common stock, $1.00 par value,—Authorized 50,000,000 Issued 30,832,449 and 30,832,449, Outstanding 26,871,942 and 26,895,188 shares | 30,832 | 30,832 |
| Additional paid-in capital | 8,862 | 4,650 |
| Accumulated other comprehensive income | 504,338 | 413,712 |
| Retained earnings | 3,954,731 | 3,838,821 |
| Treasury stock, at cost | (101,941) | (97,441) |
| Total American National stockholders' equity | 4,396,822 | 4,190,574 |
| Noncontrolling interest | 12,279 | 12,757 |
| **Total stockholders' equity** | **4,409,101** | **4,203,331** |
| **Total liabilities and stockholders' equity** | **$23,460,700** | **$23,324,883** |

*See accompanying notes to the consolidated financial statements.*

**AMERICAN NATIONAL INSURANCE COMPANY**
**CONSOLIDATED STATEMENTS OF OPERATIONS**
(Unaudited and in thousands, except for share and per share data)

|  | Three months ended September 30, | | Nine months ended September 30, | |
|---|---:|---:|---:|---:|
|  | 2014 | 2013 | 2014 | 2013 |
| **PREMIUMS AND OTHER REVENUE** | | | | |
| Premiums | | | | |
|   Life | $ 79,492 | $ 75,278 | $ 224,165 | $ 215,479 |
|   Annuity | 34,661 | 23,412 | 148,250 | 89,733 |
|   Accident and health | 53,454 | 52,839 | 164,169 | 159,100 |
|   Property and casualty | 279,429 | 271,270 | 820,953 | 801,106 |
| Other policy revenues | 55,255 | 52,975 | 167,041 | 152,910 |
| Net investment income | 236,489 | 254,336 | 697,604 | 752,488 |
| Realized investment gains (losses) | (649) | 43,795 | 27,548 | 107,473 |
| Other-than-temporary impairments | (1,608) | (312) | (3,045) | (3,503) |
| Other income | 9,647 | 11,911 | 26,707 | 29,423 |
| **Total premiums and other revenues** | **746,170** | **785,504** | **2,273,392** | **2,304,209** |
| **BENEFITS, LOSSES AND EXPENSES** | | | | |
| Policyholder benefits | | | | |
|   Life | 83,740 | 83,821 | 257,505 | 246,896 |

|  |  |  |  |  |
|---|---:|---:|---:|---:|
| Annuity | 43,893 | 34,860 | 180,372 | 118,155 |
| Claims incurred |  |  |  |  |
|     Accident and health | 33,193 | 34,404 | 109,859 | 106,378 |
|     Property and casualty | 180,413 | 182,809 | 563,650 | 581,042 |
| Interest credited to policyholders' account balances | 83,746 | 98,862 | 258,952 | 309,738 |
| Commissions for acquiring and servicing policies | 97,608 | 94,504 | 299,992 | 273,360 |
| Other operating expenses | 118,002 | 128,115 | 357,043 | 381,850 |
| Change in deferred policy acquisition costs | 10,800 | 7,265 | 10,854 | 19,568 |
| **Total benefits, losses and expenses** | 651,395 | 664,640 | 2,038,227 | 2,036,987 |
| **Income (loss) before federal income tax and equity in earnings/losses of unconsolidated affiliates** | 94,775 | 120,864 | 235,165 | 267,222 |
| Less: Provision (benefit) for federal income taxes |  |  |  |  |
|     Current | 23,639 | 36,541 | 55,690 | 63,920 |
|     Deferred | 3,110 | (782) | 9,974 | 7,959 |
| Total provision (benefit) for federal income taxes | 26,749 | 35,759 | 65,664 | 71,879 |
| Equity in earnings (losses) of unconsolidated affiliates, net of tax | 2,735 | 121 | 10,405 | 9,774 |
| **Net income (loss)** | 70,761 | 85,226 | 179,906 | 205,117 |
| Less: Net income (loss) attributable to noncontrolling interest, net of tax | 2,877 | 2,613 | 1,883 | 4,364 |
| **Net income (loss) attributable to American National** | $ 67,884 | $ 82,613 | $ 178,023 | $ 200,753 |
| **Amounts available to American National common stockholders** |  |  |  |  |
| Earnings per share |  |  |  |  |
|     Basic | $ 2.53 | $ 3.08 | $ 6.64 | $ 7.49 |
|     Diluted | 2.52 | 3.07 | 6.61 | 7.46 |
| Cash dividends to common stockholders | 0.77 | 0.77 | 2.31 | 2.31 |
| Weighted average common shares outstanding | 26,805,535 | 26,780,313 | 26,800,835 | 26,789,564 |

|  | | | | |
|---|---|---|---|---|
| Weighted average common shares outstanding and dilutive potential common shares | 26,911,507 | 26,905,093 | 26,919,414 | 26,910,017 |

*See accompanying notes to the consolidated financial statements.*

4

## AMERICAN NATIONAL INSURANCE COMPANY
## CONSOLIDATED STATEMENTS OF COMPREHENSIVE INCOME (LOSS)
(Unaudited and in thousands)

|  | Three months ended September 30, | | Nine months ended September 30, | |
|---|---|---|---|---|
|  | 2014 | 2013 | 2014 | 2013 |
| Net income (loss) | $ 70,761 | $ 85,226 | $ 179,906 | $ 205,117 |
| Other comprehensive income (loss), net of tax | | | | |
|    Change in net unrealized gain (loss) on securities | (17,708) | 26,747 | 89,051 | 31,569 |
|    Foreign currency transaction and translation adjustments | (476) | (625) | (577) | (211) |
|    Defined pension benefit plan adjustment | 718 | 2,876 | 2,152 | 8,627 |
| Other comprehensive income (loss), net of tax | (17,466) | 28,998 | 90,626 | 39,985 |
| **Total comprehensive income (loss)** | **53,295** | **114,224** | **270,532** | **245,102** |
|    Less: Comprehensive income (loss) attributable to noncontrolling interest | 2,877 | 2,613 | 1,883 | 4,364 |
| **Total comprehensive income (loss) attributable to American National** | **$ 50,418** | **$ 111,611** | **$ 268,649** | **$ 240,738** |

## AMERICAN NATIONAL INSURANCE COMPANY
## CONSOLIDATED STATEMENTS OF CHANGES IN STOCKHOLDERS' EQUITY
(Unaudited and in thousands, except for per share data)

|  | Nine months ended September 30, | |
|---|---|---|
|  | 2014 | 2013 |
| **Common Stock** | | |
|    Balance at beginning and end of the period | $ 30,832 | $ 30,832 |
| **Additional Paid-In Capital** | | |
|    Balance as of January 1, | 4,650 | — |
|    Reissuance of treasury shares | 1,635 | 3,012 |
|    Income tax effect from restricted stock arrangement | — | 80 |
|    Amortization of restricted stock | 2,577 | 1,028 |
|      Balance at end of period | 8,862 | 4,120 |
| **Accumulated Other Comprehensive Income (Loss)** | | |
|    Balance as of January 1, | 413,712 | 242,010 |

|  | | |
|---|---:|---:|
| Other comprehensive income (loss) | 90,626 | 39,985 |
| Balance at end of the period | 504,338 | 281,995 |
| **Retained Earnings** | | |
| Balance as of January 1, | 3,838,821 | 3,653,280 |
| Net income (loss) attributable to American National | 178,023 | 200,753 |
| Cash dividends to common stockholders | (62,113) | (62,122) |
| Balance at end of the period | 3,954,731 | 3,791,911 |
| **Treasury Stock** | | |
| Balance as of January 1, | (97,441) | (98,286) |
| Reissuance (purchases) of treasury shares | (4,500) | 844 |
| Balance at end of the period | (101,941) | (97,442) |
| **Noncontrolling Interest** | | |
| Balance as of January 1, | 12,757 | 11,491 |
| Contributions | 478 | 456 |
| Distributions | (2,839) | (2,675) |
| Gain (loss) attributable to noncontrolling interest | 1,883 | 4,364 |
| Balance at end of the period | 12,279 | 13,636 |
| **Total Stockholders' Equity** | $ 4,409,101 | $ 4,025,052 |

*See accompanying notes to the consolidated financial statements.*

**AMERICAN NATIONAL INSURANCE COMPANY**
**CONSOLIDATED STATEMENTS OF CASH FLOWS**
(Unaudited and in thousands)

|  | Nine months ended September 30, | |
|---|---:|---:|
|  | **2014** | **2013** |
| **OPERATING ACTIVITIES** | | |
| Net income (loss) | $ 179,906 | $ 205,117 |
| Adjustments to reconcile net income (loss) to net cash provided by operating activities | | |
| Realized investment (gains) losses | (27,548) | (107,473) |
| Other-than-temporary impairments | 3,045 | 3,503 |
| Accretion (amortization) of discounts, premiums and loan origination fees | 6,316 | 4,460 |
| Net capitalized interest on policy loans and mortgage loans | (23,988) | (20,156) |
| Depreciation | 26,421 | 24,873 |
| Interest credited to policyholders' account balances | 258,952 | 309,738 |
| Charges to policyholders' account balances | (167,041) | (152,910) |
| Deferred federal income tax (benefit) expense | 9,974 | 7,959 |
| Equity in (earnings) losses of unconsolidated affiliates | (10,405) | (9,774) |
| Distributions from equity method investments | 679 | 18,925 |
| Changes in | | |
| Policyholder liabilities | 166,392 | 48,816 |
| Deferred policy acquisition costs | 10,854 | 19,568 |
| Reinsurance recoverables | 4,218 | 17,883 |
| Premiums due and other receivables | (15,189) | (26,248) |
| Prepaid reinsurance premiums | 2,188 | 4,945 |
| Accrued investment income | (3,729) | 3,630 |
| Current tax receivable/payable | 14,104 | 30,975 |

|  |  |  |
|---|---:|---:|
| Liability for retirement benefits | (17,453) | 8,093 |
| Other, net | (44,626) | (38,730) |
| **Net cash provided by (used in) operating activities** | **373,070** | **353,194** |
| **INVESTING ACTIVITIES** |  |  |
| Proceeds from sale/maturity/prepayment of |  |  |
| Held-to-maturity securities | 442,748 | 1,209,058 |
| Available-for-sale securities | 705,681 | 702,625 |
| Investment real estate | 45,843 | 84,371 |
| Mortgage loans | 421,023 | 446,480 |
| Policy loans | 41,331 | 43,911 |
| Other invested assets | 34,537 | 11,021 |
| Disposals of property and equipment | 2,571 | 674 |
| Distributions from unconsolidated affiliates | 49,403 | 22,834 |
| Payment for the purchase/origination of |  |  |
| Held-to-maturity securities | (356,452) | (856,086) |
| Available-for-sale securities | (883,346) | (737,342) |
| Investment real estate | (28,865) | (35,240) |
| Mortgage loans | (444,140) | (638,690) |
| Policy loans | (21,721) | (19,564) |
| Other invested assets | (14,376) | (13,690) |
| Additions to property and equipment | (13,038) | (17,958) |
| Contributions to unconsolidated affiliates | (40,333) | (94,078) |
| Change in short-term investments | 149,043 | (26,393) |
| Other, net | 3,834 | 8,561 |
| **Net cash provided by (used in) investing activities** | **93,743** | **90,494** |
| **FINANCING ACTIVITIES** |  |  |
| Policyholders' account deposits | 783,255 | 654,346 |
| Policyholders' account withdrawals | (1,162,898) | (1,164,806) |
| Change in notes payable | (4,500) | (49,258) |
| Dividends to stockholders | (62,113) | (62,122) |
| Proceeds from (payments to) noncontrolling interest | (2,361) | (2,219) |
| **Net cash provided by (used in) financing activities** | **(448,617)** | **(624,059)** |
| **NET INCREASE (DECREASE) IN CASH AND CASH EQUIVALENTS** | 18,196 | (180,371) |
| Beginning of the period | 117,946 | 303,008 |
| **End of period** | $ 136,142 | $ 122,637 |

*See accompanying notes to the consolidated financial statements.*

## NOTES TO THE CONSOLIDATED FINANCIAL STATEMENTS

### 1. NATURE OF OPERATIONS

American National Insurance Company and its consolidated subsidiaries (collectively "American National") offer a broad spectrum of insurance products, including individual and group life insurance, annuities, health insurance, and property and casualty insurance. Business is conducted in 50 states, the District of Columbia, Puerto Rico, Guam and American Samoa.

### 2. SUMMARY OF SIGNIFICANT ACCOUNTING POLICIES AND PRACTICES

The consolidated financial statements and notes thereto have been prepared in conformity with U.S. generally accepted accounting principles ("GAAP") and are reported in U.S. currency. American National consolidates entities that are wholly-owned and those in which American National owns less than 100% but controls, as well as variable interest entities in which American National is the primary beneficiary. Intercompany balances and transactions with consolidated entities have been eliminated. Investments in unconsolidated affiliates are accounted for using the equity method of accounting. Certain amounts in prior years have been reclassified to conform to current year presentation.

The interim consolidated financial statements and notes herein are unaudited and reflect all adjustments which management considers necessary for the fair presentation of the interim consolidated statements of financial position, operations, comprehensive income (loss), changes in stockholders' equity, and cash flows.

The interim consolidated financial statements and notes should be read in conjunction with the annual consolidated financial statements and notes thereto included in American National's Annual Report on Form 10-K as of and for the year ended December 31, 2013. The consolidated results of operations for the interim periods should not be considered indicative of results to be expected for the full year.

The preparation of the consolidated financial statements in conformity with GAAP requires the use of estimates and assumptions that affect the reported consolidated financial statement balances. Actual results could differ from those estimates.

### 3. RECENTLY ISSUED ACCOUNTING PRONOUNCEMENTS

**Adoption of New Accounting Standards**—The Financial Accounting Standards Board ("FASB") issued the following accounting guidance relevant to American National, including technical amendments and corrections to make the accounting standards easier to understand and fair value measurement easier to apply. Each became effective for American National on January 1, 2014 and, unless stated otherwise, did not have a material effect on the consolidated financial statements.

> Amended guidance for the recognition, measurement, and disclosure of obligations resulting from joint and several liability arrangements for which the total amount of the obligation within the scope of the guidance is fixed at the reporting date. The amended guidance requires the entity to measure obligations resulting from joint and several liability arrangements as the sum of the amount the reporting entity agreed with co-obligors to pay and any additional amounts it expects to pay on behalf of one or more co-obligors.

**Future Adoption of New Accounting Standards**—The FASB issued the following accounting standards relevant to American National:

> Guidance that allows investors to elect the use of proportional amortization method to account for investments in qualified affordable housing projects, if certain conditions are met. The new guidance replaces the effective yield method and allows an investor to amortize the cost of its investment, in proportion to the tax credits and other tax benefits it receives, to income tax expense. The guidance requires new disclosure for all investors for all investments in qualified affordable housing projects, regardless of the accounting method used for those investments.

> Guidance that will supersede most existing revenue recognition requirements in U.S. Generally Accepted Accounting Principles. The Standard will become effective for American National on January 1, 2017 and allows for both retrospective and prospective methods of

adoption. American National is in the process of determining the adoption method and is currently assessing the impact of this standard.

## 4. INVESTMENTS IN SECURITIES

The cost or amortized cost and fair value of investments in securities are shown below (in thousands):

|  | September 30, 2014 | | | |
|---|---|---|---|---|
|  | Cost or Amortized Cost | Gross Unrealized Gains | Gross Unrealized (Losses) | Fair Value |
| **Fixed maturity securities, bonds held-to-maturity** | | | | |
| U.S. states and political subdivisions | $ 327,022 | $ 25,144 | $ (67) | $ 352,099 |
| Foreign governments | 29,122 | 1,641 | — | 30,763 |
| Corporate debt securities | 7,636,327 | 453,220 | (40,292) | 8,049,255 |
| Residential mortgage-backed securities | 353,444 | 22,178 | (1,921) | 373,701 |
| Collateralized debt securities | 2,236 | 223 | — | 2,459 |
| Other debt securities | 16,580 | 1,396 | — | 17,976 |
| **Total bonds held-to-maturity** | **8,364,731** | **503,802** | **(42,280)** | **8,826,253** |
| **Fixed maturity securities, bonds available-for-sale** | | | | |
| U.S. treasury and government | 24,073 | 783 | — | 24,856 |
| U.S. states and political subdivisions | 746,801 | 33,661 | (2,940) | 777,522 |
| Foreign governments | 5,000 | 1,900 | — | 6,900 |
| Corporate debt securities | 3,866,518 | 206,396 | (16,342) | 4,056,572 |
| Residential mortgage-backed securities | 45,644 | 2,112 | (754) | 47,002 |
| Collateralized debt securities | 12,199 | 1,175 | (8) | 13,366 |
| **Total bonds available-for-sale** | **4,700,235** | **246,027** | **(20,044)** | **4,926,218** |
| **Equity securities** | | | | |
| Common stock | 722,015 | 734,419 | (3,791) | 1,452,643 |
| Preferred stock | 23,718 | 18,123 | (13) | 41,828 |
| **Total equity securities** | **745,733** | **752,542** | **(3,804)** | **1,494,471** |
| **Total investments in securities** | **$ 13,810,699** | **$1,502,371** | **$(66,128)** | **$15,246,942** |

|  | December 31, 2013 | | | |
|---|---|---|---|---|
|  | Cost or Amortized Cost | Gross Unrealized Gains | Gross Unrealized (Losses) | Fair Value |
| **Fixed maturity securities, bonds held-to-maturity** | | | | |
| U.S. treasury and government | $ 1,738 | $ 6 | $ — | $ 1,744 |

| | Amortized Cost | Gross Unrealized Gains | Gross Unrealized Losses | Fair Value |
|---|---:|---:|---:|---:|
| U.S. states and political subdivisions | 346,240 | 16,945 | (529) | 362,656 |
| Foreign governments | 29,099 | 2,505 | — | 31,604 |
| Corporate debt securities | 7,700,559 | 410,232 | (116,900) | 7,993,891 |
| Residential mortgage-backed securities | 400,619 | 20,711 | (2,647) | 418,683 |
| Collateralized debt securities | 2,366 | 225 | — | 2,591 |
| Other debt securities | 10,726 | 1,173 | — | 11,899 |
| **Total bonds held-to-maturity** | **8,491,347** | **451,797** | **(120,076)** | **8,823,068** |
| Fixed maturity securities, bonds available-for-sale | | | | |
| U.S. treasury and government | 21,751 | 725 | — | 22,476 |
| U.S. states and political subdivisions | 630,199 | 22,118 | (13,756) | 638,561 |
| Foreign governments | 5,000 | 1,649 | — | 6,649 |
| Corporate debt securities | 3,689,349 | 171,717 | (54,033) | 3,807,033 |
| Residential mortgage-backed securities | 61,135 | 2,940 | (1,068) | 63,007 |
| Commercial mortgage-backed securities | 18,223 | 11,037 | — | 29,260 |
| Collateralized debt securities | 13,884 | 1,320 | (18) | 15,186 |
| Other debt securities | 16,850 | 679 | (28) | 17,501 |
| **Total bonds available-for-sale** | **4,456,391** | **212,185** | **(68,903)** | **4,599,673** |
| Equity securities | | | | |
| Common stock | 717,390 | 653,967 | (2,362) | 1,368,995 |
| Preferred stock | 23,690 | 18,301 | (378) | 41,613 |
| **Total equity securities** | **741,080** | **672,268** | **(2,740)** | **1,410,608** |
| **Total investments in securities** | **$13,688,818** | **$1,336,250** | **$(191,719)** | **$14,833,349** |

The amortized costs and fair values, by contractual maturity, of fixed maturity securities are shown below (in thousands):

| | September 30, 2014 | | | |
|---|---:|---:|---:|---:|
| | Bonds Held-to-Maturity | | Bonds Available-for-Sale | |
| | Amortized Cost | Fair Value | Amortized Cost | Fair Value |
| Due in one year or less | $ 902,160 | $ 921,894 | $ 345,538 | $ 351,549 |
| Due after one year through five years | 2,046,277 | 2,257,421 | 855,878 | 932,247 |
| Due after five years through ten years | 4,988,483 | 5,196,155 | 3,029,503 | 3,154,290 |
| Due after ten years | 421,961 | 445,711 | 464,316 | 483,132 |
| Without single maturity date | 5,850 | 5,072 | 5,000 | 5,000 |
| **Total** | **$ 8,364,731** | **$8,826,253** | **$ 4,700,235** | **$4,926,218** |

Actual maturities differ from contractual maturities because borrowers may have the right to call or prepay obligations with or without call or prepayment penalties. Residential and commercial mortgage-backed securities, which are not due at a single maturity, have been allocated to their respective categories based on the year of final contractual maturity.

Proceeds from sales of available-for-sale securities, with the related gross realized gains and losses, are shown below (in thousands):

|  | Three months ended September 30, | | Nine months ended September 30, | |
|---|---|---|---|---|
|  | 2014 | 2013 | 2014 | 2013 |
| Proceeds from sales of available-for-sale securities | $ 2,671 | $ 33,390 | $ 139,137 | $ 189,438 |
| Gross realized gains | 228 | 10,349 | 24,994 | 33,699 |
| Gross realized losses | — | (97) | (2,123) | (623) |

All gains and losses for securities sold throughout the periods presented were determined using specific identification of the securities sold. During the nine months ended September 30, 2014 and 2013, bonds with a carrying value of $44,781,000 and $13,492,000, respectively, were transferred from held-to-maturity to available-for-sale after a significant deterioration in the issuers' creditworthiness became evident. An unrealized gain of $1,301,000 and unrealized loss of $263,000 were established in 2014 and 2013, respectively following the transfers at fair value.

### Change in net unrealized gains (losses) on securities

The components of the change in net unrealized gains (losses) on securities are shown below (in thousands):

|  | Nine months ended September 30, | |
|---|---|---|
|  | 2014 | 2013 |
| Bonds available-for-sale | $ 82,701 | $ (163,493) |
| Equity securities | 79,211 | 165,613 |
| Change in net unrealized gains (losses) on securities during the year | 161,912 | 2,120 |
| Adjustments for |  |  |
| Deferred policy acquisition costs | (17,175) | 46,643 |
| Participating policyholders' interest | (8,526) | 1,018 |
| Deferred federal income tax benefit (expense) | (47,160) | (18,212) |
| **Change in net unrealized gains (losses) on securities, net of tax** | $ 89,051 | $ 31,569 |

10

The gross unrealized losses and fair value of the investment securities, aggregated by investment category and length of time that individual securities have been in a continuous unrealized loss position, are shown below (in thousands):

|  | September 30, 2014 | | | | | |
|---|---|---|---|---|---|---|
|  | Less than 12 months | | 12 Months or more | | Total | |
|  | Unrealized (Losses) | Fair Value | Unrealized (Losses) | Fair Value | Unrealized (Losses) | Fair Value |
| Fixed maturity securities, bonds held-to-maturity |  |  |  |  |  |  |

|  | Less than 12 months | | 12 Months or more | | Total | |
| --- | ---: | ---: | ---: | ---: | ---: | ---: |
|  | Unrealized (Losses) | Fair Value | Unrealized (Losses) | Fair Value | Unrealized (Losses) | Fair Value |
| U.S. states and political subdivisions | $ (2) | $ 588 | $ (65) | $ 2,455 | $ (67) | $ 3,043 |
| Corporate debt securities | (7,727) | 511,249 | (32,565) | 799,719 | (40,292) | 1,310,968 |
| Residential mortgage-backed securities | (225) | 18,589 | (1,696) | 31,203 | (1,921) | 49,792 |
| **Total bonds held-to-maturity** | **(7,954)** | **530,426** | **(34,326)** | **833,377** | **(42,280)** | **1,363,803** |
| Fixed maturity securities, bonds available-for-sale | | | | | | |
| U.S. Treasury & other U.S. Gov corporations and agencies | — | 476 | — | — | — | 476 |
| U.S. states and political subdivisions | (449) | 37,887 | (2,491) | 79,485 | (2,940) | 117,372 |
| Corporate debt securities | (5,167) | 372,578 | (11,175) | 338,870 | (16,342) | 711,448 |
| Residential mortgage-backed securities | (147) | 10,908 | (607) | 13,835 | (754) | 24,743 |
| Collateralized debt securities | (1) | 117 | (7) | 361 | (8) | 478 |
| Other Debt Securities | — | — | — | — | — | — |
| **Total bonds available-for-sale** | **(5,764)** | **421,966** | **(14,280)** | **432,551** | **(20,044)** | **854,517** |
| Equity securities | | | | | | |
| Common stock | (3,791) | 37,132 | — | — | (3,791) | 37,132 |
| Preferred stock | (13) | 1,874 | — | — | (13) | 1,874 |
| **Total equity securities** | **(3,804)** | **39,006** | — | — | **(3,804)** | **39,006** |
| **Total** | **$ (17,522)** | **$ 991,398** | **$(48,606)** | **$1,265,928** | **$ (66,128)** | **$2,257,326** |

December 31, 2013

|  | Less than 12 months | | 12 Months or more | | Total | |
| --- | ---: | ---: | ---: | ---: | ---: | ---: |
|  | Unrealized (Losses) | Fair Value | Unrealized (Losses) | Fair Value | Unrealized (Losses) | Fair Value |

Fixed maturity securities, bonds

| | Unrealized Losses | Fair Value | Unrealized Losses | Fair Value | Unrealized Losses | Fair Value |
|---|---:|---:|---:|---:|---:|---:|
| **held-to-maturity** | | | | | | |
| U.S. states and political subdivisions | $ (529) | $ 22,430 | $ — | $ — | $ (529) | $ 22,430 |
| Corporate debt securities | (104,308) | 1,916,758 | (12,592) | 109,603 | (116,900) | 2,026,361 |
| Residential mortgage-backed securities | (1,718) | 31,715 | (929) | 13,514 | (2,647) | 45,229 |
| **Total bonds held-to-maturity** | **(106,555)** | **1,970,903** | **(13,521)** | **123,117** | **(120,076)** | **2,094,020** |
| Fixed maturity securities, bonds available-for-sale | | | | | | |
| U.S. Treasury & other U.S. Gov corporations and agencies | — | 725 | — | — | — | 725 |
| U.S. states and political subdivisions | (13,271) | 168,093 | (485) | 2,905 | (13,756) | 170,998 |
| Corporate debt securities | (49,198) | 1,083,677 | (4,835) | 92,004 | (54,033) | 1,175,681 |
| Residential mortgage-backed securities | (978) | 16,835 | (90) | 1,872 | (1,068) | 18,707 |
| Collateralized debt securities | (3) | 205 | (15) | 587 | (18) | 792 |
| Other debt securities | (28) | 10,027 | — | — | (28) | 10,027 |
| **Total bonds available-for-sale** | **(63,478)** | **1,279,562** | **(5,425)** | **97,368** | **(68,903)** | **1,376,930** |
| Equity securities | | | | | | |
| Common stock | (2,362) | 29,978 | — | — | (2,362) | 29,978 |
| Preferred stock | (378) | 6,123 | — | — | (378) | 6,123 |
| **Total equity securities** | **(2,740)** | **36,101** | **—** | **—** | **(2,740)** | **36,101** |
| **Total** | **$(172,773)** | **$3,286,566** | **$(18,946)** | **$ 220,485** | **$(191,719)** | **$3,507,051** |

As of September 30, 2014, the securities with unrealized losses were not deemed to be other-than-temporarily impaired, including those with the duration of the unrealized losses exceeding one year. American National has the ability and intent to hold those securities until a market price recovery or maturity. Further, it is not more-likely-than-not that American National will be required to sell them prior to recovery, and recovery is expected in a reasonable period of time. It is possible an issuer's financial circumstances may be different in the future, which may lead to a different impairment conclusion in future periods.

## Credit Risk Management

Bonds distributed by credit quality rating, using both S&P and Moody's ratings, are shown below:

|  | September 30, 2014 | December 31, 2013 |
|---|---|---|
| AAA | 4.9% | 4.9% |
| AA | 12.5 | 11.3 |
| A | 40.1 | 40.7 |
| BBB | 39.0 | 39.2 |
| BB and below | 3.5 | 3.9 |
| **Total** | **100.0%** | **100.0%** |

Equity securities by market sector distribution are shown below:

|  | September 30, 2014 | December 31, 2013 |
|---|---|---|
| Consumer goods | 19.2% | 19.8% |
| Energy and utilities | 14.7 | 15.0 |
| Financials | 18.8 | 19.3 |
| Healthcare | 13.8 | 12.7 |
| Industrials | 8.4 | 9.0 |
| Information technology | 16.3 | 15.7 |
| Other | 8.8 | 8.5 |
| **Total** | **100.0%** | **100.0%** |

## 5. MORTGAGE LOANS

Generally, commercial mortgage loans are secured by first liens on income-producing real estate. American National attempts to maintain a diversified portfolio by considering the property-type and location of the underlying collateral. Mortgage loans by property-type and geographic distribution are as follows:

|  | September 30, 2014 | December 31, 2013 |
|---|---|---|
| Hotel and motel | 11.3% | 10.0% |
| Industrial | 21.2 | 24.9 |
| Office | 35.6 | 34.0 |
| Retail | 18.2 | 19.6 |
| Other | 13.7 | 11.5 |
| **Total** | **100.0%** | **100.0%** |

|  | September 30, 2014 | December 31, 2013 |
|---|---|---|
| East North Central | 19.5% | 19.3% |
| East South Central | 5.0 | 6.8 |
| Mountain | 10.3 | 10.0 |
| Pacific | 12.3 | 12.3 |
| South Atlantic | 21.0 | 19.6 |
| West South Central | 25.1 | 26.4 |
| Other | 6.8 | 5.6 |
| **Total** | **100.0%** | **100.0%** |

As of September 30, 2014, American National was in the process of foreclosure on two loans with a recorded investment of $15,945,000; there was one loan foreclosed in the same period in 2013 with a recorded investment of $5,600,000. No loans were sold in the nine months ended September 30, 2014 and 2013.

## Credit Quality

The credit quality of the mortgage loan portfolio is assessed by evaluating the credit risk of each borrower. A loan is classified as performing or non-performing based on whether all of the contractual terms of the loan have been met.

The age analysis of past due commercial mortgage loans is shown below (in thousands):

|  | 30-59 Days Past Due | 60-89 Days Past Due | Greater Than 90 Days | Total Past Due | Current | Total Mortgage Loans |
|---|---|---|---|---|---|---|
| **September 30, 2014** |  |  |  |  |  |  |
| Industrial | $ — | $ — | $ — | $ — | $ 705,801 | $ 705,801 |
| Office | — | — | — | — | 1,191,525 | 1,191,525 |
| Retail | — | — | — | — | 610,335 | 610,335 |
| Other | — | — | — | — | 828,496 | 828,496 |
| Total | $ — | $ — | $ — | $ — | **$3,336,157** | 3,336,157 |
| Allowance for loan losses |  |  |  |  |  | 17,605 |
| **Mortgage loans on real estate, net of allowance** |  |  |  |  |  | **$ 3,318,552** |
| **December 31, 2013** |  |  |  |  |  |  |
| Industrial | $ — | $ — | $ 2,739 | $ 2,739 | $ 821,741 | $ 824,480 |
| Office | — | — | — | — | 1,124,818 | 1,124,818 |
| Retail | — | — | — | — | 651,236 | 651,236 |
| Other | — | — | — | — | 710,889 | 710,889 |
| Total | $ — | $ — | $ 2,739 | $ 2,739 | **$3,308,684** | 3,311,423 |
| Allowance for loan losses |  |  |  |  |  | 12,181 |
| **Mortgage loans on real estate, net of allowance** |  |  |  |  |  | **$ 3,299,242** |

Commercial mortgage loans placed on nonaccrual status are shown below (in thousands):

|  | September 30, 2014 | December 31, 2013 |
|---|---|---|
| Industrial | $ — | $ 2,739 |

Total mortgage loans are net of unamortized discounts of $708,000 and $852,000 and unamortized origination fees of $16,378,000 and $15,709,000 at September 30, 2014 and December 31, 2013, respectively. No unearned income is included in these amounts.

## Allowance for Credit Losses

Loans not evaluated individually for collectability are segregated by property-type and location, and allowance factors are applied. These factors are developed annually and reviewed quarterly based on our historical loss experience adjusted for the expected trend in the rate of foreclosure losses. Allowance factors are higher for loans of certain property types and in certain regions based on loss experience or a blended historical loss factor.

The change in allowance for credit losses in commercial mortgage loans is shown below (in thousands):

|  | Nine months ended September 30, 2014 | |
|---|---|---|
|  | Collectively Evaluated for Impairment | Individually Evaluated for Impairment |
| **Beginning balance, 2014** | $ 11,688 | $ 493 |
| Change Due to Factor Development | (441) | — |
| Change in allowance | 775 | 5,090 |
| **Ending balance, 2014** | $ 12,022 | $ 5,583 |

At September 30, 2014 and December 31, 2013, the recorded investment for loans collectively evaluated for impairment was $3,279,133,000 and $3,294,235,000, respectively, and the recorded investment for loans individually evaluated for impairment was $57,024,000 and $17,188,000, respectively.

13

Loans individually evaluated for impairment with and without an allowance are shown below (in thousands):

|  | September 30, 2014 | | September 30, 2013 | |
|---|---|---|---|---|
|  | Average Recorded Investment | Interest Income Recognized | Average Recorded Investment | Interest Income Recognized |
| **Three months ended** | | | | |
| **With an allowance recorded** | | | | |
| Office | $ 27,564 | $ 547 | $ 23,159 | $ 393 |
| Retail | — | — | 493 | — |
| Total | $ 27,564 | $ 547 | $ 23,652 | $ 393 |
| **Without an allowance recorded** | | | | |
| Office | $ 26,941 | $ 431 | $ 6,432 | $ 110 |
| Industrial | 2,702 | 36 | — | — |
| Retail | 851 | 11 | — | — |
| Total | $ 30,494 | $ 478 | $ 6,432 | $ 110 |
| **Nine months ended** | | | | |
| **With an allowance recorded** | | | | |
| Office | $ 29,421 | $ 1,663 | $ 23,234 | $ 1,192 |
| Retail | — | — | 493 | — |
| Total | $ 29,421 | $ 1,663 | $ 23,727 | $ 1,192 |
| **Without an allowance recorded** | | | | |
| Office | $ 27,019 | $ 1,298 | $ 6,439 | $ 331 |
| Industrial | 2,721 | 110 | — | — |
| Retail | 1,149 | 16 | — | — |
| Total | $ 30,889 | $ 1,424 | $ 6,439 | $ 331 |

|  | September 30, 2014 | | December 31, 2013 | |
|---|---|---|---|---|
|  | Recorded Investment | Unpaid Principal Balance | Recorded Investment | Unpaid Principal Balance |

|  | | | | |
|---|---:|---:|---:|---:|
| **With an allowance recorded** | | | | |
| Office | $ 26,662 | $ 27,947 | $ — | $ — |
| Retail | — | — | 493 | 493 |
| Total | **$ 26,662** | **$ 27,947** | **$ 493** | **$ 493** |
| **Without an allowance recorded** | | | | |
| Office | $ 26,941 | $ 26,941 | $ 12,377 | $ 12,377 |
| Industrial | 2,702 | 2,702 | 2,739 | 2,739 |
| Retail | 719 | 719 | 1,579 | 1,579 |
| Total | **$ 30,362** | **$ 30,362** | **$ 16,695** | **$ 16,695** |

**Troubled Debt Restructurings**

American National has granted concessions to mortgage loan borrowers related to their ability to pay the loans which are classified as troubled debt restructurings. Concessions are generally one of, or a combination of, a delay in payment of principal or interest, a reduction of the contractual interest rate or an extension of the maturity date. American National considers the amount, timing and extent of concessions in determining any impairment or changes in the specific allowance for loan losses recorded in connection with a troubled debt restructuring. The carrying value after specific allowance, before and after modification in a troubled debt restructuring, may not decrease significantly, or may increase if the expected recovery is higher than the pre-modification recovery assessment.

The number of mortgage loans and recorded investments in troubled debt restructuring are as follows (in thousands except for number of contracts):

| | \multicolumn{6}{c}{Nine months ended September 30,} | | | | | |
|---|---|---|---|---|---|---|
| | \multicolumn{3}{c}{2014} | \multicolumn{3}{c}{2013} |
| | Number of contracts | Recorded investment pre-modification | Recorded investment post modification | Number of contracts | Recorded investment pre-modification | Recorded investment post modification |
| Office | 3 | $ 34,400 | $ 30,996 | 1 | $ 6,432 | $ 6,432 |

There were no commitments to lend additional funds to debtors whose loans have been modified in troubled debt restructuring. One restructured loan is in the process of foreclosure.

## 6. INVESTMENT REAL ESTATE

Investment real estate by property-type and geographic distribution are as follows:

| | September 30, 2014 | December 31, 2013 |
|---|---:|---:|
| Industrial | 13.8% | 12.3% |
| Office | 20.7 | 23.1 |
| Retail | 46.4 | 43.4 |
| Other | 19.1 | 21.2 |
| **Total** | **100.0%** | **100.0%** |

| | September 30, 2014 | December 31, 2013 |
|---|---:|---:|
| East North Central | 4.8% | 7.8% |
| East South Central | 4.8 | 5.4 |
| Mountain | 6.5 | 6.0 |
| Pacific | 7.4 | 5.5 |
| South Atlantic | 12.7 | 13.4 |
| West South Central | 57.1 | 59.0 |

|  |  |  |
|---|---|---|
| Other | 6.7 | 2.9 |
| **Total** | **100.0%** | **100.0%** |

American National regularly invests in real estate partnerships and joint ventures. American National frequently participates in the design of these entities with the sponsor, but in most cases, its involvement is limited to financing. Through analysis performed by American National, some of these partnerships and joint ventures have been determined to be variable interest entities ("VIEs"). In certain instances, in addition to an economic interest in the entity, American National holds the power to direct the most significant activities of the entity and is deemed the primary beneficiary or consolidator of the entity. The assets of the consolidated VIEs are restricted and must first be used to settle their liabilities. Creditors or beneficial interest holders of these VIEs have no recourse to the general credit of American National, as American National's obligation is limited to the amount of its committed investment. American National has not provided financial or other support to the VIEs in the form of liquidity arrangements, guarantees, or other commitments to third parties that may affect the fair value or risk of its variable interest in the VIEs in 2014 or 2013.

15

The assets and liabilities relating to the VIEs included in the consolidated financial statements are as follows (in thousands):

|  | September 30, 2014 | December 31, 2013 |
|---|---|---|
| Investment real estate | $ 138,994 | $ 123,624 |
| Cash and cash equivalents | 1,761 | 2,154 |
| Accrued investment income | 412 | 2,197 |
| Other receivables | 7,986 | 8,488 |
| Other assets | 5,686 | 6,016 |
| Total assets of consolidated VIEs | $ 154,839 | $ 142,479 |
| Notes payable | $ 109,349 | $ 113,849 |
| Other liabilities | 4,595 | 6,680 |
| Total liabilities of consolidated VIEs | $ 113,944 | $ 120,529 |

The notes payable in the consolidated statements of financial position pertain to the borrowings of the consolidated VIEs. The liability of American National Insurance Company relating to notes payable of the consolidated VIEs is limited to the amount of its direct or indirect investment in the respective ventures, which totaled $14,948,000 and $12,782,000 at September 30, 2014 and December 31, 2013, respectively. The current portion of notes payable was $543,000 and $3,199,000 at September 30, 2014 and December 31, 2013, respectively. The average interest rate on the current portion of the notes payable was 4.25% during 2014. The total long-term portion of notes payable consists of three notes with the following interest rates: 4.0 %, and adjusted LIBOR plus 1.0%. Of the long-term notes payable, $9,375,000 will mature in 2016, with the remainder maturing beyond 5 years.

For other VIEs in which American National invests, it is not the primary beneficiary and these entities were not consolidated, as the major decisions that most significantly impact the economic activities of the VIE require unanimous consent of all owners. The following table presents the carrying amount and maximum exposure to loss relating to unconsolidated VIEs (in thousands):

|  | September 30, 2014 | | December 31, 2013 | |
|---|---|---|---|---|
|  | Carrying Amount | Maximum Exposure to Loss | Carrying Amount | Maximum Exposure to Loss |

|  |  |  |  |  |
|---|---|---|---|---|
| Investment in unconsolidated affiliates | $195,794 | $195,794 | $195,794 | $195,794 |
| Mortgage loans | 153,626 | 153,626 | 101,648 | 101,648 |
| Accrued investment income | 617 | 617 | 454 | 454 |

## 7. DERIVATIVE INSTRUMENTS

American National purchases over-the-counter equity-indexed options as economic hedges against fluctuations in the equity markets to which equity-indexed policies are exposed. Equity-indexed policies include a fixed host universal-life insurance or annuity policy and an equity-indexed embedded derivative. The detail of derivative instruments is shown below (in thousands, except the number of instruments):

| Derivatives Not Designated as Hedging Instruments | Location in the Consolidated Statements of Financial Position | September 30, 2014 | | December 31, 2013 | |
|---|---|---|---|---|---|
| | | Number of Instruments | Notional Amounts / Estimated Fair Value | Number of Instruments | Notional Amounts / Estimated Fair Value |
| Equity-indexed options | Other invested assets | 416 | 1,034,600 $ / 170,343 | 394 | 951,400 $ / 164,753 |
| Equity-indexed embedded derivative | Policyholders' account balances | 39,723 | 957,600 / 191,760 | 33,579 | 819,200 / 148,435 |

| Derivatives Not Designated as Hedging Instruments | Location in the Consolidated Statements of Operations | Gains (Losses) Recognized in Income on Derivatives | | | |
|---|---|---|---|---|---|
| | | Three months ended September 30, | | Nine months ended September 30, | |
| | | 2014 | 2013 | 2014 | 2013 |
| Equity-indexed options | Net investment income | $ 6,562 | $ 13,260 | $ 29,011 | $ 48,019 |
| Equity-indexed embedded derivative | Interest credited to policyholders' account balances | (1,762) | (11,056) | (16,484) | (39,750) |

## 8. NET INVESTMENT INCOME AND REALIZED INVESTMENT GAINS (LOSSES)

Net investment income is shown below (in thousands):

| | Three months ended September 30, | | Nine months ended September 30, | |
|---|---|---|---|---|
| | 2014 | 2013 | 2014 | 2013 |
| Bonds | $ 148,715 | $ 157,888 | $ 450,110 | $ 479,296 |
| Equity securities | 8,146 | 7,417 | 26,488 | 22,653 |
| Mortgage loans | 51,652 | 55,629 | 159,010 | 163,497 |
| Real estate | 14,245 | 11,297 | 11,347 | 10,228 |
| Options | 6,562 | 13,260 | 29,011 | 48,019 |
| Other invested assets | 7,169 | 8,845 | 21,638 | 28,795 |
| Total | $ 236,489 | $ 254,336 | $ 697,604 | $ 752,488 |

Realized investment gains (losses) are shown below (in thousands):

| | Three months ended September 30, | | Nine months ended September 30, | |
|---|---|---|---|---|
| | 2014 | 2013 | 2014 | 2013 |
| Bonds | $ 1,925 | $ 9,907 | $ 21,837 | $ 16,826 |
| Equity securities | 229 | 10,149 | 10,293 | 30,668 |
| Mortgage loans | (1,551) | (1,561) | (5,424) | (1,172) |
| Real estate | (1,242) | 25,311 | 1,787 | 61,257 |
| Other invested assets | (10) | (11) | (945) | (106) |
| Total | $ (649) | $ 43,795 | $ 27,548 | $ 107,473 |

The other-than-temporary-impairment losses are shown below (in thousands):

|  | Three months ended September 30, | | Nine months ended September 30, | |
| --- | --- | --- | --- | --- |
|  | 2014 | 2013 | 2014 | 2013 |
| Bonds | $  — | $  — | $  (41) | $  — |
| Equity securities | (1,608) | (312) | (3,004) | (3,503) |
| **Total** | **$ (1,608)** | **$ (312)** | **$ (3,045)** | **$ (3,503)** |

## 9. FAIR VALUE OF FINANCIAL INSTRUMENTS

The carrying amount and fair value of financial instruments are shown below (in thousands):

|  | September 30, 2014 | | December 31, 2013 | |
| --- | --- | --- | --- | --- |
|  | Carrying Amount | Fair Value | Carrying Amount | Fair Value |
| **Financial assets** | | | | |
| Fixed maturity securities, bonds held-to-maturity | $ 8,364,731 | $ 8,826,253 | $ 8,491,347 | $ 8,823,068 |
| Fixed maturity securities, bonds available-for-sale | 4,926,218 | 4,926,218 | 4,599,673 | 4,599,673 |
| Equity securities | 1,494,471 | 1,494,471 | 1,410,608 | 1,410,608 |
| Equity-indexed options | 170,343 | 170,343 | 164,753 | 164,753 |
| Mortgage loans on real estate, net of allowance | 3,318,552 | 3,515,463 | 3,299,242 | 3,470,663 |
| Policy loans | 404,705 | 404,705 | 397,407 | 397,407 |
| Short-term investments | 346,343 | 346,343 | 495,386 | 495,386 |
| Separate account assets | 992,615 | 992,615 | 970,954 | 970,954 |
| **Total financial assets** | **$20,017,978** | **$20,676,411** | **$19,829,370** | **$20,332,512** |
| **Financial liabilities** | | | | |
| Investment contracts | $ 9,039,356 | $ 9,039,356 | $ 9,423,122 | $ 9,423,122 |
| Embedded derivative liability for equity-indexed contracts | 191,760 | 191,760 | 148,435 | 148,435 |
| Notes payable | 109,349 | 109,349 | 113,849 | 113,849 |
| Separate account liabilities | 992,615 | 992,615 | 970,954 | 970,954 |
| **Total financial liabilities** | **$10,333,080** | **$10,333,080** | **$10,656,360** | **$10,656,360** |

Fair value is defined as the price that would be received to sell an asset or paid to transfer a liability. A fair value hierarchy is used to determine fair value based on a hypothetical transaction at the measurement date from the perspective of a market participant. American National has evaluated the types of securities in its investment portfolio to determine an appropriate hierarchy level based upon trading activity and the observability of market inputs. The classification of assets or liabilities within the fair value hierarchy is based on the lowest level of significant input to its valuation. The input levels are defined as follows:

Level 1     Unadjusted quoted prices in active markets for identical assets or liabilities.

Level 2     Quoted prices in markets that are not active or inputs that are observable directly or indirectly. Level 2 inputs include quoted prices for similar assets or liabilities other than quoted prices in Level 1; quoted prices in markets that are not active; or other inputs that are observable or can be derived principally from or corroborated by observable market data for substantially the full term of the assets or liabilities.

Level 3     Unobservable inputs that are supported by little or no market activity and are significant to the fair value of the assets or liabilities. Unobservable inputs reflect American National's own assumptions about the assumptions that market participants would use in pricing the asset or liability. Level 3 assets and liabilities include financial instruments whose values are determined using pricing models and third-party evaluation, as well as instruments for which the determination of fair value requires significant management judgment or estimation.

18

**Fixed Maturity Securities and Equity Options**—American National utilizes a pricing service to estimate fair value measurements. The estimates of fair value for most fixed maturity securities, including municipal bonds, provided by the pricing service are disclosed as Level 2 measurements as the estimates are based on observable market information rather than market quotes.

The pricing service utilizes market quotations for fixed maturity securities that have quoted prices in active markets. Since fixed maturity securities generally do not trade on a daily basis, the pricing service prepares estimates of fair value measurements for these securities using its proprietary pricing applications, which include available relevant market information, benchmark curves, benchmarking of like securities, sector groupings and matrix pricing. Additionally, an option adjusted spread model is used to develop prepayment and interest rate scenarios.

The pricing service evaluates each asset class based on relevant market information, credit information, perceived market movements and sector news. The market inputs utilized in the pricing evaluation, listed in the approximate order of priority, include: benchmark yields, reported trades, broker/dealer quotes, issuer spreads, two-sided markets, benchmark securities, bids, offers, reference data, and economic events. The extent of the use of each market input depends on the asset class and the market conditions. Depending on the security, the priority of the use of inputs may change or some market inputs may not be relevant. For some securities, additional inputs may be necessary.

American National has reviewed the inputs and methodology used and the techniques applied by the pricing service to produce quotes that represent the fair value of a specific security. The review confirms that the pricing service is utilizing information from observable transactions or a technique that represents a market participant's assumptions. American National does not adjust quotes received from the pricing service. The pricing service utilized by American National has indicated that they will produce an estimate of fair value only if there is objectively verifiable information available.

American National holds a small amount of private placement debt and fixed maturity securities that have characteristics that make them unsuitable for matrix pricing. For these securities, a quote from an independent broker (typically a market maker) is obtained. Due to the disclaimers on the quotes that indicate that the price is indicative only, American National includes these fair value estimates in Level 3.

For securities priced using a quote from an independent broker, such as the equity options and certain fixed maturity securities, American National uses a market-based fair value analysis to validate the reasonableness of prices received from an independent broker. Price variances above a certain threshold are analyzed further to determine if any pricing issue exists. This analysis is performed quarterly.

**Equity Securities**—For publicly-traded equity securities, prices are received from a nationally recognized pricing service that are based on observable market transactions, and these securities are classified as Level 1 measurements. For certain preferred stock, current market quotes in active markets are unavailable. In these instances, an estimate of fair value is received from the pricing service. The service utilizes similar methodologies to price preferred stocks as it does for fixed maturity securities. These estimates are disclosed as Level 2 measurements. American National tests the accuracy of the information provided by reference to other services regularly.

**Mortgage Loans**—The estimated fair value of mortgage loans is determined on a loan by loan basis by applying a discount rate to expected cash flows from future installment and balloon payments. The discount rate takes into account general market trends and specific credit risk trends for the individual loan. Factors used to arrive at the discount rate include inputs from spreads based on U.S. Treasury notes and the loan's credit quality, region, property type, lien priority, payment type and current status.

**Embedded Derivative**—The embedded derivative liability for equity-indexed contracts is measured at fair value and is recalculated each reporting period using equity option pricing models. To validate the assumptions used to price the embedded derivative liability, American National measures and compares embedded derivative returns against the returns of equity options held to hedge the liability cash flows.

The significant unobservable input used to calculate the fair value of the embedded derivatives is equity option implied volatility. An increase in implied volatility will result in an increase in the value of the equity-indexed embedded derivatives, all other things being equal. At September 30, 2014 and December 31, 2013, the one year implied volatility used to estimate embedded derivative value was 16.0% and 15.0%, respectively.

**Other Financial Instruments**—Other financial instruments classified as Level 3 measurements, as there is little or no market activity, are as follows:

Policy loans—The carrying value of policy loans is the outstanding balance plus any accrued interest. Due to the collateralized nature of policy loans, that it cannot be separated from the policy contract and the unpredictable timing of repayments and that settlement is at outstanding value, American National believes the carrying value of policy loans approximates fair value.

Investment contracts —The carrying value of investment contracts is equivalent to the accrued account balance. The accrued account balance consists of deposits, net of withdrawals, plus or minus interest credited, fees and charges assessed and other adjustments. American National believes that the carrying value of investment contracts approximates fair value because the majority of these contracts' interest rates reset to current rates offered at anniversary.

Notes payable—Notes payable are carried at outstanding principal balance. The carrying value of the notes payable approximates fair value because the underlying interest rates approximate market rates at the balance sheet date.

**Quantitative Disclosures**

The fair value hierarchy measurements of the financial instruments are shown below (in thousands):

|  | Fair Value Measurement as of September 30, 2014 | | | |
|---|---:|---:|---:|---:|
|  | Total Fair Value | Level 1 | Level 2 | Level 3 |
| **Financial assets** | | | | |
| Fixed maturity securities, bonds held-to-maturity | | | | |
|   U.S. states and political subdivisions | $ 352,099 | $ — | $ 352,099 | $ — |
|   Foreign governments | 30,763 | — | 30,763 | — |
|   Corporate debt securities | 8,049,255 | — | 7,998,901 | 50,354 |
|   Residential mortgage-backed securities | 373,701 | — | 372,724 | 977 |
|   Collateralized debt securities | 2,459 | — | — | 2,459 |
|   Other debt securities | 17,976 | — | 13,113 | 4,863 |
| **Total bonds held-to-maturity** | **8,826,253** | **—** | **8,767,600** | **58,653** |
| Fixed maturity securities, bonds available-for-sale | | | | |
|   U.S. treasury and government | 24,856 | — | 24,856 | — |
|   U.S. states and political subdivisions | 777,522 | — | 775,012 | 2,510 |
|   Foreign governments | 6,900 | — | 6,900 | — |
|   Corporate debt securities | 4,056,572 | — | 4,021,030 | 35,542 |
|   Residential mortgage-backed securities | 47,002 | — | 45,076 | 1,926 |
|   Collateralized debt securities | 13,366 | — | 11,200 | 2,166 |
| **Total bonds available-for-sale** | **4,926,218** | **—** | **4,884,074** | **42,144** |
| Equity securities | | | | |
|   Common stock | 1,452,643 | 1,452,643 | — | — |
|   Preferred stock | 41,828 | 41,828 | — | — |
| **Total equity securities** | **1,494,471** | **1,494,471** | **—** | **—** |
| Options | 170,343 | — | — | 170,343 |
| Mortgage loans on real | 3,515,463 | — | 3,515,463 | — |

| | | | | |
|---|---|---|---|---|
| estate | | | | |
| Policy loans | 404,705 | — | — | 404,705 |
| Short-term investments | 346,343 | — | 346,343 | — |
| Separate account assets | 992,615 | — | 992,615 | — |
| **Total financial assets** | **$20,676,411** | **$1,494,471** | **$18,506,095** | **$ 675,845** |
| Financial liabilities | | | | |
| Investment contracts | $ 9,039,356 | $ — | $ — | $9,039,356 |
| Embedded derivative liability for equity-indexed contracts | 191,760 | — | — | 191,760 |
| Notes payable | 109,349 | — | — | 109,349 |
| Separate account liabilities | 992,615 | — | 992,615 | — |
| **Total financial liabilities** | **$10,333,080** | **$ —** | **$ 992,615** | **$9,340,465** |

| | Total Fair Value | Level 1 | Level 2 | Level 3 |
|---|---|---|---|---|
| Financial assets | | | | |
| Fixed maturity securities, bonds held-to-maturity | | | | |
| U.S. treasury and government | $ 1,744 | $ — | $ 1,744 | $ — |
| U.S. states and political subdivisions | 362,656 | — | 362,656 | — |
| Foreign governments | 31,604 | — | 31,604 | — |
| Corporate debt securities | 7,993,891 | — | 7,950,418 | 43,473 |
| Residential mortgage-backed securities | 418,683 | — | 417,688 | 995 |
| Collateralized debt securities | 2,591 | — | — | 2,591 |
| Other debt securities | 11,899 | — | 11,899 | — |
| **Total bonds held-to-maturity** | **8,823,068** | **—** | **8,776,009** | **47,059** |
| Fixed maturity securities, bonds available-for-sale | | | | |
| U.S. treasury and government | 22,476 | — | 22,476 | — |
| U.S. states and political subdivisions | 638,561 | — | 636,041 | 2,520 |
| Foreign governments | 6,649 | — | 6,649 | — |
| Corporate debt securities | 3,807,033 | — | 3,794,809 | 12,224 |
| Residential mortgage-backed | 63,007 | — | 60,841 | 2,166 |

|  | | | | |
|---|---:|---:|---:|---:|
| securities | | | | |
| Commercial mortgage-backed securities | 29,260 | — | — | 29,260 |
| Collateralized debt securities | 15,186 | — | 13,052 | 2,134 |
| Other debt securities | 17,501 | — | 17,501 | — |
| **Total bonds available-for-sale** | **4,599,673** | **—** | **4,551,369** | **48,304** |
| Equity securities | | | | |
| Common stock | 1,368,995 | 1,368,995 | — | — |
| Preferred stock | 41,613 | 41,613 | — | — |
| **Total equity securities** | **1,410,608** | **1,410,608** | **—** | **—** |
| Options | 164,753 | — | — | 164,753 |
| Mortgage loans on real estate | 3,470,663 | — | 3,470,663 | — |
| Policy loans | 397,407 | — | — | 397,407 |
| Short-term investments | 495,386 | — | 495,386 | — |
| Separate account assets | 970,954 | — | 970,954 | — |
| **Total financial assets** | **$20,332,512** | **$1,410,608** | **$18,264,381** | **$ 657,523** |
| Financial liabilities | | | | |
| Investment contracts | $ 9,423,122 | $ — | $ — | $9,423,122 |
| Embedded derivative liability for equity-indexed contracts | 148,435 | — | — | 148,435 |
| Notes payable | 113,849 | — | — | 113,849 |
| Separate account liabilities | 970,954 | — | 970,954 | — |
| **Total financial liabilities** | **$10,656,360** | **$ —** | **$ 970,954** | **$9,685,406** |

For financial instruments measured at fair value on a recurring basis using Level 3 inputs during the period, a reconciliation of the beginning and ending balances is shown below (in thousands):

| | Level 3 | | | | | |
|---|---|---|---|---|---|---|
| | Three months ended September 30, | | | Nine months ended September 30, | | |
| | Assets | | Liability | Assets | | Liability |
| | Investment Securities | Equity-Indexed Options | Embedded Derivative | Investment Securities | Equity-Indexed Options | Embedded Derivative |
| **Beginning balance, 2014** | $ 11,932 | $163,861 | $186,261 | $ 48,304 | $164,753 | $148,435 |
| Total realized and unrealized investment gains/losses included in other comprehensive income | 138 | — | — | (11,735) | — | — |
| Net fair value change included in realized gains/losses | — | — | — | 13,056 | — | — |
| Net gain (loss) for derivatives included in net investment income | — | 4,998 | — | — | 23,788 | — |

| | | | | | | |
|---|---|---|---|---|---|---|
| Net change included in interest credited | — | — | 1,762 | — | — | 16,484 |
| Purchases, sales and settlements or maturities | | | | | | |
|   Purchases | — | 3,655 | — | — | 12,345 | — |
|   Sales | (120) | — | — | (37,670) | — | — |
|   Settlements or maturities | (5) | (2,171) | — | (10) | (30,543) | — |
| Premiums less benefits | | | 3,737 | | | 26,841 |
| Gross transfers into Level 3 | 30,199 | — | — | 30,199 | — | — |
| Gross transfers out of Level 3 | — | — | — | — | — | — |
| **Ending balance September 30, 2014** | $ 42,144 | $170,343 | $191,760 | $ 42,144 | $170,343 | $191,760 |
| **Beginning balance, 2013** | $ 55,558 | $115,558 | $100,963 | $107,036 | $ 82,625 | $ 75,032 |
| Total realized and unrealized investment gains/losses included in other comprehensive income | (633) | — | — | 10,496 | — | — |
| Net fair value change included in realized gains/losses | (1) | — | — | 218 | — | — |
| Net gain (loss) for derivatives included in net investment income | — | 11,775 | — | — | 42,941 | — |
| Net change included in interest credited | — | — | 11,056 | — | — | 39,750 |
| Purchases, sales and settlements or maturities | | | | | | |
|   Purchases | 45 | 4,470 | — | 2,115 | 12,178 | — |
|   Sales | (138) | — | — | (14,272) | — | — |
|   Settlements or maturities | — | (2,054) | — | — | (7,995) | — |
|   Premiums less benefits | — | — | (730) | — | — | (3,493) |
| Gross transfers into Level 3 | 157 | — | — | 157 | — | — |
| Gross transfers out of Level 3 | (2,840) | — | — | (53,602) | — | — |
| **Ending balance September 30, 2013** | $ 52,148 | $129,749 | $111,289 | $ 52,148 | $129,749 | $111,289 |

Within the net gain (loss) for derivatives included in net investment income were unrealized gain/(loss) of $7,395,000 and $39,652,000 relating to assets still held at September 30, 2014 and 2013, respectively.

## 10. DEFERRED POLICY ACQUISITION COSTS

Deferred policy acquisition costs are shown below (in thousands):

|  | Life | Annuity | Accident & Health | Property & Casualty | Total |
|---|---|---|---|---|---|
| **Beginning balance 2014** | $684,084 | $424,158 | $ 47,220 | $ 122,271 | $1,277,733 |
| Additions | 77,261 | 36,413 | 14,949 | 161,978 | 290,601 |
| Amortization | (61,488) | (58,469) | (14,084) | (167,414) | (301,455) |
| Effect of change in unrealized gains on available-for-sale securities | (4,147) | (13,028) | — | — | (17,175) |
| Net change | 11,626 | (35,084) | 865 | (5,436) | (28,029) |
| **Ending balance at September 30, 2014** | **$695,710** | **$389,074** | **$ 48,085** | **$ 116,835** | **$1,249,704** |

## 11. LIABILITY FOR UNPAID CLAIMS AND CLAIM ADJUSTMENT EXPENSES

The liability for unpaid claims and claim adjustment expenses ("claims") for accident and health, and property and casualty insurance is included in the "Policy and contract claims" in the consolidated statements of financial position and represents the amount estimated for claims that have been reported but not settled and IBNR claims. Liability for unpaid claims are estimated based upon American National's historical experience and actuarial assumptions that consider the effects of current developments, anticipated trends and risk management programs, reduced for anticipated salvage and subrogation. The effects of the changes are included in the consolidated results of operations in the period in which the changes occur.

Information regarding the liability for unpaid claims is shown below (in thousands):

|  | Nine months ended September 30, | |
|---|---|---|
|  | 2014 | 2013 |
| Unpaid claims balance, beginning | $ 1,096,299 | $ 1,168,047 |
| Less reinsurance recoverables | 215,161 | 256,885 |
| **Net beginning balance** | **881,138** | **911,162** |
| Incurred related to |  |  |
| Current | 706,824 | 743,194 |
| Prior years | (29,044) | (50,553) |
| **Total incurred claims** | **677,780** | **692,641** |
| Paid claims related to |  |  |
| Current | 410,077 | 442,100 |
| Prior years | 252,082 | 266,472 |
| **Total paid claims** | **662,159** | **708,572** |
| Net balance | 896,759 | 895,231 |
| Plus reinsurance recoverables | 235,485 | 226,822 |
| **Unpaid claims balance, ending** | **$ 1,132,244** | **$ 1,122,053** |

The net and gross reserve calculations have shown favorable development for the last several years as a result of favorable loss emergence compared to what was implied by the loss development patterns used in the original estimation of losses in prior years. Estimates for ultimate incurred claims attributable to insured events of prior years decreased by approximately $29,044,000 during the first nine months of 2014 and $50,553,000 during the same period in 2013.

## 12. FEDERAL INCOME TAXES

A reconciliation of the effective tax rate to the statutory federal tax rate is shown below (in thousands, except percentages):

|  | Three months ended September 30, | | | | Nine months ended September 30, | | | |
|---|---|---|---|---|---|---|---|---|
|  | 2014 | | 2013 | | 2014 | | 2013 | |
|  | Amount | Rate | Amount | Rate | Amount | Rate | Amount | Rate |
| Income tax (benefit) on pre-tax income | $33,171 | 35.0% | $42,302 | 35.0% | $82,308 | 35.0% | $93,527 | 35.0% |
| Tax-exempt investment income | (1,742) | (1.8) | (1,502) | (1.2) | (4,897) | (2.1) | (4,700) | (1.8) |
| Dividend exclusion | (1,700) | (1.8) | (1,710) | (1.4) | (5,253) | (2.2) | (4,802) | (1.8) |
| Miscellaneous tax credits, net | (2,658) | (2.8) | (1,930) | (1.6) | (5,873) | (2.5) | (5,820) | (2.2) |
| Other items, net | (322) | (0.3) | (1,401) | (1.2) | (621) | (0.3) | (6,326) | (2.3) |
|  | $26,749 | 28.3% | $35,759 | 29.6% | $65,664 | 27.9% | $71,879 | 26.9% |

American National made federal tax payments of $41,121,000 during the nine months ended September 30, 2014 and $37,784,000 during the nine months ended September 30, 2013.

Management believes a sufficient level of taxable income will be achieved over time to utilize the deferred tax assets in the consolidated federal tax return; therefore, no valuation allowance was recorded as of September 30, 2014 and December 31, 2013. However, if not utilized beforehand, approximately $2,260,000 of ordinary loss tax carryforwards will expire on December 31, 2034.

The statute of limitations for the examination of federal income tax returns by the Internal Revenue Service for years 2006 to 2009 has been extended. In the opinion of management, all prior year deficiencies have been paid or adequate provisions have been made for any tax deficiencies that may be upheld. No provision for penalties was established, and no interest expense was incurred for 2014 or 2013, relating to uncertain tax positions. Management does not believe there are any uncertain tax benefits that could be recognized within the next twelve months that would decrease American National's effective tax rate.

## 13. ACCUMULATED OTHER COMPREHENSIVE INCOME (LOSS)

The components of and changes in the accumulated other comprehensive income (loss) ("AOCI"), and the related tax effects, are shown below (in thousands):

|  | Net Unrealized Gains/(Losses) on Securities | Defined Benefit Pension Plan Adjustments | Foreign Currency Adjustments | AOCI |
|---|---|---|---|---|
| **Beginning balance 2014** | $ 457,937 | $ (43,884) | $ (341) | $413,712 |
| Amounts reclassified from AOCI (net of tax benefit $8,906 and expense $1,159) | (16,539) | 2,152 | — | (14,387) |
| Unrealized holding gains (losses) arising during the period (net of tax expense $65,575) | 121,782 |  |  | 121,782 |

|  | | | | |
|---|---:|---:|---:|---:|
| Unrealized adjustment to DAC (net of tax benefit $6,525) | (10,650) | | | (10,650) |
| Unrealized (gains) losses on investments attributable to participating policyholders' interest (net of tax benefit $2,984) | (5,542) | | | (5,542) |
| Foreign currency adjustment (net of tax benefit $311) | | | (577) | (577) |
| **Ending balance at September 30, 2014** | $ 546,988 | $ (41,732) | $ (918) | $504,338 |

|  | Net Unrealized Gains/(Losses) on Securities | Defined Benefit Pension Plan Adjustments | Foreign Currency Adjustments | AOCI |
|---|---:|---:|---:|---:|
| **Beginning balance 2013** | $ 370,842 | $ (129,003) | $ 171 | $242,010 |
| Amounts reclassified from AOCI (net of tax benefit $12,720 and expense $4,645) | (23,095) | 8,627 | — | (14,468) |
| Unrealized holding gains (losses) arising during the period (net of tax expense $13,277) | 24,658 | | | 24,658 |
| Unrealized adjustment to DAC (net of tax expense $17,299) | 29,344 | | | 29,344 |
| Unrealized (gains) losses on investments attributable to participating policyholders' interest (net of tax expense $356) | 662 | | | 662 |
| Foreign currency adjustment (net of tax benefit $114) | | | (211) | (211) |
| **Ending balance at September 30, 2013** | $ 402,411 | $ (120,376) | $ (40) | $281,995 |

## 14. STOCKHOLDERS' EQUITY AND NONCONTROLLING INTERESTS

American National has one class of common stock with a par value of $1.00 per share and 50,000,000 authorized shares. The amounts outstanding at the dates indicated are shown below:

|  | September 30, 2014 | December 31, 2013 |
|---|---|---|
| **Common stock** | | |
| Shares issued | 30,832,449 | 30,832,449 |
| Treasury shares | (3,960,507) | (3,937,261) |
| **Outstanding shares** | **26,871,942** | **26,895,188** |
| Restricted shares | (142,667) | (190,667) |
| **Unrestricted outstanding shares** | **26,729,275** | **26,704,521** |

### Stock-based compensation

American National has one stock-based compensation plan, which allows for grants of Non-Qualified Stock Options, Stock Appreciation Rights ("SAR"), Restricted Stock ("RS") Awards, Restricted Stock Units ("RSU"), Performance Awards, Incentive Awards or any combination thereof. This plan is administered by the American National Board Compensation Committee. The Board Compensation Committee makes incentive awards under this plan to our executives after meeting established performance objectives. All awards are subject to review by the Board of Directors, both when setting applicable performance objectives and at the payment of the awards. The number of shares available for grants under the plan cannot exceed 2,900,000, and no more than 200,000 shares may be granted to any one individual in any calendar year. Grants are made to certain officers and directors as compensation and to align their interests with those of other shareholders.

SAR, RS and RSU information for the periods indicated is shown below:

|  | SAR | | RS Shares | | RS Units | |
|---|---|---|---|---|---|---|
|  | Shares | Weighted-Average Grant Date Fair Value | Shares | Weighted-Average Grant Date Fair Value | Units | Weighted-Average Grant Date Fair Value |
| Outstanding at December 31, 2013 | 74,435 | $ 114.08 | 190,667 | $ 107.54 | 121,369 | $ 76.23 |
| Granted | — | — | — | — | 66,383 | 113.49 |
| Exercised | (2,817) | 95.58 | (48,000) | 108.00 | (59,438) | 76.53 |
| Forfeited | — | — | — | — | (100) | 113.49 |
| Expired | (15,279) | 115.23 | — | — | — | — |
| Outstanding at September 30, 2014 | 56,339 | $ 114.69 | 142,667 | $ 107.39 | 128,214 | $ 95.82 |

|  | SAR | RS Shares | RS Units |
|---|---|---|---|
| Weighted-average contractual remaining life (in years) | 2.0 | 4.1 | 2.0 |
| Exercisable shares Weighted-average exercise price | $ 114.69 | $ 107.39 | $ 95.82 |
| Weighted-average exercise | 114.78 | N/A | N/A |

|  |  |  |  |
|---|---:|---:|---:|
| price exercisable shares | | | |
| Compensation expense (credits) | | | |
| Three months ended September 30, 2014 | $ (19,000) | $ 496,000 | $ 522,000 |
| Three months ended September 30, 2013 | 87,000 | 674,000 | 409,000 |
| Nine months ended September 30, 2014 | (33,000) | 2,577,000 | 6,447,000 |
| Nine months ended September 30, 2013 | 160,000 | 1,703,000 | 8,692,000 |
| Fair value of liability award | | | |
| September 30, 2014 | $157,000 | N/A | $15,039,000 |
| December 31, 2013 | 376,000 | N/A | 15,018,000 |

The SARs give the holder the right to cash compensation based on the difference between the price of a share of stock on the grant date and the price on the exercise date. The SARs vest at a rate of 20% per year for five years and expire five years after vesting.

RS Awards entitle the participant to full dividend and voting rights. Each award has the value of one share of restricted stock and vests 10 years from the grant date. Unvested shares are restricted as to disposition, and are subject to forfeiture under certain circumstances. Compensation expense is recognized over the vesting period. The restrictions on these awards lapse after 10 years and these awards generally feature a graded vesting schedule in the case of the retirement of an award holder. Restricted stock for 350,334 shares has been granted at an exercise price of zero, of which 142,667 shares are unvested.

Effective December 31, 2012, the settlement provision within outstanding RSU awards was modified to allow the recipient of the awards to settle the vested RSUs in either cash or American National's common stock. This change in the settlement provision is expected to apply to all future issuance of RSU awards. Prior to the modification, vested RSUs were converted to American National's common stock on a one-for-one basis. This modification changes the award classification from equity to liability award. At the date of modification, American National recorded a liability of $7,974,000 with a corresponding reduction in additional paid-in capital. The liability will be remeasured and adjusted for changes in the fair value each reporting period through the vesting date. RSUs generally vest after a three-year graded vesting requirement. Certain awards vest over a shorter period as a result of retirement provisions. The modification, which was applied consistently to all participants, resulted in an incremental cost of $5,310,000 for the nine months ended September 30, 2014 and added an incremental cost of $2,947,000 during the nine months ended September 30, 2013.

## Earnings per share

Basic earnings per share were calculated using a weighted average number of shares outstanding. The Restricted Stock awards and units resulted in diluted earnings per share as follows (in thousands, except for share and per share data):

|  | Three months ended September 30, | | Nine months ended September 30, | |
|---|---:|---:|---:|---:|
|  | 2014 | 2013 | 2014 | 2013 |
| Weighted average shares outstanding | 26,805,535 | 26,780,313 | 26,800,835 | 26,789,564 |
| Incremental shares from RS awards and RSUs | 105,972 | 124,780 | 118,579 | 120,453 |
| **Total shares for** | **26,911,507** | **26,905,093** | **26,919,414** | **26,910,017** |

|  | | | | | | | | |
|---|---|---|---|---|---|---|---|---|
| diluted calculations | | | | | | | | |
| Net income (loss) attributable to American National | $ | 67,884 | $ | 82,613 | $ | 178,023 | $ | 200,753 |
| Basic earnings per share | $ | 2.53 | $ | 3.08 | $ | 6.64 | $ | 7.49 |
| Diluted earnings per share | | 2.52 | | 3.07 | | 6.61 | | 7.46 |

**Statutory Capital and Surplus**

Risk Based Capital ("RBC") requirements are measures insurance regulators use to evaluate the capital adequacy of American National Insurance Company and its insurance subsidiaries. RBC is calculated using formulas applied to certain financial balances and activities that consider, among other things, risks related to the type and quality of the invested assets, insurance risks associated with an insurer's products and liabilities, interest rate risks and general business risks. Insurance companies that do not maintain capital and surplus at a level at least 200% of the authorized control level RBC are required to take certain actions. At September 30, 2014 and December 31, 2013, American National Insurance Company's statutory capital and surplus was $2,842,984,000 and $2,667,858,000, respectively. Additionally, each of the insurance subsidiaries had statutory capital and surplus at September 30, 2014 and December 31, 2013, substantially above each subsidiary's authorized control level RBC.

American National's insurance subsidiaries prepare statutory-basis financial statements in accordance with statutory accounting practices prescribed or permitted by the insurance department of the state of domicile, which include certain components of the National Association of Insurance Commissioners' Codification of Statutory Accounting Principles ("NAIC Codification"). NAIC Codification is intended to standardize regulatory accounting and reporting to state insurance departments. However, statutory accounting practices continue to be established by individual state laws and permitted practices. Modifications by the various state insurance departments may impact the statutory capital and surplus of American National Insurance Company and its insurance subsidiaries.

Statutory accounting differs from GAAP primarily by charging policy acquisition costs to expense as incurred, establishing future policy benefit liabilities using different actuarial assumptions, and valuing securities on a different basis. In addition, certain assets are not admitted under statutory accounting principles and are charged directly to surplus.

One of American National's insurance subsidiaries has been granted a permitted practice from the Missouri Department of Insurance to record as the valuation of its investment in a wholly-owned subsidiary that is the attorney-in-fact for a Texas domiciled insurer, the statutory capital and surplus of the Texas domiciled insurer. This permitted practice increases the statutory capital and surplus of both American National Insurance Company and the Missouri domiciled insurance subsidiary by $60,732,000 and $56,205,000 at September 30, 2014 and 2013, respectively. The statutory capital and surplus of both American National Insurance Company and the Missouri domiciled insurance subsidiary would have remained substantially above the company action level RBC had it not used the permitted practice.

28

The statutory capital and surplus and net income (loss) of our insurance entities in accordance with statutory accounting practices are shown below (in thousands):

|  | September 30, 2014 | December 31, 2013 |
|---|---|---|
| **Statutory capital and surplus** | | |

|  | | | | |
|---|---|---|---|---|
| Life insurance entities | | $ 1,898,939 | | $ 1,771,999 |
| Property and casualty insurance entities | | 952,964 | | 904,557 |

|  | Three months ended September 30, | | Nine months ended September 30, | |
|---|---|---|---|---|
|  | 2014 | 2013 | 2014 | 2013 |
| **Statutory net income** | | | | |
| Life insurance entities | $43,447 | $59,602 | $139,564 | $159,286 |
| Property and casualty insurance entities | 22,718 | 20,205 | 44,852 | 26,136 |

### Dividends

American National Insurance Company's payment of dividends to stockholders is restricted by state laws. The restrictions require life insurance companies to maintain minimum amounts of capital and surplus, and in the absence of special approval, limit the payment of dividends to the greater of prior year statutory net income from operations on an annual, non-cumulative basis, or 10% of prior year statutory surplus. Under Texas insurance law, American National Insurance Company is permitted to pay total dividends of $266,786,000 during 2014 without prior approval of the Texas Department of Insurance. Similar restrictions on amounts that can transfer in the form of dividends, loans, or advances to American National Insurance Company apply to its insurance subsidiaries.

### Noncontrolling interests

American National County Mutual Insurance Company ("County Mutual") is a mutual insurance company that is owned by its policyholders. American National has a management agreement that effectively gives it control of County Mutual. As a result, County Mutual is included in the consolidated financial statements of American National. Policyholder interests in the financial position of County Mutual are reflected as noncontrolling interest of $6,750,000 at September 30, 2014 and December 31, 2013.

American National Insurance Company and its subsidiaries exercise significant control or ownership of various joint ventures, resulting in their consolidation into American National's consolidated financial statements. The interests of the other partners in the consolidated joint ventures are shown as noncontrolling interests of $5,529,000 and $6,007,000 at September 30, 2014 and December 31, 2013, respectively.

### 15. SEGMENT INFORMATION

Management organizes the business into five operating segments:

- Life—markets whole, term, universal, indexed and variable life insurance on a national basis primarily through career and multiple-line agents, independent agents and direct marketing channels.

- Annuity—offers fixed, indexed, and variable annuity products. These products are sold through independent agents, brokers, and financial institutions, along with multiple-line and career agents.

- Health—primary lines of business are Medicare Supplement, stop loss, other supplemental health products and credit disability insurance. Health products are typically distributed through independent agents and managing general underwriters.

- Property and Casualty—writes personal and commercial coverages and credit-related property insurance. These products are sold through multiple-line and independent agents.

- Corporate and Other—consists of net investment income from investments not allocated to the insurance segments and revenues from non-insurance operations.

The accounting policies of the segments are the same as those described in Note 2 to American National's annual report on form 10-K. All revenue and expense amounts specifically attributable to policy transactions are recorded directly to the appropriate operating segment. Revenues and expenses not specifically attributable to policy transactions are allocated to each segment as follows:

- Recurring income from bonds and mortgage loans is allocated based on the assets allocated to each line of business at the average yield available from these assets.

- Net investment income from all other assets is allocated to the insurance segments in accordance with the amount of capital allocated to each segment, with the remainder recorded in the Corporate and Other business segment.

- Expenses are allocated based upon various factors, including premium and commission ratios within the respective operating segments.

The following summarizes results of operations by operating segments (in thousands):

|  | Three months ended September 30, | | Nine months ended September 30, | |
|---|---|---|---|---|
|  | 2014 | 2013 | 2014 | 2013 |
| Income (loss) from continuing operations before federal income taxes, and equity in earnings/losses of unconsolidated affiliates |  |  |  |  |
| Life | $10,794 | $ 9,005 | $ 22,076 | $ 23,420 |
| Annuity | 24,366 | 18,631 | 70,415 | 69,633 |
| Health | 9,304 | 7,170 | 19,579 | 16,164 |
| Property and casualty | 30,088 | 24,634 | 59,790 | 33,198 |
| Corporate and other | 20,223 | 61,424 | 63,305 | 124,807 |
| **Total** | **$94,775** | **$120,864** | **$235,165** | **$267,222** |

### 16. COMMITMENTS AND CONTINGENCIES

**Commitments**

American National had aggregate commitments at September 30, 2014, to purchase, expand or improve real estate, to fund fixed interest rate mortgage loans, and to purchase other invested assets of $452,166,000 of which $176,259,000 is expected to be funded in 2014. The remaining $275,907,000 will be funded in 2015 and beyond.

American National has a $100,000,000 short-term variable rate borrowing facility containing a $55,000,000 sub-feature for the issuance of letters of credit. Borrowings under the facility are at the discretion of the lender and would be used only for funding working capital requirements. The combination of borrowings and outstanding letters of credit cannot exceed $100,000,000 at any time. As of September 30, 2014 and December 31, 2013, the outstanding letters of credit were $12,191,000 and $15,560,000, respectively, and there were no borrowings on this facility. This facility expires on October 30, 2015. American National expects it will be renewed on substantially equivalent terms upon expiration.

**Guarantees**

American National has guaranteed bank loans for customers of a third-party marketing operation. The bank loans are used to fund premium payments on life insurance policies issued by American National. The loans are secured by the cash values of the life insurance policies. If the customer were to default on the bank loan, American National would be obligated to pay off the loans. As the cash values of the life insurance policies always equal or exceed the balance of the loans, management does not foresee any loss on these guarantees. The total amount of the guarantees outstanding as of September 30, 2014, was approximately $206,376,000, while the total cash values of the related life insurance policies was approximately $208,418,000.

**Litigation**

American National Insurance Company and certain subsidiaries, in common with the insurance industry in general, are defendants in various lawsuits concerning alleged breaches of contracts, various employment matters, allegedly deceptive insurance sales and marketing practices, and miscellaneous other causes of action arising in the ordinary course of operations. Certain of these lawsuits include claims for compensatory and punitive damages. We provide accruals for these items to the extent we deem the losses probable and reasonably estimable. After reviewing these matters with legal counsel, based upon information presently available, management is of the opinion that the ultimate resultant liability, if any, would not have a material adverse effect on American National's consolidated financial position, liquidity or results of operations; however, assessing the eventual outcome of litigation necessarily involves forward-looking speculation as to judgments to be made by judges, juries and appellate courts in the future. Such speculation warrants caution, as the frequency of large damage awards, which bear little or no relation to the economic damages incurred by plaintiffs in some jurisdictions, continues to create the potential for an unpredictable judgment in any given lawsuit. These lawsuits are in various stages of development, and future facts and circumstances could result in management's changing its conclusions. It is possible that, if the defenses in these lawsuits are not successful, and the judgments are greater than management can anticipate, the resulting liability could have a material impact on our consolidated financial position, liquidity or results of operations. With respect to the existing litigation, management currently believes that the possibility of a material judgment adverse to American National is remote and no estimate of range can be made for loss contingencies that are at least reasonably possible but not accrued.

## 17. RELATED PARTY TRANSACTIONS

American National has entered into recurring transactions and agreements with certain related parties. These include mortgage loans, management contracts, agency commission contracts, marketing agreements, accident and health insurance contracts and legal services. The impact on the consolidated financial statements of the significant related party transactions is shown below (in thousands):

| Related Party | Financial Statement Line Impacted | Dollar Amount of Transactions Nine months ended September 30, | | Amount due to/(from) American National | |
|---|---|---|---|---|---|
| | | 2014 | 2013 | September 30, 2014 | December 31, 2013 |
| Gal-Tex Hotel Corporation | Mortgage loan on real estate | $ 917 | $ 853 | $ 6,825 | $ 7,742 |
| Gal-Tex Hotel Corporation | Net investment income | 399 | 463 | 41 | 47 |
| Greer, Herz and Ada | Other operating | 8,037 | 7,484 | (404) | (284) |

ms, LLP                          expenses

*Mortgage Loans to Gal-Tex Hotel Corporation ("Gal-Tex")*: The Moody Foundation and the Libbie Shearn Moody Trust own 34.0% and 50.2%, respectively, of Gal-Tex Hotel Corporation. The Moody Foundation and the Libbie Shearn Moody Trust also own approximately 22.9% and 37.1%, respectively, of American National. American National holds a first mortgage loan originated in 1999, with an interest rate of 7.30% and final maturity date of April 1, 2019 issued to Gal-Tex, which is collateralized by a hotel property in San Antonio, Texas. This loan is current as to principal and interest payments.

*Transactions with Greer, Herz & Adams, L.L.P.*: Irwin M. Herz, Jr. is an American National advisory director and a Partner with Greer, Herz Adams, L.L.P., which serves as American National's General Counsel.

## ITEM 2. MANAGEMENT'S DISCUSSION AND ANALYSIS OF FINANCIAL CONDITION AND RESULTS OF OPERATIONS

Set forth on the following pages is management's discussion and analysis ("MD&A") of financial condition and results of operations for the three and nine months ended September 30, 2014 and 2013 of American National Insurance Company and its subsidiaries (referred to in this document as "we", "our", "us", or the "Company"). This information should be read in conjunction with our consolidated financial statements included in Item 1, Financial Statements (unaudited), of this Form 10-Q.

**Forward-Looking Statements**

This document contains forward-looking statements that reflect our estimates and assumptions related to business, economic, competitive and legislative developments. Forward-looking statements generally are indicated by words such as "expects," "intends," "anticipates," "plans," "believes," "estimates," "will" or words of similar meaning and include, without limitation, statements regarding the outlook of our business and expected financial performance. Forward-looking statements are not guarantees of future performance and involve various risks and uncertainties. Moreover, forward-looking statements speak only as of the date made, and we undertake no obligation to update them. Certain important factors could cause our actual results to differ, possibly materially, from our expectations or estimates. These factors are described in greater detail in Item IA, Risk Factors, in our 2013 Annual Report on Form 10-K filed with the SEC on February 28th, 2014, and they include among others:

- **Economic Risk Factors**
    - difficult conditions in the economy, which may not improve in the near future, and risks related to persistently low or unpredictable interest rates;

- **Operational Risk Factors**
    - differences between actual experience regarding mortality, morbidity, persistency, expense, surrenders and investment returns, and our assumptions for establishing liabilities and reserves or for other purposes;
    - potential ineffectiveness of our risk management policies and procedures;
    - changes in our experience related to deferred policy acquisition costs;
    - failures or limitations of our computer, data security and administration systems;

- potential employee error or misconduct, which may result in fraud or adversely affect the execution and administration of our policies and claims;

- **Investment and Financial Market Risk Factors**
    - fluctuations in the markets for fixed maturity securities, equity securities, and commercial real estate, which could adversely affect the valuation of our investment portfolio, our net investment income, our retirement expense, and sales of or fees from certain of our products;
    - lack of liquidity for certain of our investments;
    - risk of investment losses and defaults;

- **Catastrophic Event Risk Factors**
    - natural or man-made catastrophes, pandemic disease, or other events resulting in increased claims activity from catastrophic loss of life or property;
    - the effects of unanticipated events on our disaster recovery and business continuity planning;

- **Marketplace Risk Factors**
    - the highly competitive nature of the insurance and annuity business;
    - potential difficulty in attraction and retention of qualified employees and agents;
    - the introduction of alternative healthcare solutions or changes in federal healthcare policy, both of which could impact our supplement healthcare business;

- **Litigation and Regulation Risk Factors**
    - adverse determinations in litigation or regulatory proceedings which may result in significant financial losses and harm our reputation;

- the effects of extensive government regulation;
- changes in tax law;
- changes in statutory or U.S. generally accepted accounting principles ("GAAP"), practices or policies;

- **Reinsurance and Counterparty Risk Factors**
    - potential changes in the availability, affordability and adequacy of reinsurance protection;
    - potential default or failure to perform by the counterparties to our reinsurance arrangements and derivative instruments;

- **Other Risk Factors**
    - potentially adverse rating agency actions; and
    - control of our company by a small number of stockholders.

## Overview

We are a diversified insurance and financial services company offering a broad spectrum of insurance products. Chartered in 1905, we are headquartered in Galveston, Texas. We operate in all 50 states, the District of Columbia, Guam, American Samoa and Puerto Rico.

## General Trends

American National had no material changes to the general trends, as discussed in the MD&A included in our 2013 Annual Report on Form 10-K filed with the SEC on February 28, 2014.

### Critical Accounting Estimates

The unaudited interim consolidated financial statements have been prepared in conformity with GAAP. In addition to GAAP, insurance companies apply specific SEC regulations when preparing the consolidated financial statements. The preparation of the consolidated financial statements and notes requires us to make estimates and assumptions that affect the amounts reported. Actual results could differ from results reported using those estimates and assumptions. Our accounting policies inherently require the use of judgments relating to a variety of assumptions and estimates, particularly expectations of current and future mortality, morbidity, persistency, expenses, interest rates, and property and casualty loss frequency, severity, claim reporting and settlement patterns. Due to the inherent uncertainty when using the assumptions and estimates, the effect of certain accounting policies under different conditions or assumptions could vary from those reported in the consolidated financial statements.

For a discussion of our critical accounting estimates, see the MD&A in our 2013 Annual Report on Form 10-K filed with the SEC on February 28, 2014. There have been no material changes in accounting policies since December 31, 2013.

### Recently Issued Accounting Pronouncements

Refer to Note 3, Recently Issued Accounting Pronouncements, of the Notes to the Unaudited Consolidated Financial Statements in Item 1.

## Consolidated Results of Operations

The following sets forth the consolidated results of operations (in thousands):

| | Three months ended September 30, | | | Nine months ended September 30, | | |
|---|---|---|---|---|---|---|
| | 2014 | 2013 | Change | 2014 | 2013 | Change |
| **Premiums and other revenues** | | | | | | |
| Premiums | $ 447,036 | $ 422,799 | $ 24,237 | $ 1,357,537 | $ 1,265,418 | $ 92,119 |
| Other policy revenues | 55,255 | 52,975 | 2,280 | 167,041 | 152,910 | 14,131 |
| Net investment income | 236,489 | 254,336 | (17,847) | 697,604 | 752,488 | (54,884) |
| Realized investments gains (losses), net | (2,257) | 43,483 | (45,740) | 24,503 | 103,970 | (79,467) |

| | | | | | | |
|---|---|---|---|---|---|---|
| Other income | 9,647 | 11,911 | (2,264) | 26,707 | 29,423 | (2,716) |
| **Total premiums and other revenues** | 746,170 | 785,504 | (39,334) | 2,273,392 | 2,304,209 | (30,817) |
| **Benefits, losses and expenses** | | | | | | |
| Policyholder benefits | 127,633 | 118,681 | 8,952 | 437,877 | 365,051 | 72,826 |
| Claims incurred | 213,606 | 217,213 | (3,607) | 673,509 | 687,420 | (13,911) |
| Interest credited to policyholders' account balances | 83,746 | 98,862 | (15,116) | 258,952 | 309,738 | (50,786) |
| Commissions for acquiring and servicing policies | 97,608 | 94,504 | 3,104 | 299,992 | 273,360 | 26,632 |
| Other operating expenses | 118,002 | 128,115 | (10,113) | 357,043 | 381,850 | (24,807) |
| Change in deferred policy acquisition costs [1] | 10,800 | 7,265 | 3,535 | 10,854 | 19,568 | (8,714) |
| **Total benefits and expenses** | 651,395 | 664,640 | (13,245) | 2,038,227 | 2,036,987 | 1,240 |
| **Income (loss) before other items and federal income taxes** | $ 94,775 | $ 120,864 | $ (26,089) | $ 235,165 | $ 267,222 | $ (32,057) |

(1) A negative amount of net change indicates more expense was deferred than amortized and represents a decrease to expenses in the period indicated, a positive net change indicates less expense was deferred than amortized and represents an increase to expenses in the period indicated.

Earnings (income before other items and taxes) decreased for the quarter and nine months ended September 30, 2014 compared to the same periods in 2013, primarily a result of lower realized investment gains (losses) net. Earnings excluding realized investment gains (losses) increased for the quarter and nine months ended September 30, 2014 compared to 2013.

## Life

Life segment financial results for the periods indicated were as follows (in thousands):

|  | Three months ended September 30, | | | Nine months ended September 30, | | |
|---|---|---|---|---|---|---|
|  | 2014 | 2013 | Change | 2014 | 2013 | Change |
| **Premiums and other revenues** | | | | | | |
| Premiums | $ 79,492 | $ 75,278 | $ 4,214 | $ 224,165 | $ 215,479 | $ 8,686 |
| Other policy revenues | 51,751 | 49,158 | 2,593 | 155,355 | 142,034 | 13,321 |
| Net investment income | 57,598 | 57,008 | 590 | 172,633 | 173,195 | (562) |
| Other income | 338 | 708 | (370) | 1,027 | 2,093 | (1,066) |
| **Total premiums and other revenues** | **189,179** | **182,152** | **7,027** | **553,180** | **532,801** | **20,379** |
| **Benefits, losses and expenses** | | | | | | |
| Policyholder benefits | 83,740 | 83,821 | (81) | 257,505 | 246,896 | 10,609 |
| Interest credited to policyholders' account balances | 16,649 | 13,653 | 2,996 | 48,265 | 40,750 | 7,515 |
| Commissions for acquiring and servicing policies | 30,239 | 30,341 | (102) | 91,971 | 86,491 | 5,480 |
| Other operating expenses | 47,622 | 52,042 | (4,420) | 149,136 | 156,269 | (7,133) |
| Change in deferred policy acquisition costs [1] | 135 | (6,710) | 6,845 | (15,773) | (21,025) | 5,252 |
| **Total benefits and expenses** | **178,385** | **173,147** | **5,238** | **531,104** | **509,381** | **21,723** |
| Income before other items and federal income taxes | $ 10,794 | $ 9,005 | $ 1,789 | $ 22,076 | $ 23,420 | $ (1,344) |

(1) A negative amount of net change indicates more expense was deferred than amortized and represents a decrease to expenses in the period indicated, a positive net change indicates less expense was deferred than amortized and represents an increase to expenses in the period indicated.

Earnings increased during the quarter ended September 30, 2014 compared to 2013 due to a decrease in operating expenses. Earnings decreased during the nine months ended September 30, 2014 compared to 2013 primarily due to an increase in policyholder benefits, a result of higher than expected claims in the first quarter of 2014.

*Premiums and other policy revenues*

Premiums increased during the three and nine months ended September 30, 2014 compared to 2013. The increases were primarily driven by the continued growth of the in-force block of business of term products.

Other policy revenues include mortality charges, earned policy service fees and surrender charges on interest-sensitive life insurance policies. An increase in interest-sensitive life policies contributed to the increases in these charges during the three and nine months ended September 30, 2014 compared to 2013.

**Life insurance sales**

The following table presents life insurance sales as measured by annualized premium, a non-GAAP measure used by the insurance industry, which allows a comparison of new policies written by an insurance company during the period (in thousands):

|  | Three months ended September 30, | | | Nine months ended September 30, | | |
|---|---|---|---|---|---|---|
|  | 2014 | 2013 | Change | 2014 | 2013 | Change |
| Whole life | $ 5,656 | $ 5,643 | $ 13 | $ 19,387 | $ 19,044 | $ 343 |
| Term life | 6,890 | 7,756 | (866) | 22,049 | 24,436 | (2,387) |
| Universal life | 8,427 | 8,920 | (493) | 26,409 | 26,759 | (350) |
| Total recurring | $ 20,973 | $ 22,319 | $ (1,346) | $ 67,845 | $ 70,239 | $ (2,394) |
| Single and excess [1] | $ 505 | $ 584 | $ (79) | $ 1,466 | $ 1,676 | $ (210) |
| Credit life [1] | 1,046 | 1,107 | (61) | 2,978 | 3,108 | (130) |

[1] These are weighted amounts representing 10% of single and excess premiums and 15% of credit life premuims.

35

Life insurance sales are based on the total yearly premium that insurance companies would expect to receive if all recurring premium policies would remain in force, plus 10% of single and excess premiums and 15% of credit life premium. Life insurance sales measure activity associated with gaining new insurance business in the current period whereas GAAP premium revenues are associated with policies sold in current and prior periods; therefore, a reconciliation of premium revenues and insurance sales is not meaningful.

Life insurance sales decreased during the three and nine months ended September 30, 2014 compared to 2013 driven primarily by a decline in term life sales. Marketing activities at financial institutions with whom the Company markets life insurance have been curtailed at the financial institutions to ensure compliance with Consumer Financial Protection Bureau views on appropriate marketing practices.

*Benefits, losses and expenses*

Policyholder benefits increased during the nine months ended September 30, 2014 compared to 2013 primarily due to higher than expected claims in the first quarter of 2014.

The increase in commissions during the nine months ended September 30, 2014 compared to 2013 is primarily due to an increase in first year premiums on term and equity-indexed universal life products.

Other operating expenses decreased during the three and nine months ended September 30, 2014 compared to 2013.

The following table presents the components of the change in DAC (in thousands), which increased expenses due to a decrease in acquisition cost capitalized.

|  | Three months ended September 30, | | | Nine months ended September 30, | | |
|---|---|---|---|---|---|---|
|  | 2014 | 2013 | Change | 2014 | 2013 | Change |
| Acquisition cost capitalized | $ 26,271 | $ 30,999 | $ (4,728) | $ 77,261 | $ 80,226 | $ (2,965) |
| Amortization of DAC | (26,406) | (24,289) | (2,117) | (61,488) | (59,201) | (2,287) |
| Net change in DAC (1) | $ (135) | $ 6,710 | $ (6,845) | $ 15,773 | $ 21,025 | $ (5,252) |

(1) A positive amount of net change indicates more expense was deferred than amortized and represents a decrease to expenses in the period indicated, a negative net change indicates less expense was deferred than amortized and represents an increase to expenses in the period indicated.

*Policy in-force information*

The following table summarizes changes in the life insurance in-force amounts (in thousands) and number of policies in-force:

|  | September 30, 2014 | December 31, 2013 | Change |
|---|---|---|---|
| **Life insurance in-force** | | | |
| Traditional life | $58,249,120 | $54,788,898 | $3,460,222 |
| Interest-sensitive life | 25,803,248 | 25,281,391 | 521,857 |
| **Total life insurance in-force** | $84,052,368 | $80,070,289 | $3,982,079 |
| **Number of policies in-force** | | | |
| Traditional life | 1,961,707 | 2,002,602 | (40,895) |
| Interest-sensitive life | 202,748 | 196,949 | 5,799 |
| **Total number of policies** | 2,164,455 | 2,199,551 | (35,096) |

Total life insurance in-force increased during 2014 compared to 2013, while the total number of policies decreased reflecting the transition to fewer but larger face amount policies.

**Annuity**

Annuity segment financial results for the periods indicated were as follows (in thousands):

| | Three months ended September 30, | | | Nine months ended September 30, | | |
|---|---|---|---|---|---|---|
| | 2014 | 2013 | Change | 2014 | 2013 | Change |
| **Premiums and other revenues** | | | | | | |
| Premiums | $ 34,661 | $ 23,412 | $ 11,249 | $ 148,250 | $ 89,733 | $ 58,517 |
| Other policy revenues | 3,504 | 3,817 | (313) | 11,686 | 10,876 | 810 |
| Net investment income | 128,890 | 148,322 | (19,432) | 404,347 | 463,530 | (59,183) |
| Other income | (1) | 96 | (97) | (1) | 241 | (242) |
| Total premiums and other revenues | 167,054 | 175,647 | (8,593) | 564,282 | 564,380 | (98) |
| **Benefits, losses and expenses** | | | | | | |
| Policyholder benefits | 43,893 | 34,860 | 9,033 | 180,372 | 118,155 | 62,217 |
| Interest credited to policyholders' account balances | 67,097 | 85,208 | (18,111) | 210,687 | 268,987 | (58,300) |
| Commissions for acquiring and servicing policies | 10,787 | 10,303 | 484 | 37,358 | 31,890 | 5,468 |
| Other operating expenses | 12,465 | 16,242 | (3,777) | 43,394 | 48,053 | (4,659) |
| Change in deferred policy acquisition costs [(1)] | 8,446 | 10,403 | (1,957) | 22,056 | 27,662 | (5,606) |
| Total benefits and expenses | 142,688 | 157,016 | (14,328) | 493,867 | 494,747 | (880) |
| Income before other items and federal | $ 24,366 | $ 18,631 | $ 5,735 | $ 70,415 | $ 69,633 | $ 782 |

income taxes

(1) A negative amount of net change indicates more expense was deferred than amortized and represents a decrease to expenses in the period indicated, a positive net change indicates less expense was deferred than amortized and represents an increase to expenses in the period indicated.

Earnings increased during the three and nine months ended September 30, 2014 compared to 2013, primarily due to lower operating expenses.

*Premiums and other policy revenues*

Annuity premium and deposit amounts received are shown below (in thousands):

|  | Three months ended September 30, | | | Nine months ended September 30, | | |
|---|---|---|---|---|---|---|
|  | 2014 | 2013 | Change | 2014 | 2013 | Change |
| Fixed deferred annuity | $ 67,414 | $ 53,250 | $ 14,164 | $ 261,123 | $ 186,765 | $ 74,358 |
| Single premium immediate annuity | 40,996 | 32,245 | 8,751 | 171,244 | 127,146 | 44,098 |
| Equity-indexed deferred annuity | 67,524 | 47,405 | 20,119 | 185,602 | 126,898 | 58,704 |
| Variable deferred annuity | 24,514 | 30,485 | (5,971) | 84,960 | 94,553 | (9,593) |
| Total premium and deposits | 200,448 | 163,385 | 37,063 | 702,929 | 535,362 | 167,567 |
| Less: Policy deposits | 165,787 | 139,973 | 25,814 | 554,679 | 445,629 | 109,050 |
| Total earned premiums | $ 34,661 | $ 23,412 | $ 11,249 | $ 148,250 | $ 89,733 | $ 58,517 |

37

We monitor account values and changes in those values as key indicators of performance in our Annuity segment. Changes in account values are mainly the result of net inflows, surrenders, policy fees, interest credited and market value changes (shown below in thousands):

|  | Nine months ended September 30, | |
|---|---|---|
|  | 2014 | 2013 |
| **Fixed deferred and equity-indexed annuity** | | |
| Account value, beginning of period | $ 9,355,946 | $ 9,803,197 |
| Net inflows | 322,605 | 183,832 |
| Surrenders | (875,968) | (842,436) |

|  |  |  |
|---|---:|---:|
| Fees | (7,174) | (6,795) |
| Interest credited | 203,460 | 262,472 |
| **Account value, end of period** | **$ 8,998,869** | **$ 9,400,270** |
| **Single premium immediate annuity** | | |
| Reserve, beginning of period | $ 1,199,276 | $ 1,075,638 |
| Net inflows | 75,450 | 36,436 |
| Interest and mortality | 35,374 | 32,726 |
| **Reserve, end of period** | **$ 1,310,100** | **$ 1,144,800** |
| **Variable deferred annuity** | | |
| Account value, beginning of period | $ 489,305 | $ 417,645 |
| Net inflows | 83,843 | 91,664 |
| Surrenders | (95,054) | (84,866) |
| Fees | (4,308) | (3,945) |
| Change in market value and other | 19,854 | 52,440 |
| **Account value, end of period** | **$ 493,640** | **$ 472,938** |

Deferred and single premium immediate annuity sales increased compared to last year, which resulted in the increase in fund inflows to these products. The Company has increased its focus on the annuity channel, expanding distribution through the introduction of additional marketing programs and the development of new accounts. The Company also introduced a new indexed annuity.

Variable deferred annuities have no guaranted minimum withdrawal benefits. Our total direct exposure on the guaranteed minimum death benefits associated with these products was $1.3 million and $1.6 million as of September 30, 2014 and 2013, respectively. After reinsurance, which is with reinsurers rated "A" or higher by A.M. Best, the net exposure was $0.2 million and $0.3 million, as of September 30, 2014 and 2013, respectively.

*Benefits, losses and expenses*

Policyholder benefits are highly correlated to the sales volume of Single Premium Immediate Annuity ("SPIA") contracts and increased for 2014 compared to 2013.

These benefits consist of annuity payments and reserve increases for annuity contracts. Commissions increased for the three and nine months ended September 30, 2014 compared to 2013 primarily as a result of increased annuity sales.

Other operating expenses decreased during the three and nine months ended September 30, 2014 compared to 2013.

The change in DAC represents acquisition costs capitalized less the amortization of existing DAC, which is calculated in proportion to expected gross profits. The following table shows the components of the change in DAC (in thousands):

|  | Three months ended September 30, | | | Nine months ended September 30, | | |
|---|---:|---:|---:|---:|---:|---:|
|  | 2014 | 2013 | Change | 2014 | 2013 | Change |
| Acquisition cost capitalized | $ 12,219 | $ 13,315 | $(1,096) | $ 36,413 | $ 36,370 | $ 43 |

|  | | | | | | |
|---|---:|---:|---:|---:|---:|---:|
| Amortization of DAC | (20,665) | (23,718) | 3,053 | (58,469) | (64,032) | 5,563 |
| Net change in DAC (1) | $ (8,446) | $ (10,403) | $ 1,957 | $ (22,056) | $ (27,662) | $5,606 |

(1) A positive amount of net change indicates more expense was deferred than amortized and represents a decrease to expenses in the period indicated, a negative net change indicates less expense was deferred than amortized and represents an increase to expenses in the period indicated.

The amortization of DAC as a percentage of gross profits is an important ratio for the Annuity segment. Changes in this ratio reflect the impact of items such as surrenders which impact the DAC amortization relative to gross margins. The ratios for the three months ended September 30, 2014 and 2013 were 36.9% and 42.7%, respectively. The ratios for the nine months ended September 30, 2014 and 2013 were 33.8% and 36.1%, respectively.

*Options and Derivatives*

Shown below is the incremental impact of the option return to net investment income, and the impact of the equity-indexed annuity embedded derivatives to interest credited to policyholders' account balances (in thousands):

|  | Three months ended September 30, | | | Nine months ended September 30, | | |
|---|---:|---:|---:|---:|---:|---:|
|  | 2014 | 2013 | Change | 2014 | 2013 | Change |
| **Net investment income** | | | | | | |
| Without option return | $ 122,684 | $ 135,304 | $ (12,620) | $ 376,841 | $ 416,132 | $ (39,291) |
| Option return | 6,206 | 13,018 | (6,812) | 27,506 | 47,398 | (19,892) |
| **Interest credited to policy account balances** | | | | | | |
| Without embedded derivatives | 65,333 | 74,261 | (8,928) | 194,877 | 229,681 | (34,804) |
| Equity-indexed annuity embedded derivatives | 1,764 | 10,947 | (9,183) | 15,810 | 39,306 | (23,496) |

Advanced Risk Management

Net investment income without option return decreased for the three and nine months ended September 30, 2014 compared to 2013 primarily due to lower portfolio yield and aggregate account values. Fixed interest credited to policyholders' account balances without embedded derivatives decreased during the three and nine months ended September 30, 2014 compared to 2013 due to these same two factors.

The returns from options and the related equity-indexed embedded derivative return, decreased during the three and nine months ended September 30, 2014 compared to the same period in 2013, due to the relative change in the S&P 500 Index during the respective periods. These option returns correlate to the 0.6% and 4.7% change in the S&P 500 Index during the quarters ended September 30, 2014 and 2013, respectively. For the nine months ended September 30, 2014 and 2013 the decrease correlates to the 6.7% and 17.9% return in the S&P 500, respectively.

**Health**

Health segment results for the periods indicated were as follows (in thousands):

|  | Three months ended September 30, | | | Nine months ended September 30, | | |
|---|---|---|---|---|---|---|
|  | 2014 | 2013 | Change | 2014 | 2013 | Change |
| **Premiums and other revenues** | | | | | | |
| Premiums | $ 53,454 | $ 52,839 | $ 615 | $ 164,169 | $ 159,100 | $5,069 |
| Net investment income | 2,971 | 2,941 | 30 | 8,806 | 8,645 | 161 |
| Other income | 5,075 | 4,439 | 636 | 15,330 | 13,255 | 2,075 |
| **Total premiums and other revenues** | 61,500 | 60,219 | 1,281 | 188,305 | 181,000 | 7,305 |
| **Benefits, losses and expenses** | | | | | | |
| Claims incurred | 33,193 | 34,404 | (1,211) | 109,859 | 106,378 | 3,481 |
| Commissions for acquiring and servicing policies | 9,688 | 7,316 | 2,372 | 27,031 | 20,568 | 6,463 |
| Other operating expenses | 10,009 | 11,222 | (1,213) | 32,701 | 35,810 | (3,109) |
| Change in deferred policy acquisition | (694) | 107 | (801) | (865) | 2,080 | (2,945) |

|  | | | | | | |
|---|---|---|---|---|---|---|
| costs [1] | | | | | | |
| Total benefits and expenses | 52,196 | 53,049 | (853) | 168,726 | 164,836 | 3,890 |
| Income before other items and federal income taxes | $ 9,304 | $ 7,170 | $2,134 | $ 19,579 | $ 16,164 | $3,415 |

(1) A negative amount of net change indicates more expense was deferred than amortized and represents a decrease to expenses in the period indicated, a positive net change indicates less expense was deferred than amortized and represents an increase to expenses in the period indicated.

Earnings increased during the three months ended September 30, 2014 versus 2013 due to a decrease in claims and operating expenses. Earnings increased during the nine months ended September 30, 2014 compared to 2013, primarily due to lower operating expenses and an increase in other income primarily from continued growth in the MGU business block.

*Premiums and other revenues*

Health earned premiums for the periods indicated are as follows (in thousands, except percentages):

|  | Three months ended September 30, | | | | Nine months ended September 30, | | | |
|---|---|---|---|---|---|---|---|---|
|  | 2014 | | 2013 | | 2014 | | 2013 | |
|  | Amount | Percentage | Amount | Percentage | Amount | Percentage | Amount | Percentage |
| Medicare Supplement | $ 21,060 | 39.4 % | $ 22,591 | 42.8 % | $64,413 | 39.2 % | $68,509 | 43.1 % |
| Medical expense | 4,985 | 9.3 | 7,463 | 14.1 | 16,750 | 10.2 | 23,168 | 14.6 |
| Group health | 7,051 | 13.2 | 9,291 | 17.6 | 25,811 | 15.7 | 27,556 | 17.3 |
| Credit accident and health | 3,738 | 7.0 | 3,721 | 7.0 | 11,049 | 6.7 | 11,438 | 7.2 |
| MGU | 6,301 | 11.8 | 4,822 | 9.1 | 18,183 | 11.1 | 14,750 | 9.3 |
| Supplemental insurance | 8,785 | 16.4 | 3,409 | 6.5 | 23,110 | 14.1 | 8,571 | 5.4 |
| All other | 1,534 | 2.9 | 1,542 | 2.9 | 4,853 | 3.0 | 5,108 | 3.1 |
| Total | $ 53,454 | 100.0 % | $ 52,839 | 100.0 % | $ 164,169 | 100.0 % | $ 159,100 | 100.0 % |

Premiums increased during the three and nine months ended September 30, 2014 compared to 2013, primarily from the sales of individual limited benefit supplemental insurance products as well as growth in the MGU business. Medicare Supplement premiums declined due to policy lapses outpacing new sales which have a lower average premium per policy.

Our in-force certificates or policies as of the dates indicated are as follows:

|  | September 30, 2014 | | December 31, 2013 | |
|---|---|---|---|---|
|  | Number of Policies | Percentage of Total Policies | Number of Policies | Percentage of Total Policies |
| Medicare Supplement | 38,120 | 5.7% | 40,064 | 6.4% |
| Medical expense | 3,551 | 0.5 | 4,633 | 0.7 |
| Group | 16,306 | 2.4 | 19,679 | 3.1 |
| Credit accident and health | 229,441 | 34.2 | 235,014 | 37.5 |
| MGU | 270,416 | 40.3 | 221,811 | 35.3 |
| Supplemental insurance | 70,694 | 10.5 | 61,342 | 9.8 |
| All other | 42,341 | 6.4 | 45,369 | 7.2 |
| **Total** | **670,869** | **100.0%** | **627,912** | **100.0%** |

Total in-force policies increased during the nine months ended September 30, 2014 compared to 2013 primarily due to increases in the MGU and supplemental insurance lines. The MGU line increased as a result of our continued expansion in the MGU market as employers are using the stop loss market to manage the cost of providing health insurance for employees. The supplemental insurance line continues to increase with the demand for individual limited benefit products.

*Benefits, losses and expenses*

Claims incurred decreased during the quarter ended September 30, 2014 compared to 2013 primarily as a result of the continued decline in the closed medical expense block and a decrease in group claim submissions.

Claims incurred increased during the nine months ended September 30, 2014 compared to 2013 primarily due to a judicial determination that the Company could not rescind a reinsurance agreement in dispute. Although the Company is appealing the determination, it has accrued for claims the reinsurer has asserted are due under the agreement.

Other operating expenses decreased during the three and nine months ended September 30, 2014 compared to 2013.

*Change in Deferred Policy Acquisition Costs*

The following table presents the components of the change in DAC (in thousands):

|  | Three months ended September 30, | | | Nine months ended September 30, | | |
|---|---|---|---|---|---|---|
|  | 2014 | 2013 | Change | 2014 | 2013 | Change |
| Acquisition cost capitalized | $ 5,486 | $ 4,017 | $1,469 | $ 14,949 | $ 9,457 | $ 5,492 |
| Amortization of DAC | (4,792) | (4,124) | (668) | (14,084) | (11,537) | (2,547) |
| **Net change in DAC** | $ 694 | $ (107) | $ 801 | $ 865 | $ (2,080) | $ 2,945 |

(1) A positive amount of net change indicates more expense was deferred than amortized and represents a decrease to expenses in the period indicated, a negative net change indicates less expense was deferred than amortized and represents an increase to expenses in the period indicated.

The net change in DAC increased for the three and nine months ended September 30, 2014 compared to 2013, primarily due to higher commissions from increased sales of individual limited benefit supplemental insurance products.

## Property and Casualty

Property and Casualty results for the periods indicated were as follows (in thousands, except percentages):

|  | Three months ended September 30, | | | Nine months ended September 30, | | |
|---|---|---|---|---|---|---|
|  | 2014 | 2013 | Change | 2014 | 2013 | Change |
| **Net premiums written** | $282,058 | $272,524 | $ 9,534 | $854,593 | $823,284 | $ 31,309 |
| **Premiums and other revenues** | | | | | | |
| Net premiums earned | $279,429 | $271,270 | $ 8,159 | $820,953 | $801,106 | $ 19,847 |
| Net investment income | 14,523 | 17,081 | (2,558) | 44,452 | 50,199 | (5,747) |
| Other income | 905 | 2,177 | (1,272) | 3,550 | 4,827 | (1,277) |
| Total premiums and other revenues | 294,857 | 290,528 | 4,329 | 868,955 | 856,132 | 12,823 |
| **Benefits, losses and expenses** | | | | | | |
| Claims incurred | 180,413 | 182,809 | (2,396) | 563,650 | 581,042 | (17,392) |
| Commissions for acquiring and servicing policies | 46,894 | 46,533 | 361 | 143,632 | 134,190 | 9,442 |
| Other operating expenses | 34,549 | 33,087 | 1,462 | 96,447 | 96,851 | (404) |
| Change in deferred policy acquisition costs (1) | 2,913 | 3,465 | (552) | 5,436 | 10,851 | (5,415) |
| Total benefits and expenses | 264,769 | 265,894 | (1,125) | 809,165 | 822,934 | (13,769) |
| **Income (loss) before other items and federal income taxes** | $ 30,088 | $ 24,634 | $ 5,454 | $ 59,790 | $ 33,198 | $ 26,592 |
| Loss ratio | 64.6% | 67.4% | (2.8) | 68.7% | 72.5% | (3.8) |
| Underwriting expense | 30.2 | 30.6 | (0.4) | 29.9 | 30.2 | (0.3) |

| | | | | | | |
|---|---|---|---|---|---|---|
| ratio | | | | | | |
| Combined ratio | 94.8% | 98.0% | (3.2) | 98.6% | 102.7% | (4.1) |
| Impact of catastrophe events on combined ratio | 5.3 | 4.1 | 1.2 | 7.1 | 9.6 | (2.5) |
| Combined ratio without impact of catastrophe events | 89.5% | 93.9% | (4.4) | 91.5% | 93.1% | (1.6) |
| Gross catastrophe losses | $ 14,487 | $ 10,871 | $ 3,616 | $ 55,592 | $ 84,744 | $(29,152) |
| Net catastrophe losses | 14,652 | 11,613 | 3,039 | 56,795 | 76,555 | (19,760) |

(1) A negative amount of net change indicates more expense was deferred than amortized and represents a decrease to expenses in the period indicated, a positive net change indicates less expense was deferred than amortized and represents an increase to expenses in the period indicated.

Property and Casualty results for the quarter improved compared to 2013 due to an improved rate adequacy and underwriting improvements which were partially offset by increases in catastrophe claims and commissions. Results improved during the nine months ended September 30, 2014 compared to 2013, primarily as a result of decreases in catastrophe losses and improved rate adequacy.

### Benefits, losses and expenses

Claims incurred decreased during the three months ended September 30, 2014 compared to 2013, as a result of lower non-catastrophe losses. Claims incurred decreased during the nine months ended September 30, 2014 compared to 2013, as a result of fewer catastrophe losses. The decrease year-to-date is due primarily to the decreases in the severity of catastrophes in 2014 compared to 2013.

Commissions increased for the three and nine months ended September 30, 2014 compared to 2013, primarily due to an increase in premium as well as an increase in certain variable commissions driven by the improvement in the loss ratio.

### Products

Our Property and Casualty segment consists of: (i) Personal products, which we market primarily to individuals, representing 62.2% of net premiums written, (ii) Commercial products, which focus primarily on agricultural and other commercial markets, representing 29.6% of net premiums written, and (iii) Credit-related property insurance products, which are marketed to and through financial institutions and retailers, representing 8.2% of net premiums written.

### Personal Products

Personal Products results for the periods indicated were as follows (in thousands, except percentages):

| | Three months ended September 30, | | | Nine months ended September 30, | | |
|---|---|---|---|---|---|---|
| | 2014 | 2013 | Change | 2014 | 2013 | Change |
| **Net premiums written** | | | | | | |
| Auto | $102,678 | $102,643 | $ 35 | $304,776 | $306,640 | $ (1,864) |
| Homeowner | 63,073 | 60,515 | 2,558 | 172,294 | 164,661 | 7,633 |

|  | | | | | | |
|---|---|---|---|---|---|---|
| Other Personal | 9,718 | 9,556 | 162 | 28,998 | 28,712 | 286 |
| **Total net premiums written** | **$175,469** | **$172,714** | **$ 2,755** | **$506,068** | **$500,013** | **$ 6,055** |
| **Net premiums earned** | | | | | | |
| Auto | $ 99,957 | $101,478 | $(1,521) | $298,612 | $302,711 | $ (4,099) |
| Homeowner | 56,720 | 53,351 | 3,369 | 164,799 | 154,752 | 10,047 |
| Other Personal | 9,303 | 9,234 | 69 | 27,055 | 27,106 | (51) |
| **Total net premiums earned** | **$165,980** | **$164,063** | **$ 1,917** | **$490,466** | **$484,569** | **$ 5,897** |
| **Loss ratio** | | | | | | |
| Auto | 79.4% | 75.9% | 3.5 | 76.1% | 77.7% | (1.6) |
| Homeowner | 55.3 | 80.0 | (24.7) | 73.3 | 96.8 | (23.5) |
| Other Personal | 69.3 | 57.0 | 12.3 | 42.3 | 53.7 | (11.4) |
| **Personal line loss ratio** | **70.6%** | **76.2%** | **(5.6)** | **73.3%** | **82.5%** | **(9.2)** |
| **Combined Ratio** | | | | | | |
| Auto | 103.8% | 99.4% | 4.4 | 99.1% | 100.6% | (1.5) |
| Homeowner | 81.6 | 105.7 | (24.1) | 98.5 | 121.8 | (23.3) |
| Other Personal | 92.3 | 79.6 | 12.7 | 61.7 | 76.3 | (14.6) |
| **Personal line combined ratio** | **95.5%** | **100.3%** | **(4.8)** | **96.8%** | **106.0%** | **(9.2)** |

*Personal Automobile*: Net premiums written and earned decreased in our personal automobile line during the nine months ended September 30, 2014 compared to 2013, primarily due to a decline in policies in-force. The loss and combined ratios improved year-to-date during 2014 compared to 2013 due to a decline in catastrophe losses.

*Homeowners*: Net premiums written and earned increased during the three and nine months ended September 30, 2014 compared to 2013 primarily due to increasing premium rates over the time period. The loss and combined ratios improved for the three and nine months ended September 30, 2014 compared to 2013 due to a decrease in weather-related losses and improved rate adequacy.

*Other Personal*: These products include watercraft, rental-owner and umbrella coverages for individuals seeking to protect their personal property and liability not covered within their homeowner and auto policies. Low volume and volatility with these lines can lead to some quarterly fluctuations. The loss and combined ratios decreased during the nine months ended September 30, 2014 compared to 2013, in line with trends on the larger personal lines.

*Commercial Products*

Commercial Products results for the periods indicated were as follows (in thousands, except percentages):

|  | Three months ended September 30, | | | Nine months ended September 30, | | |
|---|---|---|---|---|---|---|
|  | 2014 | 2013 | Change | 2014 | 2013 | Change |
| **Net premiums written** | | | | | | |
| Other Commercial | $33,072 | $31,116 | $1,956 | $117,594 | $109,437 | $ 8,157 |
| Agricultural Business | 31,515 | 27,976 | 3,539 | 94,311 | 83,655 | 10,656 |
| Commercial | 18,952 | 17,471 | 1,481 | 69,103 | 64,635 | 4,468 |

| | | | | | | |
|---|---|---|---|---|---|---|
| Automobile | | | | | | |
| **Total net premiums written** | **$83,539** | **$76,563** | **$6,976** | **$281,008** | **$257,727** | **$23,281** |
| **Net premiums earned** | | | | | | |
| Other Commercial | $37,820 | $32,826 | $4,994 | $106,026 | $ 95,058 | $10,968 |
| Agricultural Business | 28,545 | 28,073 | 472 | 87,408 | 81,759 | 5,649 |
| Commercial Automobile | 22,595 | 19,698 | 2,897 | 61,377 | 58,243 | 3,134 |
| **Total net premiums earned** | **$88,960** | **$80,597** | **$8,363** | **$254,811** | **$235,060** | **$19,751** |
| **Loss ratio** | | | | | | |
| Other Commercial | 60.3% | 42.1% | 18.2 | 79.6% | 58.3% | 21.3 |
| Agricultural Business | 61.7 | 78.0 | (16.3) | 62.2 | 78.8 | (16.6) |
| Commercial Automobile | 66.2 | 81.5 | (15.3) | 69.1 | 74.9 | (5.8) |
| **Commercial line loss ratio** | **62.2%** | **64.2%** | **(2.0)** | **71.1%** | **69.5%** | **1.6** |
| **Combined ratio** | | | | | | |
| Other Commercial | 86.2% | 69.6% | 16.6 | 107.2% | 86.8% | 20.4 |
| Agricultural Business | 101.7 | 115.5 | (13.8) | 99.6 | 115.7 | (16.1) |
| Commercial Automobile | 87.6 | 103.7 | (16.1) | 93.1 | 98.7 | (5.6) |
| **Commercial line combined ratio** | **91.5%** | **93.9%** | **(2.4)** | **101.2%** | **99.8%** | **1.4** |

*Other Commercial*: Net premiums written and earned increased during the three and nine months ended September 30, 2014 compared to 2013, primarily attributable to increased sales in the workers' compensation and business owners' lines. The loss and combined ratios for the three and nine months ended September 30, 2014 increased due to larger than anticipated reserve increases on workers' compensation claims.

*Agricultural Business*: Our agricultural business product allows policyholders to customize and cover their agriculture exposure using a package policy which includes coverage for residences and household contents, farm buildings and building contents, personal and commercial liability and personal property. Net premiums written and earned increased during the three and nine months ended September 30, 2014 compared to 2013, primarily as a result of rate increases and a decrease in ceded premiums. The loss and combined ratio improved for the three and nine months ended September 30, 2014 primarily due to a reduction in overall claim frequency, as well as a combination of rate and underwriting actions.

*Commercial Automobile*: Net premiums written and earned increased primarily due to rate increases over the three and nine months ended September 30, 2014 compared to 2013. The loss and combined ratio improved for the three and nine months ended September 30, 2014 primarily due to a reduction in overall claim frequency.

**Credit Products**

Credit-related property products for the periods indicated were as follows (in thousands, except percentages):

|  | Three months ended September 30, | | | Nine months ended September 30, | | |
| --- | --- | --- | --- | --- | --- | --- |
|  | 2014 | 2013 | Change | 2014 | 2013 | Change |
| Net premiums written | $23,050 | $23,247 | $ (197) | $67,518 | $65,544 | $ 1,974 |
| Net premiums earned | 24,489 | 26,610 | (2,121) | 75,676 | 81,477 | (5,801) |
| Loss ratio | 32.2 | 22.9 | 9.3 | 30.2 | 22.2 | 8.0 |
| Combined ratio | 101.6 | 100.0 | 1.6 | 102.2 | 97.2 | 5.0 |

Credit-related property products are offered on automobiles, furniture and appliances in connection with the financing of those items. These policies pay an amount if the insured property is lost or damaged and the amount paid is not directly related to an event affecting the consumer's ability to pay the debt.

Net premiums written increased for the nine months ended September 30, 2014 compared to 2013 primarily due to an increase in our Guaranteed Auto Protection business. Net premiums earned decreased as premiums shifted from Guaranteed Auto Protection Insurance to Guaranteed Auto Protection Waiver, a lower premium debt protection product.

The loss and combined ratios increased during the three and nine months ended 2014 compared to 2013 primarily due to an increase in claims in our collateral protection business.

**Corporate and Other**

Corporate and Other segment financial results for the periods indicated were as follows (in thousands):

|  | Three months ended September 30, | | | Nine months ended September 30, | | |
| --- | --- | --- | --- | --- | --- | --- |
|  | 2014 | 2013 | Change | 2014 | 2013 | Change |
| **Premiums and other revenues** | | | | | | |
| Net investment income | $32,507 | $28,984 | $ 3,523 | $67,366 | $ 56,919 | $ 10,447 |
| Realized investments gains, net | (2,257) | 43,483 | (45,740) | 24,503 | 103,970 | (79,467) |
| Other Income | 3,330 | 4,491 | (1,161) | 6,801 | 9,007 | (2,206) |
| **Total premiums and other revenues** | 33,580 | 76,958 | (43,378) | 98,670 | 169,896 | (71,226) |
| **Benefits, losses and expenses** | | | | | | |
| Commissions | — | 11 | (11) | — | 221 | (221) |
| Other operating expenses | 13,357 | 15,523 | (2,166) | 35,365 | 44,868 | (9,503) |
| **Total benefits, losses and expenses** | 13,357 | 15,534 | (2,177) | 35,365 | 45,089 | (9,724) |
| **Income before other items and federal income taxes** | $20,223 | $61,424 | $(41,201) | $63,305 | $124,807 | $(61,502) |

Earnings decreased during the three months ended September 30, 2014 compared to 2013 primarily due to lower realized investment gains. The decrease in realized gains is attributable to lower gains in equity securities and less real estate sale activity.

The Corporate and Other business segment recorded other-than-temporary impairments of $3,045,000 and $3,503,000 in the nine months ended September 30, 2014 and 2013, respectively, which are included in "Realized investment gains, net."

## Investments

We manage our investment portfolio to optimize the rate of return commensurate with sound and prudent asset selection and to maintain a well-diversified portfolio. Our investment operations are regulated primarily by the state insurance departments where we or our insurance subsidiaries are domiciled. Investment activities, including setting investment policies and defining acceptable risk levels, are subject to review and approval by our Board of Directors, which is assisted by our Finance Committee and Management Risk Committee.

Our insurance and annuity products are primarily supported by investment-grade bonds and, to a lesser extent collateralized mortgage obligations and commercial mortgage loans. We purchase fixed maturity securities and designate them as either held-to-maturity or available-for-sale considering our estimated future cash flow needs. We also monitor the composition of our fixed maturity securities classified as held-to-maturity and available-for-sale and adjust the mix within the portfolio as investments mature or new investments are purchased.

We invest in commercial mortgage loans when the yield and credit risk compare favorably with fixed maturity securities. Individual residential mortgage loans including sub-prime or Alt A mortgage loans have not been and are not expected to be part of our investment portfolio. We invest in real estate and equity securities based on a risk and reward analysis where we believe there are opportunities for enhanced returns.

The following summarizes the carrying values of our invested assets (other than investments in unconsolidated affiliates) by asset class (in thousands, except percentages):

|  | September 30, 2014 | | December 31, 2013 | |
| --- | --- | --- | --- | --- |
|  | Amount | Percent | Amount | Percent |
| Bonds held-to-maturity, at amortized cost | $ 8,364,731 | 42.9% | $ 8,491,347 | 43.8% |
| Bonds available-for-sale, at fair value | 4,926,218 | 25.2 | 4,599,673 | 23.7 |
| Equity securities, at fair value | 1,494,471 | 7.7 | 1,410,608 | 7.3 |
| Mortgage loans on real estate, net of allowance | 3,318,552 | 17.0 | 3,299,242 | 17.0 |
| Policy loans | 404,705 | 2.1 | 397,407 | 2.0 |
| Investment real estate, net of accumulated depreciation | 458,116 | 2.3 | 507,142 | 2.6 |
| Short-term investments | 346,343 | 1.8 | 495,386 | 2.6 |
| Other invested assets | 202,131 | 1.0 | 201,442 | 1.0 |
| **Total investments** | **$19,515,267** | **100.0%** | **$19,402,247** | **100.0%** |

The increase in our total investments at September 30, 2014 as compared to December 31, 2013 was primarily a result of an increase in bonds and the market value of equity securities, partially offset by decreases in short term investments.

Each component of our invested assets and their related revenues are described further in the Notes to the Unaudited Consolidated Financial Statements. Additionally, Note 2, Summary of Significant Accounting Policies and Practices, of the Notes to the Consolidated Financial Statements within our Annual Report on Form 10-K for the year ended December 31, 2013 filed with the SEC on February 28, 2014 contains a detailed description of the Company's methodology for evaluating other-than-temporary impairment losses on its investments.

*Bonds:* We allocate most of our fixed maturity securities to support our insurance business. As of September 30, 2014, our fixed maturity securities had an estimated fair value of $13.8 billion, which was $0.7 billion, or 5.3%, above amortized cost. At December 31, 2013, our fixed maturity securities had an estimated fair value of $13.4 billion, which was $0.5 billion, or 3.7%, above amortized cost. At September 30, 2014 fixed maturity securities' estimated fair value, due in one year or less, were $1.2 billion which was unchanged compared to December 31, 2013.

The following table identifies the total bonds by credit quality rating, using both Standard & Poor's and Moody's ratings (in thousands, except percentages):

|  | September 30, 2014 | | | December 31, 2013 | | |
| --- | --- | --- | --- | --- | --- | --- |
|  | Amortized Cost | Estimated Fair Value | % of Fair Value | Amortized Cost | Estimated Fair Value | % of Fair Value |
| AAA | $ 629,985 | $ 667,466 | 4.9 | $ 621,527 | $ 649,161 | 4.9 |
| AA | 1,636,392 | 1,715,944 | 12.5 | 1,472,221 | 1,511,517 | 11.3 |
| A | 5,228,300 | 5,511,482 | 40.0 | 5,260,435 | 5,466,136 | 40.7 |
| BBB | 5,094,673 | 5,367,709 | 39.0 | 5,094,589 | 5,272,246 | 39.2 |
| BB and below | 477,080 | 489,870 | 3.6 | 498,966 | 523,681 | 3.9 |
| Total | $13,066,430 | $13,752,471 | 100.0 | $12,947,738 | $13,422,741 | 100.0 |

We expect the exposure to below investment grade securities to decrease as these bonds approach maturity. We do not own direct investments in sovereign debt issued by Greece, Ireland, Italy, Portugal or Spain.

*Mortgage Loans:* We invest in commercial mortgage loans that are diversified by property-type and geography to support our insurance business. Generally, mortgage loans are secured by first liens on income-producing real estate with a loan-to-value ratio of up to 75%. Mortgage loans held-for-investment are carried at outstanding principal balances, adjusted for any unamortized premium or discount, deferred fees or expenses, and net of allowances. The weighted average coupon yield on the principal funded for mortgage loans was 5.3% and 5.2% at September 30, 2014 and December 31, 2013, respectively. It is likely that the weighted average yield on funded mortgage loans will decline as loans mature and new loans are originated with lower rates in the current interest rate environment.

*Equity Securities*: Our equity portfolio is in companies publicly traded on national U.S. stock exchanges; the cost and estimated fair value of the equity securities are as follows (in thousands):

|  | September 30, 2014 | | | | |
| --- | --- | --- | --- | --- | --- |
|  | Cost | Unrealized Gains | Unrealized Losses | Fair Value | % of Fair Value |
| Common stock | $722,015 | $734,419 | $ (3,791) | $1,452,643 | 97.2 |
| Preferred stock | 23,718 | 18,123 | (13) | 41,828 | 2.8 |
| Total | $745,733 | $752,542 | $ (3,804) | $1,494,471 | 100.0 |

|  | December 31, 2013 | | | | |
| --- | --- | --- | --- | --- | --- |
|  | Cost | Unrealized Gains | Unrealized Losses | Fair Value | % of Fair Value |
| Common stock | $717,390 | $653,967 | $ (2,362) | $1,368,995 | 97.0 |
| Preferred stock | 23,690 | 18,301 | (378) | 41,613 | 3.0 |
| Total | $741,080 | $672,268 | $ (2,740) | $1,410,608 | 100.0 |

*Investment Real Estate*: We invest in commercial real estate where positive cash flows and/or appreciation in value is expected. Real estate may be owned directly by our insurance companies or non-insurance affiliates or indirectly in joint ventures with real estate developers or investors we determine share our perspective regarding risk and return relationships. The carrying value of real estate is stated at cost, less accumulated depreciation and prior impairments, if any. Depreciation is provided over the estimated useful lives of the properties.

*Short-Term Investments*: Short-term investments are primarily commercial paper rated A2/P2 or better by Standard & Poor's and Moody's, respectively. The amount fluctuates depending on the available long-term investment opportunities and our liquidity needs, including mortgage investment-funding commitments.

*Policy Loans*: For certain life insurance products, policyholders may borrow funds using the policy's cash value as collateral. The maximum amount of the policy loan depends upon the policy's surrender value and the number of years since policy origination. As of September 30, 2014, we had $404.7 million in policy loans with a loan to surrender value of 56.7%, and at December 31, 2013, we had $397.4 million in policy loans with a loan to surrender value of 67.9%. Interest rates on policy loans primarily range from 3.0% to 12.0% per annum. Policy loans may be repaid at any time by the policyholder and have priority to any claims on the policy. If the policyholder fails to repay the policy loan, funds are withdrawn from the policy's benefits.

### Net Investment Income and Realized Gains (Losses)

Net investment income decreased $54.9 million during the nine months ended September 30, 2014 primarily due to a decrease in income from options and bonds. Net investment income from options decreased $19.0 million during 2014 due to a smaller change in the S&P 500 index from which our option values are derived. Net investment income from bonds decreased $29.2 million during the nine months ended September 30, 2014 primarily due to bonds with lower interest yields making up a larger percentage of our portfolio as older bonds, which were purchased when interest rates were higher, matured.

Realized gains decreased $79.9 million during the nine months ended September 30, 2014 compared to 2013 primarily as a result of decrease in realized gains on sales of investment real estate. Other-than-temporary impairment on investment securities increased $0.5 million during the nine months ended September 30, 2014 compared to 2013.

### Net Unrealized Gains and Losses

The net unrealized gains on available-for-sale securities at September 30, 2014 and December 31, 2013 were $974.7 million and $812.8 million, respectively. Unrealized gains or losses on available-for-sale securities are recognized as other comprehensive income or loss which has no impact on earnings. The gross unrealized gains on available-for-sale securities increased $114.0 million to $998.6 million during 2014 resulting from increases in the value of bonds and equity securities. The gross unrealized losses on available-for-sale securities decreased to $23.8 million at September 30, 2014 from $71.6 million at December 31, 2013. The gross unrealized gains on held-to-maturity securities increased $52.0 million to $503.8 million, and gross unrealized losses decreased from $120.1 million in 2013 to $42.3 million in 2014. The decrease in gross unrealized losses of available-for-sale and held-to-maturity securities during 2014 is primarily attributable to corporate debt securities and the impact changes in interest rates have on fixed income securities.

The fair value of our investment securities is affected by various factors, including volatility of financial markets, changes in interest rates and fluctuations in credit spread. We have the ability and intent to hold those securities in unrealized loss positions until a market price recovery or maturity. Further, it is unlikely that we will be required to sell them prior to recovery, and recovery is expected in a reasonable period of time.

## Liquidity

Our liquidity requirements have been and are expected to continue to be met by funds from operations, comprised of premiums received from our customers and investment income. The primary use of cash has been and is expected to continue to be payment of policyholder benefits and claims incurred. Current and expected patterns of claim frequency and severity may change from period to period but continue to be within historical norms. Management considers our current liquidity position to be sufficient to meet anticipated demands over the next twelve months. Our contractual obligations are not expected to have a significant negative impact to cash flow from operations.

Changes in interest rates during 2014 and market expectations for potentially higher rates through 2015 will likely lead to increases in the volume of annuity contracts, which may be partially offset by increases in surrenders. Freezing our defined benefit pension plans effective December 31, 2013, will lessen the impact of changes in interest rates on our contributions to these plans, and future contributions to our defined benefit plans may be smaller than historical contributions. A portion of the contributions will be used for employer contributions to defined contribution retirement plans, which will provide employees with the potential to accumulate assets for retirement. There are no other known trends or uncertainties regarding product pricing, changes in product lines or rising costs, which would have a significant impact to cash flows from operations. No unusually large capital expenditures are expected in the next 12-24 months. Additionally, we have paid dividends to stockholders for over 100 consecutive years and expect to continue this trend.

To ensure we will be able to continue to pay future commitments, the funds received as premium payments and deposits are invested in bonds and commercial mortgages. Funds are invested with the intent that income from the investments and proceeds from the maturities will meet our ongoing cash flow needs. We historically have not had to liquidate invested assets in order to cover cash flow needs. We believe our portfolio of highly liquid available-for-sale investment securities, including equity securities, is sufficient to meet future liquidity needs as necessary.

Our cash and cash equivalents and short-term investment position was $482.5 million at September 30, 2014 compared to $613.3 million at December 31, 2013. The decrease relates primarily to a reduction in short-term investments.

A downgrade or a potential downgrade in our financial strength ratings could result in a loss of business and could adversely affect our cash flow from operations. Further information regarding additional sources or uses of cash is described in Note 19, Commitments and Contingencies, of the Notes to the Consolidated Financial Statements.

## Capital Resources

Our capital resources are summarized below (in thousands):

|  | September 30, 2014 | December 31, 2013 |
|---|---|---|
| American National stockholders' equity, excluding accumulated other comprehensive income (loss), net of tax ("AOCI") | $ 3,892,484 | $ 3,776,862 |
| AOCI | 504,338 | 413,712 |
| **Total American National stockholders' equity** | **$ 4,396,822** | **$ 4,190,574** |

We have notes payable relating to borrowings by real estate joint ventures that we consolidate into our financial statements that are not part of our capital resources. The lenders for the notes payable have no recourse against us in the event of default by the joint ventures. Therefore, the liability we have for these notes payable is limited to our investment in the respective ventures, which totaled $14.9 million at September 30, 2014 and $12.8 million at December 31, 2013, respectively.

The changes in our capital resources are summarized below (in thousands):

|  | Nine months ended September 30, 2014 |
|---|---:|
| Net income | $ 178,023 |
| Increase in net unrealized gains | 89,051 |
| Defined benefit pension plan adjustment | 2,152 |
| Dividends to shareholders | (62,113) |
| Other | (865) |
| **Total** | **$ 206,248** |

During the nine months ended September 30, 2014, our capital resources increased substantially compared to the same period in 2013 primarily due to net income and increases in unrealized gains from our equity investment portfolio partially offset by dividends to stockholders.

*Statutory Capital and Surplus and Risk-based Capital*

Statutory capital and surplus is the capital of our insurance companies reported in accordance with accounting practices prescribed or permitted by the applicable state insurance departments. RBC is calculated using formulas applied to certain financial balances and activities that consider, among other things, risks related to the type and quality of the invested assets, insurance risks associated with an insurer's products and liabilities, interest rate risks and general business risks. Insurance companies that do not maintain capital and surplus at a level at least 200% of the authorized control level RBC are required to take certain regulatory actions. At September 30, 2014 and December 31, 2013, American National Insurance Company's statutory capital and surplus was $2,842,984,000 and $2,667,858,000, respectively. Additionally, each of the insurance subsidiaries had statutory capital and surplus at September 30, 2014 and December 31, 2013, substantially above its authorized control level RBC.

The achievement of long-term growth will require growth in American National Insurance Company's and our insurance subsidiaries' statutory capital and surplus. Our subsidiaries may obtain additional statutory capital through various sources, such as retained statutory earnings or equity contributions from us. As of December 31, 2013, the levels of our and our insurance subsidiaries' capital and surplus exceeded the minimum RBC requirements.

**Contractual Obligations**

Our future cash payments associated with claims and claims adjustment expenses, life, annuity and disability obligations, contractual obligations pursuant to operating leases for office space and equipment, and notes payable have not materially changed since December 31, 2013. We expect to have the capacity to pay our obligations as they come due.

**Off-Balance Sheet Arrangements**

We have off-balance sheet arrangements relating to third-party marketing operation bank loans as discussed in Note 16, Commitments and Contingencies, of the Notes to the unaudited

Consolidated Financial Statements. We could be exposed to a liability for these loans, which are supported by the cash value of the underlying insurance contracts. The cash value of the life insurance policies is designed to always equal or exceed the balance of the loans. Accordingly, management does not foresee any loss related to these arrangements.

**Related-Party Transactions**

We have various agency, consulting and service arrangements with individuals and entities considered to be related parties. Each of these arrangements has been reviewed and approved by our Audit Committee, which retains final decision-making authority for these transactions. The amounts involved, both individually and in the aggregate, with these arrangements are not material to any segment or to our overall operations. For additional details see Note 17, Related Party Transactions, of the Notes to the unaudited Consolidated Financial Statements.

## ITEM 3. QUANTITATIVE AND QUALITATIVE DISCLOSURES ABOUT MARKET RISK

Our market risks have not changed materially from those disclosed in our 2013 Annual Report on Form 10-K filed with the SEC on February 28, 2014.

## ITEM 4. CONTROLS AND PROCEDURES

The Company maintains disclosure controls and procedures (as that term is defined in Rules 13a-15(e) and 15d-15(e) under the Securities Exchange Act of 1934, as amended (Exchange Act)) that are designed to ensure that information required to be disclosed in the Company's reports under the Exchange Act is recorded, processed, summarized and reported within the time periods specified in the Securities and Exchange Commission's rules and forms, and that such information is accumulated and communicated to the Company's management, including its Chief Executive Officer and Corporate Chief Financial Officer, as appropriate, to allow timely decisions regarding required disclosures.

Any controls and procedures, no matter how well designed and operated, can provide only reasonable assurance of achieving the desired control objectives. The Company's management, with the participation of the Company's Chief Executive Officer and Corporate Chief Financial Officer, has evaluated the effectiveness of the design and operation of the Company's disclosure controls and procedures as of September 30, 2014. Based upon that evaluation and subject to the foregoing, the Company's Chief Executive Officer and Corporate Chief Financial Officer concluded that, as of September 30, 2014, the design and operation of the Company's disclosure controls and procedures were effective to accomplish their objectives at the reasonable assurance level.

Management has monitored the internal controls over financial reporting, including any material changes to the internal control over financial reporting. There were no changes in the Company's internal control over financial reporting (as that term is defined in Rules 13a-15(f) and 15d-15(f) under the Exchange Act) that occurred during the quarter ended September 30, 2014 that have materially affected, or are reasonably likely to materially affect, the Company's internal control over financial reporting.

## PART II – OTHER INFORMATION

### ITEM 1. LEGAL PROCEEDINGS

Information required for Item 1 is incorporated by reference to the discussion under the heading "Litigation" in Note 16, Commitments and Contingencies, of the Notes to the Unaudited Consolidated Financial Statements.

### ITEM 1A. RISK FACTORS

There have been no material changes with respect to the risk factors as previously disclosed in our 2013 Annual Report on Form 10-K filed with the SEC on February 28, 2014.

### ITEM 2. UNREGISTERED SALES OF EQUITY SECURITIES AND USE OF PROCEEDS

None.

### ITEM 3. DEFAULTS UPON SENIOR SECURITIES

None.

### ITEM 4. MINE SAFETY DISCLOSURES

Not Applicable.

### ITEM 5. OTHER INFORMATION

None.

### ITEM 6. EXHIBITS

| Exhibit Number | Basic Documents |
| --- | --- |
| 3.1 | Restated Articles of Incorporation, as amended (incorporated by reference to Exhibit No. 3.1 to the registrant's Registration Statement on Form 10-12B filed April 10, 2009). |
| 3.2 | Amended and Restated Bylaws (incorporated by reference to Exhibit No. 3.2 to the registrant's Current Report on Form 8-K filed May 2, 2012). |
| 31.1 | Certification of the principal executive officer pursuant to Section 302 of the Sarbanes-Oxley Act of 2002 (filed herewith). |
| 31.2 | Certification of the principal financial officer pursuant to Section 302 of the Sarbanes-Oxley Act of 2002 (filed herewith). |
| 32.1 | Certification of the principal executive officer and principal financial officer pursuant to Section 906 of the Sarbanes-Oxley Act of 2002 (filed herewith). |
| 101 | The following unaudited financial information from American National Insurance Company's Quarterly Report on Form 10-Q for Nine months ended September 30, 2014 formatted in eXtensible Business Reporting Language ("XBRL"): (i) Consolidated Statements of Financial Position, (ii) Consolidated Statements of Operations, |

(iii) Consolidated Statements of Comprehensive Income (Loss), (iv) Consolidated Statements of Changes in Stockholders' Equity, (v) Consolidated Statements of Cash Flows, and (vi) Notes to the Unaudited Consolidated Financial Statements.

## SIGNATURES

Pursuant to the requirements of the Securities Exchange Act of 1934, the Registrant has duly caused this report to be signed on its behalf by the undersigned thereunto duly authorized.

By: /s/ Robert L. Moody
Name: Robert L. Moody
Title: *Chairman of the Board, Chief Executive Officer*

By: /s/ John J. Dunn, Jr.
Name: John J. Dunn, Jr.,
Title: *Executive Vice President, Corporate Chief Financial Officer*

Date: November 07, 2014

# PRINCIPAL FINANCIAL GROUP INC
# FORM 10-K
# (Annual Report)

Filed 02/12/14 for the Period Ending 12/31/13

Address 711 HIGH STREET
DES MOINES, IA 50392-0300
Telephone 5152475111
CIK 0001126328
Symbol PFG
SIC Code 6321 - Accident and Health Insurance
Industry Insurance (Accident & Health)
Sector Financial
Fiscal Year 02/24

UNITED STATES SECURITIES AND EXCHANGE COMMISSION
Washington, D.C. 20549
FORM 10-K
PART I

**Item 1. Business**
Principal Financial Group, Inc. ("PFG") is a global investment management leader offering retirement services, insurance solutions and asset management. We offer businesses, individuals and institutional clients a wide range of financial products and services, including retirement, asset management and insurance through our diverse family of financial services companies. We have $483.2 billion in assets under management ("AUM") and approximately 19.4 million customers worldwide as of December 31, 2013.

We primarily focus on small and medium-sized businesses, which we define as companies with less than 1,000 employees, providing a broad array of retirement and employee benefit solutions to meet the needs of the business, the business owner and their employees. We are the leading provider of corporate defined contribution plans in the U.S., according to Spectrem Group. We are also the leading employee stock
ownership plan consultant. In addition, we are a leading provider of nonqualified plans, defined benefit plans and plan termination annuities. We are also one of the largest providers of specialty benefits insurance product solutions. We believe small and medium-sized businesses are an underserved market, offering attractive growth opportunities in the U.S. in

retirement services and other employee benefits. We also believe there is a significant opportunity to leverage our U.S. retirement expertise into select international markets that have adopted or are moving toward private sector defined contribution pension systems. This opportunity is particularly compelling as aging populations around the world are driving increased demand for retirement accumulation, retirement asset management and retirement income management solutions.

**Our Reportable Segments**

We organize our businesses into the following reportable segments:
- Retirement and Investor Services;
- Principal Global Investors;
- Principal International and
- U.S. Insurance Solutions.

We also have a Corporate segment, which consists of the assets and activities that have not been allocated to any other segment.
See Item 8. "Financial Statements and Supplementary Data, Notes to Consolidated Financial Statements, Note 16, Segment Information" for financial results of our segments, including our operating revenues for our products and services described in each of the subsequent segment discussions.

**Retirement and Investor Services Segment**

Our asset accumulation activities in the U.S. date back to the 1940s when we first began providing pension plan products and services. We
now offer a comprehensive portfolio of asset accumulation products and services for retirement savings and investment:
- To businesses of all sizes with a concentration on small and medium-sized businesses, we offer products and services for defined
contribution pension plans, including 401(k) and 403(b) plans, defined benefit pension plans, nonqualified executive benefit plans
and employee stock ownership plan ("ESOP") consulting services. For more basic investment needs, we offer SIMPLE Individual
Retirement Accounts ("IRA") and payroll deduction plans;
- To large institutional clients, we also offer investment-only products, including guaranteed investment contracts ("GICs") and
funding agreements and
- To employees of businesses and other individuals, we offer the ability to accumulate savings for retirement and other purposes
through mutual funds, individual annuities and bank products.

We organize our Retirement and Investor Services ("RIS") operations into two business groupings:

- Accumulation business — which includes full service accumulation, Principal Funds (our mutual fund business), individual annuities and bank and trust services; and
- Guaranteed business — which includes investment only and full service payout.

## Accumulation Business
### *Full Service Accumulation*
*Products*

We offer a wide variety of investment and administrative products for defined contribution pension plans, including 401(k) and 403(b) plans, defined benefit pension plans, nonqualified executive benefit plans and ESOPs. A 403(b) plan is a plan described in Section 403(b) of the Internal Revenue Code that provides retirement benefits for employees of tax-exempt organizations and public schools.

Full service accumulation products respond to the needs of plan sponsors seeking both administrative and investment services for defined contribution plans or defined benefit plans. The investment component of both the defined contribution and defined benefit plans may be in the form of a general account, separate account, a mutual fund offering or a collective investment trust. In addition, defined contribution plans may also offer their own employer security as an investment option.

We deliver both administrative and investment services to our defined contribution plan and defined benefit plan customers through annuities and mutual funds. Group annuities and the underlying investment options are not required to be registered with the United States Securities and Exchange Commission ("SEC"). Our mutual fund offering is called Principal Advantage. It is a qualified plan product based on our series mutual fund, Principal Funds, Inc. ("PFI"). We offer investments covering the full range of stable value, equity, fixed income, real estate and international investment options managed by our Principal Global Investors segment as well as third-party asset managers.

As of December 31, 2013, we provided full service accumulation products to (a) over 32,600 defined contribution pension plans, of which approximately 27,400 were 401(k) plans, including $113.8 billion in assets and covering 3.8 million eligible plan participants, and (b) to over 2,300 defined benefit pension plans, including $17.2 billion in assets and covering over 338,000 eligible plan participants. As of December 31, 2013, approximately 58% of our full service accumulation account values were managed by our Principal Global Investors segment. Third-party asset managers provide asset management services with respect to the remaining assets.

**Markets and Distribution**

We offer our full service accumulation products and services to employer-sponsored pension plans, including qualified and nonqualified defined contribution plans and defined benefit plans. Our primary target market is plans sponsored by small and medium-sized businesses, which we believe remains under-penetrated. According to Spectrem Group, in 2012, only 22% of businesses with between 10 and 49 employees, 52% of businesses with between 50 and 99 employees, 54% of businesses with between 100 and 249 employees and 72% of businesses with between 250 and 500 employees offered a 401(k) plan. The same study indicates that 75% of employers with between 500 and 1,000 employees, 82% of employers with between 1,000 and 5,000 employees and 83% of employers with 5,000 or more employees offered a 401(k) plan in 2012.

We distribute our full service accumulation products and services nationally, primarily through a captive retirement services sales force. As of December 31, 2013, 117 retirement services sales representatives in 42 offices, operating as a wholesale distribution network, maintained relationships with over 13,500 independent brokers, consultants and agents. Retirement services sales representatives are an integral part of the sales process alongside the referring consultant or independent broker. We compensate retirement services sales representatives through a blend of salary and production-based incentives, while we pay independent brokers, consultants and agents a commission or fee.

As of December 31, 2013, we had a separate staff of over 280 service and education specialists located in the sales offices who play a key role in the ongoing servicing of pension plans by providing local services to our customers, such as reviewing plan performance, investment options and plan design; communicating the customers' needs and feedback to us and helping employees understand the benefits of their pension plans. The following summarizes our distribution channels:

• We distribute our annuity-based products through sales representatives, agents and brokers who are primarily state licensed individuals.

• Principal Advantage, our mutual fund-based product, is targeted at defined contribution plans through broker-dealer distribution channels. Principal Advantage gives us access to Financial Industry Regulatory Authority-registered distributors who are not

traditional sellers of annuity-based products and broadens opportunities for us in the investment advisor and broker-dealer
distribution channels.

• Principal Retirement Income Edge® is designed to create a coordinated experience from accumulation to income management for
advisors to use with their individual clients and plan participants who are nearing or enjoying retirement. The Principal
Retirement Income Edge® program provides education and planning tools as well as a wide variety of products such as annuities,
mutual funds and bank products to provide personalized income management solutions.

• Through our Retire Secure strategy we provide financial education and assistance to individual investors who are
participants/members of employer-based accumulation solutions to help them achieve financial security.

We believe our approach to full service accumulation plan services distribution gives us a local sales and service presence that differentiates us from many of our competitors. We have also established a number of marketing and distribution relationships to increase the sales of our accumulation products.

## *Principal Funds*

We have been providing mutual funds to customers since 1969. We offer mutual funds to individuals, businesses and institutional investors for use within variable life and variable annuity contracts, for use in employer-sponsored pension plans, as a rollover investment option, and for general investment purposes.

*Products and Services*

Principal Funds plans to grow into a top advisor sold mutual fund company with a sales force focused on multiple channels. As of
December 2013, as reported by the Strategic Insight, we are ranked 17 th according to AUM (long term funds) of the top 50 intermediary sold mutual funds. We provide accounting, compliance, corporate governance and product development for all mutual funds we organize.

***Principal Funds, Inc.*** PFI is a series mutual fund that, as of December 31, 2013, offered 65 investment options. This fund's five R share classes act as the funding vehicles for Principal Advantage, the defined contribution product described above under "Retirement and Investor

Services Segment-Full Service Accumulation-Products." This fund also offers three classes of shares to individuals. One of these three share classes is for IRA rollovers (J shares) and two are for general investment purposes (A and C shares). PFI offers two additional classes of shares: (1) I shares, which are offered primarily to specified institutional investors, and (2) P shares, which are used primarily in adviser fee-based programs. As of December 31, 2013, the fund held $101.5 billion of AUM. We report the results for this fund in "Full Service Accumulation" or "Principal Funds" based on the distribution channel associated with the AUM.

***Principal Variable Contracts Funds, Inc.*** Principal Variable Contracts Funds, Inc. is a series mutual fund that, as of December 31, 2013, provided 39 investment options for variable annuity and variable life insurance contracts issued by Principal Life Insurance Company ("Principal Life") and other insurance companies not affiliated with Principal Life. As of December 31, 2013, this fund had AUM of $7.4 billion. AUM backing Principal Life variable annuity contracts is reported in this segment under "Individual Annuities." AUM backing Principal Life variable life insurance contracts is reported in the U.S. Insurance Solutions segment.

***Principal Managed Portfolio.*** Principal Managed Portfolio is an advisory product offered by one of our registered investment advisers, Princor Financial Services Corporation ("Princor"), which permits the client to invest primarily in mutual funds of Principal Funds, Inc. The other investments offered through the program are municipal bond funds comprising the fixed income component in the tax-sensitive nonqualified Model Portfolios and a limited number of mutual funds and Exchange Traded Funds ("ETFs") representing alternative asset classes and investment strategies. Clients are charged a quarterly asset-based fee on this product. As of December 31, 2013, Principal Managed Portfolio had accumulated $852.4 million in assets.

***Principal Advisory Select and Principal Dynamic Portfolios.*** These are advisory products offered by one of our registered investment advisors, Princor, which permits the client to invest in a broad array of investments. Clients are charged a quarterly asset-based fee on these products. As of December 31, 2013, these products had accumulated $2.6 billion in assets.

## Markets and Distribution

Our markets for PFI's retail share classes are individuals seeking to accumulate savings for retirement and other purposes, as well as nonqualified individual savings plans utilizing payroll deductions. We also market PFI's retail share classes to participants in pension plans who are departing their plans and reinvesting their retirement assets into individual retirement accounts.

We sell PFI's share classes primarily through registered representatives from other broker-dealers; affiliated financial representatives; independent brokers registered with our securities broker-dealer, Princor; direct deposits from our employees and others and Principal Connection. As of December 31, 2013, 62 retail sales representatives across the United States, operating as a wholesale distribution network, maintained relationships with over 50,000 independent brokers, consultants and agents. Principal Connection is our direct response distribution channel for retail financial services products to individuals. Principal Connection's services are available over the phone, on the Internet or by mail. Princor recruits, trains and supervises registered representatives selling our products through Principal Connection.

### *Individual Annuities*

Individual annuities offer a tax-deferred means of accumulating retirement savings, as well as a tax-efficient source of income during the payout period.

*Products*

We offer both fixed and variable annuities to individuals and pension plans. Individual annuities may be categorized in two ways:
(1) deferred, in which case assets accumulate until the contract is surrendered, the customer dies or the customer begins receiving benefits under
an annuity payout option, or (2) payout, in which case payments are made for a fixed period of time or for life.

*Fixed Deferred Annuities.* Our individual fixed deferred annuities consist of both single premium deferred annuity contracts and flexible premium deferred annuity contracts ("FPDAs"). Some FPDA contracts limit the period of time deposits are allowed (e.g., only one year). For most contracts, the principal amount is guaranteed. We credit the customer's account with a fixed interest rate for a specified number of years.

Thereafter, we reset, typically annually, the interest rate credited to the contract based upon our discretion, subject to contractual minimums, by taking into account market and other conditions. We also offer a fixed deferred annuity where the interest credited is linked to an external equity index, subject to maximum and minimum values. Our major source of income from fixed deferred annuities is the spread between the investment income earned on the underlying general account assets and the interest rate credited to the contracts. We bear the investment risk because, while we credit customers' accounts with a stated interest rate, we cannot be certain the investment income we earn on our general account assets will exceed that rate. The Principal Global Investors segment manages the assets supporting these contracts.

***Variable Deferred Annuities.*** Individual variable deferred annuities are savings vehicles through which the customer makes one or more deposits of varying amounts and intervals. Customers have the flexibility to allocate their deposits to mutual funds managed by the Principal Global Investors segment or unaffiliated third-party asset managers. As of December 31, 2013, 87% of our $8.1 billion in variable annuity account balances was allocated to mutual funds and our general account, which are managed by the Principal Global Investors segment and 13% was allocated to mutual funds managed by unaffiliated third-party asset managers. Generally speaking, the customers bear the investment risk and have the right to allocate their assets among various separate mutual funds. The value of the annuity fluctuates in accordance with the experience of the mutual funds chosen by the customer. Customers have the option to allocate all or a portion of their account to our general account, in which case we credit interest at rates we determine, subject to contractual minimums. Customers may elect a living benefit guarantee (commonly known in the industry as a guaranteed minimum withdrawal benefit, or "GMWB"). We bear the GMWB investment risk. Our goal is to hedge the GMWB investment risk through the use of sophisticated risk management techniques. As of December 31, 2013, $4.8 billion of the $8.1 billion of variable annuity account value had the GMWB rider. Our major source of revenue from variable annuities is mortality and expense fees we charge to the customer, generally determined as a percentage of the market value of the assets held in a separate investment subaccount.

Account balances of variable annuity contracts with the GMWB rider were invested in separate account investment options as follows:

***Fixed Income Annuities.*** Our individual fixed income annuities consist of single premium immediate annuity contracts ("SPIAs") and deferred income annuity contracts ("DIAs"). SPIAs and DIAs are products where the customer pays a premium in return for periodic benefit payments. SPIA payments begin immediately and DIA payments begin after a deferral period, during which a return-of-premium death benefit is included. Payments may be contingent upon the survival of one or two individuals or payments may be fixed, meaning payments are contractually guaranteed and do not depend on the continuing survival of any individual. Our major source of income from fixed immediate annuities is the spread between the investment income earned on the underlying general account assets and the interest rate implied in the calculation of annuity benefit payments. We bear the investment risk because we cannot be certain the investment income we earn on our general account assets will exceed the rate implied in the SPIA and DIA contracts. The Principal Global Investors segment manages the assets supporting these contracts.

*Markets and Distribution*

Our target markets for individual annuities include owners, executives and employees of small and medium-sized businesses and individuals seeking to accumulate and/or eventually receive distributions of assets for retirement. We market both fixed and variable annuities to individuals for both qualified and nonqualified retirement savings. We sell our individual annuity products through our affiliated financial representatives, who accounted for 47%, 46% and 50% of annuity sales for the years ended December 31, 2013, 2012 and 2011, respectively. The remaining sales were made through banks, brokerage general agencies, mutual fund companies, Principal Connection and unaffiliated broker-dealer firms. Affiliated financial representatives continued to be the primary distribution channel of our variable deferred annuities. The majority of overall annuity sales, however, were from non-affiliated distribution channels, as a result of focused efforts to increase fixed annuity sales through non-affiliated distribution channels.

## *Bank and Trust Services*

**Bank and trust services includes Principal Bank and Principal Trust Company**. Principal Bank is a federal savings bank that began its activities in February 1998. As of December 31, 2013, Principal Bank had over 262,000 customers and

7

December 31, 2013 December 31, 2012
*(in millions)*
Equity funds **$ 469.6** $ 482.5
Bond funds **256.9** 266.1
Balanced funds **4,077.2** 2,782.7
Money market funds **8.0** 7.3
Total **$ 4,811.7** $ 3,538.6
Percent of total variable annuity account values **59 %** 55 %

approximately $2.1 billion in assets. Principal Bank operates under a limited purpose charter and may only accept deposits held in a fiduciary capacity, and may not hold demand deposits or make commercial loans. Delaware Charter Guarantee & Trust Company, dba Principal Trust Company, is a Delaware state-chartered non-deposit trust company that was chartered in 1899. It is one of the largest non-deposit trust companies in the U.S. As of December 31, 2013, we served as trustee or custodian to over 240,000 accounts, which held assets of approximately $150.0 billion. Principal Trust Company may not accept deposits and cannot make personal or commercial loans. The majority of the trust assets are affiliated and reported in "Full Service Accumulation" AUM.

*Products*

Our current bank products and services include IRAs that are primarily funded by moneys rolled over from qualified retirement plans. The IRAs hold savings accounts, money market accounts and certificates of deposit. The deposit products provide a relatively stable source of funding and liquidity for Principal Bank and are used to fund purchases of investment securities and residential mortgage loans. Principal Bank does not originate any loans.

Principal Trust Company specializes in providing trust solutions for a full array of employee benefit plans and accounts including 401(k) and 403(b) plans, defined benefit pension plans, nonqualified executive benefit plans, ESOPs, and self-directed tax-advantaged savings accounts, such as IRAs. Principal Trust Company also maintains collective investment funds and provides personal trust services.

**Markets and Distribution**

Bank employees pursue asset retention strategies by offering our bank products and services to participants of qualified retirement plans, with a primary focus on helping customers understand their retirement options and accumulate savings for retirement. Principal Bank services

customers through the telephone, mail and Internet.
We deliver our directed trust services and collective investment funds to customers through our PFG affiliates and affiliated financial representatives. Administrative trust services for self-directed tax-advantaged savings accounts are sold through non-affiliated brokerage firms, clearing firms, financial advisors and asset managers.

**Guaranteed Business**

***Investment Only***
*Products*
The three primary products for which we provide investment only services are: GICs, funding agreements and other investment only products.
GICs and funding agreements pay a specified rate of return. The rate of return can be a floating rate based on an external market index or a fixed rate. Our investment only products contain provisions disallowing or limiting early surrenders, including penalties for early surrenders and minimum notice requirements.
Deposits to investment only products are predominantly in the form of single payments. As a result, the level of new deposits can fluctuate from one fiscal quarter to another. Assets invested in GICs and funding agreements generate a spread between the investment income earned by us and the amount credited to the customer. Our other investment only products consist of separate accounts invested in either equities or fixed income instruments. The Principal Global Investors segment manages the assets supporting investment only account values.
*Markets and Distribution*
We market GICs and funding agreements primarily to pension plan sponsors and other institutions. We also offer them as part of our full service accumulation products. We sell our GICs primarily to plan sponsors for funding of tax-qualified retirement plans. We sell our funding agreements directly to institutions that may or may not be pension funds and unconsolidated special purpose vehicles domiciled either in the U.S. or offshore for funding agreement-backed note programs. The funding agreements sold as part of these funding agreement-backed note programs work by having investors purchase debt obligations from the special purpose vehicle which, in turn, purchases the funding agreement from us with terms similar to those of the debt obligations. The strength of this market is dependent on debt capital market conditions. As a

result, our sales through this channel can vary widely from one quarter to another. In addition to the special purpose vehicle selling the funding agreement-backed notes to U.S. and foreign institutional investors, the special purpose vehicle may also sell notes to U.S. retail investors through a SEC-registered shelf debt issuance program.

***Full Service Payout***
*Products*
Full service payout products respond to the needs of pension plan participants who, upon retirement or termination of their employment, seek a guaranteed income stream. Plan participants who seek these services include those from pension plans we service, as well as pension plans other providers service. We primarily offer single premium group annuities, which are immediate or deferred annuities that provide a current or future specific income amount, fully guaranteed by us. These are available to defined contribution and defined benefit plan participants. We make regular payments to individuals, invest the underlying assets on their behalf and provide tax reporting to them. We also reinsure single premium immediate annuities issued by another insurer.
Single premium group annuities are traditionally used in conjunction with defined benefit plans, particularly those where the plan is being terminated. In such instances, the plan sponsor transfers all its obligations under the plan to an insurer by paying a single premium. Increasingly, these products are purchased by defined contribution plan participants who reach retirement age. Generally, plan sponsors restrict their purchases to insurance companies with superior or excellent financial quality ratings because the Department of Labor has mandated that annuities be purchased only from the "safest available" insurers.
Premium received from full service payout products are generally in the form of single payments. As a result, the level of new premiums can fluctuate depending on the number of retirements and large-scale annuity sales in a particular fiscal quarter. The Principal Global Investors segment manages the assets supporting full service payout account values.
*Markets and Distribution*
Our primary distribution channel for full service payout products is comprised of several specialized home office sales consultants working through consultants and brokers that specialize in this type of business. Our sales consultants also make sales directly to institutions. Our nationally dispersed retirement services sales representatives act as a secondary distribution channel for these products. Principal Connection

also distributes full service payout products to participants in plans we service who are terminating employment or retiring.

**Principal Global Investors Segment**

Our Principal Global Investors segment manages assets for sophisticated investors around the world, using a multi-boutique strategy that enables the segment to provide an expanded range of diverse investment capabilities including equity, fixed income, real estate, and other alternative investments. We also have experience in asset allocation, stable value management and other structured investment strategies. We focus on providing services to our other segments and third-party institutional clients. We maintain offices in Australia, Brazil, Dubai, Germany, Hong Kong, Japan, Netherlands, Singapore, the United Kingdom and the United States.

We deliver our products and services through our network of specialized investment groups and boutiques including Principal Global Investors — Equities; Principal Global Investors — Fixed Income; Principal Real Estate Investors, LLC; Principal Enterprise Capital, LLC; Spectrum Asset Management Inc.; Post Advisory Group, LLC; Columbus Circle Investors; Edge Asset Management Inc.; Morley Financial Services Inc.; Macro Currency Group; Finisterre Capital LLP; Origin Asset Management LLP; CIMB Principal Islamic Asset Management Sdn Bhd; Multi-Asset Advisors Group and Liongate Capital Management LLP. As of December 31, 2013, Principal Global Investors and its boutiques managed $292.1 billion in assets.

*Products and Services*

Our products and services are provided for a fee as defined by client mandates. Our fees are generally driven by AUM. We are diversified across the following primary asset classes.

***Equity Investments.*** As of December 31, 2013, Principal Global Investors — Equities along with Columbus Circle Investors, Edge Asset Management Inc. and Origin Asset Management LLP managed $103.1 billion in global equity assets. Our equity capabilities encompass largecap, mid-cap and small-cap stocks in developed and emerging markets worldwide. As of December 31, 2013, 45% of equity AUM was derived from our pension products, 30% from other products of PFG and the remaining 25% from third-party institutional clients.

***Fixed Income Investments.*** As of December 31, 2013, Principal Global Investors — Fixed Income along with Spectrum Asset Management Inc.; Post Advisory Group, LLC; Edge Asset Management Inc.; and Morley Financial Services Inc. managed $126.4 billion in global fixed income assets. Collectively, our experience in fixed income management spans multiple economic and credit market cycles, and encompasses all major fixed income sectors and security types. Our research and risk management capabilities in worldwide debt markets provide a strong foundation for broadly diversified "multi-sector" portfolios, tailored to specific client objectives. As of December 31, 2013, 31% of these assets were derived from our pension products, 32% from other products of PFG, and the remaining 37% from third-party institutional clients.

***Real Estate Investments.*** Principal Global Investors, through its affiliates Principal Real Estate Investors, LLC and Principal Enterprise Capital, LLC, managed a portfolio of primarily U.S. commercial real estate assets of $48.8 billion as of December 31, 2013. Principal Real Estate Investors, LLC provides our clients with a broad range of real estate investment options including private real estate equity, commercial mortgages, bridge/mezzanine loans, commercial mortgage-backed securities and real estate investment trust securities. As of December 31, 2013, 25% of the commercial real estate portfolio was derived from our pension products, 27% from other products of PFG and the remaining 48% from third-party institutional clients.

***Other Alternative Investments.*** We offer products and services through other alternative asset classes including managing currency mandates through our Macro Currency Group boutique and hedge fund mandates through the Liongate Capital Management LLP, Finisterre Capital LLP, and Columbus Circle Investors boutiques. As of December 31, 2013, we managed $13.8 billion with 2% from other products of PFG and the remaining 98% of these assets derived from thirdparty institutional clients.

Multi-Asset Advisors Group was established to provide advice on multi-asset strategies to global clients and to develop and manage customized multi-asset products to address specific client needs. Multi-Asset Advisors Group helps Principal Global Investors optimize our broad range of capabilities while enhancing our position as a thought leader and trusted advisor to large institutional clients.

*Markets and Distribution*

We employed 144 institutional sales, relationship management and client service professionals as of December 31, 2013, who worked with consultants and directly with large investors to acquire and retain third-party institutional clients. As of December 31, 2013, Principal Global Investors and its boutiques had approximately 797 third-party institutional clients with $109.4 billion of AUM in 37 countries.

**Principal International Segment**

Our Principal International segment has operations in Brazil, Chile, China, Hong Kong Special Administrative Region ("SAR"), India, Mexico and Southeast Asia. We focus on countries with growing middle classes, favorable demographics, and increasing long-term savings, ideally with defined contribution retirement markets. We entered these locations through acquisitions, start-up operations and joint ventures. The activities of our Principal International segment reflect our efforts to accelerate the growth of our AUM by capitalizing on the international trend toward private sector defined contribution pension systems and individual long-term savings. We offer retirement products and services, mutual funds, institutional asset management, annuities and life insurance accumulation products.

*Products, Markets and Distribution*

*Brazil.* We offer pension, retirement income and asset accumulation products through a co-managed joint venture, Brasilprev Seguros e Previdencia ("Brasilprev"). We own 25% of the economic interest and 50.01% of the voting shares, and the partner is Banco do Brasil ("Banco"), the largest bank in Latin America which had approximately 5,300 Brazilian branches as of September 30, 2013. According to Federação Nacional de Previdência e Vida, our joint venture ranked third in the Brazilian private pension market based upon managed assets as of November 30, 2013 and first in 2013 net sales.

Brasilprev has the exclusive distribution rights of its pension, retirement and long-term asset allocation products through the Banco network until October 2032. Our joint venture provides products for the retirement needs of individuals and employers. Banco's employees sell these products directly to individual clients through its bank branches. In addition, our joint venture reaches corporate clients through two wholesale distribution channels: (1) a network of independent brokers who sell to the public and (2) Banco's corporate account executives who sell to existing and prospective corporate clients.

We offer mutual fund and asset management services through Claritas Administração de Recursos Ltda ("Claritas"), a leading independent Brazilian mutual fund and asset management company. We own 62.7% of the economic interest and the remainder is owned by employeepartners. The company manages equity funds, balanced funds, managed accounts and other strategies for affluent clients and institutions and
sells through its multi-channel distribution network.

***Chile.*** We offer a complete array of pension accumulation and retirement payout products including mandatory employee-funded pension
plans, individual voluntary plans ("APV"), voluntary savings funds, employer-based voluntary retirement plans ("APVC"), pension products, retirement annuities, mutual funds, life insurance accumulation products, institutional asset management services and other long-term savings products.

We offer mandatory employee-funded pension, APV and voluntary savings plans through Cuprum, the company we acquired in February
2013. As of December 31, 2013 we own 94.05% of Cuprum, and the rest is publicly floated. Cuprum's products are sold through a proprietary
sales network of approximately 650 sales employees. Cuprum ranked first in the Pension Superintendence Customer Service Index for 19
consecutive trimesters (as of trimester ending August 2013).

We offer APV and APVC plans through Principal Administradora Generale de Fondos, our wholly-owned mutual fund company.

According to the Asociacion de Adminstradoras de Fondos Mutuous de Chile, we ranked first in AUM for mutual fund companies offering these plans in Chile as of November 30, 2013. The plans, together with non-qualified mutual fund products, are distributed to retail clients through our proprietary sales force, financial advisors, brokerage houses and alliances with financial institutions. We also offer institutional asset
management services to pension funds, insurance companies, sophisticated investors, mutual fund companies and investment platforms through
our proprietary sales force.

We offer mandatory retirement annuities and life insurance accumulation products through Principal Compania de Seguros de Vida
Chile S.A., our wholly owned life insurance company. Annuity products are distributed through a network of brokers and independent agents numbering approximately 385 as of December 31, 2013. Life insurance accumulation

products are also offered to individuals through brokers and financial advisors.

***China.*** We offer mutual funds and asset management services to individuals and institutions through a joint venture, CCB Principal Asset Management Company, LTD. We own 25% and China Construction Bank ("CCB") is the majority partner with 65% ownership. We sell mutual funds primarily through our partner bank, CCB. The bank provides extensive distribution capabilities for the joint venture in terms of brand awareness and the number of branch outlets, which number approximately 15,000 as of June 2013.

***Hong Kong SAR.*** We offer both defined contribution pension and mutual fund products to corporate and retail clients through wholly owned companies.

We offer Mandatory Provident Fund ("MPF") schemes to serve the mandatory retirement market. We target small and medium-sized employers and distribute products through a proprietary sales force that maintains relationships with third-party intermediaries such as insurance companies, independent financial advisors, brokers, consultants and banks. We also target individual account holders who have changed jobs or are looking to consolidate their retirement accounts. We service over 225,000 MPF accounts.

We sell mutual funds to retail customers seeking to accumulate assets for retirement and other long-term investment needs. Our mutual funds are distributed through a proprietary sales force that maintains relationships with third-party intermediaries such as banks, insurance companies and independent financial advisors. To further grow our mutual fund business we will seek to leverage our operations in the Hong Kong SAR to pursue potential opportunities created by the mutual recognition of fund products between Hong Kong and China. Mutual recognition was highlighted in Supplement 10 of the Closer Economic Partnership Arrangement agreement, and is subject to the approval of the Hong Kong and Chinese governments.

***India.*** We offer mutual funds and asset management services to both retail and corporate customers through our joint venture Principal PNB Asset Management Company Private Limited. We own 66% and the partners are Punjab National Bank (30%) and Vijaya Bank (4%), two large Indian commercial banks with a combined network of approximately 7,000 branches. Mutual funds are sold through bank branches and proprietary sales offices located throughout India, by independent distributors and direct sales.

We also have a proprietary distribution company, Principal Retirement Advisors, that focuses on promoting and advising on retirement and long term investment products in these emerging markets.

***Mexico.*** We offer defined contribution pension products, mutual funds, annuities and asset management services to institutional clients through our wholly-owned companies.

Through our AFORE pension company, we manage and administer approximately 3.8 million individual retirement accounts under the mandatory privatized social security system for all non-government and government employees in Mexico. We distribute products and services through a proprietary sales force of approximately 1,000 sales representatives as of December 31, 2013, as well as independent brokers who sell

directly to individuals. In addition, we have an agreement for the exclusive distribution of Principal AFORE's products through HSBC Bank's extensive network in Mexico through 2017.

Our mutual fund company distributes products and services through a sales force of approximately 70 employees and through distribution agreements with other financial entities. We administer previously sold annuities and life products.

Mexico has institutional asset management services, offering both domestic and international products, typically sold direct.

***Southeast Asia.*** We offer conventional and Islamic mutual funds and fund management services through our joint venture CIMBPrincipal Asset Management ("CPAM"). We own 40% and the partner is CIMB Group, the second largest Malaysian bank with a strong presence in many Asian countries. CPAM ranked second in total unit trust assets managed and second in Islamic unit trust assets managed in the Malaysian asset management industry as of December 31, 2013. CPAM also manages a significant amount of institutional asset mandates.

CPAM distributes mutual funds through the branches of its partner bank (approximately 1,300 bank branches throughout Malaysia, Indonesia, Thailand and Singapore) and through an agency sales force of approximately 5,100 agents selling to retail customers. CPAM also distributes its mutual funds through third party institutions including other banks and security houses.

As of December 31, 2013 CPAM ranked second in private retirement schemes managed in the new voluntary retirement market.
The joint venture also has wholly owned subsidiaries in Singapore (CIMB-Principal Asset Management (S) Pte Ltd), Indonesia (PT CIMBPrincipal Asset Management) and Thailand (CIMB-Principal Asset Management Company Limited).

## U.S. Insurance Solutions Segment

Our U.S. Insurance Solutions segment offers individual and group insurance solutions. We focus on providing comprehensive insurance solutions for small and medium-sized businesses and their owners and executives. We organize our operations into two divisions: Individual Life Insurance and Specialty Benefits Insurance. However, we share key resources in our core areas such as strategic leadership, distribution, and marketing.

## Individual Life Insurance

We began as an individual life insurer in 1879. Our U.S. operations administer approximately 546,000 individual life insurance policies with over $197 billion of individual life insurance in force as of December 31, 2013. We assist not only in personal insurance but also specialize in business insurance needs for small to medium-sized companies through our wide range of business and nonqualified solutions.
Small and medium-sized companies are challenged with how to build quality benefits packages for executives, how to transition the company's ownership to a partner or family member and how to save for retirement. In addition, executives and other key employees often have personal insurance needs. These needs are the focus of our products within the individual life insurance arena.

### *Products and Services*

Our Business Owner and Executive Solutions platform as well as our nonqualified deferred compensation offering combines administration and consulting to service our clients' needs. We target the business and personal insurance needs of owners and executives of small and medium sized businesses with an increasing focus on providing insurance solutions for nonqualified executive benefits. In addition, we market our products to meet traditional retail insurance needs. We offer a variety of individual life insurance products, including universal life insurance, variable universal life insurance and term life insurance.

***Universal and Variable Universal Life Insurance.*** Universal and variable universal life insurance products offer the policyholder the option of adjusting both the premium and the death benefit amounts of the insurance contract. Universal life insurance typically includes a cash value account that accumulates at a credited interest rate based on the investment returns of the block of business. Variable universal life insurance is credited with the investment returns of the various investment options selected. For the year ended December 31, 2013, 72% of individual life insurance annualized first year premium sales were generated from universal and variable universal life insurance products. Universal and variable universal life insurance represents 40% of individual life insurance in force as of December 31, 2013.

After a deduction for policy level expenses, we credit net deposits to an account maintained for the policyholder. For universal life contracts, the entire account balance is invested in the general account. Interest is credited to the policyholder's account based on the earnings on general account investments. For variable universal life contracts, the policyholder may allocate the account balance among our general account and a variety of mutual funds underlying the contract. Interest is credited on amounts allocated to the Principal Life general account in the same manner as for universal life. Net investment performance on mutual funds is allocated directly to the policyholder accounts; the policyholder bears the investment risk. Some of our universal life and variable universal life insurance contracts contain what are commonly referred to as "secondary" or "no-lapse" guarantee provisions. A no-lapse guarantee keeps the contract in force, even if the contract holder's account balance is insufficient to cover all of the contract charges, provided that the contract holder has continually paid a specified minimum premium.

***Traditional Life Insurance.*** Traditional life insurance includes participating whole life, adjustable life products and non-participating term life insurance products. Participating products and non-participating term life insurance products represented 28% of our individual life insurance annualized first year premium sales for the year ended December 31, 2013, and 60% of individual life insurance in force as of December 31, 2013. Adjustable life insurance products provide a guaranteed benefit in return for the payment of a fixed premium and allow the policyholder to set the coverage period, premium and face amount combination. Term insurance products provide a guaranteed death benefit for a specified period of time in return for the payment of a fixed premium. Policyholder dividends are not paid on term insurance.

**Specialty Benefits Insurance**

Specialty benefits insurance, which includes group dental, vision, life and disability insurance and individual disability insurance, is an important component of the employee benefit offering at small and medium-sized businesses. We offer traditional employer sponsored and voluntary products for group dental, vision, life and disability. We also offer group dental, vision, and disability on a fee-for-service basis.

*Products and Services*

*Group Dental and Vision Insurance.* We began selling group dental and vision insurance in the late 1960's. Our plans provide partial reimbursement for dental and vision expenses. As of December 31, 2013, we had over 34,000 group dental and vision insurance policies in force covering nearly 902,000 employee lives. According to Life Insurance and Market Research Association ("LIMRA"), we were the 7th largest group dental insurer in terms of number of contracts/employer groups in force in 2012. In addition to indemnity and preferred provider organization dental offered on both an employer paid and voluntary basis, we offer a prepaid dental plan in Arizona through our Employers Dental Services, Inc. subsidiary. On November 1, 2012, we finalized the purchase of a 100% interest in First Dental Health, a California based independent dental preferred provider organization. We acquired First Dental Health to expand our owned dental networks primarily in California.

*Group Life Insurance.* Group life insurance was one of our first group products beginning in the early 1940's. Our group life insurance provides coverage to employees and their dependents for a specified period. As of December 31, 2013, we had over 47,000 group policies providing nearly $117.6 billion of group life insurance in force to approximately 1.9 million employee lives. According to LIMRA in 2012, we were ranked 4th in the U.S. in terms of the number of group life insurance contracts in force. We currently sell traditional group life insurance that does not provide for accumulation of cash values on both an employer paid and voluntary basis. Our group life insurance business remains focused on the traditional, annually renewable term product. Group term life and group universal life accounted for 97% and 3%, respectively, of our total group life insurance in force as of December 31, 2013. We no longer market group universal life insurance to new employer groups.

***Group Disability Insurance.*** Group disability insurance has also been sold since the early 1940's. Our group disability insurance provides a benefit to insured employees who become disabled. In most instances, this benefit is in the form of a monthly income. Our group disability products include both short-term and long-term disability, offered on both an employer paid and voluntary basis. As of December 31, 2013, long-term disability represents 63% of total group disability premium, while short-term disability represents 37% of total group disability premium. In addition, we provide disability management services, also called rehabilitation services, to assist individuals in returning to work as quickly as possible following disability. We also work with disability claimants to improve the approval rate of Social Security benefits, thereby reducing payment of benefits by the amount of Social Security payments received. As of December 31, 2013, we served approximately 1.4 million employee lives under nearly 35,000 contracts. According to LIMRA, our group short-term disability business was ranked 6th and our group long-term disability business was ranked 4th in the U.S. as of December 31, 2012, in terms of number of contracts/employer groups in force. We recently expanded our product offering to include voluntary critical illness insurance. The insurance provides a lump-sum cash benefit to pay for additional expenses associated with the five most common critical illnesses.

***Individual Disability Insurance.*** Individual disability insurance has been sold since the early 1950's. Our individual disability insurance products provide income protection to the insured member and/or business in the event of disability. In most instances, this benefit is in the form of a monthly income. In addition to income replacement, we offer products to pay business-related costs such as overhead expenses for a disabled business owner, buy-out costs for business owners purchasing a disabled owner's interest in the business, expenditures for replacement of a key person and business loan payments. We also offer a product to protect retirement savings in the event of disability. As of December 31, 2013, we served approximately 159,000 individual disability policyholders. According to LIMRA, our individual disability business is ranked 5th in the U.S. in terms of premium in force in the non-cancellable segment of the market and 7th overall, as of December 31, 2012.

*Fee-for-Service.* We offer administration of group dental, disability and vision benefits on a fee-for-service basis.

### U.S. Insurance Solutions Markets and Distribution

For each of our products, administration and distribution channels are customized to meet customer needs and expectations for that product. We sell our individual life and individual disability income products in all 50 states and the District of Columbia, primarily targeting owners and executives of small and medium-sized businesses. Small and medium-sized business sales represented 57% of individual life sales and 63% of individual disability sales for the year ended December 31, 2013. Much of our life insurance sales efforts focus on the Business Owner & Executive Solutions market. This strategy offers solutions to address business owner financial challenges such as exiting the business, business transition, retaining key employees and retirement planning. Key employees also have needs to supplement retirement income, survivor income, and business protection. We believe the Business Owner & Executive Solutions segment offers growth opportunities and we will continue to develop strategies to capitalize on this expanding market. We distribute our individual life and individual disability insurance products through our affiliated financial representatives and independent brokers, as well as other marketing and distribution alliances. Affiliated financial representatives were responsible for 23% of individual life insurance sales based on first year annualized premium and 14% of individual disability sales for the year ended December 31, 2013. We had 1,121 affiliated financial representatives in 31 offices as of December 31, 2013. Although they are independent contractors, we have a close tie with affiliated financial representatives and we offer them benefits, training and access to tools and expertise. To meet the needs of the various marketing channels, particularly the independent brokers, we employ wholesale distributors — Regional Vice Presidents for individual life and Regional Vice Presidents for individual disability. A key differentiator in the nonqualified executive benefit sale is our Regional Vice Presidents-Nonqualified Plans, who are not only wholesalers but also consultants and subject-matter experts providing point-ofsale support in closing cases.

We market our group life, disability, dental and vision insurance products to small and medium-sized businesses, primarily targeting our sales toward owners and human resources professionals. We sell our group life, disability, dental and vision products in all 50 states and the

District of Columbia. We continually adapt our products and pricing to meet local market conditions. We market our fee-for-service capabilities to employers that self-insure their employees' dental, disability and vision benefits. We market our fee-for-service businesses in all 50 states and the District of Columbia.

The group insurance market continues to see a shift to voluntary/worksite products due to various pressures on employers. In keeping with this market change, which shifts the funding of such products from the employer to the employee, we continue to place an enhanced focus on our voluntary benefits platform. We believe the voluntary/worksite market presents growth opportunities, and we will continue to develop strategies to capitalize on this expanding market.

As of December 31, 2013, we had 108 sales representatives and 131 service representatives in 28 offices. Our sales representatives accounted for 97% of our group insurance sales for the year ended December 31, 2013. The group sales force plays a key role in the ongoing servicing of the case by providing local, responsive services to our customers and their brokers, such as renewing contracts, revising plans and solving any administrative issues; communicating the customers' needs and feedback to us and helping employees understand the benefits of their plans.

**Corporate Segment**

Our Corporate segment manages the assets representing capital that has not been allocated to any other segment. Financial results of the Corporate segment primarily reflect our financing activities (including interest expense and preferred stock dividends), income on capital not allocated to other segments, inter-segment eliminations, income tax risks and certain income, expenses and other after-tax adjustments not allocated to the segments based on the nature of such items. Results of our exited group medical insurance business are reported in this segment. For further details, see Item 7. "Management's Discussion and Analysis of Financial Condition and Results of Operations — Transactions Affecting Comparability of Results of Operations."

**Competition**

Competition in our segments is based on a number of factors including: scale, service, product features, price, investment performance, commission structure, distribution capacity, financial strength ratings and name recognition. We compete with a large number of financial

services companies such as banks, mutual funds, broker-dealers, insurers and asset managers. Some of these companies offer a broader array of products, more competitive pricing, greater diversity of distribution sources, better brand recognition or, with respect to insurers, higher financial strength ratings. Some may also have greater financial resources with which to compete or may have better investment performance at various times. We believe we distinguish ourselves from our competitors through our:
- full service platform;
- strong customer relationships;
- focus on financial performance and
- expansive product portfolio.

## Ratings

Insurance companies are assigned financial strength ratings by rating agencies based upon factors relevant to policyholders. Financial strength ratings are generally defined as opinions as to an insurer's financial strength and ability to meet ongoing obligations to policyholders. Information about ratings provides both industry participants and insurance consumers meaningful insights on specific insurance companies. Higher ratings generally indicate financial stability and a stronger ability to pay claims.

Principal Life and Principal National Life Insurance Company ("PNLIC") have been assigned the following insurer financial strength ratings:

A.M. Best's ratings for insurance companies range from "A++" to "S". A.M. Best indicates that "A++" and "A+" ratings are assigned to those companies that in A.M. Best's opinion have superior ability to meet ongoing obligations to policyholders. Fitch's ratings for insurance companies range from "AAA" to "C". Fitch "AA" ratings indicate very strong capacity to meet policyholder and contractholder obligations on a timely basis. Moody's Investors Service ratings for insurance companies range from "Aaa" to "C". Moody's Investors Service indicates that "A" ratings are assigned to those companies that have demonstrated good financial security. Standard & Poor's ratings for insurance companies range

**Rating Agency Financial Strength Rating Rating Structure**
A.M. Best Company, Inc. A+ ("Superior") with a stable outlook Second highest of 16 rating levels

Fitch Ratings Ltd. AA- ("Very Strong") with a negative outlook Fourth highest of 21 rating levels

Moody's Investors Service A1 ("Good") with a stable outlook Fifth highest of 21 rating levels

Standard & Poor's A+ ("Strong") with a stable outlook Fifth highest of 21 rating levels

from "AAA" to "R". Standard & Poor's indicates that "A" ratings are assigned to those companies that have demonstrated strong financial security characteristics. In evaluating a company's financial and operating performance, these rating agencies review its profitability, leverage and liquidity, as well as its book of business, the adequacy and soundness of its reinsurance, the quality and estimated market value of its assets, the adequacy of its policy reserves, the soundness of its risk management programs, the experience and competency of its management and other factors. All of the four rating agencies maintain a 'stable' outlook on the U.S. life insurance sector. Moody's revised its outlook to 'stable' from 'negative' in December 2013.

The rating agencies have indicated they expect gradually increasing interest rates to take some of the earnings pressure off insurers, and rising equity markets will improve performance on variable products and assets under management. They expect some stabilization of life insurers' revenues and earnings over the next 12-18 months.

We believe our strong ratings are an important factor in marketing our products to our distributors and customers, as ratings information is broadly disseminated and generally used throughout the industry. Our ratings reflect each rating agency's opinion of our financial strength, operating performance and ability to meet our obligations to policyholders and are not evaluations directed toward the protection of investors.

Such ratings are neither a rating of securities nor a recommendation to buy, hold or sell any security, including our common stock. For more information on ratings, see Item 7. "Management's Discussion and Analysis of Financial Condition and Results of Operations — Liquidity and Capital Resources — Financial Strength Rating and Credit Ratings."

**Regulation**

Our businesses are subject to regulation and supervision by U.S. federal and state regulatory authorities as well as non-U.S. regulatory authorities for our operations outside the U.S., which can have a significant effect on our business. Our businesses are also affected by U.S.

federal, state and local tax laws as well as tax laws for jurisdictions outside the U.S.

PFG, our parent holding company, is not licensed as an insurer, investment advisor, broker-dealer, bank or other regulated entity. However, because it is the holding company for all of our operations, it is subject to regulation of our regulated entities, including as an insurance holding company. We are subject to legal and regulatory requirements applicable to public companies, including public reporting and disclosure, securities trading, accounting and financial reporting and corporate governance.

### *U.S. Insurance Regulation*

We are subject to the insurance holding company laws in the states where our insurance companies are domiciled. Principal Life and PNLIC are domiciled in Iowa and their principal insurance regulatory authority is the Insurance Division of the Department of Commerce of the State of Iowa. Our other U.S. insurance companies are principally regulated by the insurance departments of the states in which they are domiciled. These laws generally require each insurance company directly or indirectly owned by the holding company to register with the insurance department in the insurance company's state of domicile and to furnish financial and other information about the operations of the companies within the holding company system. Transactions affecting the insurers in the holding company system must be fair and at arm's length. Most states have insurance laws that require regulatory approval of a direct or indirect change in control of an insurer or an insurer's holding company and laws requiring prior notification of state insurance departments of a change in control of a non-domiciliary insurance company doing business in that state.

Annually, our U.S. insurance companies must submit an opinion from a board-appointed qualified actuary to state insurance regulators, where licensed, on whether the statutory assets held backing statutory reserves are sufficient to meet contractual obligations and related expenses of the insurer. If such an opinion cannot be rendered noting the sufficiency of assets, then the insurance company must set up additional statutory reserves drawing from available statutory surplus until such an opinion can be given.

State insurance departments have broad administrative powers over the insurance business, including insurance company licensing and examination, agent licensing, establishment of reserve requirements and solvency standards, premium rate regulation, admittance of assets to statutory surplus, policy form approval, unfair trade and claims practices regulation and other matters. State insurance statutes also typically place restrictions and limitations on the amount of dividends or other distributions payable by insurance company subsidiaries to their parent companies. See Item 7. "Management's Discussion and Analysis of Financial Condition and Results of Operations — Liquidity and Capital Resources" for further details.

In order to enhance the regulation of insurer solvency, the National Association of Insurance Commissioners ("NAIC") has established riskbased
capital standards. The standards require life insurers to submit a report to state regulators on an annual basis regarding their risk-based
capital based upon four categories of risk: asset risk, insurance risk, interest rate risk and business risk. As of December 31, 2012, the statutory surplus of each of our U.S. life insurance companies exceeded the minimum level of risk-based capital requirements required before state insurance departments would take action against an insurer.

State and federal insurance and securities regulatory authorities and other state law enforcement agencies and attorneys general regularly make inquiries and conduct examinations or investigations regarding our compliance with, among other things, insurance laws and securities laws.

Each state has insurance guaranty association laws under which insurers doing business in a state can be assessed, up to prescribed limits, in order to cover contractual benefit obligations of insolvent insurance companies. The guaranty associations levy assessments on each member insurer in a jurisdiction on the basis of the proportionate share of the premiums written by such insurer in the lines of business in which the insolvent insurer is engaged. Some jurisdictions permit the member insurers to recover the assessments paid through full or partial premium tax offsets.

### *Securities Regulation*

Insurance and investment products such as variable annuities, variable life insurance and some funding agreements that constitute securities and mutual fund products are subject to securities laws and regulations, including state securities regulation as well as federal regulation under the SEC, the Financial Industry Regulatory Authority and other regulatory authorities. These regulations affect investment advice, sales and related activities for these products.

We also have entities which are registered as investment advisers with the SEC under the Investment Advisers Act of 1940.

### *Employee Retirement Income Security Act*

As we provide products and services for U.S. employee benefit plans, we are subject to regulation under the Employee Retirement Income Security Act ("ERISA"). ERISA provisions include reporting and disclosure requirements and standards of conduct.

### *Banking Regulation*

Principal Bank, a wholly owned subsidiary, is a federal savings bank regulated by the Office of the Comptroller of the Currency. Principal Bank's deposits are insured by the Federal Deposit Insurance Corporation ("FDIC") making the Bank subject to certain of the FDIC's regulations. On December 31, 2013, our application to deregister as a savings and loan holding company was approved by the Federal Reserve Board ("Federal Reserve"). As a result, we are no longer subject to oversight from or examination by the Federal Reserve.

### *Environmental Regulation*

As we own and operate real property, we are subject to federal, state and local environmental laws and could be subject to environmental liabilities and costs associated with required remediation of our properties. We routinely have environmental assessments performed for real estate being acquired or used as collateral for commercial mortgages we use for investment.

### *Regulation of International Businesses*

Our international businesses are supervised by regulatory authorities in the jurisdictions in which they operate.

### **Risk Management**

Like all financial services companies, we are exposed to a wide variety of financial, operational and other risks, as described in Item 1A. "Risk Factors." Effective enterprise risk management is, therefore, a key component of our business model. Enterprise risk management helps us to:

- identify and manage those risks that present profitable growth opportunities, and avoid those that do not and
- balance the sometimes competing demands of our various stakeholders, meet our customer obligations, satisfy regulatory

requirements and optimize shareholder returns relative to the risks we take. We utilize an integrated risk management framework to help us identify, assess, monitor, report and manage our risks within established limits and risk tolerances. The framework delivers important perspective that is used in strategic and tactical decision making and is adaptable to changes in our businesses and in the external environments in which we operate. Our approach also requires a commitment to continuous improvement and periodic validation.

Our governance structure includes Board of Director oversight, internal risk committees, a corporate risk management function and embedded risk professionals in all of our business units and functional areas. Our Board of Directors, Audit Committee, Finance Committee, Human Resource Committee and Nominating and Governance Committee provide oversight no less frequently than quarterly addressing various aspects and assessments of our risk profile. Quarterly reports on risk topics and an annual enterprise-wide risk report are provided to the Board of Directors by the Corporate Chief Risk Officer.

Our internal risk committees meet on a regular and frequent basis to discuss various issues and reflect on profile status. Each business unit and key functional area has its own risk committee that is responsible for oversight of all risks within the unit. These committees typically include key corporate leaders. We also have committees that provide oversight around a certain risk or group of related risks across the organization. This matrix approach helps us maintain comprehensive risk coverage and preserve an integrated view of risks. Two committees reside at the top of our internal risk committee hierarchy. The Corporate Strategic Working Group provides enterprise-wide oversight around our strategic risk profile and the Enterprise Risk Management Committee, comprised of members from corporate senior management, exercises enterprise-wide oversight around all other risk profiles.

The business units and functional areas are responsible for identifying, assessing, monitoring, reporting and managing their own risks. Chief Risk Officers embedded within each business unit or risk professionals in functional areas help align risk management practice with the strategies of the unit as well as with enterprise-wide objectives. The Corporate Chief Risk Officer and supporting staff are separate from the business units and provide objective oversight, framework enablement and aggregated risk analysis. Internal Audit provides independent assurance around effective risk management design and control execution. We have established risk tolerances from an overall corporate perspective, a business unit perspective, and for specific categories of risks.

We monitor a variety of risk metrics on an ongoing basis and take the appropriate steps to help us stay within our established risk tolerances. Potentially significant actions are considered in terms of the possible impact on our risk profile, including but not limited to the capital required, the impact on near term and long-term earnings and the ability to meet our targets with respect to return on equity, liquidity, debt/capital, cash coverage, business risk and operational risk. Quarterly risk reporting provides a feedback loop between the business units and the Corporate Chief Risk Officer and includes, among other things, emerging risk outlooks or incident reporting, if necessary. We have developed a Business Continuity Management Program that identifies critical business functions and includes plans for their protection and recovery in the event of a disaster or other business interruption.

We regularly build upon our already strong risk management practices to incorporate updated modeling tools, processes and metrics, which we actively use to better understand and manage our business.

**Employees**

As of December 31, 2013, we had 14,792 employees. None of our employees are subject to collective bargaining agreements governing employment with us. We believe that our employee relations are satisfactory.

**Internet Website**

Our Internet website can be found at www.principal.com. We make available free of charge on or through our Internet website, access to our annual report on Form 10-K, quarterly reports on Form 10-Q, current reports on Form 8-K and amendments to those reports filed or furnished pursuant to Section 13(a) or 15(d) of the Securities Exchange Act of 1934 as soon as reasonably practicable after such material is filed with or furnished to the SEC. Also available free of charge on our Internet website is our code of business conduct and ethics, corporate governance guidelines and charters for the Audit, Finance, Human Resources and Nominating and Governance committees of our Board of

Directors. Also see Item 10. "Directors, Executive Officers and Corporate Governance."

## Item 1A. Risk Factors
This section provides an overview of the risks that may impact our performance in the future.

**Adverse capital and credit market conditions may significantly affect our ability to meet liquidity needs, as well as our access to capital and cost of capital.**

Our results of operations, financial condition, cash flows and statutory capital position could be materially adversely affected by volatility, uncertainty and disruption in the capital and credit markets.
We maintain a level of cash and securities which, combined with expected cash inflows from investments and operations, is believed adequate to meet anticipated short-term and long-term benefit and expense payment obligations. However, withdrawal and surrender levels may differ from anticipated levels for a variety of reasons, such as changes in economic conditions or changes in our claims paying ability and financial strength ratings. For additional information regarding our exposure to interest rate risk and the impact of a downgrade in our financial strength ratings, see "— Changes in interest rates or credit spreads or a sustained low interest rate environment may adversely affect our results of operations, financial condition and liquidity, and our net income can vary from period-to-period" and "— A downgrade in our financial strength or credit ratings may increase policy surrenders and withdrawals, reduce new sales and terminate relationships with distributors, impact existing liabilities and increase our cost of capital, any of which could adversely affect our profitability and financial condition." In addition, mark-to-market adjustments on our derivative instruments may lead to fluctuations in our reported statutory capital. These fluctuations may result in the need for additional capital to maintain a targeted level of statutory capital relative to the NAIC's risk-based capital requirements. In the event our current internal sources of liquidity do not satisfy our needs, we may have to seek additional financing and, in such case, we may not be able to successfully obtain additional financing on favorable terms, or at all. The availability of additional financing will depend on a variety of factors such as market conditions, the general availability of credit, the volume of trading activities, the overall availability of credit to

the financial services industry, our credit ratings and credit capacity, as well as customers' or lenders' perception of our long- or short-term financial prospects. Similarly, our access to funds may be impaired if regulatory authorities or rating agencies take negative actions against us. Disruptions, uncertainty or volatility in the capital and credit markets may limit our access to capital required to operate our business, most significantly our insurance operations. Such market conditions may limit our ability to replace, in a timely manner, maturing liabilities; satisfy statutory capital requirements; fund redemption requests on insurance or other financial products; generate fee income and market-related revenue to meet liquidity needs and access the capital necessary to grow our business. As such, we may be forced to delay raising capital, issue shorter tenor securities than we prefer, utilize available internal resources or bear an unattractive cost of capital, which could decrease our profitability and significantly reduce our financial flexibility and liquidity.

For further discussion on liquidity risk management, see Item 7. "Management's Discussion and Analysis of Financial Condition and Results of Operations — Liquidity and Capital Resources."

**Conditions in the global capital markets and the economy generally may materially and adversely affect our business and results of operations.**

Our results of operations are materially affected by conditions in the global capital markets and the economy generally, both in the U.S. and elsewhere around the world. Our AUM and revenues may decline and our profit margins could erode. In addition, in the event of extreme prolonged market events and economic downturns, such as the recent global financial crisis, we could incur significant losses. Even in the absence of a market downturn, we are exposed to substantial risk of loss due to market volatility.

Factors such as consumer spending, business investment, government spending, the volatility and strength of the capital markets, investor and consumer confidence and inflation levels all affect the business and economic environment and, ultimately, the amount and profitability of our business. In an economic downturn characterized by higher unemployment, lower family income, lower corporate earnings, lower business investment, negative investor sentiment and lower consumer spending, the demand for our financial and insurance products could be adversely affected. In addition, we may experience an elevated incidence of claims and lapses or surrenders of policies. Our policyholders may choose to defer paying insurance premiums or stop paying insurance premiums altogether. In addition, reductions in employment levels of our existing employer customers may result in a reduction in membership levels and premium income for our specialty benefits products. Participants within the retirement plans for which we provide administrative services may elect to reduce or stop their payroll deferrals to these plans, which would reduce AUM and revenues. In addition, reductions in employment levels may result in a decline in employee deposits into retirement plans. Adverse changes in the economy could affect net income negatively and could have a material adverse effect on our business, results of operations and financial condition.

**Continued volatility or declines in the equity, bond or real estate markets could reduce our AUM and may result in investors withdrawing from the markets or decreasing their rates of investment, all of which could reduce our revenues and net income.**
Because the revenues of our asset management and accumulation businesses are, to a large extent, based on the value of AUM, a decline in domestic and global equity, bond or real estate markets will decrease our revenues. Turmoil in these markets could lead investors to withdraw from these markets, decrease their rates of investment or refrain from making new investments, which may reduce our net income, revenues and AUM.
For further discussion on equity risk management, see Item 7A. "Quantitative and Qualitative Disclosures About Market Risk — Equity Risk."

**Changes in interest rates or credit spreads or a sustained low interest rate environment may adversely affect our results of operations, financial condition and liquidity, and our net income can vary from period-to-period.**
In recent years, interest rates have remained at or near historically low levels. During periods of declining interest rates or sustained low interest rates, the interest rates we earn on our assets may be lower than the rates assumed in pricing our products, thereby reducing our profitability. For some of our products, such as GICs and funding agreements, we are unable to lower the rate we credit to customers in response

to the lower return we will earn on our investments. In addition, guaranteed minimum interest rates on our life insurance and annuity products may constrain our ability to lower the rate we credit to customers. If interest rates remain low over a sustained period of time, this may result in increases in our reserves and unlocking of our deferred acquisition cost ("DAC") asset and other actuarial balances. During periods of declining interest rates, borrowers may prepay or redeem mortgages and bonds that we own, which would force us to reinvest the proceeds at lower interest rates. Furthermore, declining interest rates may reduce the rate of policyholder surrenders and withdrawals on our life insurance and annuity products, thus increasing the duration of the liabilities and creating asset and liability duration mismatches. Low interest rates may also result in increased hedging costs. Although we take measures to manage the economic risks of investing in a changing interest rate environment, we may not be able to mitigate the interest rate risk of our assets relative to our liabilities. Declining interest rates or a sustained low interest rate environment may also result in changes to the discount rate assumption used for valuing our pension and other postretirement benefit obligations, which could negatively impact our results of operations and financial condition. In addition, certain statutory capital and reserve requirements are based on formulas or models that consider interest rates, and a prolonged period of low interest rates may increase the statutory capital we are required to hold as well as the amount of assets we must maintain to support statutory reserves.

Increases in market interest rates may also adversely affect our results of operations, financial condition, and liquidity. During periods of increasing market interest rates, we may offer higher crediting rates on our insurance and annuity products in order to keep these products competitive. Because returns on our portfolio of invested assets may not increase as quickly as current interest rates, we may have to accept lower spreads, thus reducing our profitability. Rapidly rising interest rates may also result in an increase in policy surrenders, withdrawals, and requests for policy loans as customers seek to achieve higher returns. In addition, rising interest rates would cause unrealized losses in our investment portfolio. Despite our efforts to reduce the impact of rising interest rates, we may be required to sell assets to raise the cash necessary to respond to an increase in surrenders, withdrawals and loans, thereby realizing capital losses on the assets sold. An increase in policy surrenders and withdrawals may also require us to accelerate amortization of our DAC relating to these products, which would further reduce our profitability.

We attempt to significantly reduce the impact of changes in interest rates on our results of operations and financial condition. We
accomplish this reduction primarily by managing the duration of our assets relative to the duration of our liabilities. For further discussion on
interest rate risk management, see Item 7A. "Quantitative and Qualitative Disclosures About Market Risk — Interest Rate Risk".

Our exposure to credit spreads primarily relates to market price variability and reinvestment risk associated with changes in credit spreads.
A widening of credit spreads would cause unrealized losses in our investment portfolio, would increase losses associated with credit-based derivatives we have sold that do not qualify or have not been designated for hedge accounting where we assume credit exposure and, if issuer
credit spreads increase as a result of fundamental credit deterioration, would likely result in higher other-than-temporary impairments. Credit
spread tightening will reduce net investment income associated with new purchases of fixed maturities. Credit spread tightening may also cause
an increase in the reported value of certain liabilities that are valued using a discount rate that reflects our own credit spread. In addition, market volatility may make it difficult to value certain of our securities if trading becomes less frequent. As such, valuations may include assumptions or estimates that may have significant period-to-period changes from market volatility, which could have a material adverse effect on our results of operations or financial condition.

**Our investment portfolio is subject to several risks that may diminish the value of our invested assets and the investment returns credited to customers, which could reduce our sales, revenues, AUM and net income.**

*An increase in defaults or write-downs on our fixed maturities portfolio may reduce our profitability.*

We are subject to the risk that the issuers of the fixed maturities we own will default on principal and interest payments, particularly if a
major downturn in economic activity occurs. As of December 31, 2013, our U.S. investment operations held $46.0 billion of fixed maturities, or
76% of total U.S. invested assets, of which approximately 7% were below investment grade, including $574.1 million, or 1.25% of our total

fixed maturities which we classified as either "problem," "potential problem" or "restructured." See Item 7. "Management's Discussion and Analysis of Financial Condition and Results of Operations — Investments — U.S. Investment Operations — Fixed Maturities."

Our U.S. fixed maturities portfolio includes securities collateralized by residential and commercial mortgage loans. As of December 31, 2013, our U.S. investment operations held $3.9 billion of residential mortgage-backed securities, of which $2.9 billion are Government National Mortgage Association, Federal National Mortgage Association or Federal Home Loan Mortgage Corporation pass-through securities, and $4.0 billion of commercial mortgage-backed securities, which represent in combination 17% of our total fixed maturities portfolio. For residential mortgage-backed securities, prepayment speeds, changes in mortgage delinquency or recovery rates, credit rating changes by rating agencies, changes in property values underlying the loans and the quality of service provided by service providers on securities in our portfolios could lead to write-downs on these securities. For commercial mortgage-backed securities, changes in mortgage delinquency or default rates, interest rate movements, credit quality and vintage of the underlying loans, changes in property values underlying the loans and credit rating changes by rating agencies could result in write-downs of those securities. See Item 7. "Management's Discussion and Analysis of Financial Condition and Results of Operations — Investments — U.S. Investment Operations — Fixed Maturities."

As of December 31, 2013, the international investment operations of our fully consolidated subsidiaries held $3.4 billion of fixed maturities, or 55%, of total international invested assets, of which 17% are government bonds. Some non-government bonds have been rated on the basis of the issuer's country credit rating. However, the ratings relationship between national ratings and global ratings is not linear with the U.S. The starting point for national ratings differs by country, which makes the assessment of credit quality more difficult. See Item 7. "Management's Discussion and Analysis of Financial Condition and Results of Operations — Investments — International Investment Operations." An increase in defaults on our fixed maturities portfolio could harm our financial strength and reduce our profitability.

***An increased rate of delinquency and defaults on our commercial mortgage loans, including balloon maturities with and without amortizing payments, may adversely affect our profitability.***

Our commercial mortgage loan portfolio faces both delinquency and default risk. Commercial mortgage loans of $10.3 billion represented 15% of our total invested assets as of December 31, 2013. As of December 31, 2013, loans that were in the process of foreclosure totaled $8.0 million, or 0.1% of our commercial mortgage loan portfolio. The performance of our commercial mortgage loan investments, however, may fluctuate in the future. An increase in the delinquency rate of, and defaults under, our commercial mortgage loan portfolio could harm our financial strength and decrease our profitability.

As of December 31, 2013, approximately $8.5 billion, or 82%, of our commercial mortgage loans before valuation allowance had balloon payment maturities. A balloon maturity is a loan with all or a meaningful portion of the loan amount due at the maturity of the loan. The default rate on commercial mortgage loans with balloon payment maturities has historically been higher than for commercial mortgage loans with a fully amortizing loan structure. Since a significant portion of the principal is repaid at maturity, the amount of loss on a default is generally greater than fully amortizing commercial mortgage loans. An increase in defaults on balloon maturity loans as a result of the foregoing factors could harm our financial strength and decrease our profitability.

***Mark-to-market adjustments on certain equity method investments and trading securities may reduce our profitability or cause volatility in our reported earnings.***

Our investment portfolio includes certain equity method investments and trading securities that are reported at fair value on the consolidated statements of financial position, with changes in fair value reported in net investment income on the consolidated statements of operations. Mark-to-market adjustments on these investments may reduce our profitability or cause our net income to vary from period to period. We anticipate that acquisition and investment activities may increase the number and magnitude of these investments in the future.

***We may have difficulty selling our privately placed fixed maturities, commercial mortgage loans and real estate investments because they are less liquid than our publicly traded fixed maturities.***

We hold certain investments that may lack liquidity, such as privately placed fixed maturities, mortgage loans and real estate investments. These asset classes represented approximately 42% of the value of our invested assets as of December 31, 2013.

If we require significant amounts of cash on short notice, we may have difficulty selling these investments in a timely manner, be forced to sell them for less than we otherwise would have been able to realize or both. The reported value of our relatively illiquid types of investments, our investments in the asset classes described above and, at times, our high quality, generally liquid asset classes, do not necessarily reflect the lowest possible price for the asset. If we were forced to sell certain of our assets in the current market, there can be no assurance that we will be able to sell them for the prices at which we have recorded them and we may be forced to sell them at significantly lower prices.

***The impairment of other financial institutions could adversely affect us.***
We use derivative instruments to hedge various risks we face in our businesses. See Item 7A. "Quantitative and Qualitative Disclosures About Market Risk." We enter into a variety of derivative instruments, including interest rate swaps, interest rate options, swaptions, interest rate futures, currency swaps, currency forwards, currency options, equity options, equity futures, credit default swaps and total return swaps, with a number of counterparties in the financial services industry, including brokers and dealers, commercial banks, investment banks, clearinghouses, exchanges and other institutions. For transactions where we are in-the-money, we are exposed to credit risk in the event of default of our counterparty. We establish collateral agreements with nominal thresholds for a large majority of our counterparties to limit our exposure.
However, our credit risk may be exacerbated when the collateral held by us cannot be realized or is liquidated at prices not sufficient to recover the full amount of the loan or derivative exposure. With regard to our derivative exposure, we have over-collateralization requirements on the portion of collateral we hold, based on the risk profile of the assets posted as collateral. We also have exposure to these financial institutions in the form of unsecured debt instruments and equity investments. Such losses or impairments to the carrying value of these assets may materially and adversely affect our business and results of operations.

***Our requirements to post collateral or make payments related to declines in market value of specified assets may adversely affect our liquidity and expose us to counterparty credit risk.***
Many of our derivative transactions with financial and other institutions specify the circumstances under which the parties are required to

post collateral. The amount of collateral we may be required to post under these agreements may increase under certain circumstances, which could adversely affect our liquidity. In addition, under the terms of some of our transactions we may be required to make payment to our counterparties related to any decline in the market value of the specified assets. Such payments could have an adverse effect on our liquidity. Furthermore, with respect to any such payments, we will have unsecured risk to the counterparty as these amounts are not required to be segregated from the counterparty's other funds, are not held in a third-party custodial account, and are not required to be paid to us by the counterparty until the termination of the transaction.

### *Environmental liability exposure may result from our commercial mortgage loan portfolio and real estate investments.*

Liability under environmental protection laws resulting from our commercial mortgage loan portfolio and real estate investments may harm our financial strength and reduce our profitability. Under the laws of several states, contamination of a property may give rise to a lien on the property to secure recovery of the costs of cleanup. In some states, this kind of lien has priority over the lien of an existing mortgage against the property, which would impair our ability to foreclose on that property should the related loan be in default. In addition, under the laws of some states and under the federal Comprehensive Environmental Response, Compensation and Liability Act of 1980, we may be liable for costs of addressing releases or threatened releases of hazardous substances that require remedy at a property securing a mortgage loan held by us, if our agents or employees have become sufficiently involved in the hazardous waste aspects of the operations of the related obligor on that loan, regardless of whether or not the environmental damage or threat was caused by the obligor. We also may face this liability after foreclosing on a property securing a mortgage loan held by us. This may harm our financial strength and decrease our profitability.

### *Regional concentration of our commercial mortgage loan portfolio in California may subject us to economic downturns or losses attributable to earthquakes in that state.*

Commercial mortgage lending in the state of California accounted for 21%, or $2.2 billion, of our commercial mortgage loan portfolio as of December 31, 2013. Due to this concentration of commercial mortgage loans in California, we are exposed to potential losses resulting from the risk of an economic downturn in California as well as to catastrophes, such as earthquakes, that may affect the region. While we generally do not require earthquake insurance for properties on which we make commercial mortgage loans, we do take into account property specific engineering reports, construction type and geographical concentration by fault lines in our investment underwriting guidelines. If economic conditions in California deteriorate or catastrophes occur, we may in the future experience delinquencies or defaults on the portion of our commercial mortgage loan portfolio located in California, which may harm our financial strength and reduce our profitability.

**Our valuation of fixed maturities, equity securities and derivatives may include methodologies, estimations and assumptions which are subject to differing interpretations and could result in changes to investment valuations that may materially adversely affect our results of operations or financial condition.**

Fixed maturities, equity securities and derivatives reported at fair value on our consolidated statements of financial position represented the majority of our total cash and invested assets. The fair value hierarchy prioritizes the inputs to valuation techniques used to measure fair value into three levels. The level in the fair value hierarchy is based on the priority of the inputs to the respective valuation technique. The fair value hierarchy gives the highest priority to quoted prices in active markets for identical assets or liabilities (Level 1) and the lowest priority to unobservable inputs (Level 3). An asset or liability's classification within the fair value hierarchy is based on the lowest level of significant input to its valuation.

• Level 1: Fair values are based on unadjusted quoted prices in active markets for identical assets or liabilities.

• Level 2: Fair values are based on inputs other than quoted prices within Level 1 that are observable for the asset or liability, either directly or indirectly.

• Level 3: Fair values are based on at least one significant unobservable input for the asset or liability.

Excluding separate account assets as of December 31, 2013, 1%, 98% and 1% of our net assets and liabilities reported at fair value represented Level 1, Level 2 and Level 3, respectively. Our Level 1 assets and liabilities primarily include exchange traded equity securities and U.S. Treasury bonds. Our Level 2 assets and liabilities primarily include fixed maturities (including public and private bonds), equity securities, derivatives and other investments for which public quotations are not available but that are priced by third-party pricing services or internal models using substantially all observable inputs. Our Level 3 assets and liabilities include certain fixed maturities, private equity securities, commercial mortgage loan investments and obligations of consolidated variable interest entities for which the fair value option was elected, complex derivatives, embedded derivatives and equity method real estate investments for which the fair value option was elected. Level 3 securities contain at least one significant unobservable market input and as a result considerable judgment may be used in determining the fair values. These fair values are generally obtained through the use of valuation models or methodologies using at least one significant unobservable input or broker quotes. Prices provided by independent pricing services or independent broker quotes that are used in the determination of fair value can vary for a particular security.

For additional information on our valuation methodology, see Item 8. "Financial Statements and Supplementary Data, Notes to Consolidated Financial Statements, Note 15, Fair Value Measurements." During periods of market disruption including periods of significantly rising or high interest rates, rapidly widening credit spreads or illiquidity, it may be difficult to value certain securities, for example collateralized mortgage obligations and collateralized debt obligations, if trading becomes less frequent and/or market data becomes less observable. There may be certain asset classes that were in active markets with significant observable data that become illiquid due to the current financial environment. In such cases, more securities may fall to Level 3 and thus require more subjectivity and management judgment. As such, valuations may include inputs and assumptions that are less observable or require greater estimation as well as valuation methods that require greater estimation, which could result in values that are different from the value at which the investments may be ultimately sold. Further, rapidly changing credit and equity market conditions could materially impact the valuation of securities as reported within our consolidated financial statements and the period-to-period changes in value could vary significantly. Decreases in value may have a material adverse effect on our results of operations or financial condition.

**The determination of the amount of allowances and impairments taken on our investments requires estimations and assumptions which are subject to differing interpretations and could materially impact our results of operations or financial position.**

The determination of the amount of allowances and impairments vary by investment type and is based upon our periodic evaluation and assessment of known and inherent risks associated with the respective asset class. Such evaluations and assessments are revised as conditions change and new information becomes available. There can be no assurance that our management has accurately assessed the level of impairments taken and allowances reflected in our financial statements. Furthermore, additional impairments may need to be taken or allowances provided for in the future. Historical trends may not be indicative of future impairments or allowances.

Additionally, our management considers a wide range of factors about the instrument issuer and uses their best judgment in evaluating the cause of the decline in the estimated fair value of the instrument and in assessing the prospects for recovery. Inherent in management's evaluation of the instrument are assumptions and estimates about the operations of the issuer and its future earnings potential. For further information regarding our impairment methodology, see Item 7. "Management's Discussion and Analysis of Financial Condition and Results of Operations — Investments — U.S. Investment Operations — Fixed Maturities."

**Any impairments of or valuation allowances against our deferred tax assets could adversely affect our results of operations and financial condition.**

Deferred tax liabilities and assets are determined based on the difference between the financial statement and tax bases of assets and liabilities using enacted tax rates expected to be in effect during the years in which the basis differences reverse. We are required to evaluate the recoverability of our deferred tax assets each quarter and establish a valuation allowance, if necessary, to reduce our deferred tax assets to an amount that is more-likely-than-not to be realizable. In determining the need for a valuation allowance, we consider many factors, including future reversals of existing taxable temporary differences, future taxable income exclusive of reversing temporary differences and carryforwards, taxable income in prior carryback years and implementation of any feasible and prudent tax planning strategies management would employ to realize the tax benefit.

Inherent in the provision for income taxes are estimates regarding the deductibility of certain items, the timing of income and expense recognition and the current or future realization of operating losses, capital losses and certain tax credits. In the event these estimates differ from our prior estimates due to the receipt of new information, we may be required to significantly change the provision for income taxes recorded in the consolidated financial statements. Any such change could significantly affect the amounts reported in the consolidated financial statements in the year these estimates change. A further significant decline in value of assets incorporated into our tax planning strategies could lead to an increase of our valuation allowance on deferred tax assets having an adverse effect on current and future results.

**Gross unrealized losses may be realized or result in future impairments, resulting in a reduction in our net income.**

Fixed maturities that are classified as available-for-sale ("AFS") are reported on the consolidated statements of financial position at fair value. Unrealized gains or losses on AFS securities are recognized as a component of equity and are, therefore, excluded from net income. Our U.S. investment operations held gross unrealized losses on fixed maturities of $0.8 billion pre-tax as of December 31, 2013, and the component of gross unrealized losses for securities trading down 20% or more for over six months was approximately $0.3 billion pre-tax. The accumulated change in fair value of the AFS securities is recognized in net income when the gain or loss is realized upon the sale of the asset or in the event that the decline in fair value is determined to be other than temporary (referred to as an other-than-temporary impairment). Realized losses or impairments may have a material adverse impact on our net income in a particular quarterly or annual period.

**Competition from companies that may have greater financial resources, broader arrays of products, higher ratings and stronger financial performance may impair our ability to retain existing customers, attract new customers and maintain our profitability.**

We believe that our ability to compete is based on a number of factors including scale, service, product features, price, investment performance, commission structure, distribution capacity, financial strength ratings and name recognition. We compete with a large number of financial services companies such as banks, mutual funds, broker-dealers, insurers and asset managers, many of which have advantages over us in one or more of the above competitive factors.

Each of our segments faces strong competition. The primary competitors for our Retirement and Investor Services and Principal Global

Investors segments are asset managers, banks, broker-dealers and insurers. Our ability to increase and retain AUM is directly related to the performance of our investments as measured against market averages and the performance of our competitors. Even when securities prices are generally rising, performance can be affected by investment styles. Also, there is a risk that we may not be able to attract and retain the top talent needed to compete in our industry.

Competition for our Principal International segment comes primarily from local financial services firms and other international companies operating on a stand-alone basis or in partnership with local firms.

Our U.S. Insurance Solutions segment competes with other insurance companies.

National banks, with their large existing customer bases, may increasingly compete with insurers as a result of court rulings allowing national banks to sell annuity products in some circumstances, and as a result of legislation removing restrictions on bank affiliations with insurers. Specifically, the Gramm-Leach-Bliley Act of 1999 permits mergers that combine commercial banks, insurers and securities firms under one holding company. These developments may increase competition, in particular for our asset management and accumulation businesses, by substantially increasing the number, size and financial strength of potential competitors who may be able to offer, due to economies of scale, more competitive pricing than we can.

**We may not be able to protect our intellectual property and may be subject to infringement claims.**

We rely on a combination of contractual rights and copyright, trademark, patent and trade secret laws to establish and protect our intellectual property. Although we use a broad range of measures to protect our intellectual property rights, third parties may infringe or misappropriate our intellectual property. We may have to litigate to enforce and protect our copyrights, trademarks, patents, trade secrets and know-how or to determine their scope, validity or enforceability, which represents a diversion of resources that may be significant in amount and may not prove successful. The loss of intellectual property protection or the inability to secure or enforce the protection of our intellectual property assets could have a material adverse effect on our business and our ability to compete.

We also may be subject to costly litigation in the event that another party alleges our operations or activities infringe upon such other party's intellectual property rights. Third parties may have, or may eventually be issued, patents or other protections that could be infringed by our products, methods, processes or services or could otherwise limit our ability to offer certain product features. Any party that holds such a patent could make a claim of infringement against us. We may also be subject to claims by third parties for breach of copyright, trademark, license usage rights, or misappropriation of trade secret rights. Any such claims and any resulting litigation could result in significant liability for damages. If we were found to have infringed or misappropriated a third party patent or other intellectual property rights, we could incur substantial liability, and in some circumstances could be enjoined from providing certain products or services to our customers or utilizing and benefiting from certain methods, processes, copyrights, trademarks, trade secrets or licenses, or alternatively could be required to enter into costly licensing arrangements with third parties, all of which could have a material adverse effect on our business, results of operations and financial condition.

**A downgrade in our financial strength or credit ratings may increase policy surrenders and withdrawals, reduce new sales and terminate relationships with distributors, impact existing liabilities and increase our cost of capital, any of which could adversely affect our profitability and financial condition.**

A.M. Best, Fitch, Moody's Investors Services and Standard & Poor's publish financial strength ratings on U.S. life insurance companies that are indicators of an insurance company's ability to meet contract holder and policyholder obligations. These rating agencies also assign credit ratings on non-life insurance entities, such as PFG and Principal Financial Services, Inc. ("PFS"). Credit ratings are indicators of a debt issuer's ability to meet the terms of debt obligations in a timely manner, and are important factors in overall funding profile and ability to access external capital.

Ratings are important factors in establishing the competitive position of insurance companies and maintaining public confidence in products being offered. A ratings downgrade, or the potential for such a downgrade, could, among other things:

• materially increase the number of surrenders for all or a portion of the net cash values by the owners of policies and contracts we have issued, and materially increase the number of withdrawals by policyholders of cash values from their policies;

- result in the termination of our relationships with broker-dealers, banks, agents, wholesalers and other distributors of our products and services;
- reduce new sales, particularly with respect to full service payout product and general account GICs and funding agreements purchased by pension plans and other institutions;
- cause some of our existing liabilities to be subject to acceleration, additional collateral support, changes in terms, or creation of additional financial obligations and
- increase our cost of capital and limit our access to the capital markets.

Any of these consequences could adversely affect our profitability and financial condition.

**Guarantees within certain of our products that protect policyholders may decrease our earnings or increase the volatility of our results of operations or financial position under U.S. generally accepted accounting principles ("U.S. GAAP") if our hedging or risk management strategies prove ineffective or insufficient.**

Certain of our variable annuity products include guaranteed minimum death benefits and/or guaranteed minimum withdrawal benefits.

Periods of significant and sustained downturns in equity markets, increased equity volatility or reduced interest rates could result in an increase in the valuation of the future policy benefit or policyholder account balance liabilities associated with such products, resulting in a reduction to net income. We use derivative instruments to mitigate changes in the liability exposure related to interest rate, equity market and volatility movements, and the volatility of net income associated with these liabilities. While we believe that these and other actions have mitigated the overall economic risks related to these benefits, we remain liable for the guaranteed benefits in the event that derivative counterparties are unable or unwilling to pay. The liability exposure and volatility of net income may also be influenced by changes in market credit spreads reflecting our own creditworthiness, for which we do not attempt to hedge. In addition, we are subject to the risk that hedging and other management procedures prove ineffective or that unanticipated policyholder behavior or mortality, combined with adverse market events, produces economic losses beyond the scope of the risk management techniques employed. These, individually or collectively, may have a material adverse effect on net income, financial condition or liquidity. We are also subject to the risk that the cost of hedging these guaranteed minimum benefits increases as implied volatilities increase and/or interest rates decrease, resulting in a reduction to net income.

**If we are unable to attract and retain qualified employees and sales representatives and develop new distribution sources, our results of operations, financial condition and sales of our products may be adversely impacted.**

Our continued success is largely dependent on our ability to attract and retain qualified employees. We face intense competition in attracting and retaining key employees, including investment, marketing, finance, legal, compliance and other professionals. If we are unable to attract and retain qualified employees, our results of operations and financial condition may be adversely impacted.

We distribute our asset accumulation, asset management and life and specialty benefit insurance products and services through a variety of distribution channels, including our own internal sales representatives, independent brokers, banks, broker-dealers and other third-party marketing organizations. We must attract and retain sales representatives to sell our products. Strong competition exists among financial services companies for efficient sales representatives. We compete with other financial services companies for sales representatives primarily on the basis of our financial position, support services and compensation and product features. If we are unable to attract and retain sufficient sales representatives to sell our products, our ability to compete and revenues from new sales would suffer.

**Our international businesses face political, legal, operational and other risks that could reduce our profitability in those businesses.**

Our international businesses face political, legal, operational and other risks that we do not face in our operations in the U.S. We face the risk of discriminatory regulation, nationalization or expropriation of assets, price controls and exchange controls or other restrictions that prevent us from transferring funds from these operations out of the countries in which they operate or converting local currencies we hold into U.S. dollars or other currencies. Some of our international businesses are, and are likely to continue to be, in emerging or potentially volatile markets.

In addition, we rely on local staff, including local sales forces, in these countries where there is a risk that we may encounter labor problems with local staff, especially in countries where workers' associations and trade unions are strong. Some of our international businesses are joint ventures in which we hold a minority interest. In these joint ventures, we lack complete management and operational control over the operations, which may limit our ability to take action to protect or increase the value of our investment in the joint venture.

**We may face losses if our actual experience differs significantly from our pricing and reserving assumptions.**

Our profitability depends significantly upon the extent to which our actual experience is consistent with the assumptions used in setting
prices for our products and establishing liabilities for future insurance and annuity policy benefits and claims. The premiums that we charge and the liabilities that we hold for future policy benefits are based on assumptions reflecting a number of factors, including the amount of premiums
that we will receive in the future, rate of return on assets we purchase with premiums received, expected claims, mortality, morbidity, expenses and persistency, which is the measurement of the percentage of insurance policies remaining in force from year to year. However, due to the nature of the underlying risks and the high degree of uncertainty associated with the determination of the liabilities for unpaid policy benefits and claims, we cannot determine precisely the amounts we will ultimately pay to settle these liabilities. As a result, we may experience volatility in the level of our profitability and our reserves from period-to-period. To the extent that actual experience is less favorable than our underlying assumptions, we could be required to increase our liabilities, which may harm our financial strength and reduce our profitability.

For example, if mortality rates are higher than our pricing assumptions, we will be required to make greater claims payments on our life
insurance policies than we had projected. However, this risk may be partially offset by our payout annuity business, where an increase in
mortality rates will result in a decrease in benefit payments, and our use of third party reinsurance. Our results of operations may also be
adversely impacted by an increase in morbidity rates.

Our results of operations may also be adversely impacted if our actual investment earnings differ from our pricing and reserve assumptions. Changes in economic conditions may lead to changes in market interest rates or changes in our investment strategies, either of which could cause our actual investment earnings to differ from our pricing and reserve assumptions.

For additional information on our insurance reserves, see Item 7. "Management's Discussion and Analysis of Financial Condition and

Results of Operations — Critical Accounting Policies and Estimates — Insurance Reserves."

**Our ability to pay stockholder dividends and meet our obligations may be constrained by the limitations on dividends Iowa insurance laws impose on Principal Life.**

We are an insurance holding company whose assets include all of the outstanding shares of the common stock of Principal Life and other subsidiaries. Our ability to pay dividends to our stockholders and meet our obligations, including paying operating expenses and any debt service, depends upon the receipt of dividends from Principal Life. Iowa insurance laws impose limitations on the ability of Principal Life to pay dividends to us. Any inability of Principal Life to pay dividends to us in the future may cause us to be unable to pay dividends to our stockholders and meet our other obligations. See Item 7. "Management's Discussion and Analysis of Financial Condition and Results of Operations — Liquidity and Capital Resources" for a discussion of regulatory restrictions on Principal Life's ability to pay us dividends.

**The pattern of amortizing our DAC and other actuarial balances on our universal life-type insurance contracts, participating life insurance policies and certain investment contracts may change, impacting both the level of the DAC and other actuarial balances and the timing of our net income.**

Amortization of the DAC asset and other actuarial balances depends on the actual and expected profits generated by the lines of business that incurred the expenses. Expected profits are dependent on assumptions regarding a number of factors including investment returns, benefit payments, expenses, mortality and policy lapse. Due to the uncertainty associated with establishing these assumptions, we cannot, with precision, determine the exact pattern of profit emergence. As a result, amortization of these balances will vary from period-to-period. To the extent that actual experience emerges less favorably than expected, or our expectation for future profits decreases, the DAC asset and other actuarial balances may be adjusted, reducing our profitability in the current period.

For additional information, see Item 7. "Management's Discussion and Analysis of Financial Condition and Results of Operation — Critical Accounting Policies and Estimates — Deferred Acquisition Costs and Other Actuarial Balances."

**We may need to fund deficiencies in our Closed Block assets.**

In connection with its conversion in 1998 into a stock life insurance company, Principal Life established an accounting mechanism, known as a "Closed Block" for the benefit of participating ordinary life insurance policies that had a dividend scale in force on July 1, 1998. Dividend scales are the actuarial formulas used by life insurance companies to determine amounts payable as dividends on participating policies based on experience factors relating to, among other things, investment results, mortality, lapse rates, expenses, premium taxes and policy loan interest and utilization rates. The Closed Block was designed to provide reasonable assurance to policyholders included in the Closed Block that, after the conversion, assets would be available to maintain the aggregate dividend scales in effect for 1997 if the experience underlying such scales were to continue.

We allocated assets to the Closed Block as of July 1, 1998, in an amount such that we expected their cash flows, together with anticipated revenues from the policies in the Closed Block, to be sufficient to support the Closed Block business, including payment of claims, certain direct expenses, charges and taxes and to provide for the continuation of aggregate dividend scales in accordance with the 1997 policy dividend scales if the experience underlying such scales continued, and to allow for appropriate adjustments in such scales if the experience changed. We bear the costs of administrative expenses associated with Closed Block policies and, accordingly, these costs were not funded as part of the assets allocated to the Closed Block. Any increase in such costs in the future will be borne by us. As of December 31, 2013, Closed Block assets and liabilities were $ 4,279.1 million and $ 4,951.5 million, respectively.

We will continue to pay guaranteed benefits under the policies included in the Closed Block, in accordance with their terms. The Closed Block assets, cash flows generated by the Closed Block assets and anticipated revenues from policies included in the Closed Block may not be sufficient to provide for the benefits guaranteed under these policies. If they are not sufficient, we must fund the shortfall. Even if they are sufficient, we may choose for business reasons to support dividend payments on policies in the Closed Block with our general account funds.

The Closed Block assets, cash flows generated by the Closed Block assets and anticipated revenues from policies in the Closed Block will benefit only the holders of those policies. In addition, to the extent that these amounts are greater than the amounts estimated at the time we funded the Closed Block, dividends payable in respect of the policies included in the Closed Block may be greater than they would have been in the absence of a Closed Block. Any excess net income will be available for distribution over time to Closed Block policyholders but will not be available to our stockholders.

**A pandemic, terrorist attack, military action or other catastrophic event could adversely affect our net income.**

Our mortality and morbidity experience could be adversely impacted by a catastrophic event. In addition, a severe catastrophic event may cause significant volatility in global financial markets, disruptions to commerce and reduced economic activity. The resulting macroeconomic conditions could adversely affect our cash flows, as well as the value and liquidity of our invested assets. We may also experience operational disruptions if our employees are unable or unwilling to come to work due to a pandemic or other catastrophe. We have developed extensive contingency plans to minimize the risk of operational disruptions. In addition, our use of reinsurance reduces our exposure to adverse mortality experience. Despite these measures, we may still be exposed to losses in the event of a pandemic, terrorist attack, military action or other catastrophe.

**Our reinsurers could default on their obligations or increase their rates, which could adversely impact our net income and financial condition.**

We cede life, disability and health insurance to other insurance companies through reinsurance. See Item 8. "Financial Statements and Supplementary Data, Notes to Consolidated Financial Statements, Note 1, Nature of Operations and Significant Accounting Policies." However, we remain liable to the policyholder, even if the reinsurer defaults on its obligations with respect to the ceded business. In addition, a reinsurer's insolvency may cause us to lose our reserve credits on the ceded business, in which case we would be required to establish additional reserves.

The premium rates that we charge are based, in part, on the assumption that reinsurance will be available at a certain cost. Most of our reinsurance contracts contain provisions which limit the reinsurer's ability to increase rates on in-force business; however, some do not. If a reinsurer raises the rates that it charges on a block of in-force business, our profitability may be negatively impacted if we are not able to pass the increased costs on to the customer. If reinsurers raise the rates that they charge on new business, we may be forced to raise the premiums that we charge, which could have a negative impact on our competitive position. To mitigate the risks associated with the use of reinsurance, we carefully select our reinsurers, and we monitor their ratings and financial condition on a regular basis. We also spread our business among several reinsurers, in order to diversify our risk exposure.

**We face risks arising from acquisitions of businesses.**

We have engaged in acquisitions of businesses in the past, and expect to continue to do so in the future. We face a number of risks arising from acquisition transactions, including difficulties in integrating the acquired business into our operations, difficulties in assimilating and retaining employees and intermediaries, difficulties in retaining the existing customers of the acquired entity, unforeseen liabilities that arise in connection with the acquired business and unfavorable market conditions that could negatively impact our growth expectations for the acquired business. These risks may prevent us from realizing the expected benefits from acquisitions and could result in the impairment of goodwill and/or intangible assets recognized at the time of acquisition.

For additional information on our goodwill and other intangible assets, see Item 7. "Management's Discussion and Analysis of Financial Condition and Results of Operations — Critical Accounting Policies and Estimates — Goodwill and Other Intangible Assets."

**Changes in laws or regulations may reduce our profitability.**

*Changes in regulations may reduce our profitability.*

Our insurance business is subject to comprehensive state regulation and supervision throughout the U.S. and in the international markets in which we operate. We are also impacted by federal legislation and administrative policies in areas such as employee benefit plan regulation, financial services regulations and federal taxation. The primary purpose of state regulation of the insurance business is to protect policyholders, not stockholders. The laws of the various states establish insurance departments with broad powers to regulate such matters as:

• licensing companies to transact business,
• licensing agents,
• admitting statutory assets,
• mandating a number of insurance benefits,
• regulating premium rates,
• approving policy forms,
• regulating unfair trade and claims practices,
• establishing statutory reserve requirements and solvency standards,
• regulating insurer use of affiliated reinsurance companies,
• fixing maximum interest rates on life insurance policy loans and minimum rates for accumulation of surrender values,
• restricting various transactions between affiliates and

- regulating the types, amounts and valuation of investments.

State insurance regulators, federal regulators and the NAIC continually reexamine existing laws and regulations, and may impose changes in the future.

State insurance guaranty associations have the right to assess insurance companies doing business in their state for funds to help pay the obligations of insolvent insurance companies to policyholders and claimants. Because the amount and timing of an assessment is beyond our control, the liabilities we have established for these potential assessments may not be adequate. In addition, regulators may change their interpretation or application of existing laws and regulations. Changes in laws or regulations or the interpretation thereof could significantly increase our compliance costs and adversely affect our profitability and financial strength.

Federal legislation and administrative policies in areas such as employee benefit plan regulation, financial services regulation and federal taxation can reduce our profitability. We provide products and services to certain employee benefit plans that are subject to ERISA or the Internal Revenue Code of 1986, as amended. The U.S. Congress has, from time to time, considered legislation relating to changes in ERISA to permit application of state law remedies, such as consequential and punitive damages, in lawsuits for wrongful denial of benefits, which, if adopted, could increase our liability for damages in future litigation. Additionally, in 2010, the Department of Labor issued a proposed regulation that would, if adopted, significantly broaden the circumstances under which a person or entity would be deemed a fiduciary by virtue of providing investment advice with respect to ERISA plans or IRAs. In September, 2011, the Department of Labor announced that it will repropose these regulations; a new proposal is expected in 2014. New interpretations of existing laws and the passage of new legislation may harm our ability to sell new policies and increase our claims exposure on policies we issued previously. In addition, reductions in contribution levels to defined contribution plans may decrease our profitability.

We have implemented reinsurance transactions utilizing affiliated reinsurers to mitigate the capital impact of Regulation XXX and AG38 on our term and universal life insurance business. We currently use, and currently expect to be able to continue using, affiliated reinsurance companies in various structures. However, the NAIC has established a subgroup to study the use of captives and special purpose vehicles to transfer insurance risk in relation to existing state laws and regulations, which issued a Captives and Special Purpose Vehicles White Paper, which was recently adopted by the NAIC Financial Condition ("E") Committee and Executive Committee/Plenary. The Financial Condition Committee also adopted an "interim solution for captives" in the form of a new charge for the Financial Analysis Working Group ("FAWG"), which will review captive transactions submitted by the states in a peer review and comment process, while the remaining recommendations in the White Paper are divided among the NAIC Reinsurance ("E") Task Force and the Principles Based Reserving Implementation ("EX") Task Force. Also, the Federal Advisory Committee on Insurance ("FACI") took up the issue of captives at a recent meeting, and a task force was created. Any regulatory action that materially adversely affects our use or materially increases our cost of using affiliated reinsurers, either retroactively or prospectively, could have a material adverse impact on our financial condition or results of operations. If we were required to discontinue our use of captives for intercompany reinsurance transactions on a retroactive basis, adverse impacts could include diminished capital position and a higher cost of capital. Additionally, finding alternative means to support policy liabilities efficiently is an unknown factor that would be dependent, in part, on future market conditions and our ability to obtain required regulatory approvals. On a prospective basis, discontinuation of the use of captives could impact the types, amounts and pricing of products offered by our insurance subsidiaries. For additional information regarding our use of affiliated reinsurance transactions, see Item 8, "Financial Statements and Supplementary Data, Notes to Consolidated Financial Statements, Note 16, Statutory Insurance Financial Information.

Our international businesses are also subject to comprehensive regulation and supervision from central and/or local governmental authorities in each country in which we operate. New interpretations of existing laws and regulations or the adoption of new laws and regulations may harm our international businesses and reduce our profitability in those businesses.

In addition, the International Association of Insurance Supervisors (the "IAIS") has proposed a common framework for the supervision of Internationally Active Insurance Groups ("IAIGs"), which is scheduled to be effective in 2019. Under the proposed framework, insurance groups designated as IAIGs may be required by their regulators to comply with new global capital requirements, which may exceed the sum of local capital requirements. In addition, the IAIS is developing a model framework for the supervision of IAIGs that contemplates "group wide supervision" across national boundaries, which requires each IAIG to conduct its own risk and solvency assessment to monitor and manage its overall solvency. It is possible that we may be designated as an IAIG, in which case we may be subject to supervision and capital requirements beyond those applicable to any competitors who are not classified as an IAIG.

***Changes in tax laws could increase our tax costs and reduce sales of our insurance, annuity and investment products.***

Current federal income tax laws generally permit the tax-deferred accumulation of earnings on the premiums paid by the holders of annuities and life insurance products. Taxes, if any, are payable on income attributable to a distribution under the contract for the year in which the distribution is made. The U.S. Congress has, from time to time, considered legislation that would reduce or eliminate the benefit of such deferral of taxation on the accretion of value within life insurance and nonqualified annuity contracts. Enactment of this legislation, including a simplified "flat tax" income structure with an exemption from taxation for investment income, could result in fewer sales of our insurance, annuity and investment products. In addition, changes in the federal estate tax laws could negatively affect the demand for the types of life insurance used in estate planning.

In addition, we benefit from certain tax items, including but not limited to, tax-exempt bond interest, dividends-received deductions, tax credits (such as foreign tax credits) and insurance reserve deductions. From time to time, the U.S. Congress, as well as foreign, state and local governments, considers legislation that could reduce or eliminate the benefits associated with these tax items. If such legislation is adopted, our profitability could be negatively impacted. We continue to evaluate the impact that potential tax reform, which lacks sufficient detail and is relatively uncertain, may have on our future results of operations and financial condition.

***Changes in federal, state and foreign securities laws may reduce our profitability.***

Our asset management and accumulation and life insurance businesses are subject to various levels of regulation under federal, state and foreign securities laws. These laws and regulations are primarily intended to protect investors in the securities markets or investment advisory or brokerage clients and generally grant supervisory agencies broad administrative powers, including the power to limit or restrict the conduct of business for failure to comply with such laws and regulations. Changes to these laws or regulations — or the interpretation thereof — that restrict the conduct of our business could significantly increase our compliance costs and reduce our profitability.

***Financial services regulatory reform may reduce our profitability, impact how we do business or limit our ability to engage in certain capital expenditures.***

On July 21, 2010, the Dodd-Frank Act became law. The Dodd-Frank Act makes extensive changes to the laws regulating financial services firms and requires various federal agencies to adopt a broad range of new implementation rules and regulations, including regulations surrounding the use of derivatives. The federal agencies were given significant discretion in drafting the implementation rules and regulations, and consequently, some of the impacts of the Dodd-Frank Act are not fully known yet. It is possible that aspects of the law may increase hedging costs for the company and possibly cause fundamental shifts to the way risks are hedged.

**We may be unable to mitigate the impact of Regulation XXX and Actuarial Guideline 38, potentially resulting in a negative impact to our capital position and/or a reduction in sales of term and universal life insurance products.**

The NAIC Model Regulation entitled "Valuation of Life Insurance Policies," commonly known as "Regulation XXX", establishes statutory reserve requirements for term life insurance policies and universal life insurance policies with secondary guarantees. Actuarial Guideline 38 ("AG38") clarifies the application of Regulation XXX with respect to certain universal life insurance products with secondary guarantees.

The NAIC amended AG38 in 2012 in an effort to create more clarity around reserving practices for certain policies that are accounted for under this guideline. The effects of the changes to AG38 are two-fold:

• Reserves for certain inforce policies are subject to additional statutory reserve minimums effective for the December 31, 2012, reporting period and

• Reserves for products designed in a specific manner and sold after January 1, 2013 are subject to a higher statutory reserve basis.

**Changes in accounting standards may reduce the transparency of our reported profitability and financial condition.**

Accounting standards are subject to change and can reduce the transparency of our reported profitability. See Item 8, "Financial Statements and Supplementary Data, Notes to Consolidated Financial Statements, Note 1, Nature of Operations and Significant Accounting Policies". The Financial Accounting Standards Board is currently working on several joint projects in conjunction with the International Accounting Standards Board. These projects could result in significant changes to U.S. GAAP, including the accounting standards for insurance contracts. There is still significant uncertainty surrounding the effective dates and transition methods for the proposed changes. If adopted, the proposed changes in accounting standards could reduce the transparency of our financial results and therefore may make it more difficult for investors and regulators to accurately assess our financial condition and profitability. In addition, the required adoption of new accounting standards may result in significant incremental costs associated with initial implementation and on-going compliance.

**A computer system failure or security breach could disrupt our business, damage our reputation and adversely impact our profitability.**

We rely on computer systems to conduct business, including customer service, marketing and sales activities, customer relationship management and producing financial statements. While we have policies, procedures, automation and backup plans designed to prevent or limit the effect of failure, our computer systems may be vulnerable to disruptions or breaches as the result of natural disasters, man-made disasters, criminal activity, pandemics, or other events beyond our control. The failure of our computer systems for any reason could disrupt our operations, result in the loss of customer business and adversely impact our profitability.

We retain confidential information on our computer systems, including customer information and proprietary business information. Any compromise of the security of our computer systems that results in the disclosure of personally identifiable customer information could damage our reputation, expose us to litigation, increase regulatory scrutiny and require us to incur significant technical, legal and other expenses.

**Loss of key vendor relationships or failure of a vendor to protect information of our customers or employees could adversely affect our business or result in losses.**

We rely on services and products provided by many vendors in the United States and abroad. These include, for example, vendors of computer hardware and software and vendors of services. In the event that one or more of our vendors suffers a bankruptcy or otherwise becomes unable to continue to provide products or services, or fails to protect personal information of our customers or employees, we may suffer operational impairments, reputational damage and financial losses.

**Results of litigation and regulatory investigations may affect our financial strength or reduce our profitability.**

We are regularly involved in litigation, both as a defendant and as a plaintiff, but primarily as a defendant. Litigation naming us as a defendant ordinarily arises out of our business operations as a provider of asset management and accumulation products and services; life and disability insurance; and our investment activities.

We are, from time to time, also involved in various governmental, regulatory and administrative proceedings and inquiries. We have received regulatory inquiries from certain state insurance regulators and other officials relating to compliance with unclaimed property laws and the use of data available on the U.S. Social Security Administration's Death Master File (or a similar database) to identify instances where benefits under life insurance policies, annuities and retained asset accounts are payable. It is possible that other jurisdictions may pursue similar inquiries and that such inquiries may result in payments to beneficiaries, escheatment of funds deemed abandoned under state laws and changes to procedures for the identification and escheatment of abandoned property. These factors may affect our financial strength or reduce our profitability. For further discussion on litigation and regulatory investigation risk, see Item 3. "Legal Proceedings," Item 8. "Financial Statements and Supplementary Data, Notes to Consolidated Financial Statements, Note 13, Contingencies, Guarantees and Indemnifications" under the caption, "Litigation and Regulatory Contingencies" and Item 8. "Financial Statements and Supplementary Data, Notes to Consolidated Financial Statements, Note 11, Income Taxes."

**From time to time we may become subject to tax audits, tax litigation or similar proceedings, and as a result we may owe additional taxes, interest and penalties in amounts that may be material.**

We are subject to income taxes in the United States as well as many other jurisdictions. In determining our provisions for income taxes and our accounting for tax-related matters in general, we are required to exercise judgment. We regularly make estimates where the ultimate tax determination is uncertain. The final determination of any tax audit, appeal of the decision of a taxing authority, tax litigation or similar proceedings may be materially different from that reflected in our historical financial statements. The assessment of additional taxes, interest and penalties could be materially adverse to our current and future results of operations and financial condition.

**Fluctuations in foreign currency exchange rates could adversely impact our profitability and financial condition.**

Principal International writes policies denominated in various local currencies and generally invests the associated assets in local currencies. For diversification purposes, assets backing the products may be partially invested in non-local currencies, and the associated foreign currency exchange risk is hedged or managed to specific risk tolerances. Although our investment and hedging strategies limit the effect of currency exchange rate fluctuation on local operating results, fluctuations in such rates affect the translation of these results into our consolidated financial statements. For further discussion on foreign currency exchange risk, see Item 7A. "Quantitative and Qualitative Disclosures About Market Risk — Foreign Currency Risk."

**Applicable laws and our certificate of incorporation and by-laws may discourage takeovers and business combinations that some stockholders might consider in their best interests.**

State laws and our certificate of incorporation and by-laws may delay, defer, prevent, or render more difficult a takeover attempt that some stockholders might consider in their best interests. For instance, they may prevent our stockholders from receiving the benefit from any premium to the market price of our common stock offered by a bidder in a takeover context. Even in the absence of a takeover attempt, the existence of these provisions may adversely affect the prevailing market price of our common stock if they are viewed as discouraging takeover attempts in the future.

State laws and our certificate of incorporation and by-laws may also make it difficult for stockholders to replace or remove our management. These provisions may facilitate management entrenchment, which may delay, defer or prevent a change in our control, which may not be in the best interests of our stockholders.

The following provisions, included in our certificate of incorporation and by-laws, may also have anti-takeover effects and may delay, defer or prevent a takeover attempt that some stockholders might consider in their best interests. In particular, our certificate of incorporation and bylaws:

- permit our Board of Directors to issue one or more series of preferred stock;
- divide our Board of Directors into three classes;
- limit the ability of stockholders to remove directors;
- prohibit stockholders from filling vacancies on our Board of Directors;
- prohibit stockholders from calling special meetings of stockholders;
- impose advance notice requirements for stockholder proposals and nominations of directors to be considered at stockholder meetings and
- require the approval of at least 75% of the voting power of our outstanding common stock for the amendment of our by-laws and provisions of our certificate of incorporation governing:
- the classified board,
- the director's discretion in determining what he or she reasonably believes to be in the best interests of Principal Financial Group, Inc.,
- the liability of directors,
- the removal of directors by shareholders,
- the prohibition on stockholder actions by written consent and
- the supermajority voting requirements.

In addition, Section 203 of the General Corporation Law of the State of Delaware may limit the ability of an "interested stockholder" to engage in business combinations with us. An interested stockholder is defined to include persons owning 15% or more of our outstanding voting stock.

**Our financial results may be adversely impacted by global climate changes.**

Atmospheric concentrations of carbon dioxide and other greenhouse gases have increased dramatically since the industrial revolution, resulting in a gradual increase in global average temperatures and an increase in the frequency and severity of natural disasters. These trends are expected to continue in the future and have the potential to impact nearly all sectors of the economy to varying degrees. Our initial research indicates that climate change does not pose an imminent or significant threat to our operations or business, but we will continue to monitor new developments in the future.

Potential impacts may include the following:
- Changes in temperatures and air quality may adversely impact our mortality and morbidity rates. For example, increases in the

level of pollution and airborne allergens may cause an increase in upper respiratory and cardiovascular diseases, leading to
increased claims in our insurance businesses. However, the risk of increased mortality on our life insurance business may be
partly offset by our payout annuity business, where an increase in mortality results in a decrease in benefit payments.
• Climate change may impact asset prices, as well as general economic conditions. For example, rising sea levels may lead to
decreases in real estate values in coastal areas. Additionally, government policies to slow climate change (e.g., setting limits on
carbon emissions) may have an adverse impact on sectors such as utilities, transportation and manufacturing. Changes in asset
prices may impact the value of our fixed income, real estate and commercial mortgage investments. We manage our investment
risks by maintaining a well-diversified portfolio, both geographically and by sector. We also monitor our investments on an
ongoing basis, allowing us to adjust our exposure to sectors and/or geographical areas that face severe risks due to climate
change.
• A natural disaster that affects one of our office locations could disrupt our operations and pose a threat to the safety of our
employees. However, we have extensive Business Continuity and Disaster Recovery planning programs in place to help mitigate
this risk.

**Item 1B. Unresolved Staff Comments**

None.

**Item 2. Properties**

As of December 31, 2013, we own 33 properties in our home office complex in Des Moines, Iowa, and in various other locations. Of these
33 properties, 18 are office buildings, 1 is a warehouse facility, 11 are parking lots and ramps, 1 is a park/green space, 1 is a childcare center and
1 is a power generation plant. Of the office and warehouse space, we occupy approximately 92% of the 2.7 million square feet of space in these
buildings. The balance of the space in these buildings is rented to commercial tenants or is occupied by the property management company
servicing these properties. We lease office space for various offices located throughout the U.S. and internationally. We believe that our owned
and leased properties are suitable and adequate for our current business operations.

**Item 3. Legal Proceedings**

Disclosure concerning material legal proceedings can be found in Item 8. "Financial Statements and Supplementary Data, Notes to Consolidated Financial Statements, Note 13, Contingencies, Guarantees and Indemnifications" under the caption, "Litigation and Regulatory Contingencies" and Item 8. "Financial Statements and Supplementary Data, Notes to Consolidated Financial Statements, Note 11, Income Taxes" under the caption, "Other Tax Information," which are incorporated here by this reference.

**Executive Officers of the Registrant**

The following information is furnished with respect to our executive officers, each of whom is elected by and serves at the pleasure of the Board of Directors.

*Timothy M. Dunbar, 56,* has been Executive Vice President and Chief Investment Officer of the Company and Principal Life since January 1, 2014. Prior to that date, he served as Senior Vice President of the Company and Principal Life since 2011, and Chief Investment Officer of the Company and Principal Life since January 2013. Prior to that date, Mr. Dunbar was in charge of Strategy and Finance for the Company and Principal Life in 2011 and 2012, overseeing the business management and strategic direction of the capital markets, corporate strategy and corporate treasury areas. He retains his responsibility for capital markets. Mr. Dunbar previously served as the executive director and head of equities for Principal Global Investors from 2004 until 2011.

*Gregory B. Elming, 53*, has been Senior Vice President and Chief Risk Officer of the Company and Principal Life since March 2011. Prior to that time, he was Senior Vice President and Controller of the Company and Principal Life since 2007 and Vice President and Controller of the Company and Principal Life since 2002.

*Ralph C. Eucher, 61,* has been Executive Vice President of the Company and Principal Life since March 2013, responsible for global human resources, corporate real estate and aviation operations. Prior to that time, he was Senior Vice President of the Company and Principal Life since 2002, overseeing human resources and corporate real estate since 2008.

*Daniel J. Houston, 52*, who heads the Retirement and Investor Services and U.S. Insurance Solutions segments of our operations, was named President, Retirement, Insurance and Financial Services of the Company and Principal Life on January 1, 2010. He was President, Retirement and Investor Services of the Company and Principal Life from February 2008 until January 2010, and was Executive Vice President,

Retirement and Investor Services of the Company and Principal Life from June 2006 to February 2008.

*Terrance J. Lillis, 61,* has been Senior Vice President and Chief Financial Officer of the Company and Principal Life since August 2008 and Senior Vice President of the Company and Principal Life since May 2008. Prior to that time, he was Chief Financial Officer — Retirement and Investor Services division of Principal Life since December 2001.

*James P. McCaughan, 60,* who heads the Principal Global Investors segment of our operations, has been President, Principal Global Investors of the Company and Principal Life since December 2003. Prior to that time, he served as Executive Vice President and global head of asset management for the Company and Principal Life since April 2002. From 2000 to 2002, he was Chief Executive Officer of the Americas division of Credit Suisse Asset Management in New York, New York.

*Mary A. O'Keefe, 57,* who heads Corporate Relations, has been Senior Vice President and Chief Marketing Officer of the Company and Principal Life since February 2005, Senior Vice President of the Company since April 2001, and Senior Vice President of Principal Life since January 1998.

*Gary P. Scholten, 56,* has been Senior Vice President and Chief Information Officer of the Company and Principal Life since November 2002. From 1998 to 2002, he was Vice President of retail information services of Principal Life.

*Karen E. Shaff, 59,* has been Executive Vice President and General Counsel of the Company and Principal Life since February 2004 and, in addition, Secretary of the Company and Principal Life since January 2014. Prior thereto, she was Senior Vice President and General Counsel of the Company since April 2001, and Senior Vice President and General Counsel of Principal Life since January 2000.

*Luis Valdes, 56,* who has been the head of the Principal International segment of our operations since March 2012, has been President, Principal International of the Company and Principal Life since March 2011. Prior to his current position, he has been Senior Vice President and President — PFG Latin America of the Company and Principal Life since March 2010, and was Vice President — Principal International of Principal Life from 2000 until March 2010.

*Larry D. Zimpleman, 62,* has been a Director of the Company and Principal Life since 2006. He has been Chairman, President and Chief Executive Officer of the Company and Principal Life since May 2009 and was President and Chief Executive Officer of the Company and

Principal Life from May 2008 to May 2009. Prior thereto, he was President and Chief Operating Officer of the Company and Principal Life from 2006 to May 2008. He was President, Retirement and Investor Services of the Company and Principal Life from December 2003 through May 2006. Mr. Zimpleman served as chairman of the board and a director of the Principal Funds from December 2001 to December 2008.

## *Fixed Maturities Exposure*

Economic and fiscal conditions in select European countries, including Greece, Ireland, Italy, Portugal and Spain, continue to cause credit concerns particularly to financial institutions and banks with exposure to the European periphery region. Our exposure to the region within our International investment operations fixed maturities portfolio is manageable, representing 5.8% and 6.2% of our total International invested assets as of December 31, 2013 and December 31, 2012, respectively. Portfolio holdings with exposure to this region consist of fixed maturities issued in the same countries as our International operations by local subsidiaries of the European parent. Nearly all of the exposure is to bonds issued in Chile. In addition, we did not hold any sovereign debt issuances of the selected countries and had not bought or sold credit protection on sovereign issuances as of December 31, 2013 and December 31, 2012. Financial sector exposure is to local subsidiary banks, subject to local capital requirements and banking regulation. The current financial exposure carries an average AA- local rating from S&P and the average time to maturity is 17 years. Non-financial sector exposure consists primarily of infrastructure bonds, which are backed by the project itself, often with minimum revenue guarantees from the government. The current non-financial exposure carries an average AA- local rating from S&P. The current Italian exposure has an average time to maturity of 14 years. In addition, the current Spanish exposure has an average time to maturity of 13 years. As of December 31, 2013, our total portfolio exposure had an average price of 107 (carrying value/amortized cost). The following table presents the carrying amount of our European periphery zone fixed maturities exposure for the periods indicated.

For further details on our U.S. investment operations exposure to these European countries, see "U.S. Investment Operations — Fixed Maturities."

## Item 7A. Quantitative and Qualitative Disclosures About Market Risk
## Market Risk Exposures and Risk Management

Market risk is the risk we will incur losses due to adverse fluctuations in market rates and prices. Our primary market risk exposures are to

interest rates, equity markets, foreign currency exchange rates, and credit risk. The active management of market risk is an integral part of our operations. We manage our overall market risk exposure within established risk tolerance ranges by using the following approaches:
- rebalance our existing asset or liability portfolios;
- control the risk structure of newly acquired assets and liabilities or
- use derivative instruments to modify the market risk characteristics of existing assets or liabilities or assets expected to be
purchased.

## Interest Rate Risk

Interest rate risk is the risk we will incur economic losses due to adverse changes in interest rates. We are exposed to interest rate risk from several sources:
- Due to the inherent difficulty in obtaining assets that mature or have their rate reset at the exact same time as the liabilities they
support, assets may have to be reinvested or sold in the future to meet the liability cash flows in unknown interest rate
environments.
- There may be timing differences between when new liabilities are priced and when assets are purchased or procured that can
cause fluctuations in profitability if interest rates move materially in the interim.
- Prepayment options embedded within asset and liability contracts can alter the cash flow profiles from what was originally
expected.

|  | December 31, 2013 | | | December 31, 2012 | | |
|---|---|---|---|---|---|---|
| **Select European Exposure** | **Italy** | **Spain** | **Total** | **Italy** | **Spain** | **Total** |
| *(in millions)* | | | | | | |
| Non-Sovereign: | | | | | | |
| Financial institutions | $ — | $ 215.5 | $ 215.5 | $ — | $ 237.3 | $ 237.3 |
| Non-financial institutions | 14.2 | 122.7 | 136.9 | 11.1 | 125.4 | 136.5 |
| Total | $ 14.2 | $ 338.2 | $ 352.4 | $ 11.1 | $ 362.7 | $ 373.8 |

- The spreads between the investment income we earn and the interest we credit to customers who own products with guaranteed
minimum interest rates may decrease (or potentially become negative) during periods of sustained low interest rates.
- During periods of sustained low interest rates, the interest rates that we earn on our assets may be lower than the rates assumed in
pricing our insurance products, thereby reducing our profitability. If interest rates remain low over a sustained period of time, this

may result in increases in our reserves and/or unlocking of our DAC asset and other actuarial balances.

• During periods of rising interest rates, policy surrenders, withdrawals, and requests for policy loans may increase as customers
seek to achieve higher returns. This may result in unlocking of our DAC and other actuarial balances. We may be required to sell
assets to raise the cash necessary to respond to such surrenders, withdrawals and loans, thereby realizing capital losses on the
assets sold.

• For our long-term borrowings, we are exposed to interest rate risk at the time of maturity or early redemption, when we may be
required to refinance our obligations.

• We are exposed to interest rate risk based upon the discount rate assumption used for purposes of valuing our pension and other postretirement benefit obligations.

An increase in market interest rates may cause the fair value of our financial assets to decline. The reduction in the fair value of our
financial assets would be partly offset by a corresponding reduction in the fair value of our financial liabilities. The following tables show the net
estimated potential loss in fair value at total company level from a hypothetical 100 basis point immediate, parallel increase in interest rates as
of December 31, 2013, and December 31, 2012. Our selection of a 100 basis point immediate, parallel increase in interest rates is a hypothetical
rate scenario we use to demonstrate potential risk. While a 100 basis point immediate, parallel increase does not represent our view of future
market changes, it is a near term reasonably possible hypothetical change that illustrates the potential impact of such events. While these fair
value measurements provide a representation of interest rate sensitivity, they are based on our portfolio exposures at a point in time and may not
be representative of future market results. These exposures will change as a result of ongoing portfolio transactions in response to new business,
management's assessment of changing market conditions and available investment opportunities.

**As of December 31, 2013 Notional Asset (liability) fair value Hypothetical fair value after +100 basis point parallel yield curve shift Hypothetical changes in fair value** *(in millions)*

Financial assets with interest rate risk:
Fixed maturities, available-for-sale **$ 48,757.1 $ 46,522.2 $ (2,234.9 )**
Fixed maturities, trading **563.1 540.4 (22.7 )**

Mortgage loans **11,773.5 11,291.1 (482.4 )**
Policy loans **963.3 891.3 (72.0 )**
Equity securities, trading **416.5 400.4 (16.1 )**
Other investments **118.0 120.8 2.8**
Financial liabilities with interest rate risk:
Investment-type insurance contracts **(30,100.0 ) (29,274.0 ) 826.0**
Long-term debt **(2,692.1 ) (2,455.9 ) 236.2**
Bank deposits **(1,951.1 ) (1,941.7 ) 9.4**
Derivatives with interest rate risk
Interest rate swaps **$ 20,570.8 (365.4 ) (459.3 ) (93.9 )**
Currency swaps **2,367.5 106.0 110.8 4.8**
Equity options **1,719.7 (125.4 ) (152.1 ) (26.7 )**
Interest rate options **4,100.0 41.7 57.5 15.8**
Swaptions **325.0 1.0 3.5 2.5**
Interest rate futures **92.5 (1.1 ) 3.0 4.1**
Net estimated potential loss in fair value **$ (1,847.1 )**
Table of Contents

The tables include only the portion of assets and liabilities that are interest rate sensitive. Separate account assets and liabilities, which are interest rate sensitive, are not included in the tables, as any interest rate risk is borne by the holder of the separate account. The fair value sensitivities of our U.S. operations' foreign financial assets and liabilities have been netted within the currency swaps line item due to fully hedging the foreign exposure.

The tables above do not include approximately $29,426.9 million of liabilities relating to insurance contracts involving significant mortality or morbidity risk as of December 31, 2013 and $28,815.5 million as of December 31, 2012, which are not considered financial liabilities. We believe the interest rate sensitivities of these insurance liabilities would economically serve as a partial offset to the net interest rate risk of the financial assets and liabilities that are set forth in these tables.

The fair value sensitivity table above replaces our 2012 Form 10-K sensitivity table, which showed the duration gap between our liabilities and the assets backing them, as well as the net fair value change for a 100 basis point immediate, parallel increase in interest rates. We believe the new disclosure provides more useful information, as it presents our assets and liabilities at a more granular level. The new disclosure also provides better perspective on the sensitivity of AOCI to interest rate changes. Therefore, we believe the new disclosure provides a clearer and more comprehensive indication of the potential impact on our consolidated statements of financial position from a 100 basis point change in interest rates.

Our net estimated potential loss in fair value as of December 31, 2013, increased $73.9 million from December 31, 2012, primarily due to a slight increase in the duration of our financial assets and a slight decrease in the duration of our financial liabilities.

| | As of December 31, 2012 | | |
|---|---|---|---|
| | Notional | Asset (liability) fair value | Hypothetical fair value after +100 basis point parallel yield curve shift | Hypothetical changes in fair value |

*(in millions)*

Financial assets with interest rate risk:
Fixed maturities, available-for-sale $ 50,939.3 $ 48,651.7 $ (2,287.6 )
Fixed maturities, trading 626.7 600.6 (26.1 )
Mortgage loans 12,163.7 11,686.6 (477.1 )
Policy loans 1,056.8 985.9 (70.9 )
Equity securities, trading 81.1 76.0 (5.1 )
Other investments 119.8 117.7 (2.1 )
Financial liabilities with interest rate risk:
Investment-type insurance contracts (32,702.1 ) (31,754.6 ) 947.5
Long-term debt (2,951.4 ) (2,671.6 ) 279.8
Bank deposits (2,177.7 ) (2,166.3 ) 11.4
Derivatives with interest rate risk
Interest rate swaps $ 18,381.2 (296.1 ) (377.2 ) (81.1 )
Currency swaps 3,454.1 102.2 101.3 (0.9 )
Equity options 1,559.7 34.5 (1.7 ) (36.2 )
Interest rate options 500.0 48.5 19.2 (29.3 )
Swaptions 325.0 0.7 2.6 1.9
Interest rate futures 82.0 — 2.6 2.6
Net estimated potential loss in fair value $ (1,773.2 )

The following table provides detail on the differences between the interest rates being credited to contract holders as of December 31, 2013, and the respective guaranteed minimum interest rates ("GMIRs"), broken down by GMIR level within the Retirement and Investor Services and U.S. Insurance Solutions segments.

During periods of low or declining interest rates, our margin of investment income above our interest credited to our liabilities ("investment margins") may be negatively impacted. Assuming a hypothetical scenario where market interest rates immediately fall by 25 basis points from their December 31, 2013 levels and then remain unchanged thereafter, we estimate that the impact of such an environment could reduce our investment margins for our domestic business by approximately $2 million and $4 million pre-tax during the 12 months ending December 31, 2014 and 2015, respectively, compared to a scenario where market interest rates remain unchanged from their December 31, 2013 levels. This hypothetical scenario reflects only the impact related to the approximately $21 billion of in-force contracts with guaranteed minimum interest rates shown above, and does not reflect potential impacts on our DAC asset and other actuarial balances. In determining the potential impact, we have reflected the impact of potential changes in crediting rates to policyholders, limited by any restrictions on our ability to adjust crediting rates due to guaranteed minimum interest rates. Our estimates of future margins include the impact of expected premium payments, lapses, and withdrawals on existing policies, but they do not include the impact of new sales. Our selection of a 25 basis point immediate, parallel decrease in interest rates is a hypothetical rate scenario we use to demonstrate potential risk. While a 25 basis point immediate, parallel decrease does not represent our view of future market changes, it is a near term reasonably possible hypothetical change that illustrates the potential impact of such events.

We manage interest rate risk through the use of an integrated risk management framework that helps us identify, assess, monitor, report and manage our risks within established limits and risk tolerances. Our internal risk committees monitor and discuss our risk profile and identify necessary actions to mitigate impacts from interest rate risk.

We also limit our exposure to interest rate risk through our business mix and strategy. We have intentionally limited our exposure to specific products where investment margins are critical to the product's profitability, and we continue to emphasize the sale of products that generate revenues in the form of fees for service or premiums for insurance coverage and expose us to minimal interest rate risk.

One of the measures we use to quantify our exposure to interest rate risk is duration, which is a measure of the sensitivity of the fair value of assets and liabilities to changes in interest rates. Differences in durations between assets and liabilities are measured and kept within acceptable tolerances. Derivatives are also commonly used to mitigate interest rate risk due to cash flow mismatches and timing differences. Prepayment risk is controlled by limiting our exposure to investments that are prepayable without penalty prior to maturity at the option of the issuer. We also require additional yield on these investments to compensate for the risk the issuer will exercise such option. Prepayment risk is also controlled by limiting the sales of liabilities with features such as puts or other options that can be exercised against the company at inopportune times. We manage the interest rate risk associated with our long-term borrowings by monitoring the interest rate environment and evaluating refinancing opportunities as maturity dates approach.

See Item 7. "Management's Discussion and Analysis of Financial Condition and Results of Operations — Critical Accounting Policies and Estimates — Valuation and Impairment of Fixed Income Investments" for additional discussion of the impact interest rate increases would have on fixed maturities, available-for-sale.

**Account values (1)**
**Excess of crediting rates over GMIR:**
**At GMIR**
**Up to 0.50% above GMIR**
**0.51% to 1.00% above GMIR**
**1.01% to 2.00% above GMIR**
**2.01% or more above GMIR Total**
*($ in millions)*
**Guaranteed minimum interest rate**
**Retirement and Investor Services**

| | | | | | | |
|---|---|---|---|---|---|---|
| Up to 1.00% | $ 465.5 | $ 670.1 | $ 3,557.6 | $ 808.4 | $ 48.5 | $ 5,550.1 |
| 1.01% - 2.00% | 321.8 | 135.6 | 286.5 | 60.4 | — | 804.3 |
| 2.01% - 3.00% | 8,659.6 | 72.9 | 235.1 | 308.8 | 1.6 | 9,278.0 |
| 3.01% - 4.00% | 246.6 | — | — | — | — | 246.6 |
| Subtotal | 9,693.5 | 878.6 | 4,079.2 | 1,177.6 | 50.1 | 15,879.0 |
| **U.S. Insurance Solutions** | | | | | | |
| Up to 1.00% | — | — | 23.7 | 11.8 | — | 35.5 |
| 1.01% - 2.00% | 259.0 | — | 105.1 | 50.9 | 6.4 | 421.4 |
| 2.01% - 3.00% | 1,820.1 | 1,005.3 | 166.3 | 71.0 | 0.1 | 3,062.8 |
| 3.01% - 4.00% | 1,426.8 | 21.6 | 16.3 | 44.1 | 6.4 | 1,515.2 |
| 4.01% - 5.00% | 153.7 | 92.1 | 77.9 | 21.3 | — | 345.0 |
| Subtotal | 3,659.6 | 1,119.0 | 389.3 | 199.1 | 12.9 | 5,379.9 |
| Total | $ 13,353.1 | $ 1,997.6 | $ 4,468.5 | $ 1,376.7 | $ 63.0 | $ 21,258.9 |
| Percentage of total | 62.8 % | 9.4 % | 21.0 % | 6.5 % | 0.3 % | 100.0 % |

(1) Includes only the account values, net of policy loans, for products with GMIRs and discretionary crediting rates.

The plan fiduciaries use a Dynamic Asset Allocation strategy for our qualified defined benefit pension plan, which strategically allocates an increasing portion of the assets of the pension plan to fixed income securities as the funding status improves. The intended purpose of using the Dynamic Asset Allocation strategy is that the expected change in the value of the plan assets and the change in pension benefit obligation due to market movements are more likely to have more correlation versus a static allocation of assets between categories. For more information see Item 7. "Management's Discussion and Analysis of Financial Condition and Results of Operations — Critical Accounting Policies and Estimates — Benefit Plans" and Item 8. "Financial Statements and Supplementary Data, Notes to Consolidated Financial Statements, Note 12, Employee and Agent Benefits."

**Use of Derivatives to Manage Interest Rate Risk.** We use or have previously used various derivative financial instruments to manage our exposure to fluctuations in interest rates, including interest rate swaps, interest rate collars, swaptions and futures. We use interest rate swaps and futures contracts to hedge changes in interest rates subsequent to the issuance of an insurance liability, such as a guaranteed investment contract, but prior to the purchase of a supporting asset, or during periods of holding assets in anticipation of near term liability sales. We use interest rate swaps primarily to more closely match the interest rate characteristics of assets and liabilities. They can be used to change the sensitivity to the interest rate of specific assets and liabilities as well as an entire portfolio. We use interest rate collars to manage interest rate risk related to GMIR liabilities in our individual annuities contracts and lapse risk associated with higher interest rates. We purchase swaptions to offset or modify existing exposures.

**Foreign Currency Risk**

Foreign currency risk is the risk we will incur economic losses due to adverse fluctuations in foreign currency exchange rates. This risk arises from foreign currency-denominated funding agreements issued to nonqualified institutional investors in the international market, foreign currency-denominated fixed maturities and our international operations, including potential acquisition and divestiture activity.

We estimate that as of December 31, 2013, a 10% immediate unfavorable change in each of the foreign currency exchange rates to which we are exposed would result in no material change to the net fair value of our foreign currency denominated instruments identified above because we effectively hedge foreign currency denominated instruments to minimize exchange rate impacts, which is consistent with our estimate as of December 31, 2012. However, fluctuations in foreign currency exchange rates do affect the translation of operating earnings and equity of our international operations into our consolidated financial statements.

For our Principal International segment, we estimate that a 10% immediate unfavorable change in each of the foreign currency exchange rates to which we were exposed would have resulted in a $306.1 million, or 10%, reduction in the total equity excluding noncontrolling interests of our international operations as of December 31, 2013, as compared to an estimated $184.2 million, or 10%, reduction as of December 31, 2012. We estimate that a 10% unfavorable change in the average foreign currency exchange rates to which we were exposed through our international operations would have resulted in a $24.2 million, or 11%, reduction in the operating earnings of our international operations for the year ended December 31, 2013, as compared to an estimated $17.5 million, or 11%, reduction for the year ended December 31, 2012. The Cuprum acquisition increased total net assets and earnings exposed to foreign currency risk compared to December 31, 2012.

The selection of a 10% immediate unfavorable change in all currency exchange rates should not be construed as a prediction by us of future market events, but rather as an illustration of the potential impact of such an event. These exposures will change as a result of a change in the size and mix of our foreign operations.

**Use of Derivatives to Manage Foreign Currency Risk.** The foreign currency risk on funding agreements and fixed maturities in our U.S. operations is mitigated by using currency swaps that swap the foreign currency interest and principal payments to our functional currency. The notional amount of our currency swap agreements associated with foreign-denominated liabilities was $1,425.0 million and $2,209.6 million as of December 31, 2013 and December 31, 2012, respectively. The notional amount of our currency swap agreements associated with foreigndenominated fixed maturities was $822.1 million and $1,164.0 million as of December 31, 2013 and December 31, 2012, respectively.

With regard to our international operations, in order to enhance the diversification of our investment portfolios we may invest in bonds denominated in a currency that is different than the currency of our liabilities. We use foreign exchange derivatives to economically hedge the currency mismatch. Our operations in Chile had currency swaps with a notional amount of $120.4 million and $80.5 million as of December 31, 2013 and December 31, 2012, respectively. Chile also utilized currency forwards with a notional amount of $247.4 million and $257.2 million as of December 31, 2013 and December 31, 2012, respectively.

We used currency options with a notional amount of $1,400.0 million and currency forwards with a notional amount of $300.0 million as of December 31, 2012, to manage the foreign currency risk associated with a business combination. There were no hedges of business combinations outstanding at December 31, 2013. Additionally, from time to time we take measures to hedge our net equity investments in our foreign subsidiaries from currency risks. There were no outstanding net equity investment hedges in 2013 or 2012.

**Equity Risk**

Equity risk is the risk we will incur economic losses due to adverse fluctuations in common stock prices. As of December 31, 2013 and December 31, 2012, the fair value of our equity securities was $827.4 million and $389.3 million, respectively. The increase is primarily due to equity securities that we acquired as part of the Cuprum acquisition that was completed in first quarter 2013. As of December 31, 2013, we estimate that a 10% decline in the value of the equity securities would result in a decline in fair value of the equity securities of $82.7 million, as compared to a decline in fair value of the equity securities of $38.9 million as of December 31, 2012.

We are also exposed to the risk that asset-based fees decrease as a result of declines in assets under management due to changes in investment prices and the risk that asset management fees calculated by reference to performance could be lower. The risk of decreased assetbased and asset management fees could also impact our estimates of total gross profits used as a basis for amortizing deferred acquisition costs and other actuarial balances. We estimate that an immediate 10% decline in the S&P index, followed by a 2% per quarter increase would reduce our annual operating earnings by approximately 4% to 6%. For further discussion, see Item 7. "Management's Discussion and Analysis of Financial Condition and Results of Operations — Critical Accounting Policies and Estimates — Deferred Acquisition Costs and Other Actuarial Balances."

The selection of a 10% unfavorable change in the equity markets should not be construed as a prediction by us of future market events, but rather as an illustration of the potential impact of such an event. Our exposure will change as a result of changes in our mix of business.

We also have equity risk associated with (1) fixed deferred annuity and universal life contracts that credit interest to customers based on changes in an external equity index; (2) variable annuity contracts that have a GMWB rider that allows the customer to make withdrawals of a specified annual amount, either for a fixed number of years or for the lifetime of the customer, even if the account value is reduced to zero; (3) variable annuity contracts that have a guaranteed minimum death benefit ("GMDB") that allows the death benefit to be paid, even if the account value has fallen below the GMDB amount and (4) investment-type contracts in which the return is subject to minimum contractual guarantees. We are also subject to equity risk based upon the assets that support our employee benefit plans. For further discussion of equity risk associated with these plans, see Item 7. "Management's Discussion and Analysis of Financial Condition and Results of Operations — Critical Accounting Policies and Estimates — Benefit Plans."

**Use of Derivatives to Manage Equity Risk.** We economically hedge the fixed deferred annuity and universal life products, where the interest credited is linked to an external equity index, by purchasing options that match the product's profile. We economically hedge the GMWB exposure, which includes interest rate risk and equity risk, using futures, options and interest rate swaps with notional amounts of $365.9 million, $1,719.7 million, and $3,263.5 million, respectively, as of December 31, 2013, and notional amounts of $455.6 million, $1,539.7 million, and $2,904.8 million, respectively, as of December 31, 2012. The fair value of both the GMWB embedded derivative and associated hedging instruments are sensitive to financial market conditions and the variance related to the change in fair value of these items for a given period is largely dependent on market conditions at the end of the period.

**Credit Risk**

Credit risk relates to the uncertainty associated with the continued ability of a given obligor to make timely payments of principal and interest. Our ability to manage credit risk is essential to our business and our profitability. See Item 7. "Management's Discussion and Analysis of Financial Condition and Results of Operations — Investments" for additional information about credit risk.

**Use of Derivatives to Diversify or Hedge Credit Risk.** We purchase credit default swaps to hedge certain credit exposures in our investment portfolio and total return swaps and futures to hedge a portion of our investment portfolio from credit losses. We sell credit default swaps to offer credit protection to investors when entering into synthetic replicating transactions. When selling credit protection, if there is an event of default by the referenced name, we are obligated to pay the counterparty the referenced amount of the contract and receive in return the referenced security. For further information on credit derivatives sold, see Item 8. "Financial Statements and Supplementary Data, Notes to Consolidated Financial Statements, Note 6, Derivative Financial Instruments" under the caption, "Credit Derivatives Sold."

We economically hedged credit exposure in our portfolio by purchasing credit default swaps with a notional amount of $334.3 million and $359.8 million, total return swaps of $90.0 million and $100.0 million, and futures of $9.1 million and $0.0 million as of December 31, 2013 and December 31, 2012, respectively. We had credit exposure through credit default swaps with a notional amount of $110.4 million and $110.4 million as of December 31, 2013 and December 31, 2012, respectively, by investing in various tranches of a synthetic collateralized debt obligation. In addition, we sold credit default swaps creating replicated assets with a notional amount of $708.5 million and $908.1 million as of December 31, 2013 and December 31, 2012, respectively.

**Derivative Counterparty Risk**

In conjunction with our use of derivatives, we are exposed to counterparty risk, or the risk that the counterparty fails to perform the terms of the derivative contract. We actively manage this risk by:
• obtaining approval of all new counterparties by the Investment Committee;
• establishing exposure limits that take into account non-derivative exposure we have with the counterparty as well as derivative exposure;
• performing similar credit analysis prior to approval on each derivatives counterparty that we do when lending money on a longterm basis;
• diversifying our risk across numerous approved counterparties;
• implementing credit support annex (collateral) agreements ("CSAs") for over-the-counter derivative transactions or similar agreements with a majority of our counterparties to further limit counterparty exposures, which provide for netting of exposures;
• limiting exposure to A credit or better for over-the-counter derivative counterparties without CSAs;
• conducting stress-test analysis to determine the maximum exposure created during the life of a prospective transaction
• daily monitoring of counterparty credit ratings, exposures and associated collateral levels and
• trading mandatorily cleared contracts through centralized clearinghouses.
We believe the risk of incurring losses due to nonperformance by our counterparties is manageable. For further information on derivatives, see Item 8. "Financial Statements and Supplementary Data, Notes to Consolidated Financial Statements, Note 6, Derivative Financial Instruments."
Based on our accounting policy, our disclosed exposure measures the fair value of derivatives that have become favorable to us and, therefore, is a combined credit exposure if all of the involved counterparties failed to fulfill their obligations. For further information on derivative exposure, see Item 8. "Financial Statements and Supplementary Data, Notes to Consolidated Financial Statements, Note 6, Derivative Financial Instruments" under the caption, "Exposure."

We manage our exposure on a net basis, whereby we net positive and negative exposures for each counterparty with agreements in place. For further information on derivative exposure, see Item 8. "Financial Statements and Supplementary Data, Notes to Consolidated Financial Statements, Note 5, Investments" under the caption, "Balance Sheet Offsetting." We have not incurred any material losses on derivative financial instruments due to counterparty nonperformance. As a result of our management of counterparty risk and the collateralization of our derivative portfolio, any credit exposure to derivative counterparties is immaterial as of December 31, 2013.

Des Moines, Iowa

# THE NAIC

The National Association of Insurance Commissioners (NAIC) is the U.S. standard-setting and regulatory support organization created and governed by the chief insurance regulators from the 50 states, the District of Columbia and five U.S. territories. Through the NAIC, state insurance regulators establish standards and best practices, conduct peer review, and coordinate their regulatory oversight. NAIC staff supports these efforts and represents the collective views of state regulators domestically and internationally. NAIC members, together with the central resources of the NAIC, form the national system of state-based insurance regulation in the U.S.

NAIC members are the elected or appointed state government officials who along with their departments and staff, regulate the conduct of insurance companies and agents in their respective state or territory.

## *OUR MISSION*

The mission of the NAIC is to assist state insurance regulators, individually and collectively, in serving the public interest and achieving the following fundamental insurance regulatory goals in a responsive, efficient and cost effective manner, consistent with the wishes of its members

www.ingramcontent.com/pod-product-compliance
Lightning Source LLC
Chambersburg PA
CBHW080232180526
45167CB00006B/2250